# SPSS

W9-AYB-216

## SPSS® Base 7.5 for Windows® User's Guide

SPSS Inc.

SPSS Inc.
444 N. Michigan Avenue
Chicago, Illinois 60611
Tel: (312) 329-2400
Fax: (312) 329-3668

SPSS Federal Systems (U.S.)
SPSS Argentina srl
SPSS Asia Pacific Pte. Ltd.
SPSS Australasia Pty. Ltd.
SPSS Belgium
SPSS Benelux BV
SPSS Central and Eastern Europe
SPSS France SARL
SPSS Germany
SPSS Hellas SA
SPSS Hispanoportuguesa S.L.
SPSS Ireland
SPSS Israel Ltd.
SPSS Italia srl
SPSS Japan Inc.
SPSS Korea
SPSS Latin America
SPSS Malaysia Sdn Bhd
SPSS Mexico SA de CV
SPSS Middle East and Africa
SPSS Scandinavia AB
SPSS Schweiz AG
SPSS Singapore Pte. Ltd.
SPSS UK Ltd.

Ser. # 3155567

Lic. Code: 30373 06814 71207

53761 67054 4951

For more information about SPSS® software products, please visit our WWW site at *http://www.spss.com* or contact

Marketing Department
SPSS Inc.
444 North Michigan Avenue
Chicago, IL 60611
Tel: (312) 329-2400
Fax: (312) 329-3668

SPSS® Base 7.5 for Windows® User's Guide
Copyright © 1997 by SPSS Inc.
All rights reserved.
Printed in the United States of America.

1 2 3 4 5 6 7 8 9 0    03 02 01 00 99 98 97

ISBN 0-13-657214-6

Library of Congress Catalog Card Number: 96-069620

# Preface

SPSS 7.5 is a comprehensive system for analyzing data. SPSS can take data from almost any type of file and use them to generate tabulated reports, charts, and plots of distributions and trends, descriptive statistics, and complex statistical analyses.

SPSS makes statistical analysis accessible for the casual user and convenient for the experienced user. The Data Editor offers a simple and efficient spreadsheet-like facility for entering data and browsing the working data file. High-resolution, presentation-quality charts and plots are integral parts of the Base system. Output from the Base system and Tables option takes the form of flexible pivot tables that you can modify quickly and copy directly into other applications. The Output Navigator makes it easy to organize and manage your tables and charts using a familiar tree structure. When you have questions about an item in a dialog box, a statistic in your output, or the steps needed to accomplish a task, help is only a click or two away. New features in SPSS 7.5 include a scripting facility that provides more automatic control over output and many parts of the system, a customizable toolbar and other convenience features, both new and extended statistical procedures, and a re-allocation of procedures among the options that provides more powerful procedures in the Base. See the overview (Chapter 1) for a list of new features and an introduction to the Base system.

This manual, the *SPSS Base 7.5 for Windows User's Guide,* documents the graphical user interface of SPSS for Windows. A companion book, the *SPSS Base 7.5 Applications Guide*, provides examples of statistical procedures and related data transformations, with advice on screening data, using appropriate procedures, and interpreting the output. Beneath the menus and dialog boxes, SPSS uses a command language that can be used to create and run production jobs. Dialog boxes can "paste" commands into a syntax window, where they can be modified and saved; a few features of the system can be accessed only via command syntax. Complete command syntax is documented in the *SPSS Base 7.5 Syntax Reference Guide,* which is included on the CD version of the software and is available for purchase separately in print. The Help system contains brief syntax diagrams in addition to full help on the graphical user interface.

## SPSS Options

The SPSS family of products includes add-on enhancements to the SPSS Base system, which are available on several computer platforms. With the addition of statistical procedures to the Base, the contents of Professional Statistics and Advanced Statistics have changed. Contact your local SPSS office or sales representative about availability of the following options:

- **SPSS Professional Statistics**™ provides more advanced regression techniques, including weighted and two-stage least-squares, logistic regression, and nonlinear regression, plus multidimensional scaling and reliability analysis.

- **SPSS Advanced Statistics**™ includes sophisticated techniques such as general linear models, variance component analysis, loglinear and probit analysis, Cox regression, and Kaplan-Meier and actuarial survival analysis.

- **SPSS Tables**™ creates a variety of presentation-quality tabular reports, including complex stub-and-banner tables and displays of multiple response data.

- **SPSS Trends**™ performs comprehensive forecasting and time series analyses with multiple curve-fitting models, smoothing models, and methods for estimating autoregressive functions.

- **SPSS Categories**® performs conjoint analysis and optimal scaling procedures, including correspondence analysis.

- **SPSS CHAID**™ simplifies tabular analysis of categorical data, develops predictive models, screens out extraneous predictor variables, and produces easy-to-read tree diagrams that segment a population into subgroups that share similar characteristics.

- **SPSS Exact Tests**™ calculates exact $p$ values for statistical tests when small or very unevenly distributed samples could make the usual tests inaccurate.

- **Neural Connection**™ provides state-of-the-art neural network power and flexibility for prediction, classification, time series analysis, and data segmentation.

- **MapInfo**® creates thematic maps for data visualization. Choose geographic regions from country to street level or create your own boundary files.

- **allCLEAR**™ III is a full-featured flowchart program. Create diagrams for causes and effects, process flow, network and deployment; build decision trees, organizational charts, and procedural charts.

## Compatibility

The SPSS Base 7.5 system is designed to operate on computer systems running either Windows 95 or Windows NT 3.51.

## Serial Numbers

Your serial number is your identification number with SPSS Inc. You will need this serial number when you call SPSS Inc. for information regarding support, payment, or an upgraded system. The serial number was provided with your Base system. Before using the system, please copy this number to the registration card.

## Registration Card

Don't put it off: *fill out and send us your registration card.* Until we receive your registration card, you have an unregistered system. Even if you have previously sent a card to us, please fill out and return the card enclosed in your Base system package. Registering your system entitles you to:

- Technical support services
- New product announcements and upgrade announcements

## Customer Service

If you have any questions concerning your shipment or account, contact your local office, listed on p. vii. Please have your serial number ready for identification when calling.

## Training Seminars

SPSS Inc. provides both public and onsite training seminars for SPSS. All seminars feature hands-on workshops. SPSS seminars will be offered in major U.S. and European cities on a regular basis. For more information on these seminars, call your local office, listed on p. vii.

## Technical Support

The services of SPSS Technical Support are available to registered customers of SPSS. Customers may contact Technical Support for assistance in using SPSS products or for installation help for one of the supported hardware environments. To reach Technical Support, see the SPSS home page on the World Wide Web at *http://www.spss.com*, or call your local office, listed on p. vii. Be prepared to identify yourself, your organization, and the serial number of your system.

## Additional Publications

Additional copies of SPSS product manuals may be purchased from Prentice Hall, the distributor of SPSS publications. To order, fill out and mail the Publications order form included with your system, or call toll-free. If you represent a bookstore or have an account with Prentice Hall, call 1-800-223-1360. If you are not an account customer, call 1-800-374-1200. In Canada, call 1-800-567-3800. Outside of North America, contact your local Prentice Hall office.

Except for academic course adoptions, manuals can also be purchased from SPSS Inc. Contact your local SPSS office, listed on p. vii.

## Tell Us Your Thoughts

Your comments are important. Please send us a letter and let us know about your experiences with SPSS products. We especially like to hear about new and interesting applications using the SPSS system. Write to SPSS Inc. Marketing Department, Attn: Director of Product Planning, 444 N. Michigan Avenue, Chicago, IL 60611.

## Contacting SPSS Inc.

If you would like to be on our mailing list, contact one of our offices below. We will send you a copy of our newsletter and let you know about SPSS Inc. activities in your area.

**SPSS Inc.**
Chicago, Illinois, U.S.A.
Tel: 1.312.329.2400
Fax: 1.312.329.3668
Customer Service:
1.800.521.1337
Sales:
1.800.543.2185
sales@spss.com
Training:
1-800-543-6607
Technical Support:
1.312.329.3410
support@spss.com

**SPSS Federal Systems**
Arlington, Virginia, U.S.A.
Tel: 1.703.527.6777
Fax: 1.703.527.6866

**SPSS Argentina srl**
Buenos Aires, Argentina
Tel: +541.816.4086
Fax: +541.814.5030

**SPSS Asia Pacific Pte. Ltd.**
Singapore, Singapore
Tel: +65.3922.738
Fax: +65.3922.739

**SPSS Australasia Pty. Ltd.**
Sydney, Australia
Tel: +61.2.9954.5660
Fax: +61.2.9954.5616

**SPSS Belgium**
Heverlee, Belgium
Tel: +32.162.389.82
Fax: +32.1620.0888

**SPSS Benelux BV**
Gorinchem, The Netherlands
Tel: +31.183.636711
Fax: +31.183.635839

**SPSS Central and
Eastern Europe**
Woking, Surrey, U.K.
Tel: +44.(0)1483.719200
Fax: +44.(0)1483.719290

**SPSS France SARL**
Boulogne, France
Tel: +33.1.4699.9670
Fax: +33.1.4684.0180

**SPSS Germany**
Munich, Germany
Tel: +49.89.4890740
Fax: +49,89.4483115

**SPSS Hellas SA**
Athens, Greece
Tel: +30.1.7251925
Fax: +30.1.7249124

**SPSS Hispanoportuguesa S.L.**
Madrid, Spain
Tel: +34.1.547.3703
Fax: +34.1.548.1346

**SPSS Ireland**
Dublin, Ireland
Tel: +353.1.66.13788
Fax: +353.1.661.5200

**SPSS Israel Ltd.**
Herzlia, Israel
Tel: +972.9.526700
Fax: +972.9.526715

**SPSS Italia srl**
Bologna, Italy
Tel: +39.51.252573
Fax: +39.51.253285

**SPSS Japan Inc.**
Tokyo, Japan
Tel: +81.3.5474.0341
Fax: +81.3.5474.2678

**SPSS Korea**
Seoul, Korea
Tel: +82.2.552.9415
Fax: +82.2.539.0136

**SPSS Latin America**
Chicago, Illinois, U.S.A.
Tel: 1.312.494.3226
Fax: 1.312. 494.3227

**SPSS Malaysia Sdn Bhd**
Selangor, Malaysia
Tel: +60.3.7045877
Fax: +60.3.7045790

**SPSS Mexico SA de CV**
Mexico DF, Mexico
Tel: +52.5.575.3091
Fax: +52.5.575.3094

**SPSS Middle East and Africa**
Woking, Surrey, U.K.
Tel: +44.(0)1483.719200
Fax: +44.(0)1483.719290

**SPSS Scandinavia AB**
Stockholm, Sweden
Tel: +46.8.102610
Fax: +46.8.102550

**SPSS Schweiz AG
Zurich, Switzerland
Tel: +41.1.201.0930**
Fax: +41.1.201.0921

**SPSS Singapore Pte. Ltd.**
Singapore, Singapore
Tel: +65.2991238
Fax: +65.2990849

**SPSS UK Ltd.**
Woking, Surrey, U.K.
Tel: +44.(0)1483.719200
Fax: +44.(0)1483.719290

# Contents

## 8   Working with Command Syntax   155

## 9   Frequencies   161

## 28  Multiple Response Analysis  305

## 29  Reporting Results  315

## 30 Overview of the SPSS Chart Facility    329

## 31 Bar, Line, Area, and Pie Charts    341

# 1

# Overview

SPSS for Windows provides a powerful statistical analysis and data management system in a graphical environment, using descriptive menus and simple dialog boxes to do most of the work for you. Most tasks can be accomplished simply by pointing and clicking the mouse.

In addition to the simple point-and-click interface for statistical analysis, SPSS for Windows provides:

**Data Editor.** A versatile spreadsheet-like system for defining, entering, editing, and displaying data.

**Output Navigator.** The new Output Navigator makes it easy to browse your results, selectively show and hide output, change the display order results, and move presentation-quality tables and charts between SPSS and other applications.

**High-resolution graphics.** High-resolution, full-color pie charts, bar charts, histograms, scatterplots, 3-D graphics, and more are now included as a standard feature in the SPSS Base system.

## What's New in SPSS 7.5?

New features available in SPSS 7.5 include:

**Scripting and automation**. With new scripting features and OLE automation, you can automate many tasks in SPSS, including customizing pivot table output. You can use the sample scripts provided with SPSS, customize them to meet your needs, or create your own scripts.

- Use Options on the Edit menu and select the Scripts tab on the Options dialog box to select autoscripts (scripts that run automatically each time you create a specified table type) and select specific autoscript functions.

- Use Create/Modify Autoscripts on the Utilities menu to create new autoscript functions for the currently selected output object type in the Output Navigator.

- Use Run Scripts on the Edit menu to run a personal script on the currently selected output object in the Output Navigator (a variety of sample personal scripts are supplied with SPSS).
- Use Open or New on the File menu to modify any personal script or create a new personal script.

**HTML and ASCII format for exporting output.** You can export output in HTML (HTML 3.0) and ASCII text format. For HTML format, pivot tables can be exported as HTML tables, and charts can be exported in JPEG format and automatically embedded by reference in your HTML document. Use *Export* on the File menu of the Output Navigator to export output.

**Expanded features for reading databases.** The new Database Capture Wizard enables you to specify multiple joins, including both inner and outer joins. Use Database Capture on the File menu to read databases into SPSS.

**Customizable toolbars.** You can modify SPSS toolbars and create your own toolbars to include the features you use often, including personal scripts and any items available on the SPSS menus. Use Toolbars on the View menu to customize toolbars.

**Statistics Coach.** For users who are not familiar with SPSS or with the statistical procedures available in SPSS, the Statistics Coach can help you get started with many of the basic statistical techniques in the SPSS Base system.

**More statistical procedures in the Base system.** Factor analysis, discriminant analysis, cluster analysis, and proximity and distance measures are now included in the SPSS Base system (Statistics menu) and feature new, flexible, pivot table output.

**Variance Components Analysis.** A new procedure in the Advanced Statistics option, Variance Components Analysis extends the analytic capabilities of the General Linear Model procedures.

**Statistical enhancements.** Many statistical procedures now have additional features:
- **Crosstabs.** McNemar test and clustered bar charts.
- **Frequencies.** Pie charts.
- **Factor Analysis.** Promax rotation method.
- **Discriminant Analysis.** Leave-one-out classification (similar to jackknifing).
- **Logistic Regression** (Professional Statistics). Pseudo $R^2$ measures and Hosmer-Lemeshow goodness-of-fit statistics.
- **General Linear Model** (Advanced Statistics). Expanded set of analysis options and techniques.

**New tables features.** With the Tables option, you can save multiple response set information, and pivoting features have been enhanced to provide greater flexibility for pivoting tables.

**More printing control**. Printing features have been expanded to include alignment control of individual output items, user-specified page and column breaks in large tables, and widow and orphan control for tables that break across pages.

- Use Align Left, Center, or Align Right on the Format menu in the Output Navigator to change the alignment for the selected output item.

- Use Break on the Format menu in an activated pivot table to specify a page or column break at the selected row or column. Use Keep Together to prevent page or column breaks between rows or columns you want to remain together.

- Use Table Properties on the Format menu in an activated pivot table to change widow/orphan settings.

**More pivot table control**. Features for modifying pivot tables have been expanded to include the ability to: reorder categories by dragging and dropping selected rows or columns, rotate row and column labels, and create groups of related rows and columns with group labels.

- Use Rotate on the Format menu in an activated pivot table to rotate inner column or outer row labels.

- Use Group on the Edit menu in an activated pivot table to create groups of related rows or columns with group labels.

**Other new features**. Other new features in SPSS 7.5 include:

- Variable labels up to 256 characters.
- Ability to read SYSTAT 6.0 for Windows files directly.
- Direct link to the SPSS Internet home page.

# Windows

There are seven types of windows in SPSS:

**Data Editor.** This window displays the contents of the data file. You can create new data files or modify existing ones with the Data Editor. The Data Editor window opens automatically when you start an SPSS session. You can have only one data file open at a time.

**Output Navigator.** All statistical results, tables, and charts are displayed in the Output Navigator. You can edit the output and save it for later use. An Output Navigator window opens automatically the first time you run a procedure that generates output.

**Pivot Table Editor.** Output displayed in pivot tables can be modified in many ways with the Pivot Table Editor. You can edit text, swap data in rows and columns, add color, create multidimensional tables, and selectively hide and show results.

**Chart Editor.** You can modify high-resolution charts and plots in chart windows. You can change the colors, select different type fonts or sizes, switch the horizontal and vertical axes, rotate 3-D scatterplots, and even change the chart type.

**Text Output Editor.** Text output not displayed in pivot tables can be modified with the Text Output Editor. You can edit the output and change font characteristics (type, style, color, size).

**Syntax Editor.** You can paste your dialog box choices into a syntax window, where your selections appear in the form of command syntax. You can then edit the command syntax to utilize special features of SPSS not available through dialog boxes. You can save these commands in a file for use in subsequent SPSS sessions.

**Script Editor.** Scripting and OLE automation allow you to customize and automate many tasks in SPSS. Use the Script Editor to create and modify Basic scripts.

**Figure 1.1    Data Editor and Output Navigator**

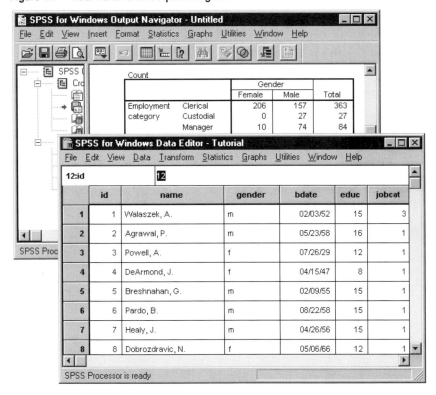

## Designated versus Active Window

If you have more than one open Output Navigator window, output is routed to the **designated** Output Navigator window. If you have more than one open Syntax Editor window, command syntax is pasted into the designated Syntax Editor window. The designated windows are indicated by an exclamation point (!) in the status bar. You can change the designated windows at any time.

The designated window should not be confused with the **active** window, which is the currently selected window. If you have overlapping windows, the active window appears in the foreground. If you open a new Syntax Editor or Output Navigator window, that window automatically becomes the active window and the designated window.

### To Change the Designated Output Navigator or Syntax Editor Window

▶ Make the window you want to designate the active window (click anywhere in the window).

▶ Click the Designate Window tool on the toolbar (the one with the exclamation point)

*or*

▶ From the menus choose:

Utilities
  Designate Window

**Figure 1.2    Designate Window tool**

Changes the designated window

# Menus

Many of the tasks you want to perform with SPSS start with menu selections. Each window in SPSS has its own menu bar with menu selections appropriate for that window type.

The Statistics and Graphs menus are available on all windows, making it easy to generate new output without having to switch windows.

## Data Editor Menus

**File.** Use the File menu to open and save data files, to read in spreadsheet or database files created by other software programs, and to print the contents of the Data Editor.

**Edit.** Use the Edit menu to cut, copy, and paste data values; to find data values; and to change Options settings.

**View.** Use the View menu to customize toolbars, to turn the status bar on and off, to turn grid lines on and off, and to control the display of value labels and data values.

**Data.** Use the Data menu to make global changes to SPSS data files, such as transposing variables and cases, creating subsets of cases for analysis, and merging files.

**Transform.** Use the Transform menu to make changes to selected variables in the data file and to compute new variables based on the values of existing ones.

**Statistics.** Use the Statistics menu to select the various statistical procedures you want to use, such as crosstabulation, analysis of variance, correlation, and linear regression.

**Graphs.** Use the Graphs menu to create bar charts, pie charts, histograms, scatterplots, and other full-color, high-resolution graphs.

**Utilities.** Use the Utilities menu to get information about variables in the working data file, to control the list of variables that appears in dialog boxes, to run scripts, and to customize menus.

**Window.** Use the Window menu to switch between SPSS windows or to minimize all open SPSS windows.

**Help.** Use the Help menu to link to the SPSS Internet home page and to access online Help on the many features available in SPSS. Context-sensitive Help is also available in dialog boxes and activated pivot tables by clicking the right mouse button on the item you want to know about.

## Output Navigator Menus

**File.** Use the File menu to open, save, and print output files.

**Edit.** Use the Edit menu to cut, copy, and paste output; to move output; to change the outline level of items in the outline pane; and to change Options settings.

**View.** Use the View menu to customize toolbars, to turn the status bar on and off, to show and hide items, and to collapse and expand the outline view.

**Insert.** Use the Insert menu to insert page breaks, titles, charts, text, and objects from other applications.

**Format.** Use the Format menu to change alignment for the selected output item.

**Statistics.** Use the Statistics menu to select the various statistical procedures you want to use, such as crosstabulation, analysis of variance, correlation, and linear regression.

**Graphs.** Use the Graphs menu to create bar charts, pie charts, histograms, scatterplots, and other full-color, high-resolution graphs.

**Utilities.** Use the Utilities menu to get information about variables in the working data file, to control the list of variables that appears in dialog boxes, to change the designated Output Navigator window, to run scripts, to create and edit autoscripts, and to customize menus.

**Window.** Use the Window menu to switch between SPSS windows or to minimize all open SPSS windows.

**Help.** Use the Help menu to link to the SPSS Internet home page and to access online Help on the many features available in SPSS. Context-sensitive Help is also available in dialog boxes and activated pivot tables by clicking the right mouse button on the item you want to know about.

## Pivot Table Editor Menus

Double-clicking on a pivot table activates the Pivot Table Editor, and the Pivot Table Editor menus replace the Output Navigator menus.

**File.** Use the File menu to open, save, and print output files.

**Edit.** Use the Edit menu to cut, copy, and paste data values and to undo and redo pivoting actions.

**View.** Use the View menu to turn toolbars on and off, to show and hide table elements, and to turn the display of table cell gridlines on and off. (Table cell gridlines do not appear in printed output.)

**Insert.** Use the Insert menu to insert titles, captions, and footnotes.

**Pivot.** Use the Pivot menu to perform basic pivoting tasks, to turn pivoting trays on and off, and to go to specific layers in a multidimensional pivot table.

**Format.** Use the Format menu to modify table and cell properties; to apply and change TableLook formats; to change font characteristics, footnote markers, and the width of data cells; and to control table breaks.

**Statistics.** Use the Statistics menu to select the various statistical procedures you want to use, such as crosstabulation, analysis of variance, correlation, and linear regression.

**Graphs.** Use the Graphs menu to create bar charts, pie charts, histograms, scatterplots, and other full-color, high-resolution graphs.

**Utilities.** Use the Utilities menu to get information about variables in the working data file and to customize menus.

**Window.** Use the Window menu to minimize all open SPSS windows.

**Help.** Use the Help menu to access online Help on the many features available in SPSS. Context-sensitive Help is also available in dialog boxes and activated pivot tables by clicking the right mouse button on the item you want to know about.

## Chart Editor Menus

**File.** Use the File menu to save chart templates and export charts in external formats (for example, Windows metafile or TIFF).

**Edit.** Use the Edit menu to copy charts for pasting into other applications and to change Options settings.

**View.** Use the View menu to customize toolbars and to turn the status bar on and off.

**Gallery.** Use the Gallery menu to change the chart type (for example, you could change from a bar chart to a pie chart).

**Chart.** Use the Chart menu to modify layout and labeling characteristics of your chart, such as the scaling and labeling of axes, all titles and labels, inner and outer frames, and whether the chart should expand to fill areas where titles are not assigned.

**Series.** Use the Series menu to select data series and categories to display or omit and to transpose data. For bar, line, and area charts, you can select whether each series should be displayed as a line, an area, or a set of bars.

**Format.** Use the Format menu to select fill patterns, colors, line styles, bar style, bar label styles (for displaying values within bars), interpolation type, and text fonts and sizes. You can also swap axes of plots, explode one or more slices of a pie chart, change the treatment of missing values in lines, and rotate 3-D scatterplots.

**Statistics.** Use the Statistics menu to select the various statistical procedures you want to use, such as crosstabulation, analysis of variance, correlation, and linear regression.

**Graphs.** Use the Graphs menu to create bar charts, pie charts, histograms, scatterplots, and other full-color, high-resolution graphs.

**Help.** Use the Help menu to link to the SPSS Internet home page and to access online Help on the many features available in SPSS. Context-sensitive Help is also available in dialog boxes and activated pivot tables by clicking the right mouse button on the item you want to know about.

## Text Output Editor Menus

Double-clicking on text output activates the Text Output Editor, and the Text Output Editor menus replace the Output Navigator menus.

**File.** Use the File menu to open, save, and print files.

**Edit.** Use the Edit menu to cut, copy, and paste output; to find and replace text strings; and to change color settings.

**View.** Use the View menu to turn toolbars and the status bar on and off.

**Insert.** Use the Insert menu to insert page breaks.

**Format.** Use the Format menu to change font characteristics and alignment.

**Statistics.** Use the Statistics menu to select the various statistical procedures you want to use, such as crosstabulation, analysis of variance, correlation, and linear regression.

**Graphs.** Use the Graphs menu to create bar charts, pie charts, histograms, scatterplots, and other full-color, high-resolution graphs.

**Utilities.** Use the Utilities menu to get information about variables in the working data file and to customize menus.

**Window.** Use the Window menu to minimize all open SPSS windows.

**Help.** Use the Help menu to access online Help on the many features available in SPSS. Context-sensitive Help is also available in dialog boxes and activated pivot tables by clicking the right mouse button on the item you want to know about.

## Syntax Editor Menus

**File.** Use the File menu to open, save, and print files.

**Edit.** Use the Edit menu to cut, copy, and paste text; to find and replace text strings; and to change Options settings.

**View.** Use the View menu to customize toolbars, to turn the status bar on and off, and to change fonts.

**Statistics.** Use the Statistics menu to select the various statistical procedures you want to use, such as crosstabulation, analysis of variance, correlation, and linear regression.

**Graphs.** Use the Graphs menu to create bar charts, pie charts, histograms, scatterplots, and other full-color, high-resolution graphs.

**Utilities.** Use the Utilities menu to get information about variables in the working data file, to control the list of variables that appears in dialog boxes, to change the designated Syntax Editor window, and to customize menus.

**Run**. Use the Run menu to run all or part of the current syntax file.

**Window.** Use the Window menu to switch between SPSS windows or to minimize all open SPSS windows.

**Help.** Use the Help menu to link to the SPSS Internet home page and to access online Help on the many features available in SPSS. Context-sensitive Help is also available in dialog boxes and activated pivot tables by clicking the right mouse button on the item you want to know about.

## Script Editor Menus

**File.** Use the File menu to open, save, and print files.

**Edit.** Use the Edit menu to cut, copy, and paste text; to find and replace text strings; and to change Options settings.

**View.** Use the View menu to customize toolbars and to turn the status bar on and off.

**Script**. Use the Script menu to create new subroutines and functions, access the dialog box editor, run scripts, and modify font characteristics of script elements such as color and font used to identify reserved keywords and comments.

**Debug**. Use the Debug menu to debug your Basic scripts and access the Object Browser, which provides information on OLE automation methods and properties and allows you to paste selected methods into scripts.

**Statistics.** Use the Statistics menu to select the various statistical procedures you want to use, such as crosstabulation, analysis of variance, correlation, and linear regression.

**Graphs.** Use the Graphs menu to create bar charts, pie charts, histograms, scatterplots, and other full-color, high-resolution graphs.

**Utilities.** Use the Utilities menu to get information about variables in the working data file, to control the list of variables that appears in dialog boxes, and to customize menus.

**Window.** Use the Window menu to switch between SPSS windows or to minimize all open SPSS windows.

**Help.** Use the Help menu to link to the SPSS Internet home page and to access online Help for SPSS and the Basic scripting language.

## Menu Editor

You can use the Menu Editor to customize your SPSS menus. With the Menu Editor you can:

- Add menu items that run customized SPSS scripts.
- Add menu items that run SPSS command syntax files.
- Add menu items that launch other applications and automatically send SPSS data to other applications.

SPSS can send data to other applications in the following formats: SPSS, Excel 4.0, Lotus 1-2-3 release 3, SYLK, tab-delimited, and dBASE IV.

## To Add Items to the SPSS Menus

▶ From the menus choose:
Utilities
  Menu Editor...

▶ In the Menu Editor dialog box, double-click the menu where you want to add a new item.

▶  Select the menu item above which you want the new item to appear.

▶  Click *Insert Item* to insert a new menu item.

▶  Select the File Type for the new item (script file, command syntax file, or external application).

▶  Click Browse to select a file to attach to the menu item.

**Figure 1.3    Menu Editor dialog box**

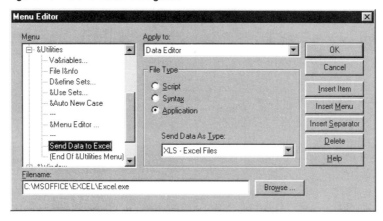

You can also add entirely new menus and separators between menu items.

Optionally, you can automatically send the contents of the Data Editor to another application when you select that application on the SPSS menus.

# Toolbars

Each SPSS window has its own toolbar that provides quick, easy access to common tasks. Some windows have more than one toolbar. ToolTips provide a brief description of each tool when you put the mouse pointer on the tool.

**Figure 1.4    Toolbar with ToolTip Help**

You can control the display of toolbars in several ways:

• Show or hide toolbars.

• Display toolbars vertically or horizontally, attached to the left, right, top, or bottom of the window.

• Display toolbars as floating palettes anywhere inside or outside the window.

• Customize toolbars to contain the features you use most often, including scripts.

## To Show or Hide a Toolbar

▶ From the menus choose:

View
  Toolbars...

▶ In the Show Toolbars dialog box, select the toolbars you want to show (or hide).

## To Move a Toolbar

▶ Click anywhere in the toolbar outside the toolbar buttons.

▶ Drag the toolbar where you want it.

• Dragging the toolbar to the left or right side of the window attaches a toolbar vertically to that side.

• Dragging the toolbar to the top or bottom of the window attaches the toolbar horizontally.

• Dragging the toolbar anywhere other than the window borders creates a detached, floating toolbar.

**Figure 1.5    Floating toolbars**

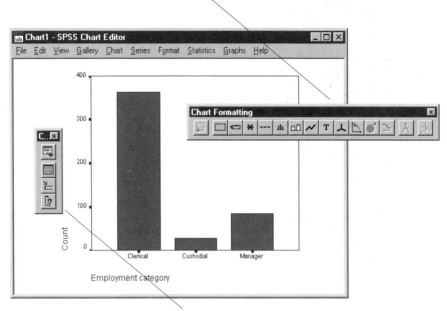

Click and drag to create a floating toolbar

Resize the toolbar by dragging the corner

## Customizing Toolbars

You can customize SPSS toolbars and create new toolbars. Toolbars can contain any of the tools available with SPSS, including tools for all menu actions. They can also contain custom tools that launch other applications, run command syntax files, or run script files.

### Show Toolbars

Use Show Toolbars to show or hide toolbars, customize toolbars, and create new toolbars. Toolbars can contain any of the tools available with SPSS, including tools for all menu actions. They can also contain custom tools that launch other applications, run command syntax files, or run script files.

**Figure 1.6    Show Toolbars dialog box**

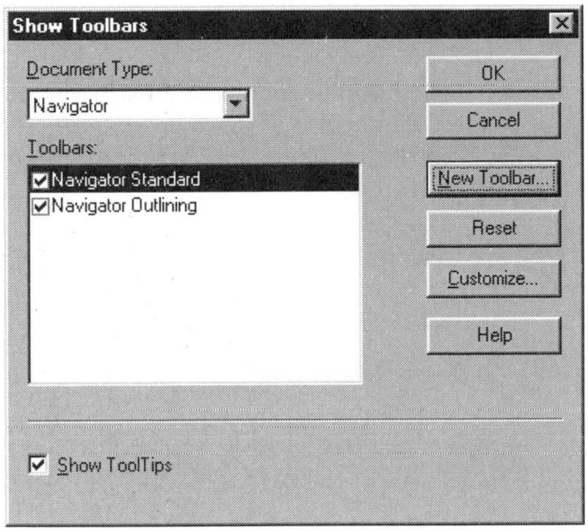

## To Customize Toolbars

▶ From the menus choose:

View
 Toolbars...

▶ Select the toolbar you want to customize and click *Customize*, or click *New Toolbar* to create a new toolbar.

▶ For new toolbars, enter a name for the toolbar, select the windows in which you want the toolbar to appear, and click *Customize*.

▶ Select an item in the Categories list to display available tools in that category.

▶ Drag and drop the tools you want on to the toolbar displayed in the dialog box.

▶ To remove a tool from the toolbar, drag it anywhere off the toolbar displayed in the dialog box.

To create a custom tool to open a file, run a command syntax file, or run a script:

▶ Click *New Tool* in the Customize Toolbar dialog box.

▶ Enter a descriptive label for the tool.

▶ Select the action you want for the tool (open a file, run a command syntax file, or run a script).

▶ Click *Browse* to select a file or application to associate with the tool.

New tools are displayed in the User-Defined category, which also contains user-defined menu items.

### Toolbar Properties

Use Toolbar Properties to select the window types in which you want the selected toolbar to appear. This dialog box is also used for creating names for new toolbars.

**Figure 1.7    Toolbar Properties dialog box**

**To Set Toolbar Properties**

▶ From the menus choose:

View
  Toolbars...

▶ For existing toolbars, click *Customize*, and then click *Properties* in the Customize Toolbar dialog box.

▶ For new toolbars, click *New Tool*.

▶ Select the window types in which you want the toolbar to appear. For new toolbars, also
enter a toolbar name.

**Customize Toolbar**

Use the Customize Toolbar dialog box to customize existing toolbars and create new
toolbars. Toolbars can contain any of the tools available with SPSS, including tools for
all menu actions. They can also contain custom tools that launch other applications, run
command syntax files, or run script files.

Figure 1.8    Customize Toolbar dialog box

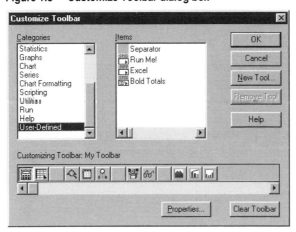

### Create New Tool

Use the New Tool dialog box to create custom tools to launch other applications, run command syntax files, and run script files.

Figure 1.9    Create New Tool dialog box

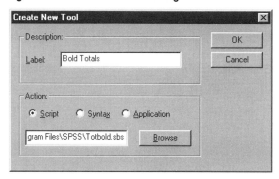

### Bitmap Editor

Use the bitmap editor to create custom icons for toolbar buttons. This is particularly useful for custom tools you create to run scripts, syntax, and other applications.

Figure 1.10    Bitmap Editor

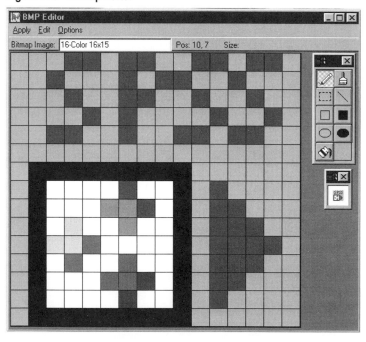

### To Edit Toolbar Bitmaps

▶ From the menus choose:
  View
    Toolbars...

▶ Select the toolbar you want to customize and click *Customize*.

▶ Click the tool with the bitmap icon you want to edit on the example toolbar.

▶ Click *Edit Tool*.

▶ Use the toolbox and the color palette to modify the bitmap or create a new bitmap icon.

# Status Bar

The status bar at the bottom of each SPSS window provides the following information:

**Command status.** For each procedure or command you run, a case counter indicates the number of cases processed so far. For statistical procedures that require iterative processing, the number of iterations is displayed.

**Filter status.** If you have selected a random sample or a subset of cases for analysis, the message *Filter on* indicates that some type of case filtering is currently in effect and not all cases in the data file are included in the analysis.

**Weight status.** The message *Weight on* indicates that a weight variable is being used to weight cases for analysis.

**Split File status.** The message *Split File on* indicates that the data file has been split into separate groups for analysis, based on the values of one or more grouping variables.

### To Show or Hide the Status Bar

▶ From the menus choose:
  View
    Status Bar

# Dialog Boxes

Most menu selections in SPSS open dialog boxes. You use dialog boxes to select variables and options for analysis.

Each main dialog box for statistical procedures and charts has several basic components:

**Source variable list.** A list of variables in the working data file. Only variables types allowed by the selected procedure are displayed in the source list. Use of short-string and long-string variables is restricted in many procedures.

**Target variable list(s).** One or more lists indicating the variables you have chosen for the analysis, such as dependent and independent variable lists.

**Command pushbuttons.** Buttons that instruct SPSS to perform an action, such as run the procedure, display Help, or open a subdialog box to make additional specifications.

For information on individual controls in a dialog box, click the control with the right mouse button.

**Figure 1.11   Dialog box controls**

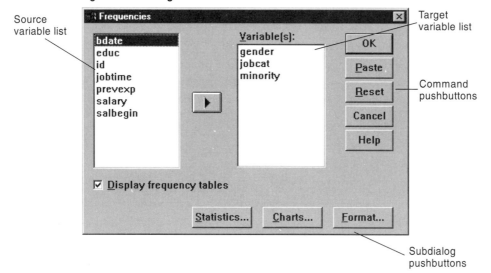

## Dialog Box Pushbuttons

There are five standard command pushbuttons in most SPSS dialog boxes:

**OK.** Runs the procedure. After you select your variables and choose any additional specifications, click *OK* to run the procedure. This also closes the dialog box.

**Paste.** Generates command syntax from the dialog box selections and pastes the syntax into a syntax window. You can then customize the commands with additional SPSS features not available from dialog boxes.

**Reset.** Deselects any variables in the selected variable list(s) and resets all specifications in the dialog box and any subdialog boxes to the default state.

**Cancel.** Cancels any changes in the dialog box settings since the last time it was opened and closes the dialog box. Within an SPSS session, dialog box settings are persistent. A dialog box retains your last set of specifications until you override them.

**Help.** Context-sensitive Help. This takes you to a standard Microsoft Help window that contains information about the current dialog box. You can also get help on individual dialog box controls by clicking the control with the right mouse button.

## Subdialog Boxes

Since most SPSS procedures provide a great deal of flexibility, not all of the possible choices can be contained in a single dialog box. The main dialog box usually contains the minimum information required to run a procedure. Additional specifications are made in subdialog boxes.

In the main dialog box, pushbuttons with an ellipsis (...) after the name indicate a subdialog box will be displayed.

## Selecting Variables

To select a single variable, you simply highlight it on the source variable list and click the right arrow button next to the target variable list box. If there is only one target variable list, you can double-click individual variables to move them from the source list to the target list.

You can also select multiple variables:

- To highlight multiple variables that are grouped together on the variable list, click and drag the mouse cursor over the variables you want. Alternatively, you can click the first one and then Shift-click the last one in the group.

- To highlight multiple variables that are not grouped together on the variable list, use the Ctrl-click method. Click the first variable, then Ctrl-click the next variable, and so on.

**Figure 1.12   Selecting multiple variables with click-and-drag or Shift-click**

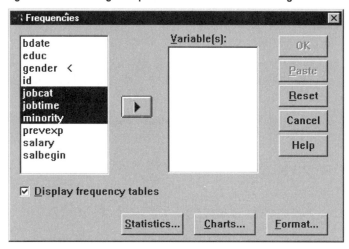

**Figure 1.13   Selecting multiple noncontiguous variables with Ctrl-click**

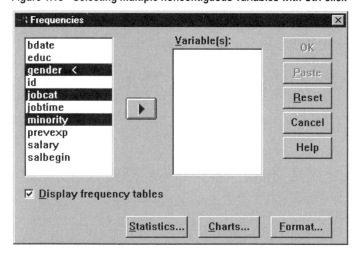

**To Get Information about Variables in a Dialog Box**

▶ Left-click a variable in a list to select it.

▶ Right-click anywhere in the list.

▶ Click *Variable Information* in the pop-up context menu.

**Figure 1.14   Variable Information with right mouse button**

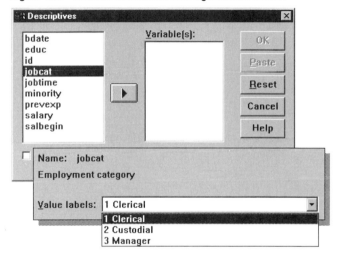

**To Get Information about Dialog Box Controls**

▶ Right-click the control you want to know about.

▶ Click *What's This?* in the pop-up context menu.

A pop-up window displays information about the control.

Figure 1.15    Right mouse button "What's This?" pop-up help for dialog box controls

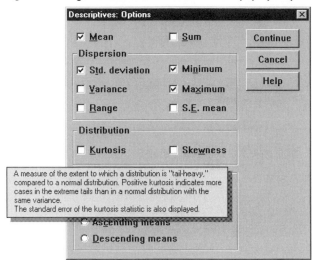

# Basic Steps in Data Analysis

Analyzing data with SPSS is easy. All you have to do is:

**Get your data into SPSS.** You can open a previously saved SPSS data file; read a spreadsheet, database, or text data file; or enter your data directly in the Data Editor.

**Select a procedure.** Select a procedure from the menus to calculate statistics or to create a chart.

**Select the variables for the analysis.** The variables in the data file are displayed in a dialog box for the procedure.

**Run the procedure and look at the results.** Results are displayed in the Output Navigator.

# Statistics Coach

If you are unfamiliar with SPSS or with the statistical procedures available in SPSS, the Statistics Coach can help you get started by prompting you with simple questions, non-technical language, and visual examples that help you select the basic statistical and charting features that are best suited for you data.

To use the Statistics Coach, from the menus in any SPSS window choose:

Help
  Statistics Coach

The Statistics Coach covers only a selected subset of procedures in the SPSS Base system. It is designed to provide general assistance for many of the basic, commonly used statistical techniques. For detailed discussions of all the statistical procedures available in SPSS, see the *SPSS Base Applications Guide* and the applications sections of the SPSS manuals that come with SPSS options (for example, *Professional Statistics* or *Advanced Statistics*).

# Finding Out More about SPSS

For a comprehensive overview of SPSS basics, see the online tutorial. From any SPSS menu bar choose:

Help
  Tutorial

# 2 Getting Help

SPSS provides online Help in several ways:

**Help menu.** Every SPSS window has a Help menu on the menu bar. *Topics* provides access to Contents, Index, and Find tabs, which you can use to find specific Help topics. *Tutorial* provides access to the SPSS introductory tutorial.

**Dialog box context menu Help.** Click the right mouse button on any control in a dialog box and select *What's This?* from the pop-up context menu to display a description of the control and how to use it.

**Dialog box Help buttons.** Most dialog boxes have a Help button that take you directly to a Help topic for that dialog box. The Help topic provides general information and links to related topics.

**Pivot table context menu Help.** Click the right mouse button on terms in an activated pivot table in the Output Navigator and select *What's This?* from the pop-up context menu to display definitions of the terms.

**SPSS tutorial.** Choose *Tutorial* on the Help menu in any SPSS window to access the online, introductory tutorial.

**CD-ROM Syntax Reference Guide.** The *SPSS Base Syntax Reference Guide*, plus syntax reference for any installed options, is available online with the CD ROM version of SPSS. The syntax reference is available from the Help menu. If you did not install the syntax reference when you installed SPSS, you will need the SPSS CD-ROM to access the syntax reference.

### To Use the SPSS Help Table of Contents

▶ From the menu bar in any SPSS window, choose:
Help
  Topics...

▶ Click the Contents tab.

▶ Double-click on items with a book icon to expand or collapse the contents.

▶ Double-click on an item to go to that Help topic.

**Figure 2.1    Contents tab and Help topic**

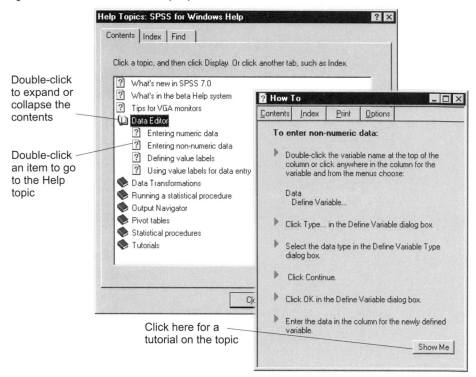

## To Use the SPSS Help Index

▶ From the menu bar in any SPSS window, choose:

Help
  Topics...

▶ Click the Index tab.

▶ Enter a term to search for in the index.

▶ Double-click on the topic you want.

The Help index uses incremental search to find the text you enter and selects the closest match in the index.

**Figure 2.2    Index tab and incremental search**

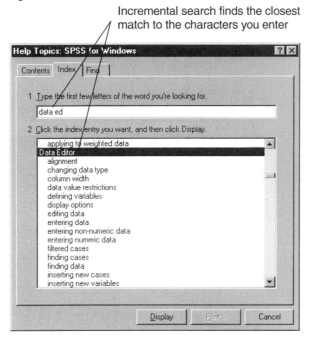

**To Use Full-Text Search in Help**

▶   From the menu bar in any SPSS window, choose:

Help
   Topics...

▶   Click the Find tab.

▶   Use the Find Setup Wizard to create a database of text in the Help system.

▶   Enter the word(s) you want to find.

▶   Double-click on one of the listed topics to display that topic.

**To Get Help for Dialog Box Controls**

▶  Click the right mouse button on the dialog box control you want to know about.

▶  Choose *What's This?* from the pop-up context menu.

A description of the control and how to use it is displayed in a pop-up window.

General information about a dialog box is available from the Help button in the dialog box.

**Figure 2.3    Dialog box control Help with right mouse button**

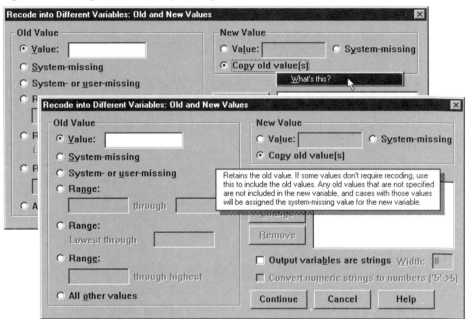

**To Get Information about Terms in Output Pivot Tables**

▶  Double-click the pivot table to activate it.

▶  Click the right mouse button on the term that you want to be explained.

▶  Choose *What's This?* from the pop-up context menu.

A definition of the term is displayed in a pop-up window.

**Figure 2.4    Activated pivot table glossary Help with right mouse button**

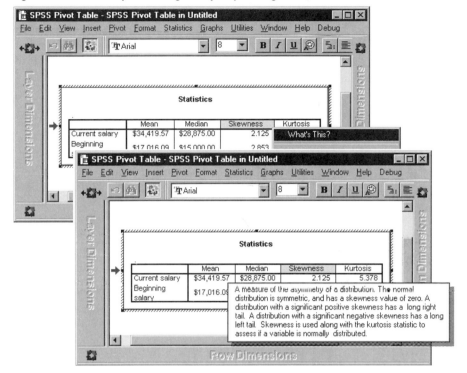

# Copying Help Text

You can copy text from the Help system and paste into other applications, including SPSS:

- You can copy whole topics or selected portions of topics in Help windows.
- You can copy the text of Help pop-ups accessed from Help windows, dialog boxes, and pivot tables.

### To Copy Help Text from a Help Window

▶ Click-and-drag to select the text you want to copy.

▶ From the Help menus choose:

Edit
  Copy

*or*

▶ Press Ctrl-C.

If no text is selected, the entire Help topic is copied. In Help windows that don't have a menu bar, use the Ctrl-C method.

## To Copy Help Text from a Pop-Up

▶ Click the right mouse button in the pop-up.

▶ Choose *Copy* on the pop-up context menu.

The entire text of the pop-up is copied.

# 3 Data Files

Data files come in a wide variety of formats, and SPSS is designed to handle many of them, including:

- Spreadsheets created with Lotus 1-2-3 and Excel
- Database files created with dBASE and various SQL formats
- Tab-delimited and other types of ASCII text files
- SPSS data files created on other systems
- SYSTAT data files

## Opening a Data File

In addition to files saved in SPSS format, you can open Excel (release 4 or earlier), Lotus 1-2-3, dBASE, and tab-delimited files without converting the files to an intermediate format or entering data definition information.

### To Open an SPSS, SYSTAT, Spreadsheet, dBASE, or Tab-Delimited Data File

▶ From the menus choose:

File
  Open…

▶ In the Open File dialog box, select the file you want to open.

▶ Click *Open*.

Optionally, you can:

- Read variable names from the first row for spreadsheet and tab-delimited files.
- Specify a range of cells to read for spreadsheet files.

## Data File Types

**SPSS.** Opens data files saved by SPSS for Windows, Macintosh, UNIX, and also by the DOS product SPSS/PC+.

**SPSS/PC+.** Opens SPSS/PC+ data files.

**SYSTAT.** Opens SYSTAT data files.

**SPSS portable.** Opens SPSS data files saved in portable format. Saving a file in portable format takes considerably longer than saving the file in SPSS format.

**Excel.** Opens spreadsheet files saved in Excel 4 or earlier versions. For Excel 5 or later versions, use Open ODBC with the appropriate Excel ODBC driver.

**Lotus 1-2-3.** Opens data files saved in 1-2-3 format for release 3.0, 2.0, or 1A of Lotus.

**SYLK.** Opens data files saved in SYLK (symbolic link) format, a format used by some spreadsheet applications.

**dBASE.** Opens dBASE format files for either dBASE IV, dBASE III or III PLUS, or dBASE II. Each case is a record. Variable and value labels and missing-value specifications are lost when you save a file in this format.

**Tab-delimited.** Opens ASCII text data files with data values separated by tabs.

## Opening File Options

**Read variable names.** For spreadsheet and tab-delimited files, you can read variable names from the first row of the file or the first row of the defined range. If the names are longer than eight characters, they are truncated. If the first eight characters do not create a unique variable name, the name is modified to create a unique variable name.

**Range.** For spreadsheet data files, you can also read a range of cells. Use the same method for specifying cell ranges as you would with the spreadsheet application.

## How SPSS Reads Spreadsheet Data

An SPSS data file is rectangular. The boundaries (or dimensions) of the data file are determined by the number of cases (rows) and variables (columns). There are no empty cells within the boundaries of the data file. All cells have a value, even if that value is *blank*. The following rules apply to reading spreadsheet data:

**Rows and columns.** Rows are cases, and columns are variables.

**Data type and width.** The data type and width for each variable are determined by the column width and data type of the first data cell in the column. Values of other types are converted to the system-missing value. If the first data cell in the column is blank, the global default data type for the spreadsheet (usually numeric) is used.

**Blank cells.** For numeric variables, blank cells are converted to the system-missing value, indicated by a period. For string variables, a blank is a valid string value, and blank cells are treated as valid string values.

**Variable names.** If you do not read variable names from the spreadsheet, SPSS uses the column letters (A, B, C, ...) for variable names for Excel and Lotus files. For SYLK files and Excel files saved in R1C1 display format, SPSS uses the column number preceded by the letter C for variable names (C1, C2, C3, ...).

**Figure 3.1    Reading a spreadsheet file with variable names**

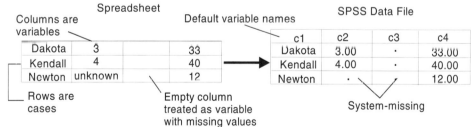

**Figure 3.2    Reading a spreadsheet file without variable names**

# How SPSS Reads dBASE Files

Database files are logically very similar to SPSS data files. The following general rules apply to dBASE files:

• Field names are automatically translated to SPSS variable names.

- Field names should comply with SPSS variable-naming conventions. Field names longer than eight characters are truncated. If the first eight characters of the field name do not produce a unique name, the field is dropped.
- Colons used in dBASE field names are translated to underscores.
- Records marked for deletion but not actually purged are included. SPSS creates a new string variable, $D\_R$, which contains an asterisk for cases marked for deletion.

## How SPSS Reads Tab-Delimited Files

The following general rules apply to reading tab-delimited files:

- Values can be either numeric or string. Any value that contains non-numeric characters is considered a string value. (Formats such as dollar and date are not recognized and are read as string values.)
- The data type and width for each variable are determined by the type and width of the first data value in the column. Values of other types are converted to the system-missing value.
- For numeric variables, the assigned width is eight digits or the number of digits in the first data value, whichever is greater. Values that exceed the defined width are rounded for display. The entire value is stored internally.
- For string variables, values that exceed the defined width are truncated.
- If you do not read variable names from the file, SPSS assigns the default names *var1*, *var2*, *var3*, and so on.

# Reading Database Files with ODBC

You can read data into SPSS from any database format for which you have an ODBC driver. You can also read Excel 5 files into SPSS using the Excel ODBC driver.

### To Read Database Files with ODBC

▶ From the menus choose:

File
  Database Capture...

▶ Select the data source. This can be a database format, an Excel file, or a text file.

▶ Select the database file.

▶ Depending on the database file, you may need to enter a login name and password.

▶ Select the table(s) and fields you want to read into SPSS.

▶ Specify any relationships between your tables.

▶ Specify any selection criteria for your data.

## Select a Data Source

Use the first dialog box to select the type of data source to read into SPSS. After you have chosen the file type, the Database Capture Wizard will prompt you for the path to your data file.

Figure 3.3    Database Capture Wizard dialog box

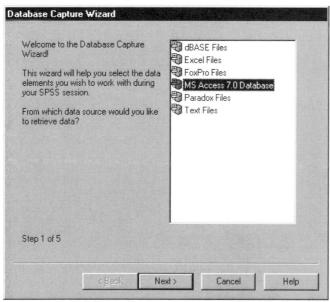

## Database Login

If your database requires a password, the Database Capture Wizard will prompt you for one before it can open the data source.

**Figure 3.4    Login dialog box**

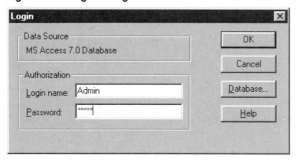

## Select Data Fields

This dialog box controls which tables and fields are read into SPSS. Database fields (columns) are read as variables in SPSS.

**Figure 3.5    Select Data dialog box**

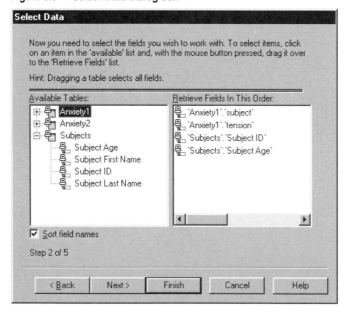

**Displaying field names.** To list the fields in a table, click the plus sign to the left of a table name. To hide the fields, click the minus sign to the left of a table name.

**To add a field.** Double-click any field in the Available Tables list, or drag it to the Retrieve Fields in This Order list. Fields can be reordered by dragging and dropping them within the selected fields list. To select all items in a list, press Ctrl-A.

**To remove a field.** Double-click any field in the Retrieve Fields in This Order list, or drag it to the Available Tables list.

**Sort field names.** If selected, the Database Capture Wizard will display your available fields in alphabetical order.

**Variable names and labels in SPSS.** The complete database field (column) name is used as the SPSS variable label. SPSS assigns variable names to each column from the database in one of two ways:

- If the name of the database field (or the first eight characters) forms a valid, unique SPSS variable name, it is used as the variable name.

- If the name of the database field does not form a valid, unique SPSS variable name, SPSS creates a unique name.

### Creating a Relationship between Tables

This dialog box allows you to define the relationships between the tables. If fields from more than one table are selected, you must define at least one join.

Figure 3.6    Relationships dialog box

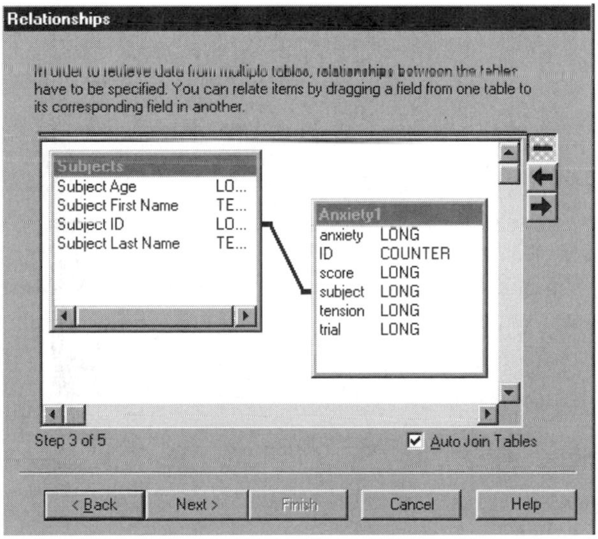

**Establishing relationships.** To create a relationship, drag a field from any table onto the field to which you want to join it. The Database Capture Wizard will draw a *join line* between the two fields, indicating their relationship. These fields must be of the same data type.

**Specifying join types.** If outer joins are supported by your driver, you can specify either inner joins, left outer joins, or right outer joins. To select the type of join, click the join line between the fields, and SPSS will display the Relationship Properties dialog box.

You can also use the icons in the upper right corner of the dialog to choose the type of join.

## Relationship Properties

This dialog box allows you to specify which type of relationship joins your tables.

**Figure 3.7    Relationship Properties dialog box**

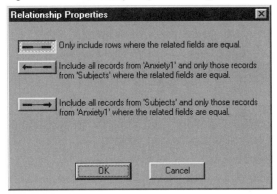

**Inner joins.** An inner join includes only rows where the related fields are equal. For example, assume that you have a database that contains the results of several psychological tests. One of those tests is a record of the patients' levels of anxiety and tension. The table for subjects contains personal information about all of the subjects that participated in the tests. Each subject is assigned an ID. The table for anxiety holds the results of their individual tests, referenced by the field ID. If you want to find the average age of subjects who participated in the anxiety test and exhibited high levels of tension, you need to define an inner join, linking the two tables on the field ID.

**Figure 3.8    Creating an inner join**

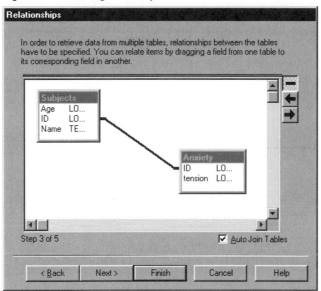

Completing this gives you an SPSS data set that contains the variables *id*, *age*, and *tension* for each subject who participated in the anxiety tests.

**Outer joins.** A left outer join includes all records from the table on the left, and only those records from the table on the right where the related fields are equal. In a right outer join, this relationship is switched, so that SPSS imports all records from the table on the right and only those records from the table on the left where the related fields are equal.

For example, of those subjects evaluated in the tests recorded in your database, only a fraction participated in the tests measuring their level of anxiety. To analyze the age of those subjects who took part in the anxiety tests in relation to the age of all the subjects, you need to define a left outer join. Once again, link the two tables for subjects and anxiety on ID. This time, specify a left outer join to include all of the subjects and the test results for those who participated in the anxiety tests.

**Figure 3.9    Creating a left outer join**

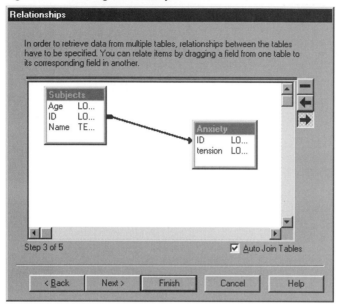

Finishing the procedure gives you an SPSS data set that contains the variables *id* and *age* for every subject in the database, whether or not they participated in the anxiety test, and *tension* levels for each person who took part in the anxiety test. For those subjects who did not take part in the anxiety test, the *tension* field remains blank.

## Selecting Cases

The Where Cases dialog box allows you to select subsets of cases (rows) using conditional expressions. A conditional expression returns a value of true, false, or missing for each case.

- If the result of a conditional expression is true, the case is selected.
- If the result of a conditional expression is false or missing, the case is not selected.

- Most conditional expressions use one or more of the six relational operators ($<$, $>$, $<=$, $>=$, $=$, $\sim=$) on the calculator pad.
- Conditional expressions can include field names, constants, arithmetic operators, numeric and other functions, logical variables, and relational operators.

**Figure 3.10   Where Cases dialog box**

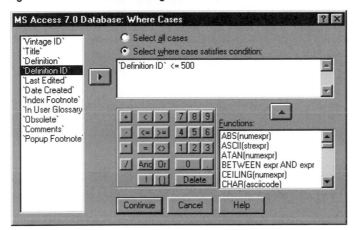

**Functions.** SPSS provides a selection of built-in arithmetic, logical, string, date, and time SQL functions. You can select a function from the list and paste it into the expression, or you can enter any valid SQL function. See your database documentation for valid SQL functions.

# Verifying Results

The Results dialog box displays the SQL syntax for your query.

**Figure 3.11    Results dialog box**

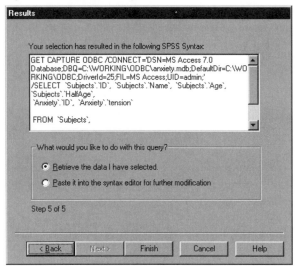

Users who are familiar with SQL can paste the query into the SPSS syntax editor to further modify it.

## To Read Excel 5 Files with ODBC

▶  In Excel, highlight the range of cells you want to read into SPSS.

▶  From the Excel menus choose:
Insert
  Name
    Define...

▶  Enter a name for the cell range and click *Add*.

▶  Save the Excel file.

▶  In SPSS, from the menus choose:
File
  Database Capture...

▶  Click the defined name for the data source list.

▶ If the defined name is not in the data source list, select *Excel Files,* and then select the Excel file.

▶ Drag and drop the defined name from the Available Tables list to the Retrieve Fields list.

▶ Click *Finish.*

# ASCII Text Data Files

If your raw data are in simple text files (standard ASCII format), you can read the data in SPSS and assign variable names and data formats. SPSS can read text data files formatted in two basic ways:

**Fixed.** Each variable is recorded in the same column location on the same record (line) for each case in the data file.

**Freefield.** The variables are recorded in the same order for each case, but not necessarily in the same locations. Spaces are interpreted as delimiters between values. More than one case can be recorded on a single line. After reading the value for the last defined variable for a case, SPSS reads the next value encountered as the first variable for the next case.

## Define Fixed Variables

Define Fixed Variables reads ASCII text data files that are in **fixed format**—each variable is recorded in the same column location on the same record (line) for each case in the data file. You can read data files that contain a wide variety of data types, including numeric, string, dollar, and date.

### To Read a Fixed-Format ASCII Text Data File

▶ From the menus choose:

File
  Read ASCII Data
    Fixed Columns

▶ Click *Browse* in the Define Fixed Variables dialog box to select the data file.

▶ For each variable, enter a variable name, the start and end column locations, and a data type.

▶ Click *Add* to enter each variable definition.

**Figure 3.12   Define Fixed Variables dialog box**

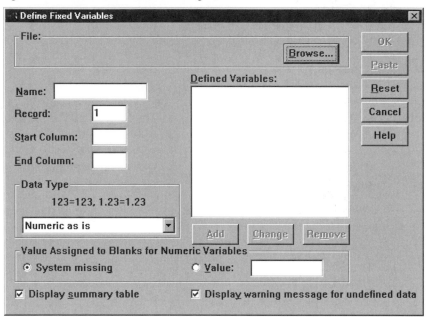

## General Rules for Reading Fixed ASCII Data

The following general rules apply:

- You can enter variables in any order. They are automatically sorted by record and start column on the list.

- You can specify multiple variables in the same or overlapping column locations. For example, you could have *bday* in columns 1–2, *bmonth* in columns 4–6, *byear* in columns 8–9, and *bdate* in columns 1–9, creating three separate variables for day, month, and year of birth, and a fourth variable combining these data for the complete date of birth.

- You can read selective data fields and/or records. You do not have to define or read all of the data in the file. SPSS reads only the columns and records you specify and skips over any data you do not define.

**Figure 3.13  Defined variables**

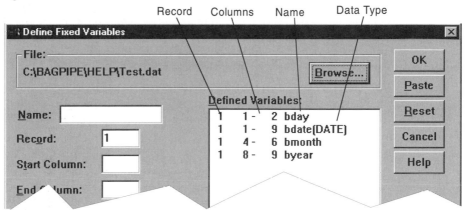

## Variable-Naming Rules

The following rules apply to variable names:

- The name must begin with a letter. The remaining characters can be any letter, any digit, a period, or the symbols @, #, _, or $.
- Variable names cannot end with a period.
- Variable names that end with an underscore should be avoided (to avoid conflict with variables automatically created by some procedures).
- The length of the name cannot exceed eight characters.
- Blanks and special characters (for example, !, ?, ', and *) cannot be used.
- Each variable name must be unique; duplication is not allowed. Variable names are not case sensitive. The names *NEWVAR*, *NewVar*, and *newvar* are all identical in SPSS.
- The following reserved keywords cannot be used as variable names:

| | | | | |
|---|---|---|---|---|
| ALL | NE | EQ | TO | LE |
| LT | BY | OR | GT | AND |
| NOT | GE | WITH | | |

## Data Types for Fixed-Format ASCII Data Files

You can define the following data types for fixed-format ASCII text data files:

**Numeric as is.** Valid values include numbers, a leading plus or minus sign, and a decimal indicator.

**Numeric 1 decimal (1).** If there is not an explicitly coded decimal indicator, one implied decimal position is assigned. For example, 123 is read as 12.3. A value with more than one explicitly coded decimal position (for example, 1.23) is read correctly but is rounded to one decimal position for display.

**Numeric 2 decimal (2).** If there is not an explicitly coded decimal indicator, two implied decimal positions are assigned. For example, 123 is read as 1.23.

**Dollar (DOLLAR).** Valid values are numbers with an optional leading dollar sign and optional commas as thousands separators.

**String (A).** Valid values include virtually any keyboard characters and embedded blanks. If the defined width is eight or fewer characters, it is a short string variable. If the defined width is more than eight characters, it is a long string variable. Short string variables can be used in many SPSS procedures; long string variables can be used in fewer procedures.

**Date (DATE).** Dates of the general format dd-mmm-yyyy. Dashes, periods, commas, slashes, or blanks can be used as delimiters. Months can be represented in digits, Roman numerals, three-letter abbreviations, or fully spelled out. Date format variables are displayed with dashes as delimiters and three-letter abbreviations for the month values. Internally, dates are stored as the number of seconds from October 14, 1582.

**American date (ADATE).** Dates of the general format mm/dd/yyyy. The conventions for the date format also apply to the American date format. ADATE format variables are displayed with slashes as delimiters and numbers for the month values.

**European date (EDATE).** Dates of the general format dd.mm.yyyy. The conventions for the date format also apply to the European date format. EDATE format variables are displayed with slashes as delimiters and numbers for the month values.

**Julian date (JDATE).** Dates of the general format yyyyddd. If the input value contains only five digits, a two-digit year is assumed and 1900 is added. Year values can be two or four digits. Two-digit year values less than 10 must contain a leading zero. All day values must be three digits. Leading zeros are required for day values less than 100.

**Quarter and year (QYR).** Dates of the general format qQyyyy. The quarter and the year are separated by the letter *Q*. Blanks can be used as additional delimiters.

**Month and year (MOYR).** Dates of the general format mm/yyyy. The date format conventions for month and year apply.

**Week and year (WKYR).** Dates of the general format wkWKyyyy. A week is expressed as a number from 1 to 53. The week and year are separated by the string *WK*. Blanks can be used as additional delimiters.

**Date and time (DATETIME).** Values containing a date and a time. The date must be written as an international date (dd-mmm-yyyy) followed by a blank and then a time value in the format hh:mm:ss.ss. The time conforms to a 24-hour clock. Fractional seconds must have the decimal indicator explicitly coded in the data value.

**Time (TIME).** Time of day or time interval values of the general format hh:mm:ss.ss. Colons, blanks, or periods can be used as delimiters between hours, minutes, and seconds. A period is required to separate seconds from fractional seconds. Internally, times are stored as the number of seconds.

**Day and time (DTIME).** Time interval that includes days in the format ddd hh:mm:ss.ss. The number of days is separated from the hours by an acceptable time delimiter—a blank, a period, or a colon. A preceding sign (+ or –) can be used. The maximum value for hours is 23.

**Day of week (WKDAY).** The day of the week expressed as a character string. Only the first two characters are significant. The remaining characters are optional. Internally, values are stored as integers from 1 to 7 (Sunday, Su, Sun=1).

**Month (MONTH).** Month of the year expressed as an integer or a character string. Only the first three characters are significant. The remaining characters are optional. Internally, values are stored as integers from 1 to 12 (January, Jan=1).

## DATA LIST Command Additional Features

The following additional data types are available with the DATA LIST command:

- Comma format—commas as thousands separators
- Dot format—commas as decimal indicators and periods as thousands separators
- Scientific notation
- Percent
- Hexadecimal
- Column binary
- Packed decimal

For a complete list of data format types, see the *SPSS Base Syntax Reference Guide*.

## Define Freefield Variables

Define Freefield Variables reads ASCII text data files in **freefield format**:

- The variables are recorded in the same order for each case, but not necessarily in the same locations.

- Spaces and commas are interpreted as delimiters between values.

- More than one case can be recorded on a single line.

- After reading the value for the last defined variable for a case, SPSS reads the next value encountered as the first variable for the next case.

- Only two data types are recognized in freefield format: simple numeric and string.

### To Read a Freefield-Format ASCII Text Data File

▶ From the menus choose:

File
  Read ASCII Data
    Freefield

▶ Click *Browse* in the Define Freefield Variables dialog box to select the data file.

▶ For each variable, enter a variable name and data type (numeric or string).

▶ For string variables, specify the variable width (maximum number of characters).

▶ Click *Add* to enter each variable definition.

Figure 3.14   Define Freefield Variables dialog box

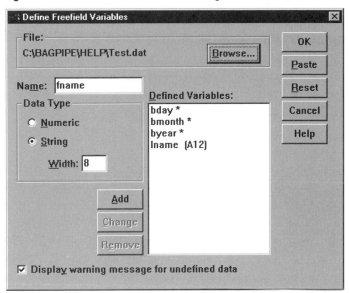

## General Rules for Reading Freefield-Format ASCII Text Data

While defining data in freefield format is relatively simple and easy, it is also easy to make mistakes. Keep the following rules in mind:

- You must enter variables in the order in which they appear in the data file. Each new variable definition is added to the bottom of the list, and SPSS reads the variables in that order.

- You must provide definitions for all variables in the file. If you omit any, the data file will be read incorrectly. SPSS determines the end of one case and the beginning of the next based on the number of defined variables.

- The data file cannot contain any missing data. Blank fields are read as delimiters between variables, and SPSS does not distinguish between single and multiple blanks. If a single observation is missing, the entire remainder of the data file will be read incorrectly.
- If your Windows Regional Settings (accessed from the Control Panel) use a period as the decimal indicator, SPSS interprets commas as delimiters between values in freefield format. For example, a value of 1,234 is read as two separate values: 1 and 234.

# File Information

An SPSS data file contains much more than raw data. It also contains any variable definition information, including:

- Variable names
- Variable formats
- Descriptive variable and value labels

This information is stored in the dictionary portion of the SPSS data file. The Data Editor provides one way to view the variable definition information. You can also display complete dictionary information for the working data file or any other SPSS data file.

### To Obtain Information about an SPSS Data File

▶ For the working data file, from the menus choose:

Utilities
  File Info

▶ For other SPSS data files, from the menus choose:

File
  Display Data Info...

▶ Select a file from the Display Data Info dialog box.

The data file information is displayed in the Output Navigator.

# Saving Data Files

Any changes you make in a data file last only for the duration of the SPSS session—unless you explicitly save the changes.

### To Save Changes to an SPSS Data File

▶ Make the Data Editor the active window (click anywhere in the window to make it active).

▶ From the menus choose:

File
  Save

The modified data file is saved, overwriting the previous version of the file.

### To Save a New SPSS Data File or Save Data in a Different Format

▶ Make the Data Editor the active window (click anywhere in the window to make it active).

▶ From the menus choose:

File
  Save As...

▶ Select a file type from the drop-down list.

▶ Enter a filename for the new data file.

To write variable names to the first row of a spreadsheet or tab-delimited data files:

▶ Click *Write variable names* in the Saving File Options dialog box.

### Saving Data: Data File Types

You can save data in the following formats:

**SPSS (\*.sav).** SPSS 7.5 for Windows. Data files saved in SPSS 7.5 format cannot be read by earlier versions of SPSS.

**SPSS 7.0 (*.sav).** SPSS 7.0 for Windows format. Data files saved in SPSS 7.0 format can be read by SPSS 7.0 and earlier version of SPSS for Windows—but do not include defined multiple response sets (Tables option) or Data Entry for Windows information.

**SPSS/PC+ (*.sys).** SPSS/PC+ format. If the data file contains more than 500 variables, only the first 500 will be saved. For variables with more than one defined user-missing value, additional user-missing values will be recoded into the first defined user-missing value.

**SPSS portable (*.por).** Portable SPSS file that can be read by other versions of SPSS on other operating systems (for example, Macintosh, UNIX).

**Tab-delimited (*.dat).** ASCII text files with values separated by tabs.

**Fixed ASCII (*.dat).** ASCII text file in fixed format, using the default write formats for all variables. There are no tabs or spaces between variable fields.

**Excel (*.xls).** Microsoft Excel 4.0 spreadsheet file. The maximum number of variables is 256.

**1-2-3 Release 3.0 (*.wk3).** Lotus 1-2-3 spreadsheet file, release 3.0. The maximum number of variables you can save is 256.

**1-2-3 Release 2.0 (*.wk1).** Lotus 1-2-3 spreadsheet file, release 2.0. The maximum number of variables you can save is 256.

**1-2-3 Release 1.0 (*.wks).** Lotus 1-2-3 spreadsheet file, release 1A. The maximum number of variables you can save is 256.

**SYLK (*.slk).** Symbolic link format for Microsoft Excel and Multiplan spreadsheet files. The maximum number of variables you can save is 256.

**dBASE IV (*.dbf).** dBASE IV format.

**dBASE III (*.dbf).** dBASE III format.

**dBASE II (*.dbf).** dBASE II format.

## Saving File Options

For spreadsheet and tab-delimited files, you can write variable names to the first row of the file.

# 4 Data Editor

The Data Editor provides a convenient, spreadsheet-like method for creating and editing SPSS data files. The Data Editor window opens automatically when you start an SPSS session.

**Figure 4.1    Data Editor**

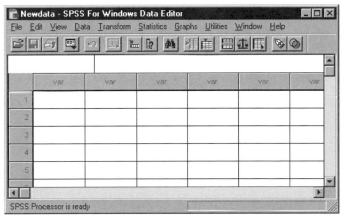

Many of the features of the Data Editor are similar to those found in spreadsheet applications. There are, however, several important distinctions:

- Rows are cases. Each row represents a case or an observation. For example, each individual respondent to a questionnaire is a case.

- Columns are variables. Each column represents a variable or a characteristic being measured. For example, each item on a questionnaire is a variable.

- Cells contain values. Each cell contains a single value of a variable for a case. The cell is the intersection of the case and the variable. Cells contain only data values. Unlike spreadsheet programs, cells in the Data Editor cannot contain formulas.

- The data file is rectangular. The dimensions of the data file are determined by the number of cases and variables. You can enter data in any cell. If you enter data in a cell outside the boundaries of the defined data file, SPSS extends the data rectangle to include any rows and/or columns between that cell and the file boundaries. There are no "empty" cells within the boundaries of the data file. For numeric variables, blank cells are converted to the system-missing value. For string variables, a blank is considered a valid value.

# Define Variable

Define Variable assigns data definition information to variables. You can define new variables or change the definition of existing variables. Data definition information includes:

- Variable name
- Data type (numeric, string, date, etc.)
- Descriptive variable and value labels
- Special codes for missing values

**Figure 4.2    Define Variable dialog box**

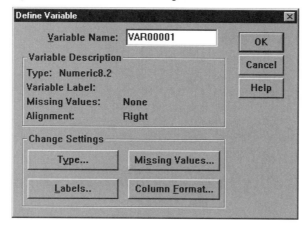

### To Define a Variable

▶  Make the Data Editor the active window.

▶  Double-click the variable name at the top of the column or click anywhere in the column for the variable, and from the menus choose:

Data
  Define Variable...

▶  Enter a variable name.

▶ Click *Type* to change the data format.

▶ Click *Labels* to assign descriptive variable and value labels.

▶ Click *Missing Values* to specify codes for missing values.

▶ Click *Column Format* to change the column width or alignment.

## Variable Names

The following rules apply to variable names:

- The name must begin with a letter. The remaining characters can be any letter, any digit, a period, or the symbols @, #, _, or $.
- Variable names cannot end with a period.
- Variable names that end with an underscore should be avoided (to avoid conflict with variables automatically created by some procedures).
- The length of the name cannot exceed eight characters.
- Blanks and special characters (for example, !, ?, ', and *) cannot be used.
- Each variable name must be unique; duplication is not allowed. Variable names are not case sensitive. The names *NEWVAR*, *NewVar*, and *newvar* are all identical in SPSS.

## Define Variable Type

Define Variable Type specifies the data type for each variable. By default, all new variables are assumed to be numeric. You can use Define Variable Type to change the data type. The contents of the Define Variable Type dialog box depend on the data type selected. For some data types, there are text boxes for width and number of decimals; for others, you can simply select a format from a scrollable list of examples.

**Figure 4.3    Define Variable Type dialog box**

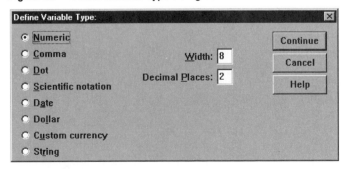

The available data types are numeric, comma, dot, scientific notation, date, dollar, custom currency, and string.

The custom currency formats CCA, CCB, CCC, CCD, and CCE are defined in the Currency tab of the Options dialog box, accessed from the Edit menu.

### Input versus Display Formats

Depending on the format, the display of values in the Data Editor may differ from the actual value as entered and stored internally. Here are some general guidelines:

- For numeric, comma, and dot formats, you can enter values with any number of decimal positions (up to 16), and the entire value is stored internally. The Data Editor displays only the defined number of decimal places, and it rounds values with more decimals. However, the complete value is used in any computations.

- For string variables, all values are right-padded to the maximum width. For a string variable with a width of 6, a value of 'No' is stored internally as 'No     ' and is not equivalent to ' No '.

- For date formats, you can use slashes, dashes, spaces, commas, or periods as delimiters between day, month, and year values, and you can enter numbers, three-letter abbreviations, or complete names for month values. Dates of the general format dd-mmm-yy are displayed with dashes as delimiters and three-letter abbreviations for the month. Dates of the general format dd/mm/yy and mm/dd/yy are displayed with slashes for delimiters and numbers for the month. Internally, dates are stored as the number of seconds from October 14, 1582.

- For time formats, you can use colons, periods, or spaces as delimiters between hours, minutes, and seconds. Times are displayed with colons as delimiters. Internally, times are stored as the number of seconds.

## Define Labels

Define Labels provides descriptive variable and value labels. Although variable names can be only 8 characters, variable labels can be up to 256 characters long, and these descriptive labels are displayed in the output.

You can assign descriptive value labels for each value of a variable. This is particularly useful if your data file uses numeric codes to represent non-numeric categories (for example, codes of 1 and 2 for male and female). Value labels can be up to 60 characters long. Value labels are not available for long string variables (string variables longer than 8 characters).

You can also modify or delete variable and value labels.

Figure 4.4    Define Labels dialog box

Define Labels: jobcat

Variable Label: Employment category

Value Labels

Value: |

Value Label:

Add
Change
Remove

1 = "Clerical"
2 = "Custodial"
3 = "Manager"

Continue
Cancel
Help

## Define Missing Values

Define Missing Values defines specified data values as user-missing. It is often useful to know why information is missing. For example, you might want to distinguish between data missing because a respondent refused to answer and data missing because the question didn't apply to that respondent. Data values specified as user-missing are flagged for special treatment and are excluded from most calculations.

Figure 4.5    Define Missing Values dialog box

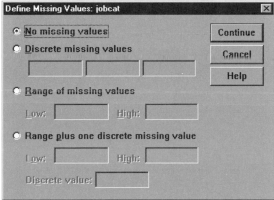

Define Missing Values: jobcat

&bull; No missing values
&bull; Discrete missing values

&bull; Range of missing values

Low:    High:

&bull; Range plus one discrete missing value

Low:    High:

Discrete value:

Continue
Cancel
Help

- You can enter up to three discreet (individual) missing values, a range of missing values, or a range plus one discreet value.
- Ranges can be specified only for numeric variables.
- You cannot define missing values for long string variables.

## Define Column Format

Define Column Format controls the width of columns in the Data Editor and the alignment of data values. Column widths can also be changed in the Data Editor by clicking and dragging the column borders.

**Figure 4.6    Define Column Format dialog box**

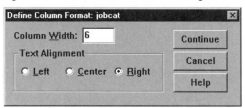

Column formats affect only the display of values in the Data Editor. Changing the column width does not change the defined width of a variable. If the defined and actual width of a value are wider than the column, asterisks (*) are displayed in the Data Editor window.

# Templates

Template provides a method for creating and applying variable definition templates. You can assign the same variable definition information to multiple variables with variable templates. For example, if you have a group of variables that all use the numeric codes 1 and 2 to represent "yes" and "no" responses and 9 to represent missing responses, you can create a template that contains those value labels and missing value specifications and apply the template to the entire group of variables.

**Figure 4.7    Template dialog box**

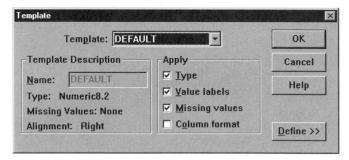

**Figure 4.8    Expanded Template dialog box**

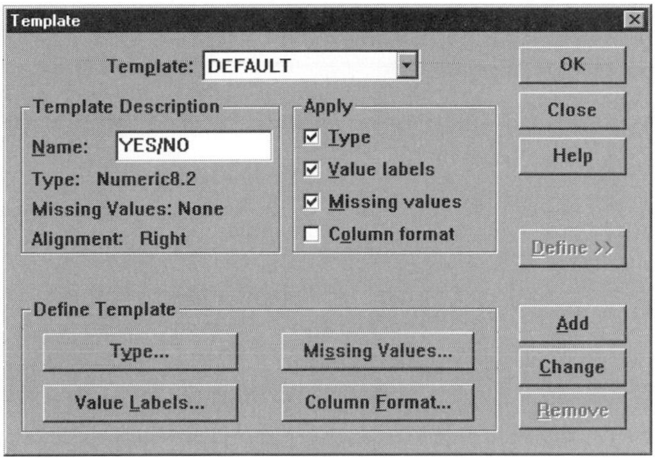

See "Define Variable" on p. 56 for descriptions of the dialog boxes for defining type, labels, missing values, and column format.

### To Create a Variable Template

▶  Make the Data Editor the active window.

▶  From the menus choose:
Data
  Templates...

▶  Click *Define* in the Template dialog box.

▶  Select the attributes you want to define.

▶  Enter a template name.

▶  Then click *Add*.

### To Modify a Variable Template

▶ Make the Data Editor the active window.

▶ From the menus choose:
Data
  Templates...

▶ Select the template from the list of template names.

▶ Click *Define*.

▶ Select the attributes you want to modify.

▶ Then click *Change*.

### To Apply a Variable Template

▶ Select the variables(s) in the Data Editor (click the variable name at the top of the column).

▶ From the menus choose:
Data
  Templates...

▶ Select the template from the list of template names.

▶ Check one or more variable definition attributes you want to apply.

▶ Click *OK* to apply the template to the selected variable(s).

# Entering Data

You can enter data directly in the Data Editor. You can enter data in any order. You can enter data by case or by variable, for selected areas or individual cells.

• The active cell is highlighted with a heavy border.

• The variable name and row number of the active cell are displayed in the top left corner of the Data Editor.

• When you select a cell and enter a data value, the value is displayed in the cell editor at the top of the Data Editor.

- Data values are not recorded until you press Enter or select another cell.
- To enter anything other than simple numeric data, you must define the variable type first.

If you enter a value in an empty column, SPSS automatically creates a new variable and assigns a variable name.

**Figure 4.9    Working data file in the Data Editor**

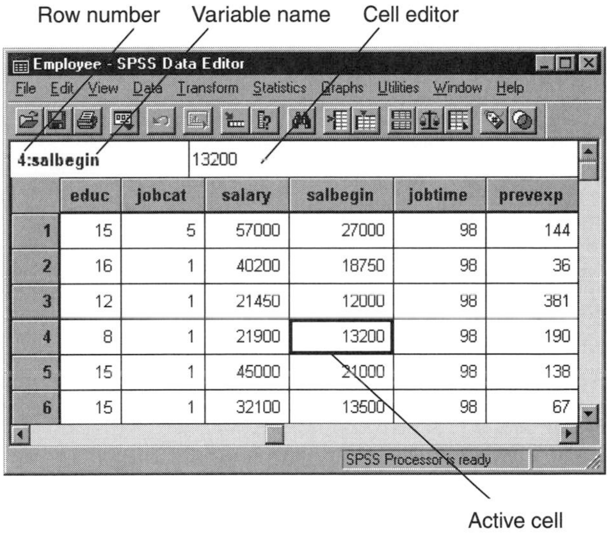

Row number    Variable name    Cell editor

Active cell

## To Enter Numeric Data

▶ Select a cell in the Data Editor.

▶ Enter the data value. The value is displayed in the cell editor at the top of the Data Editor.

▶ Press Enter or select another cell to record the value.

## To Enter Non-Numeric Data

▶ Double-click the variable name at the top of the column or click anywhere in the column for the variable, and from the menus choose:

Data
  Define Variable...

▶ Click *Type* in the Define Variable dialog box.

▶ Select the data type in the Define Variable Type dialog box.

▶ Click *Continue*.

▶ Click *OK* in the Define Variable dialog box.

▶ Enter the data in the column for the newly defined variable.

### To Use Defined Value Labels for Data Entry

▶ If value labels aren't currently displayed in the Data Editor window, from the menus choose:

View
 Value Labels

▶ Ctrl-click (press the Ctrl key and click the mouse button) on the cell in which you want to enter the value.

▶ Double-click the mouse button on the value label you want.

The value is entered and the value label is displayed in the cell.

*Note*: This works only if you have defined value labels for the variable.

## Data Value Restrictions

The defined variable type and width determine the type of value that can be entered in the cell.

• If you type a character not allowed by the defined variable type, the Data Editor beeps and does not enter the character.

• For string variables, characters beyond the defined width are not allowed.

• For numeric variables, integer values that exceed the defined width can be entered, but the Data Editor displays either scientific notation or asterisks in the cell to indicate that the value is wider than the defined width. To display the value in the cell, change the defined width of the variable. (*Note*: Changing the column width does not affect the variable width.)

# Editing Data

With the Data Editor, you can modify a data file in many ways. You can:

- Change data values.
- Cut, copy, and paste data values.
- Add and delete cases.
- Add and delete variables.
- Change the order of variables.
- Change variable definitions.

### To Replace or Modify a Data Value

To delete the old value and enter a new value:

▶ Click the cell. The cell value is displayed in the cell editor.

▶ Enter the new value. It replaces the old value in the cell editor.

▶ Press Enter (or move to another cell) to record the new value.

To modify a data value:

▶ Click the cell. The cell value appears in the cell editor.

▶ Click the cell editor.

▶ Edit the data value as you would any other text.

▶ Press Enter (or select another cell) to record the modified value.

# Cutting, Copying, and Pasting Data Values

You can cut, copy, and paste individual cell values or groups of values in the Data Editor. You can:

- Move or copy a single cell value to another cell.
- Move or copy a single cell value to a group of cells.
- Move or copy the values for a single case (row) to multiple cases.
- Move or copy the values for a single variable (column) to multiple variables.
- Move or copy a group of cell values to another group of cells.

## Data Conversion for Pasted Values in the Data Editor

If the defined variable types of the source and target cells are not the same, SPSS attempts to convert the value. If no conversion is possible, SPSS inserts the system-missing value in the target cell.

**Numeric or Date into String.** Numeric (for example, numeric, dollar, dot, or comma) and date formats are converted to strings if they are pasted into a string variable cell. The string value is the numeric value as displayed in the cell. For example, for a dollar format variable, the displayed dollar sign becomes part of the string value. Values that exceed the defined string variable width are truncated.

**String into Numeric or Date.** String values that contain acceptable characters for the numeric or date format of the target cell are converted to the equivalent numeric or date value. For example, a string value of 25/12/91 is converted to a valid date if the format type of the target cell is one of the day-month-year formats, but it is converted to system-missing if the format type of the target cell is one of the month-day-year formats.

**Date into Numeric.** Date and time values are converted to a number of seconds if the target cell is one of the numeric formats (for example, numeric, dollar, dot, or comma). Since dates are stored internally as the number of seconds since October 14, 1582, converting dates to numeric values can yield some extremely large numbers. For example, the date 10/29/91 is converted to a numeric value of 12,908,073,600.

**Numeric into Date or Time.** Numeric values are converted to dates or times if the value represents a number of seconds that can produce a valid date or time. For dates, numeric values less than 86,400 are converted to the system-missing value.

## Inserting New Cases

Entering data in a cell on a blank row automatically creates a new case. SPSS inserts the system-missing value for all of the other variables for that case. If there are any blank rows between the new case and the existing cases, the blank rows also become new cases with the system-missing value for all variables.

You can also insert new cases between existing cases.

### To Insert a New Case between Existing Cases

▶ Select any cell in the case (row) below the position in which you want to insert the new case.

▶ From the menus choose:

Data
  Insert Case

A new row is inserted for the case and all variables receive the system-missing value.

## Inserting New Variables

Entering data in a blank column automatically creates a new variable with a default variable name (the prefix *var* and a sequential five-digit number) and a default data format type (numeric). SPSS inserts the system-missing value for all cases for the new variable. If there are any blank columns between the new variable and the existing variables, these columns also become new variables with the system-missing value for all cases.

You can also insert new variables between existing variables.

### To Insert a New Variable between Existing Variables

▶ Select any cell in the variable (column) to the right of the position where you want to insert the new variable.

▶ From the menus choose:

Data
  Insert Variable

A new variable is inserted with the system-missing value for all cases.

## Moving Variables

You can move variables in the Data Editor by cutting and pasting them. If you cut and paste cell values, data definition information is not retained. If you cut and paste entire variables, all data definition information is retained.

### To Move Variables in the Data Editor

▶ If you want to move the variable between two existing variables, insert a new variable in the position where you want to move the variable.

▶ For the variable you want to move, click the variable name at the top of the column. The entire column is highlighted.

▶ From the menus choose:
Edit
  Cut

▶ Click the variable name of the column where you want to move the variable. The entire variable is highlighted.

▶ From the menus choose:
Edit
  Paste

## Changing Data Type

You can change the data type for a variable at any time using the Define Variable Type dialog box, and SPSS will attempt to convert existing values to the new type. If no conversion is possible, SPSS assigns the system-missing value. The conversion rules are the same as those for pasting data values to a variable with a different format type. If the change in data format may result in the loss of missing value specifications or value labels, SPSS displays an alert box and asks if you want to proceed with the change or cancel it.

# Go to Case

Go to Case goes to the specified case (row) number in the Data Editor.

**Figure 4.10   Go to Case dialog box**

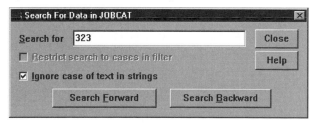

### To Go to a Case in the Data Editor

▶ Make the Data Editor the active window.

▶ From the menus choose:

Data
  Go to Case...

▶ Enter the Data Editor row number for the case.

# Search for Data

Search for Data searches for specified data values in the current variable in the Data Editor. The current variable is the variable corresponding to the active cell.

**Figure 4.11   Search for Data dialog box**

### To Find a Data Value in the Data Editor

▶ Select any cell in the column of the variable you want to search.

▶ From the menus choose:

Edit
  Find...

▶ Enter the data value you want to find.

▶ Click *Search Forward* or *Search Backward*.

Optionally, you can ignore case in string values or restrict the search to unfiltered cases.

## Case Selection Status in the Data Editor

If you have selected a subset of cases but have not discarded unselected cases, unselected cases are marked in the Data Editor with a vertical line through the row number.

**Figure 4.12 Filtered cases in Data Editor**

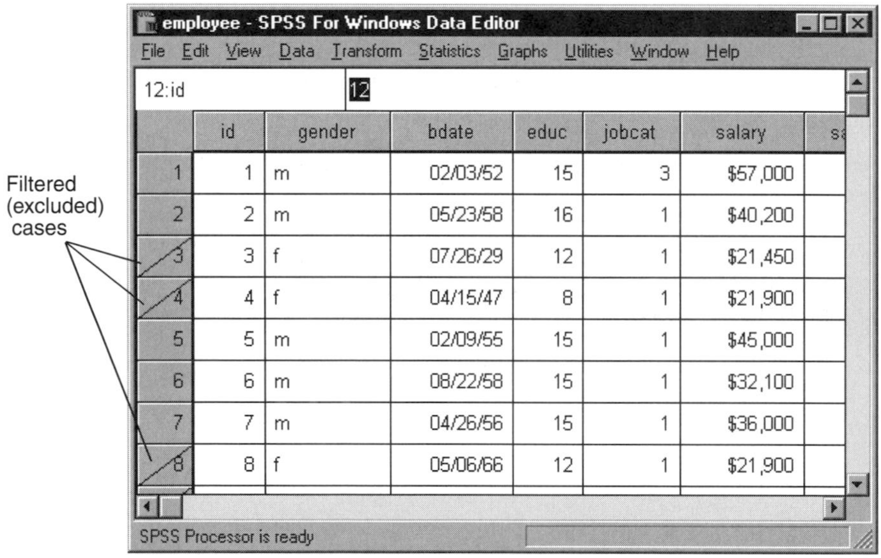
employee - SPSS For Windows Data Editor
File Edit View Data Transform Statistics Graphs Utilities Window Help
12:id
12
id gender bdate educ jobcat salary
1 1 m 02/03/52 15 3 $57,000
2 2 m 05/23/58 16 1 $40,200
3 3 f 07/26/29 12 1 $21,450
4 4 f 04/15/47 8 1 $21,900
5 5 m 02/09/55 15 1 $45,000
6 6 m 08/22/58 15 1 $32,100
7 7 m 04/26/56 15 1 $36,000
8 8 f 05/06/66 12 1 $21,900
SPSS Processor is ready
Filtered (excluded) cases

# Data Editor Display Options

The View menu provides several display options for the Data Editor:

**Fonts.** Controls the font characteristics of the data display.

**Grid Lines.** Toggles the display of gridlines on and off.

**Value Labels.** Toggles between the display of actual data values and user-defined descriptive value labels.

# 5 Data Transformations

In an ideal situation, your raw data are perfectly suitable for the type of analysis you want to perform, and any relationships between variables are either conveniently linear or neatly orthogonal. Unfortunately, this is rarely the case. Preliminary analysis may reveal inconvenient coding schemes or coding errors, or data transformations may be required in order to coax out the true relationship between variables.

With SPSS, you can perform data transformations ranging from simple tasks, such as collapsing categories for analysis, to more advanced tasks, such as creating new variables based on complex equations and conditional statements.

## Compute Variable

Compute Variable computes values for a variable based on numeric transformations of other variables.

- You can compute values for numeric or string variables.
- You can create new variables or replace the values of existing variables. For new variables, you can also specify the variable type and label.
- You can compute values selectively for subsets of data based on logical conditions.
- You can use over 70 built-in functions, including arithmetic functions, statistical functions, distribution functions, and string functions.

Figure 5.1    Compute Variable dialog box

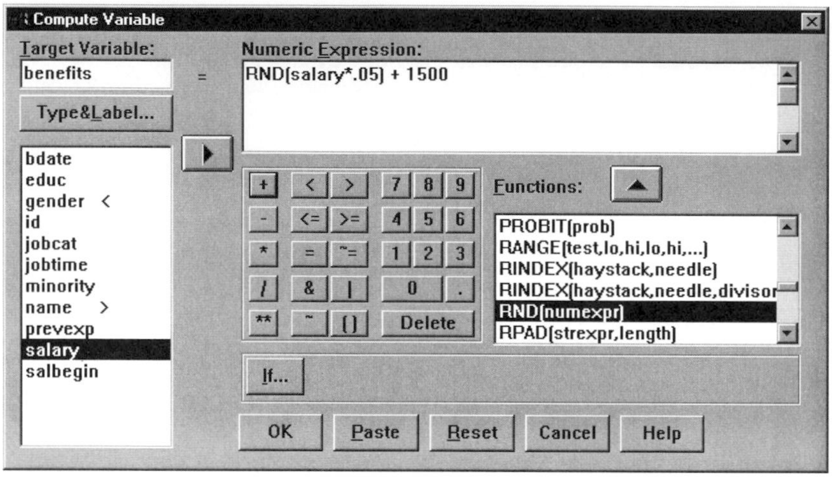

## To Compute Variables

▶  From the menus choose:

Transform
    Compute...

▶  Type the name of a single target variable. It can be an existing variable or a new variable to be added to the working data file.

▶  To build an expression, either paste components into the Expression field or type directly in the Expression field.

• Paste functions from the function list and fill in the parameters indicated by question marks.

• String constants must be enclosed in quotation marks or apostrophes.

• Numeric constants must be typed in American format, with the period (.) as the decimal indicator.

• For new string variables, you must also select *Type & Label* to specify the data type.

## Compute Variable: If Cases

The If Cases dialog box allows you to apply data transformations to selected subsets of cases, using conditional expressions. A conditional expression returns a value of *true*, *false*, or *missing* for each case.

- If the result of a conditional expression is *true*, the transformation is applied to the case.
- If the result of a conditional expression is *false* or *missing*, the transformation is not applied to the case.
- Most conditional expressions use one or more of the six relational operators (<, >, <=, >=, =, ~=) on the calculator pad.
- Conditional expressions can include variable names, constants, arithmetic operators, numeric and other functions, logical variables, and relational operators.

**Figure 5.2    If Cases dialog box**

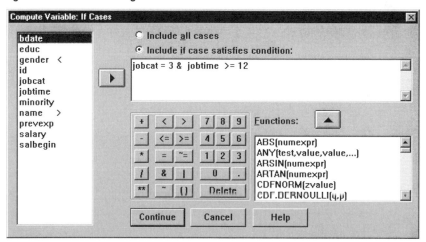

## Compute Variable: Type and Label

By default, new computed variables are numeric. To compute a new string variable, you must specify the data type and width.

**Label.** Optional, descriptive variable label up to 120 characters long. You can enter a label or use the first 110 characters of the compute expression as the label.

**Type.** Computed variables can be numeric or string (alphanumeric). String variables cannot be used in calculations.

**Figure 5.3    Type and Label dialog box**

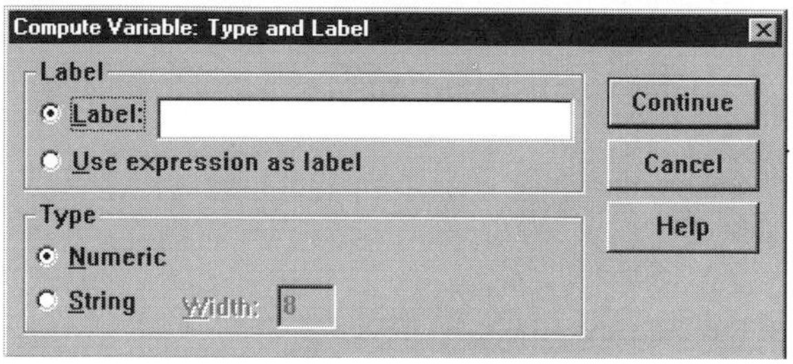

# Functions

SPSS supports many types of functions, including:

- Arithmetic functions
- Statistical functions
- String functions
- Date and time functions
- Distribution functions
- Random variable functions
- Missing value functions

Search for "functions" in the online Help system index for a complete list of SPSS functions. Click the right mouse button on a selected function in the list for a description of that function.

## Missing Values in Functions

Functions and simple arithmetic expressions treat missing values in different ways. In the expression

(var1+var2+var3)/3

the result is missing if a case has a missing value for any of the three variables.

In the expression

MEAN(var1, var2, var3)

the result is missing only if the case has missing values for all three variables.

For statistical functions, you can specify the minimum number of arguments that must have nonmissing values. To do so, type a period and the minimum number after the function name, as in

MEAN.2(var1, var2, var3)

# Random Number Seed

Random Number Seed sets the seed used by the pseudo-random number generator to a specific value so that you can reproduce a sequence of pseudo-random numbers.

The random number seed changes each time SPSS generates a random number for use in transformations (such as the UNIFORM and NORMAL functions), random sampling, or case weighting. To replicate a sequence of random numbers, use this dialog box to reset the seed to a specific value prior to each analysis that uses the random numbers.

Figure 5.4    Random Number Seed dialog box

### To Set the Random Number Seed

▶ From the menus choose:

Transform
  Random Number Seed...

▶ Select *Set seed to*.

▶ Enter a positive integer between 1 and 2,000,000,000.

# Count Occurrences of Values within Cases

This dialog box creates a variable that counts the occurrences of the same value(s) in a list of variables for each case. For example, a survey might contain a list of magazines with *yes/no* check boxes to indicate which magazines each respondent reads. You could count the number of *yes* responses for each respondent to create a new variable that contains the total number of magazines read.

**Figure 5.5   Count Occurrences dialog box**

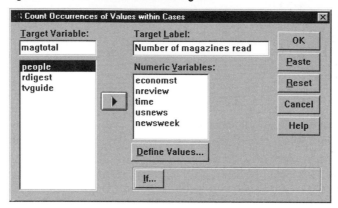

## To Count Occurrences of Values within Cases

▶   From the menus choose:

Transform
  Count...

▶   Enter a target variable name.

▶   Select two or more variables of the same type (numeric or string).

▶   Click *Define Values* and specify which value or values should be counted.

Optionally, you can define a subset of cases for which to count occurrences of values.

The If Cases dialog box for defining subsets of cases is the same as the one described for Compute Variable.

# Count Values within Cases: Values to Count

The value of the target variable (on the main dialog box) is incremented by 1 each time one of the selected variables matches a specification in the Values to Count list here. If a case matches several specifications for any variable, the target variable is incremented several times for that variable.

Value specifications can include individual values, missing or system-missing values, and ranges. Ranges include their endpoints and any user-missing values that fall within the range.

**Figure 5.6    Values to Count dialog box**

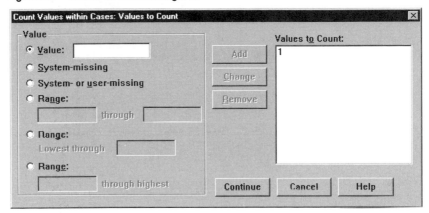

# Recoding Values

You can modify data values by recoding them. This is particularly useful for collapsing or combining categories. You can recode the values within existing variables or you can create new variables based on the recoded values of existing variables.

## Recode into Same Variables

Recode into Same Variables reassigns the values of existing variables or collapses ranges of existing values into new values. For example, you could collapse salaries into salary range categories.

You can recode numeric and string variables. If you select multiple variables, they must all be the same type. You cannot recode numeric and string variables together.

**Figure 5.7    Recode into Same Variables dialog box**

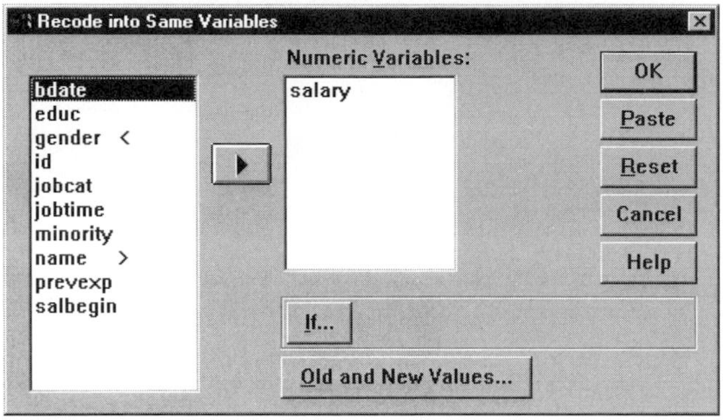

## To Recode the Values of a Variable

▶   From the menus choose:

Transform
 Recode
  Into Same Variables...

▶   Select the variables you want to recode. If you select multiple variables, they must be the same type (numeric or string).

▶   Click *Old and New Values* and specify how to recode values.

Optionally, you can define a subset of cases to recode.

The If Cases dialog box for defining subsets of cases is the same as the one described for Compute Variable.

## Recode into Same Variables: Old and New Values

You can define values to recode in this dialog box. All value specifications must be the same data type (numeric or string) as the variables selected in the main dialog box.

**Old Value**. The value(s) to be recoded. You can recode single values, ranges of values, and missing values. System-missing values and ranges cannot be selected for string variables, since neither concept applies to string variables. Ranges include their endpoints and any user-missing values that fall within the range.

**New Value.** The single value into which each old value or range of values is recoded. You can enter a value or assign the system-missing value.

**Old->New.** The list of specifications that will be used to recode the variable(s). You can add, change, and remove specifications from the list. The list is automatically sorted, based on the old value specification, using the following order: single values, missing values, ranges, and all other values. If you change a recode specification on the list, SPSS automatically re-sorts the list, if necessary, to maintain this order.

**Figure 5.8    Old and New Values dialog box**

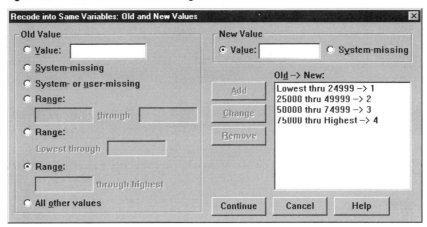

## Recode into Different Variables

Recode into Different Variables reassigns the values of existing variables or collapses ranges of existing values into new values for a new variable. For example, you could collapse salaries into a new variable containing salary-range categories.

• You can recode numeric and string variables.

• You can recode numeric variables into string variables and vice-versa.

• If you select multiple variables, they must all be the same type. You cannot recode numeric and string variables together.

**Figure 5.9    Recode into Different Variables dialog box**

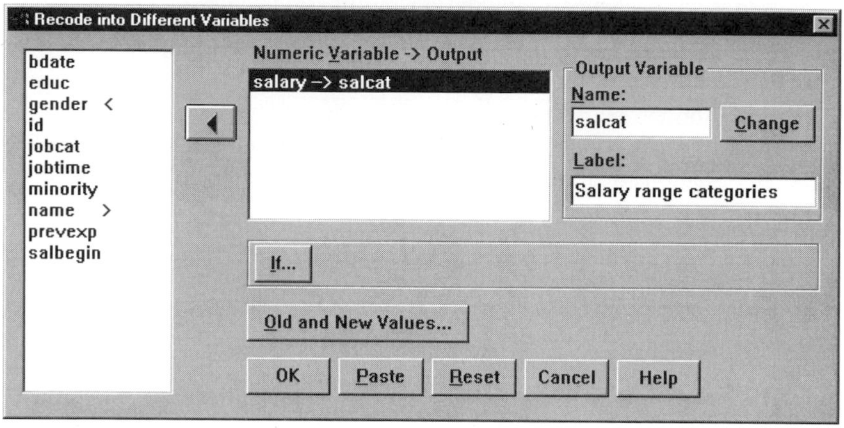

## To Recode the Values of a Variable into a New Variable

▶ From the menus choose:

Transform
  Recode
    Into Different Variables...

▶ Select the variables you want to recode. If you select multiple variables, they must be the same type (numeric or string).

▶ Enter an output (new) variable name for each new variable and click *Change*.

▶ Click *Old and New Values* and specify how to recode values.

Optionally, you can define a subset of cases to recode.

## Recode into Different Variables: Old and New Values

You can define values to recode in this dialog box.

**Old Value**. The value(s) to be recoded. You can recode single values, ranges of values, and missing values. System-missing values and ranges cannot be selected for string variables, since neither concept applies to string variables. Old values must be the same data type (numeric or string) as the original variable. Ranges include their endpoints and any user-missing values that fall within the range.

**New Value.** The single value into which each old value or range of values is recoded. New values can be numeric or string.

- If you want to recode a numeric variable into a string variable, you must also select *Output variables are strings.*

- Any old values that are not specified are not included in the new variable, and cases with those values will be assigned the system-missing value for the new variable. To include all old values that do not require recoding, select *All other values* for the old value and *Copy old value(s)* for the new value.

**Old->New.** The list of specifications that will be used to recode the variable(s). You can add, change, and remove specifications from the list. The list is automatically sorted, based on the old value specification, using the following order: single values, missing values, ranges, and all other values. If you change a recode specification on the list, SPSS automatically re-sorts the list, if necessary, to maintain this order.

**Figure 5.10   Old and New Values dialog box**

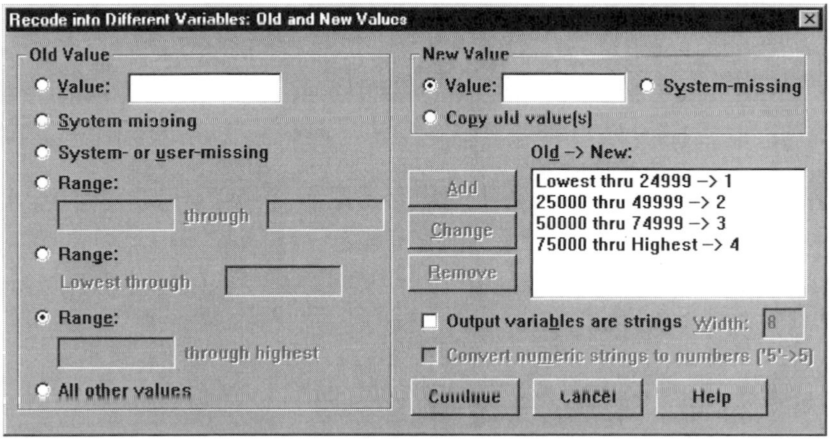

# Rank Cases

Rank Cases creates new variables containing ranks, normal and savage scores, and percentile values for numeric variables.

New variable names and descriptive variable labels are automatically generated by SPSS, based on the original variable name and the selected measure(s). A summary table lists the original variables, the new variables, and the variable labels.

Optionally, you can:

- Rank cases in ascending or descending order.

- Organize rankings into subgroups by selecting one or more grouping variables for the By list. Ranks are computed within each group. Groups are defined by the combination of values of the grouping variables. For example, if you select *gender* and *minority* as grouping variables, ranks are computed for each combination of *gender* and *minority*.

**Figure 5.11   Rank Cases dialog box**

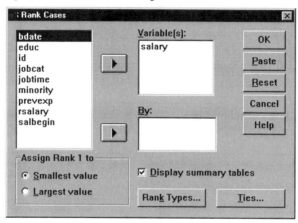

## To Rank Cases

▶   From the menus choose:

Transform
   Rank Cases...

▶   Select one or more variables to rank. You can rank only numeric variables.

Optionally, you can rank cases in ascending or descending order and organize ranks into subgroups.

# Rank Cases: Types

You can select multiple ranking methods. A separate ranking variable is created for each method. Ranking methods include simple ranks, Savage scores, fractional ranks, and percentiles. You can also create rankings based on proportion estimates and normal scores.

**Proportion Estimation Formula.** For proportion estimates and normal scores, you can select the proportion estimation formula: *Blom, Tukey, Rankit,* or *Van der Waerden.*

Figure 5.12   Rank Cases Types dialog box

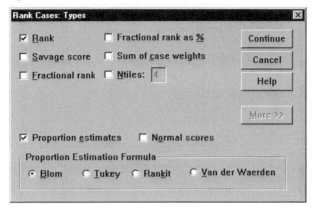

# Rank Cases: Ties

This dialog box controls the method for assigning rankings to cases with the same value on the original variable.

Figure 5.13   Rank Cases Ties dialog box

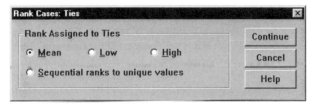

The following table shows how the different methods assign ranks to tied values:

| Value | Mean | Low | High | Sequential |
|-------|------|-----|------|------------|
| 10 | 1 | 1 | 1 | 1 |
| 15 | 3 | 2 | 4 | 2 |
| 15 | 3 | 2 | 4 | 2 |
| 15 | 3 | 2 | 4 | 2 |
| 16 | 5 | 5 | 5 | 3 |
| 20 | 6 | 6 | 6 | 4 |

# Automatic Recode

Automatic Recode converts string and numeric values into consecutive integers. When category codes are not sequential, the resulting empty cells reduce performance and increase memory requirements for many SPSS procedures. Additionally, some procedures cannot use string variables, and some require consecutive integer values for factor levels.

**Figure 5.14    Automatic Recode dialog box**

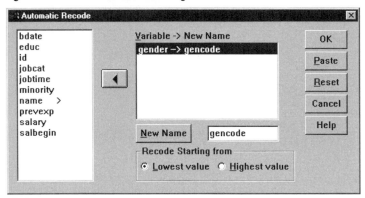

The new variable(s) created by Automatic Recode retain any defined variable and value labels from the old variable. For any values without a define value label, the original value is used as the label for the recoded value. A table displays the old and new values and value labels.

String values are recoded in alphabetical order, with uppercase letters preceding their lowercase counterparts. Missing values are recoded into missing values higher than any nonmissing values, with their order preserved. For example, if the original variable has 10 nonmissing values, the lowest missing value would be recoded to 11, and the value 11 would be a missing value for the new variable.

### To Recode String or Numeric Values into Consecutive Integers

▶   From the menus choose:

Transform
    Automatic Recode...

▶   Select one or more variables to recode.

▶   For each selected variable, enter a name for the new variable and click *New Name*.

# Time Series Data Transformations

SPSS provides several data transformations that are useful in time series analysis:

- Generate date variables to establish periodicity, and distinguish between historical, validation, and forecasting periods.

- Create new time series variables as functions of existing time series variables.

- Replace system- and user-missing values with estimates based on one of several methods.

A **time series** is obtained by measuring a variable (or set of variables) regularly over a period of time. Time series data transformations assume a data file structure in which each case (row) represents a set of observations at a different time, and the length of time between cases is uniform.

## Define Dates

Define Dates generates date variables that can be used to establish the periodicity of a time series and to label output from time series analysis.

**Figure 5.15   Define Dates dialog box**

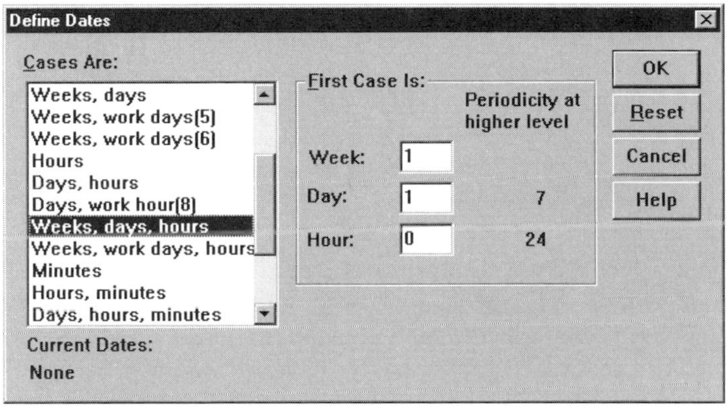

**Cases Are.** Defines the time interval used to generate dates.

- *Not dated* removes any previously defined date variables. Any variables with the following names are deleted: *year_*, *quarter_*, *month_*, *week_*, *day_*, *hour_*, *minute_*, *second_*, and *date_*.

- *Custom* indicates the presence of custom date variables created with command syntax (for example, a four-day work week). This item merely reflects the current state of the working data file. Selecting it from the list has no effect. (See the *SPSS Base*

*Syntax Reference Guide* for information on using the DATE command to create custom date variables.)

**First Case Is.** Defines the starting date value, which is assigned to the first case. Sequential values, based on the time interval, are assigned to subsequent cases.

**Periodicity at higher level.** Indicates the repetitive cyclical variation, such as the number of months in a year or the number of days in a week. The value displayed indicates the maximum value you can enter.

For each component that is used to define the date, SPSS creates a new numeric variable. The new variable names end with an underscore. A descriptive string variable, *date_*, is also created from the components. For example, if you selected *Weeks, days, hours*, four new variables are created: *week_*, *day_*, *hour_*, and *date_*.

If date variables have already been defined, they are replaced when you define new date variables that will have the same names as the existing date variables.

### To Define Dates for Time Series Data

▶  From the menus choose:

Data
  Define Dates...

▶  Select a time interval from the *Cases Are* list.

▶  Enter the value(s) that define the starting date for First Case Is, which determines the date assigned to the first case.

### Date Variables versus Date Format Variables

Date variables created with Define Dates should not be confused with date format variables, defined with Define Variable. Date variables are used to establish periodicity for time series data. Date format variables represent dates and/or times displayed in various date/time formats. Date variables are simple integers representing the number of days, weeks, hours, etc., from a user-specified starting point. Internally, most date format variables are stored as the number of seconds from October 14, 1582.

## Create Time Series

Create Time Series creates new variables based on functions of existing numeric time series variables. These transformed values are useful in many time series analysis procedures.

Default new variable names are the first six characters of the existing variable used to create it, followed by an underscore and a sequential number. For example, for the variable *price*, the new variable name would be *price_1*. The new variables retain any defined value labels from the original variables.

Available functions for creating time series variables include differences, moving averages, running medians, lag, and lead functions.

**Figure 5.16  Create Time Series dialog box**

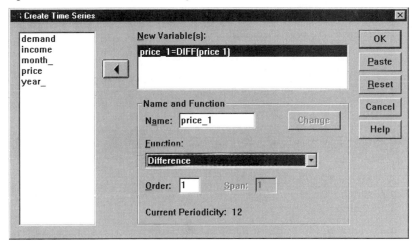

## To Create a New Time Series Variable

▶ From the menus choose:

Transform
  Create Time Series...

▶ Select the time series function you want to use to transform the original variable(s).

▶ Select the variable(s) from which you want to create new time series variables. Only numeric variables can be used.

Optionally, you can:

• Enter variable names to override the default new variable names.

• Change the function for a selected variable.

### Time Series Transformation Functions

**Difference.** Nonseasonal difference between successive values in the series. The order is the number of previous values used to calculate the difference. Since one observation is lost for each order of difference, system-missing values appear at the beginning of the series. For example, if the difference order is 2, the first two cases will have the system-missing value for the new variable.

**Seasonal difference.** Difference between series values a constant span apart. The span is based on the currently defined periodicity. To compute seasonal differences, you must have defined date variables (Data menu, Define Dates) that include a periodic component (such as months of the year). The order is the number of seasonal periods used to compute the difference. The number of cases with the system-missing value at the beginning of the series is equal to the periodicity multiplied by the order. For example, if the current periodicity is 12 and the order is 2, the first 24 cases will have the system-missing value for the new variable.

**Centered moving average.** Average of a span of series values surrounding and including the current value. The span is the number of series values used to compute the average. If the span is even, the moving average is computed by averaging each pair of uncentered means. The number of cases with the system-missing value at the beginning and at the end of the series for a span of $n$ is equal to $n/2$ for even span values and for odd span values. For example, if the span is 5, the number of cases with the system-missing value at the beginning and at the end of the series is 2.

**Prior moving average.** Average of the span of series values preceding the current value. The span is the number of preceding series values used to compute the average. The number of cases with the system-missing value at the beginning of the series is equal to the span value.

**Running median.** Median of a span of series values surrounding and including the current value. The span is the number of series values used to compute the median. If the span is even, the median is computed by averaging each pair of uncentered medians. The number of cases with the system-missing value at the beginning and at the end of the series for a span of $n$ is equal to $n/2$ for even span values and for odd span values. For example, if the span is 5, the number of cases with the system-missing value at the beginning and at the end of the series is 2.

**Cumulative sum.** Cumulative sum of series values up to and including the current value.

**Lag.** Value of a previous case, based on the specified lag order. The order is the number of cases prior to the current case from which the value is obtained. The number of cases with the system-missing value at the beginning of the series is equal to the order value.

**Lead.** Value of a subsequent case, based on the specified lead order. The order is the number of cases after the current case from which the value is obtained. The number of cases with the system-missing value at the end of the series is equal to the order value.

**Smoothing.** New series values based on a compound data smoother. The smoother starts with a running median of 4, which is centered by a running median of 2. It then resmoothes these values by applying a running median of 5, a running median of 3, and hanning (running weighted averages). Residuals are computed by subtracting the smoothed series from the original series. This whole process is then repeated on the computed residuals. Finally, the smoothed residuals are computed by subtracting the smoothed values obtained the first time through the process. This is sometimes referred to as T4253H smoothing.

## Replace Missing Values

Missing observations can be problematic in analysis, and some time series measures cannot be computed if there are missing values in the series. Replace Missing Values creates new time series variables from existing ones, replacing missing values with estimates computed with one of several methods.

Default new variable names are the first six characters of the existing variable used to create it, followed by an underscore and a sequential number. For example, for the variable *price*, the new variable name would be *price_1*. The new variables retain any defined value labels from the original variables.

Figure 5.17   Replace Missing Values dialog box

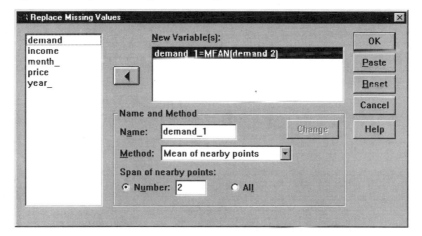

## To Replace Missing Values for Time Series Variables

▶  From the menus choose:

Transform
  Replace Missing Values...

▶  Select the estimation method you want to use to replace missing values.

▶  Select the variable(s) for which you want to replace missing values.

Optionally, you can:
- Enter variable names to override the default new variable names.
- Change the estimation method for a selected variable.

## Estimation Methods for Replacing Missing Values

**Series mean.** Replaces missing values with the mean for the entire series.

**Mean of nearby points.** Replaces missing values with the mean of valid surrounding values. The span of nearby points is the number of valid values above and below the missing value used to compute the mean.

**Median of nearby points.** Replaces missing values with the median of valid surrounding values. The span of nearby points is the number of valid values above and below the missing value used to compute the median.

**Linear interpolation.** Replaces missing values using a linear interpolation. The last valid value before the missing value and the first valid value after the missing value are used for the interpolation. If the first or last case in the series has a missing value, the missing value is not replaced.

**Linear trend at point.** Replaces missing values with the linear trend for that point. The existing series is regressed on an index variable scaled 1 to $n$. Missing values are replaced with their predicted values.

# 6

# File Handling and File Transformations

Data files are not always organized in the ideal form for your specific needs. You may want to combine data files, sort the data in a different order, select a subset of cases, or change the unit of analysis by grouping cases together. SPSS offers a wide range of file transformation capabilities, including the ability to:

**Sort data.** You can sort cases based on the value of one or more variables.

**Transpose cases and variables.** SPSS reads rows as cases and columns as variables. For data files in which this order is reversed, you can switch the rows and columns and read the data in the correct format.

**Merge files.** You can merge two or more data files together. You can combine files with the same variables but different cases or the same cases but different variables.

**Select subsets of cases.** You can restrict your analysis to a subset of cases or perform simultaneous analyses on different subsets.

**Aggregate data.** You can change the unit of analysis by aggregating cases based on the value of one or more grouping variables.

**Weight data.** Weight cases for analysis based on the value of a weight variable.

## Sort Cases

This dialog box sorts cases (rows) of the data file based on the values of one or more sorting variables. You can sort cases in ascending or descending order.

- If you select multiple sort variables, cases are sorted by each variable within categories of the prior variable on the Sort list. For example, if you select *gender* as the first sorting variable and *minority* as the second sorting variable, cases will be sorted by minority classification within each gender category.

- For string variables, uppercase letters precede their lowercase counterparts in sort order. For example, the string value "Ycs" comes before "yes" in sort order.

**Figure 6.1 Sort Cases dialog box**

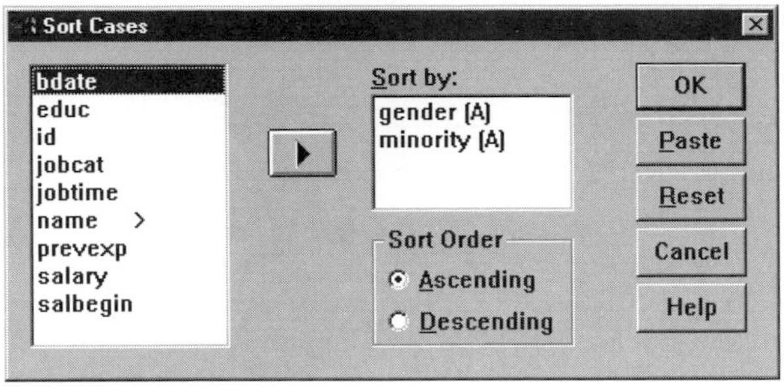

## To Sort Cases

▶ From the menus choose:

Data
  Sort Cases...

▶ Select one or more sorting variables.

# Transpose

Transpose creates a new data file in which the rows and columns in the original data file are transposed so that cases (rows) become variables and variables (columns) become cases. SPSS automatically creates new variable names and displays a list of the new variable names.

- SPSS automatically creates a new string variable, *case_lbl*, that contains the original variable names.

- If the working data file contains an ID or name variable with unique values, you can use it as the name variable, and its values will be used as variable names in the transposed data file. If it is a numeric variable, the variable names start with the letter *V*, followed by the numeric value.

- User-missing values are converted to the system-missing value in the transposed data file. To retain any of these values, change the definition of missing values (Data menu, Define Variable).

### To Transpose Variables and Cases

▶ From the menus choose:

Data
  Transpose...

▶ Select one or more variables to transpose into cases.

# Merging Data Files

With SPSS, you can merge data from two files in two different ways. You can:

- Merge files containing the same variables but different cases.
- Merge files containing the same cases but different variables.

## Add Cases

Add Cases merges the working data file with a second SPSS data file that contains the same variables but different cases. For example, you might record the same information for customers in two different sales regions and maintain the data for each region in separate files.

- The variables can be in any order in the two files. Variables are matched by name.
- Both files must be sorted in the same case order, so before you can merge the files, you must complete any necessary sorting (Data menu, Sort Cases).

Figure 6.2    Add Cases dialog box

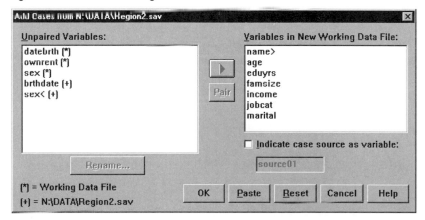

**Unpaired Variables.** Variables to be excluded from the new, merged data file. Variables from the working data file are identified with an asterisk (*). Variables from the external data file are identified with a plus sign (+). By default, this list contains:

- Variables from either data file that do not match a variable name in the other file. You can create pairs from unpaired variables and include them in the new, merged file.

- Variables defined as numeric data in one file and string data in the other file. Numeric variables cannot be merged with string variables.

- String variables of unequal width. The defined width of a string variable must be the same in both data files.

**Variables in New Working Data File.** Variables to be included in the new, merged data file. By default, all of the variables that match both the name and the data type (numeric or string) are included on the list.

- You can remove variables from the list if you don't want them to be included in the merged file.

- Any unpaired variables included in the merged file will contain missing data for cases from the file that does not contain that variable.

### To Merge Files with the Same Variables and Different Cases

▶ Open one of the data files. The cases from this file will appear first in the new, merged data file.

▶ From the menus choose:

Data
  Merge Files
    Add Cases...

▶ Select the data file to merge with the open data file.

▶ Remove any variables you don't want from the Variables in New Working Data File list.

▶ Add any variable pairs from the Unpaired Variables list that represent the same information recorded under different variable names in the two files. For example, date of birth might have the variable name *brthdate* in one file and *datebrth* in the other file.

### To Select a Pair of Unpaired Variables

▶ Click one of the variables on the Unpaired Variables list.

▶ Ctrl-click the other variable on the list. (Press the Ctrl key and click the left mouse button at the same time.)

▶ Click *Pair* to move the variable pair to the Variables in New Working Data File list. (The variable name from the working data file is used as the variable name in the merged file.).

**Figure 6.3    Selecting pairs of variables with Ctrl-click**

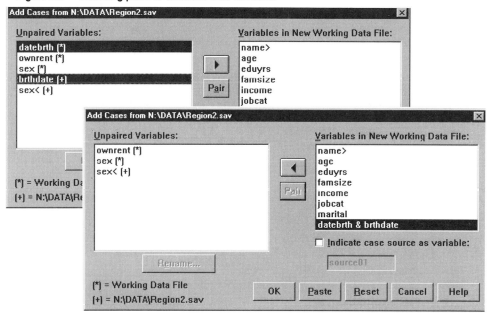

## Add Cases: Rename

You can rename variables from either the working data file or the external file before moving them from the unpaired list to the list of variables to be included in the merged data file. Renaming variables enables you to:

- Use the variable name from the external file rather than the name from the working data file for variable pairs.
- Include two variables with the same name but of unmatched types or different string widths. For example, to include both the numeric variable *sex* from the working data file and the string variable *sex* from the external file, one of them must be renamed first.

### Add Cases: Dictionary Information

Any existing dictionary information (variable and value labels, user-missing values, display formats) in the working data file is applied to the merged data file.

- If any dictionary information for a variable is undefined in the working data file, dictionary information from the external data file is used.

- If the working data file contains any defined value labels or user-missing values for a variable, any additional value labels or user-missing values for that variable in the external file are ignored.

## Add Variables

Add Variables merges the working data file with an external SPSS data file that contains the same cases but different variables. For example, you might want to merge a data file that contains pre-test results with one that contains post-test results.

- Cases must be sorted in the same order in both data files.

- If one or more key variables are used to match cases, the two data files must be sorted by ascending order of the key variable(s).

- Variable names in the second data file that duplicate variable names in the working data file are excluded by default because SPSS assumes that these variables contain duplicate information.

Figure 6.4    Add Variables dialog box

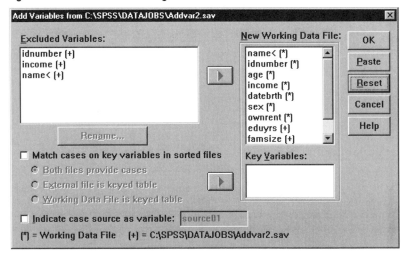

**Excluded Variables.** Variables to be excluded from the new, merged data file. By default, this list contains any variable names from the external data file that duplicate variable names in the working data file. Variables from the working data file are identified with an asterisk (*). Variables from the external data file are identified with a plus sign (+). If you want to include an excluded variable with a duplicate name in the merged file, you can rename it and add it to the list of variables to be included.

**New Working Data File.** Variables to be included in the new, merged data file. By default, all unique variable names in both data files are included on the list.

**Key Variables.** If some cases in one file do not have matching cases in the other file (that is, some cases are missing in one file), use key variables to identify and correctly match cases from the two files. You can also use key variables with table lookup files.

- The key variables must have the same names in both data files.
- Both data files must be sorted by ascending order of the key variables, and the order of variables on the Key Variables list must be the same as their sort sequence.
- Cases that do not match on the key variables are included in the merged file but are not merged with cases from the other file. Unmatched cases contain values for only the variables in the file from which they are taken; variables from the other file contain the system-missing value.

**External file or working data file is keyed table.** A keyed table, or **table lookup file**, is a file in which data for each "case" can be applied to multiple cases in the other data file. For example, if one file contains information on individual family members (such as sex, age, education) and the other file contains overall family information (such as total income, family size, location), you can use the file of family data as a table lookup file and apply the common family data to each individual family member in the merged data file.

### To Merge Files with the Same Cases but Different Variables

▶ Open one of the data files.

▶ From the menus choose:
Data
  Merge Files
    Add Variables...

▶ Select the data file to merge with the open data file.

### To Select Key Variables

▶ Select the variables from the external file variables (+) on the Excluded Variables list.

▶ Select *Match cases on key variables in sorted files*.

▶ Add the variables to the Key Variables list.

The key variables must exist in both the working data file and the external data file. Both data files must be sorted by ascending order of the key variables, and the order of variables on the Key Variables list must be the same as their sort sequence.

### Add Variables: Rename

You can rename variables from either the working data file or the external file before moving them to the list of variables to be included in the merged data file. This is useful primarily if you want to include two variables with the same name that contain different information in the two files.

# Apply SPSS Dictionary

This dialog box applies SPSS dictionary information (labels, missing values, formats) from an external SPSS data file to the working data file. Dictionary information is applied based on matching variable names. The variables don't have to be in the same order in both files, and variables that aren't present in both files are unaffected. The following rules apply:

• If the variable type (numeric or string) is the same in both files, all of the dictionary information is applied.

• If the variable type is not the same for both files, or if it is a long string (more than eight characters), only the variable label is applied.

• Numeric, dollar, dot, comma, date, and time formats are all considered numeric, and all dictionary information is applied.

• String variable widths are not affected by the applied dictionary.

• For short string variables (eight characters or less), missing values and specified values for value labels are truncated if they exceed the defined width of the variable in the working data file.

• Any applied dictionary information overwrites existing dictionary information.

### To Apply an SPSS Data Dictionary to the Working Data File

▶ From the menus choose:

File
  Apply Data Dictionary...

▶ Select the SPSS data file with the dictionary information you want to apply to the working data file.

## Applying an SPSS Dictionary to Weighted Data Files

The following rules apply when applying a data dictionary to weighted data files:

- If the working data file is weighted and the file containing the dictionary is unweighted, the working data file remains weighted.
- If the working data file is unweighted and the file containing the dictionary is weighted by a variable that exists in the working data file, the working data file is weighted by that variable.
- If both files are weighted but they are not weighted by the same variable, the weight is changed in the working data file if the weight variable in the file containing the dictionary also exists in the working data file.

# Aggregate Data

Aggregate Data combines groups of cases into single summary cases and creates a new aggregated data file. Cases are aggregated based on the value of one or more grouping variables. The new data file contains one case for each group. For example, you could aggregate county data by state and create a new data file in which state is the unit of analysis.

Figure 6.5    Aggregate Data dialog box

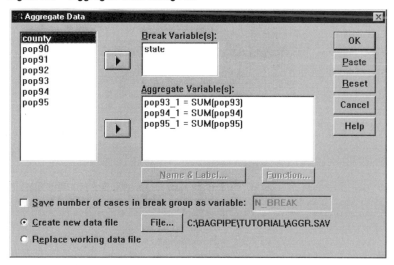

**Break Variable(s).** Cases are grouped together based on the values of the break variables. Each unique combination of break variable values defines a group and generates one case in the new aggregated file. All break variables are saved in the new file with their existing names and dictionary information. The break variable can be either numeric or string.

**Aggregate Variable(s).** Variables are used with aggregate functions to create the new variables for the aggregated file. By default, SPSS creates new aggregate variable names using the first several characters of the source variable name followed by an underscore and a sequential two-digit number. The aggregate variable name is followed by an optional variable label in quotes, the name of the aggregate function, and the source variable name in parentheses. Source variables for aggregate functions must be numeric.

You can override the default aggregate variable names with new variable names, provide descriptive variable labels, and change the functions used to compute the aggregated data values. You can also create a variable that contains the number of cases in each break group.

### To Aggregate a Data File

▶ From the menus choose:

Data
  Aggregate...

▶ Select one or more break variables that define how cases are grouped to create aggregated data.

▶ Select one or more aggregate variables to include in the new data file.

▶ Select an aggregate function for each aggregate variable.

## Aggregate Data: Aggregate Function

This dialog box specifies the function to use to calculate aggregated data values for selected variables on the Aggregate Variables list in the Aggregate Data dialog box. Aggregate functions include:

- Summary functions, including mean, standard deviation, and sum
- Percentage or fraction of values above or below a specified value
- Percentage or fraction of values inside or outside a specified range

**Figure 6.6     Aggregate Function dialog box**

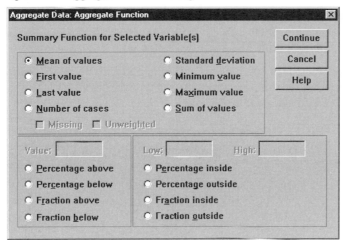

## Aggregate Data: Variable Name and Label

SPSS assigns default variable names for the aggregated variables in the new data file. This dialog box enables you to change the variable name for the selected variable on the Aggregate Variables list and provide a descriptive variable label.

- Variable names cannot exceed 8 characters.
- Variable labels can be up to 120 characters.

**Figure 6.7     Name and Label dialog box**

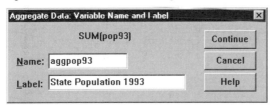

# Split File

Split File splits the data file into separate groups for analysis, based on the values of one or more grouping variables. If you select multiple grouping variables, cases are grouped by each variable within categories of the prior variable on the Groups Based On list. For example, if you select *gender* as the first grouping variable and *minority* as the second grouping variable, cases will be grouped by minority classification within each gender category.

- You can specify up to eight grouping variables.

- Each eight characters of a long string variable counts as a variable toward the limit of eight grouping variables.

- Cases should be sorted by values of the grouping variables, in the same order as variables are listed in the Groups Based On list. If the data file isn't already sorted, select *Sort the file by grouping variables.*

**Figure 6.8   Split File dialog box**

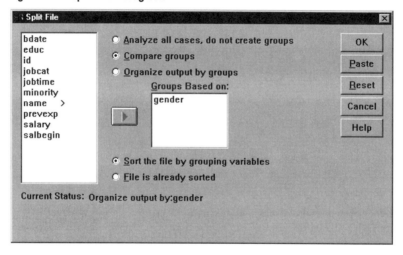

**Compare groups.** Split-file groups are presented together for comparison purposes. For pivot tables, a single pivot table is created, and each split-file variable can be moved between table dimensions. For charts, a separate chart is created for each split-file group, and the charts are displayed together in the Output Navigator.

**Organize output by groups.** All results from each procedure are displayed separately for each split-file group.

## To Split a Data File for Analysis

▶ From the menus choose:

Data
  Split File...

▶ Select *Compare groups* or *Organize output by groups.*

▶ Select one or more grouping variables.

# Select Cases

Select Cases provides several methods for selecting a subgroup of cases based on criteria that include variables and complex expressions. You can also select a random sample of cases. The criteria used to define a subgroup can include:

- Variable values and ranges
- Date and time ranges
- Case (row) numbers
- Arithmetic expressions
- Logical expressions
- Functions

**Unselected Cases.** You can **filter** or delete cases that don't meet the selection criteria. Filtered cases remain in the data file but are excluded from analysis. SPSS creates a filter variable, *filter_$*, to indicate filter status. Selected cases have a value of 1; filtered cases have a value of 0. Filtered cases are also indicated with a slash through the row number in the Data Editor. To turn filtering off and include all cases in your analysis, select *All cases*.

Deleted cases are removed from the data file and cannot be recovered if you save the data file after deleting the cases.

**Figure 6.9    Select Cases dialog box**

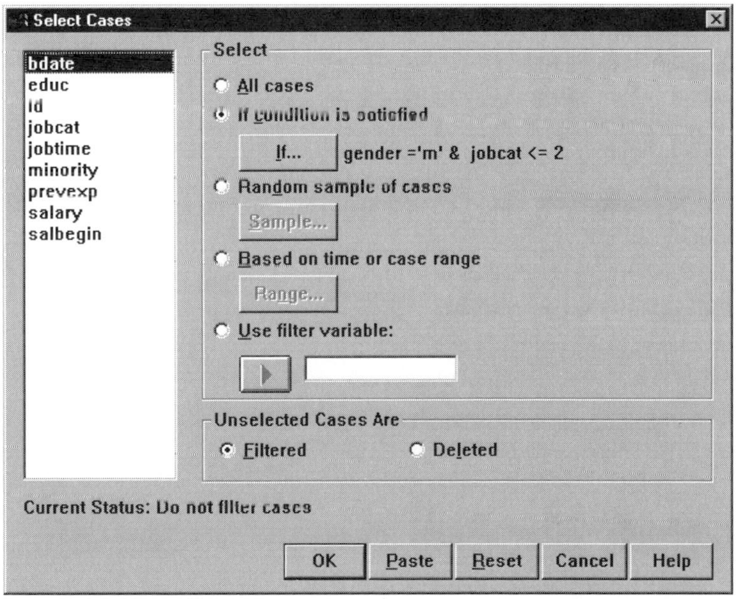

**To Select Subsets of Cases**

▶  From the menus choose:

Data
  Select Cases...

▶  Select one of the methods for selecting cases.

▶  Specify the criteria for selecting cases.

# Select Cases: If

This dialog box allows you to select subsets of cases using conditional expressions. A conditional expression returns a value of true, false, or missing for each case.

**Figure 6.10    Select Cases If dialog box**

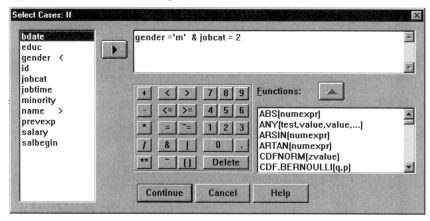

- If the result of a conditional expression is true, the case is selected.
- If the result of a conditional expression is false or missing, the case is not selected.
- Most conditional expressions use one or more of the six relational operators (<, >, <=, >=, =, ~=) on the calculator pad.
- Conditional expressions can include variable names, constants, arithmetic operators, numeric and other functions, logical variables, and relational operators.

## Select Cases: Random Sample

This dialog box allows you to select a random sample based on an approximate percentage or an exact number of cases.

**Figure 6.11   Select Cases Random Sample dialog box**

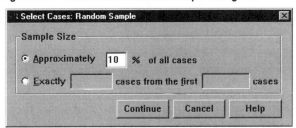

**Approximately.** SPSS generates a random sample of approximately the specified percentage of cases. Since SPSS makes an independent pseudo-random decision for each case, the percentage of cases selected can only approximate the specified percentage. The more cases there are in the data file, the closer the percentage of cases selected is to the specified percentage.

**Exactly.** A user-specified number of cases. You must also specify the number of cases from which to generate the sample. This second number should be less than or equal to the total number of cases in the data file. If the number exceeds the total number of cases in the data file, the sample will contain proportionally fewer cases than the requested number.

## Select Cases: Range

This dialog box selects cases based on a range of case numbers or a range of dates or times.

- Case ranges are based on row number as displayed in the Data Editor.
- Date and time ranges are available only for time series data with defined date variables (Data menu, Define Dates).

Figure 6.12   Select Cases Range dialog box for range of cases (no defined date variables)

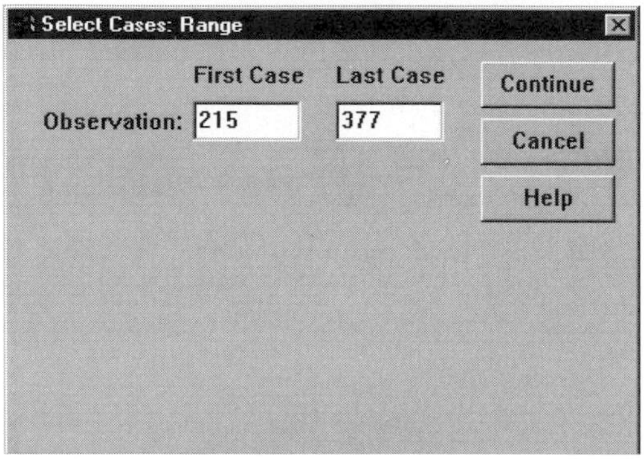

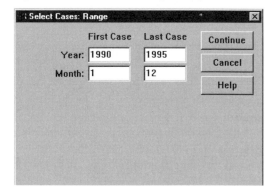

Figure 6.13   Select Cases Range dialog box for time series data with defined date variables

# Weight Cases

Weight Cases gives cases different weights (by simulated replication) for statistical analysis.

• The values of the weighting variable should indicate the number of observations represented by single cases in your data file.

• Cases with zero, negative, or missing values for the weighting variable are excluded from analysis.

- Fractional values are valid; they are used exactly where they are meaningful, and most likely where cases are tabulated (as in Crosstabs).

**Figure 6.14   Weight Cases dialog box**

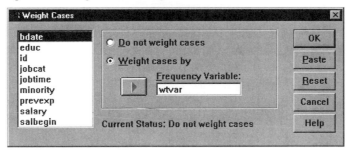

Once you apply a weight variable, it remains in effect until you select another weight variable or turn weighting off. If you save a weighted data file, weighting information is saved with the data file. You can turn weighting off at any time, even after the file has been saved in weighted form.

**Weights in scatterplots and histograms.** Scatterplots and histograms have an option for turning case weights on and off, but this does not affect cases with a negative value, zero, or a missing value for the weight variable. These cases remain excluded from the chart even if you turn weighting off from within the chart.

## To Weight Cases

▶ From the menus choose:

Data
  Weight Cases...

▶ Select *Weight cases by*.

▶ Select a frequency variable.

The values of the frequency variable are used as case weights. For example, a case with a value of 3 for the frequency variable will represent three cases in the weighted data file.

# 7 Working with Output

When you run a procedure in SPSS, the results are displayed in a window called the Output Navigator. In this window, you can easily navigate to whichever part of the output you want to see. You can also manipulate the output and create a document that contains precisely the output you want, arranged and formatted appropriately.

## Output Navigator

Results are displayed in the Output Navigator. You can use the Output Navigator to:

- Browse output results.
- Show or hide selected tables and charts.
- Change the display order of output by moving selected items.
- Edit pivot tables, charts, and text output.
- Move items between SPSS and other applications.

**Figure 7.1    Output Navigator**

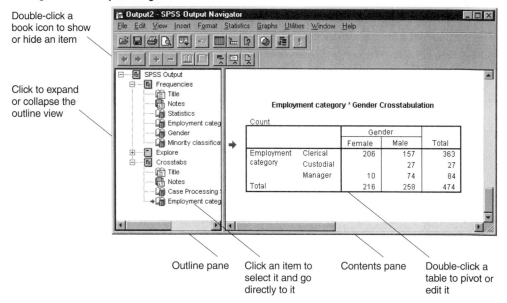

Double-click a
book icon to show
or hide an item

Click to expand
or collapse the
outline view

Outline pane

Click an item to
select it and go
directly to it

Contents pane

Double-click a
table to pivot or
edit it

The Output Navigator is divided into two panes:

• The left pane of the Output Navigator contains an outline view of the output contents.

• The right pane contains statistical tables, charts, and text output.

• You can use the scroll bars to browse the results, or you can click an item in the outline to go directly to the corresponding table or chart.

• You can click and drag the right border of the outline pane to change the width of the outline pane.

## Saving Output

The contents of the Output Navigator can be saved to a Navigator document, which you can open in SPSS. The saved document includes both panes of the Output Navigator window (the outline and the contents).

### To Save an Output Navigator Document

▶ From the Output Navigator menus choose:

File
  Save

▶ Type the name of the document and click *Save*.

To save output in external formats (for example, HTML, text), use Export on the File menu.

## Showing and Hiding Results

In the Output Navigator, you can selectively show and hide individual tables or results from an entire procedure. This is useful when you want to shorten the amount of visible output in the contents pane. You can also selectively control the initial display state (show or hidden) for new output.

### To Hide a Table or Chart without Deleting It

▶ Double-click its book icon in the outline pane of the Output Navigator.

*or*

▶ Click the item to select it.

▶ From the menus choose:

View
  Hide

*or*

▶ Click the closed book (Hide) icon on the Outlining toolbar.

The open book (Show) icon becomes the active icon, indicating that the item is now hidden.

### To Hide All of the Results from a Procedure

▶ Click the box to the left of the procedure name in the outline pane.

This hides all of the results from the procedure and collapses the outline view.

### To Control the Initial Display State for New Output

▶ From the menus choose:
Edit
  Options...

▶ Click the Navigator tab in the Options dialog box.

▶ In the Initial Output State group, select the icon for the type of item (for example, pivot table, title, notes, log) you want to show or hide whenever new output is generated.

▶ Select *Shown* or *Hidden* to specify the initial output state for that item.

## Moving, Copying, and Deleting Output

Items are displayed in the Output Navigator in the order in which the procedures were run. You can rearrange the output by copying, moving, or deleting an item or group of items.

### To Move Output in the Navigator

▶ Click an item in the outline or contents pane to select it. (Shift-click to select multiple items, or Ctrl-click to select noncontiguous items.)

▶ Use the mouse to click and drag selected items (hold down the mouse button while dragging).

▶ Release the mouse button on the item just above the location where you want to drop the moved items.

You can also move items by using Cut and Paste After on the Edit menu.

### To Delete Output in the Navigator

▶ Click an item in the outline or contents pane to select it. (Shift-click to select multiple items, or Ctrl-click to select noncontiguous items.)

▶ Press Delete.

*or*

▶ From the menus choose:

Edit
  Delete

### To Copy Output in the Navigator

▶ Click items in the outline or contents pane to select them. (Shift-click to select multiple items, or Ctrl-click to select noncontiguous items.)

▶ Hold down Ctrl while you use the mouse to click and drag selected items (hold down the mouse button while dragging).

▶ Release the mouse button to drop the items where you want them.

A plus sign is displayed while you are dragging items to be copied.

You can also copy items by using Copy and Paste After on the Edit menu or the pop-up context menu.

## Changing Output Alignment

By default, all output is initially left-aligned. You can change the initial alignment (Options on the Edit menu, Navigator tab), or you can change the alignment of selected output items at any time.

### To Change the Alignment of Output

▶ Select the items you want to align (click the items in the outline or contents pane; Shift-click or Ctrl-click to select multiple items).

▶ From the menus choose:

Format
  Align Left *or* Center *or* Align Right

*Note*: All output items are displayed left-aligned in the Output Navigator. Only the alignment of printed output is affected by the alignment settings. Centered and right-aligned items are identified by a small symbol above and to the left of the item.

## Output Navigator Outline

The outline pane provides a table of contents for all of your output in a session. You can use the outline pane to navigate through the output and control the output display. Most actions in the outline pane have a corresponding effect on the contents pane.

- Selecting an item in the outline pane selects and displays the corresponding item in the contents pane.
- Moving an item in the outline pane moves the corresponding item in the contents pane.
- Collapsing the outline view hides the output from all items in the collapsed levels.

Figure 7.2    Collapsed outline view and hidden output

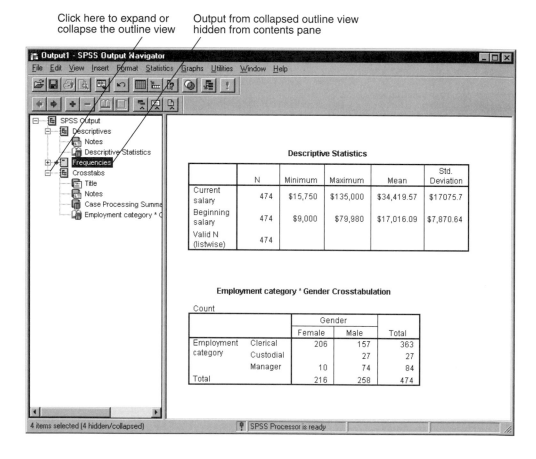

**Controlling the outline display.** To control the outline display, you can:

- Expand and collapse the outline view.
- Change the outline level for selected items.
- Change the size of items in the outline display.
- Change the font used in the outline display.

### To Collapse or Expand the Outline View

▶ Click the box to the left of the outline item you want to collapse or expand.

*or*

▶ Click the item in the outline.

▶ From the menus choose:
  View
  Collapse (*or* Expand)

### To Change the Outline Level of an Item

▶ Click the item in the outline pane to select it.

▶ Click the left arrow on the Outlining toolbar to promote the item (move the item to the left).

▶ Click the right arrow on the Outlining toolbar to demote the item (move the item to the right)

*or*

▶ From the menus choose:
  Edit
  Outline
  Promote (*or* Demote)

Changing the outline level is particularly useful after you move items in the outline level. Moving items can change the outline level of the selected items, and you can use the left and right arrow buttons on the Outlining toolbar to restore the original outline level.

**To Change the Size of Items in the Outline**

▶ From the menus choose:

View
  Outline Size
    Small (*or* Medium *or* Large)

The icons and their associated text change size.

**To Change the Font in the Outline**

▶ From the menus choose:

View
  Outline Font...

▶ Select a font.

# Pivot Tables

Much of the output in SPSS is presented in tables that can be pivoted interactively. That is, you can rearrange the rows, columns, and layers.

## Manipulating a Pivot Table

Options for manipulating a pivot table include:
- Transposing rows and columns
- Moving rows and columns
- Creating multidimensional layers
- Grouping and ungrouping rows and columns
- Showing and hiding cells
- Rotating row and column labels
- Finding definitions of terms

**To Edit a Pivot Table**

▶ Double-click the table.

This activates the Pivot Table Editor.

### To Edit Two or More Pivot Tables at a Time

▶  Click the right mouse button on the pivot table.

▶  From the pop-up context menu choose:
SPSS Pivot Table Object
 Open

▶  Repeat for each pivot table you want to edit.

Each pivot table is ready to edit in its own separate window.

### To Pivot a Table Using Icons

▶  Activate the pivot table.

▶  From the Pivot Table menus choose:
Pivot
 Pivoting Trays

▶  Hover over each icon with the mouse pointer for a ToolTip pop-up that tells you which table dimension the icon represents.

▶  Drag an icon from one tray to another.

**Figure 7.3    Pivoting trays**

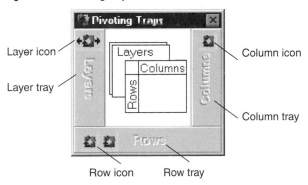

This changes the arrangement of the table. For example, suppose that the icon represents a variable with categories *Yes* and *No* and you drag the icon from the row tray to the column tray. Before the move, *Yes* and *No* were row labels; after the move, they are column labels.

### To Identify Dimensions in a Pivot Table

▶ Activate the pivot table.

▶ Click and hold down the mouse button on an icon.

This highlights the dimension labels in the pivot table.

### To Transpose Rows and Columns

▶ From the Pivot Table menus choose:

Pivot
  Transpose Rows and Columns

This has the same effect as dragging all of the row icons into the column tray and all of the column icons into the row tray.

### To Change the Display Order

The order of pivot icons in a dimension tray reflects the display order of elements in the pivot table. To change the display order of elements in a dimension:

▶ Activate the pivot table.

▶ If pivoting trays are not already on, from the Pivot Table menus choose:

Pivot
  Pivoting Trays

▶ Drag the icons in each tray to the order you want (left to right or top to bottom).

### To Move Rows or Columns in a Pivot Table

▶ Activate the pivot table.

▶ Click the label for the row or column you want to move.

▶ Click and drag the label to the new position.

▶ From the pop-up context menu, choose *Insert Before* or *Swap*.

*Note*: Make sure that Drag to Copy on the Edit menu is *not* enabled (checked). If Drag to Copy is enabled, deselect it.

## To Group Rows or Columns and Insert Group Labels

▶ Activate the pivot table.

▶ Select the labels for the rows or columns you want to group together (click and drag or Shift-click to select multiple labels).

▶ From the menus choose:

Edit
  Group

A group label is automatically inserted. Double-click the group label to edit the label text.

**Figure 7.4    Row and column groups and labels**

| | | Column Group Label | | |
|---|---|---|---|---|
| | | Female | Male | Total |
| **Row Group Label** | Clerical | 206 | 157 | 363 |
| | Custodial | | 27 | 27 |
| | Manager | 10 | 74 | 84 |

*Note*: To add rows or columns to an existing group, you must first ungroup the items currently in the group; then create a new group that includes the additional items.

## To Ungroup Rows or Columns and Delete Group Labels

▶ Activate the pivot table.

▶ Select the group label (click anywhere in the group label) for the rows or columns you want to ungroup.

▶ From the menus choose:

Edit
  Ungroup

Ungrouping automatically deletes the group label.

## To Rotate Row or Column Labels

▶ Activate the pivot table.

▶ From the menus choose:

Format
  Rotate InnerColumn Labels
  *or*
  Rotate OuterRow Labels

**Figure 7.5    Rotated column labels**

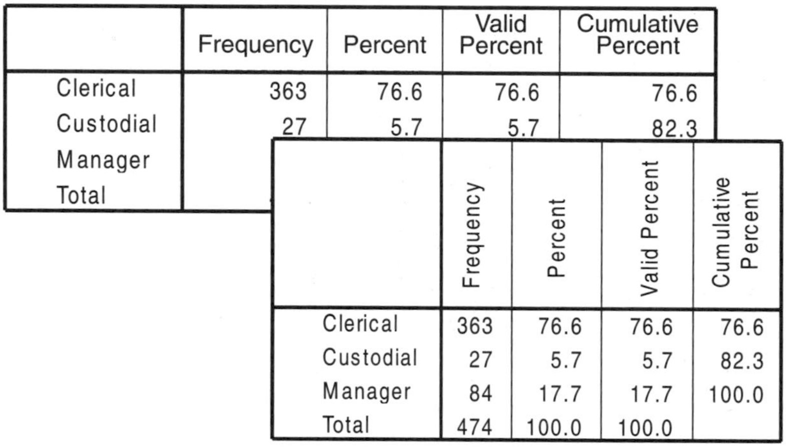

| | Frequency | Percent | Valid Percent | Cumulative Percent |
|---|---|---|---|---|
| Clerical | 363 | 76.6 | 76.6 | 76.6 |
| Custodial | 27 | 5.7 | 5.7 | 82.3 |
| Manager | | | | |
| Total | | | | |

| | Frequency | Percent | Valid Percent | Cumulative Percent |
|---|---|---|---|---|
| Clerical | 363 | 76.6 | 76.6 | 76.6 |
| Custodial | 27 | 5.7 | 5.7 | 82.3 |
| Manager | 84 | 17.7 | 17.7 | 100.0 |
| Total | 474 | 100.0 | 100.0 | |

Only the innermost column labels and the outermost row labels can be rotated.

## To Reset Pivots to Defaults

After performing one or more pivoting operations, you can return to the original arrangement of the pivot table.

▶ Choose *Reset Pivots to Defaults* from the Pivot menu.

This resets only changes that are the result of pivoting row, column, and layer elements between dimensions. It does not affect changes such as grouping or ungrouping or moving rows and columns.

## To Find the Definition of a Label in a Pivot Table

You can obtain context-sensitive Help on cell labels in pivot tables (those labels defined by SPSS). For example, if *Mean* appears as a label, you can obtain a definition of the mean.

▶ Click the right mouse button on a label cell.

▶ Choose *What's This?* from the pop-up context menu.

You must click your right mouse button on the label cell itself, rather than on the data cells in the row or column.

Context-sensitive Help is not available for user-defined labels, such as variable names or value labels.

# Working with Layers

You can display a separate two-dimensional table for each category or combination of categories. The table can be thought of as stacked in layers, with only the top layer visible.

### To Create and Display Layers

▶ Activate the pivot table and choose *Pivoting Trays* from the Pivot menu if it is not already selected.

▶ Drag an icon from the row tray or the column tray into the layer tray.

**Figure 7.6    Moving categories into layers**

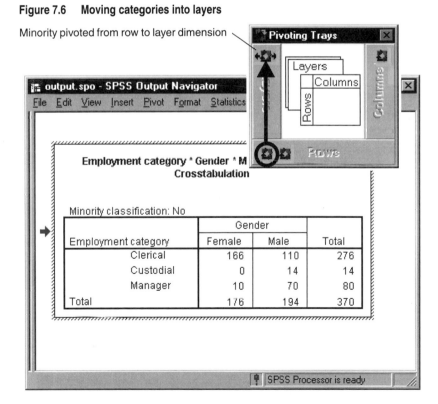

Minority pivoted from row to layer dimension

Each layer icon has left and right arrows. The visible table is the table for the top layer.

**Figure 7.7    Categories in separate layers**

| Minority classification: Yes | | | |
|---|---|---|---|

| Minority classification: No | | | | |
|---|---|---|---|---|
| | | Gender | | Total |
| | | Female | Male | |
| Employment category | Clerical | 166 | 110 | 276 |
| | Custodial | 0 | 14 | 14 |
| | Manager | 10 | 70 | 80 |
| Total | | 176 | 194 | 370 |

## To Change Layers

▶  Click one of the layer icon arrows.

 Click arrow to change layers

## Go to Layer Category

Go to Layer Category allows you to change layers in a pivot table. This dialog box is particularly useful when there is a large number of layers or when one layer has many categories.

## To Go to a Layer of a Table

▶  From the Pivot Table menus choose:
Pivot
  Go to Layer...

**Figure 7.8    Go to Layer Category dialog box**

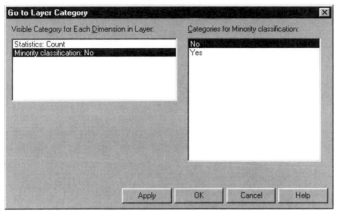

▶ Select a layer dimension in the Visible Category list. The Categories list will display all categories for the selected dimension.

▶ Select the category you want in the Categories list and click *OK*. This changes the layer and closes the dialog box.

To view another layer without closing the dialog box:

▶ Select the category and click *Apply*.

## To Move Layers to Rows or Columns

If the table you are viewing is stacked in layers with only the top layer showing, you can display all the layers at once, either down the rows or across the columns. There must be at least one icon in the layer tray.

▶ From the Pivot menu choose *Move Layers to Rows*.

*or*

▶ From the Pivot menu choose *Move Layers to Columns*.

You can also move layers to rows or columns by dragging their icons between the layer, row, and column pivoting trays.

## Showing and Hiding Cells

Many types of cells can be hidden:

- Dimension labels
- Categories, including the label cell and data cells in a row or column
- Category labels (without hiding the data cells)
- Footnotes, titles, and captions

### To Hide Rows or Columns in a Table

▶   Ctrl-Alt-click the category label of the row or column to be hidden.

▶   From the Pivot Table menus choose:

View
  Hide

*or*

▶   Right-click the highlighted row or column to show the pop-up context menu.

▶   From the pop-up context menu choose *Hide Category*.

### To Show Hidden Rows or Columns in a Table

▶   Select another label in the same dimension as the hidden row or column.

For example, if the *Female* category of the Gender dimension is hidden, click the *Male* category.

▶   From the Pivot Table menus choose:

View
  Show All Categories in *dimension name*

For example, choose *Show All Categories in Gender*.

*or*

▶   From the Pivot Table menus choose:

View
  Show All

This displays all hidden cells in the table. (If *Hide empty rows and columns* is selected in Table Properties for this table, a completely empty row or column remains hidden.)

### To Hide or Show a Dimension Label in a Table

▶ Activate the pivot table.

▶ Select the dimension label or any category label within the dimension.

▶ From the menus choose:
View
  Hide (or Show) Dimension Label

### To Hide or Show Category Labels in a Table

▶ Activate the pivot table and turn on pivoting trays if they are not already on.

▶ In the layer, row, or column dimensions tray, right-click the category icon.

▶ From the pop-up context menu choose:
Hide (or Show) All Category Labels

### To Hide or Show a Footnote in a Table

▶ Select a footnote.

▶ From the menus choose:
View
  Hide (or Show)

### To Hide or Show a Caption or Title in a Table

▶ Select a caption or title.

▶ From the menus choose:
View
  Hide (or Show)

# Editing Output

The appearance and contents of each table or text output item can be edited. You can:

- Apply a TableLook.
- Change the properties of the current table.
- Change the properties of cells in the table.
- Modify text.
- Add footnotes and captions to tables.
- Add items to the Output Navigator.
- Copy and paste output into other applications.

## Changing the Appearance of Tables

You can change the appearance of a table either by editing the table properties or by applying a TableLook. Each TableLook consists of a collection of table properties, including general appearance, footnote properties, cell properties, and borders. You can select one of the preset TableLooks or you can create and save a custom TableLook.

### TableLooks

A TableLook is a set of properties that defines the appearance of a table. You can select a previously defined TableLook or create your own.

Before or after a TableLook is applied, you can change cell formats for individual cells or groups of cells, using cell properties. The edited cell formats will remain, even when you apply a new TableLook.

For example, you might start by applying TableLook *9POINT*; then select a data column and, from the Cell Formats dialog box, change to a bold font for that column. Later, you change the TableLook to *BOXED*. The previously selected column retains the bold font while the rest of the characteristics are applied from the *BOXED* TableLook.

Optionally, you can reset all cells to the cell formats defined by the current TableLook. This resets any cells that have been edited. If *As Displayed* is selected in the TableLook files list, any edited cells are reset to the current table properties.

**Default TableLook for new pivot tables.** You can use any defined TableLook as the default TableLook for new pivot table output. The default TableLook is set in the Pivot Tables tab of the Options dialog box (Edit menu).

## To Apply a TableLook

▶ Activate a pivot table.

▶ From the menus choose:

Format
  TableLooks...

**Figure 7.9    TableLooks dialog box**

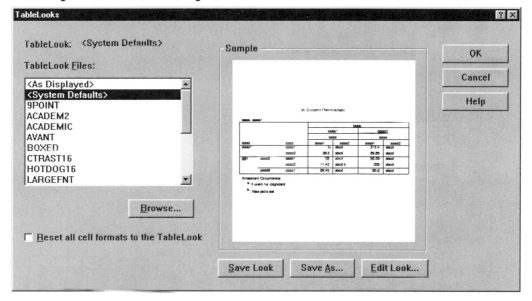

▶ Select a TableLook from the list of files. To select a file from another directory, click *Browse*.

▶ Click *OK* to apply the TableLook to the selected pivot table.

## To Edit or Create a TableLook

▶ Select a TableLook from the list of files.

▶ Click *Edit Look*.

▶ Adjust the table properties for the attributes you want and click *OK*.

▶ Click *Save Look* to save the edited TableLook or *Save As* to save it as a new TableLook.

Editing a TableLook affects only the selected pivot table. An edited TableLook is not applied to any other tables that use that TableLook unless you select those tables and reapply the TableLook.

# Table Properties

The Table Properties dialog box allows you to set general properties of a table, set cell styles for various parts of a table, and save a set of those properties as a TableLook. Using the tabs on this dialog box, you can:

- Control general properties, such as hiding empty rows or columns and adjusting printing properties.
- Control the format and position of footnote markers.
- Determine specific formats for cells in the data area, for row and column labels, and for other areas of the table.
- Control the width and color of the lines forming the borders of each area of the table.

### To Change Pivot Table Properties

▶ Activate the pivot table (double-click anywhere in the table).

▶ From the Pivot Table menus choose:

Format
  Table Properties...

▶ Select a tab (*General*, *Footnotes*, *Cell Formats*, or *Borders*).

▶ Select the options you want.

▶ Click *OK* or *Apply*.

The new properties are applied to the selected pivot table. To apply new table properties to a TableLook instead of just the selected table, edit the TableLook (Format menu, TableLooks).

### Table Properties: General

Several properties apply to the table as a whole. You can:

- Show or hide empty rows and columns. (An empty row or column has nothing in any of the data cells.)

- Control the placement of row labels. They can be in the upper left corner or nested.
- Print all layers or only the top layer of the table, and print each layer on a separate page. (This affects only printing, not the display of layers in the Output Navigator.)
- Shrink a table horizontally or vertically to fit the page for printing.
- Control widow/orphan lines—the minimum number of rows and columns that will be contained in any printed section of a table if the table is too wide and/or too long for the defined page size. (*Note*: If a table is too long to fit on the remainder of the current page because there is other output above it on the page but fits within the defined page length, it is automatically printed on a new page, regardless of the widow/orphan setting. )

**Figure 7.10    Table Properties General tab**

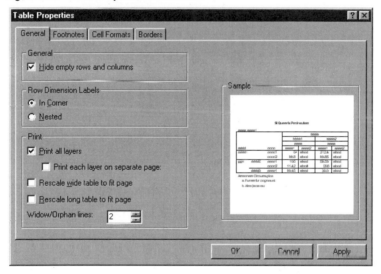

### To Change General Table Properties

▶ Select the *General* tab.

▶ Select the options you want.

▶ Click *OK* or *Apply*.

## Table Properties: Footnotes

The properties of footnote markers include style and position in relation to text.

- The style of footnote markers is either numbers (1, 2, 3, ...) or letters (a, b, c, ...).
- The footnote markers can be attached to text as superscripts or subscripts.

**Figure 7.11    Table Properties Footnotes tab**

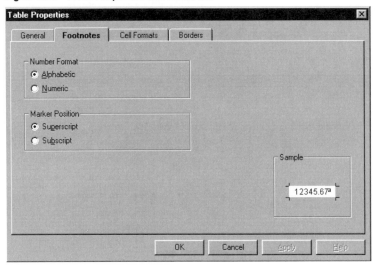

## To Change Footnote Marker Properties

▶   Select the *Footnotes* tab.

▶   Select a footnote marker format.

▶   Select a marker position.

▶   Click *OK* or *Apply*.

## Table Properties: Cell Formats

For formatting, a table is divided into areas: title, layers, corner labels, row labels, column labels, data, caption, and footnotes. For each area of a table, you can modify the associated cell formats. Cell formats include: text characteristics (font, size, color, style), horizontal and vertical alignment, cell shading, foreground and background colors, and inner cell margins.

**Figure 7.12    Areas of a table**

Title

Layers

| | |
|---|---|
| Corner labels | Column labels |
| Row labels | Data |

Caption
  Footnotes

Cell formats are applied to areas (categories of information). They are not characteristics of individual cells. This distinction is an important consideration when pivoting a table. For example:

- If you specify a bold font as a cell format of column labels, the column labels will appear bold no matter what information is currently displayed in the column dimension—and if you move an item from the column dimension to another dimension, it does not retain the bold characteristic of the column labels.

- If you make column labels bold simply by highlighting the cells in an activated pivot table and clicking the bold button on the toolbar, the contents of those cells will remain bold no matter what dimension you move them to, and the column labels will not retain the bold characteristic for other items moved into the column dimension.

**Figure 7.13    Table Properties Cell Formats tab**

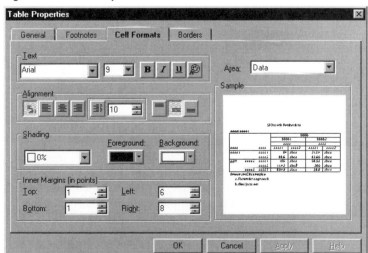

### To Change Cell Formats

▶ Select the *Cell Formats* tab.

▶ Select an area from the drop-down list or click an area of the sample.

▶ Select characteristics for the area. Your selections are reflected in the sample.

▶ Click *OK* or *Apply*.

### Table Properties: Borders

For each border location in a table, you can select a line style and a color. If you select *None* as the style, there will be no line at the selected location.

**Figure 7.14    Table Properties Borders tab**

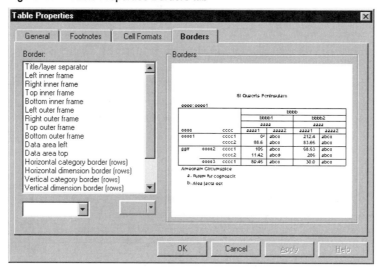

### To Change Borders in Tables

▶ Click the *Borders* tab.

▶ Select a border location, either by clicking its name in the list or by clicking a line in the Sample area. (Shift-click to select multiple names, or Ctrl-click to select noncontiguous names.)

▶ Select a line style or *None*.

▶  Select a color.

▶  Click *OK* or *Apply*.

### To Display Hidden Borders in a Pivot Table

For tables without many visible borders, you can display the hidden borders. This can make tasks like changing column widths easier. The hidden borders (gridlines) are displayed in the Output Navigator but are not printed.

▶  Activate the pivot table (double-click anywhere in the table).

▶  From the menus choose:

View
  Gridlines

## Font

A TableLook allows you to specify font characteristics for different areas of the table. You can also change the font for any individual cell. Options for the font in a cell include the font type, style, and size. You can also hide the text or underline it.

If you specify font properties in a cell, they apply in all of the table layers that have the same cell.

**Figure 7.15   Font dialog box**

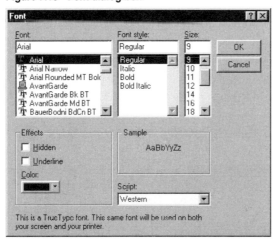

### To Change the Font in a Cell

▶ Activate the pivot table and select the text you want to change.

▶ From the Pivot Table menus choose:

Format
    Font...

Optionally, you can select a font, font style, and size; whether you want the text hidden or underlined; a color; and a script style.

## Set Data Cell Widths

Set Data Cell Widths is used to set all data cells to the same width. The units (points, inches, or centimeters) are determined by the setting for the Measurement System in Options from the Edit menu.

**Figure 7.16   Set Data Cell Width dialog box**

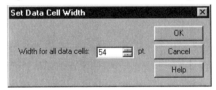

### To Change Data Cell Widths

▶ Activate the pivot table.

▶ From the menus choose:

Format
    Set Data Cell Widths...

▶ Enter a value for the cell width.

### To Change the Width of a Pivot Table Column

▶ Activate the pivot table (double-click anywhere in the table).

▶ Move the mouse pointer through the category labels until it is on the right border of the column you want to change. The pointer changes to an arrow with points on both ends.

▶ Hold down the mouse button while you drag the border to its new position.

**Figure 7.17  Changing the width of a column**

Drag column border

|  |  | Gender | | Total |
|  |  | Female | Male |  |
|---|---|---|---|---|
| Employment category | Clerical | 40 | 47 | 87 |
|  | Custodial | 0 | 13 | 13 |
|  | Manager | 0 | 4 | 4 |
| Total |  | 40 | 64 | 104 |

You can change vertical category and dimension borders in the row labels area, whether or not they are showing.

▶ Move the mouse pointer through the row labels until you see the double-pointed arrow.

▶ Drag it to the new width.

## Cell Properties

Cell Properties are applied to an individual selected cell. You can change the value format, alignment, margins, and shading. Cell properties override table properties; therefore, if you change table properties, you do not change any individually applied cell properties.

### To Change Cell Properties

▶ Activate a table and select a cell in the table.

▶ From the menus choose:
Format
  Cell Properties...

## Cell Properties: Value

This dialog box tab controls the value format for a cell. You can select formats for number, date, time, or currency, and adjust the number of decimal digits displayed.

Figure 7.18    Cell Properties Value tab

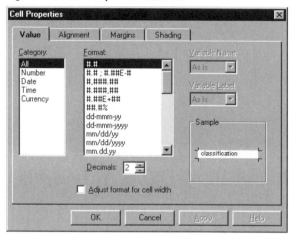

## To Change Value Formats in a Cell

▶   Click the *Value* tab.

▶   Select a category and a format.

▶   Select the number of decimal places.

## To Change Value Formats for a Column

▶   Ctrl-Alt-click on the column label.

▶   Right-click on the highlighted column.

▶   Choose *Cell Properties* from the pop-up context menu.

▶   Click the *Value* tab.

▶   Select the format you want to apply to the column.

You can use this method to suppress or add percent signs and dollar signs, change the number of decimals displayed, and switch between scientific notation and regular numeric display.

### Cell Properties: Alignment

This dialog box tab sets horizontal and vertical alignment and text direction for a cell. If you choose *Mixed*, contents of the cell are aligned according to its type (number, date, or text).

**Figure 7.19   Cell Properties Alignment tab**

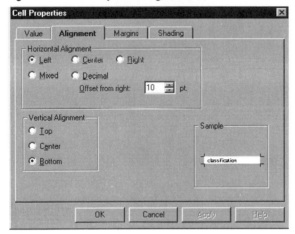

### To Change Alignment in Cells

▶   Select a cell in the table.

▶   From the Pivot Table menus choose:
    Format
      Cell Properties...

▶   Click the *Alignment* tab.

As you select the alignment properties for the cell, they are illustrated in the Sample area.

## Cell Properties: Margins

This dialog box tab specifies the inset at each edge of a cell.

**Figure 7.20   Cell Properties Margins tab**

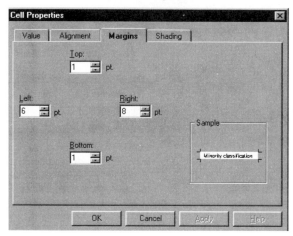

## To Change Margins in Cells

▶   Click the *Margins* tab.

▶   Select the inset for each of the four margins.

## Cell Properties: Shading

This dialog box tab specifies the percentage of shading for a cell outline, and foreground and background colors for a selected cell area. This does not change the color of the text. The cell outline is a selection on the Visual Highlights list.

**Figure 7.21    Cell Properties Shading tab**

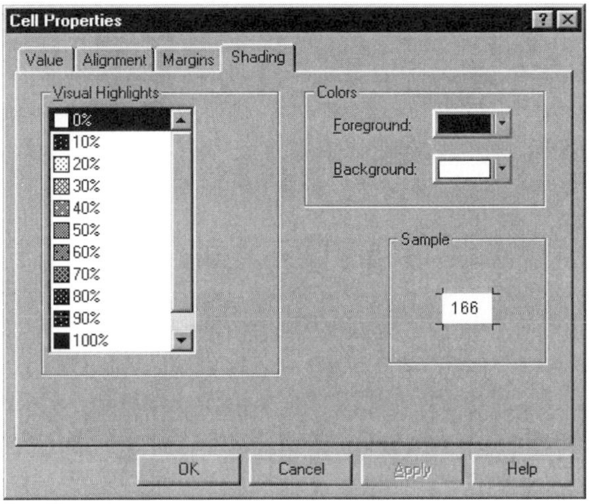

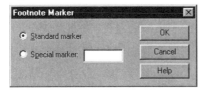

## To Change Shading in Cells

▶  Click the *Shading* tab.

▶  Select the highlights and colors for the cell.

## Footnote Marker

Footnote Marker changes the character(s) used to mark a footnote.

**Figure 7.22    Footnote Marker dialog box**

### To Change Footnote Marker Characters

▶   Select a footnote.

▶   From the Pivot Table menus choose:
Format
  Footnote Marker...

▶   Type one or two characters.

### To Renumber Footnotes

When you have pivoted a table by switching rows, columns, and layers, the footnotes may be out of order. To renumber the footnotes:

▶   Activate the pivot table.

▶   From the menus choose:
Format
  Renumber Footnotes

## Selecting Rows and Columns in Pivot Tables

The flexibility of pivot tables places some constraints on how you select entire rows and columns, and the visual highlight that indicates the selected row or column may span noncontiguous areas of the table.

### To Select a Row or Column in a Pivot Table

▶   Activate the pivot table (double-click anywhere in the table).

▶   Click on a row or column label.

▶   From the menus choose:
Edit
  Select
    Data and Label Cells

*or*

▶   Ctrl-Alt-click on the row or column label.

If the table contains more than one dimension in the row or column area, the highlighted selection may span multiple noncontiguous cells.

## Modifying Output

Text appears in the Output Navigator in many items. You can edit the text or add new text. Pivot tables can be modified by:

- Editing text within pivot table cells
- Adding captions and footnotes

Some items contain only text. They can be changed by:

- Editing text in a procedure title
- Editing text output blocks

You can also add SPSS objects and objects from other applications to an Output Navigator document.

### To Modify Text in a Table Cell

▶ Activate the pivot table.

▶ Double-click the cell or press F2.

▶ Edit the text.

▶ Press Enter to record your changes, or press Esc to revert to the previous contents of the cell.

### To Add Captions to a Table

▶ From the Pivot Table menus choose:
Insert
  Caption

The words *Table Caption* are displayed at the bottom of the table.

▶ Select the words *Table Caption* and enter your caption text over it.

### To Add a Footnote to a Table

A footnote can be attached to any item in a table.

▶ Click a title, cell, or caption within an activated pivot table.

▶ From the Pivot Table menus choose:
Insert
  Footnote

▶ Select the word *Footnote* and enter the footnote text over it.

## Working with Text Output

Some items of output are displayed as text only, not as pivot tables or charts. These text items display output in a fixed-pitch font, such as Courier New. The fixed-pitch font enables correct alignment when objects such as a stem-and-leaf plot or tables are displayed. The default font for text output is set on the Navigator tab of the Options dialog box.

### Editing Text Output and Titles

You can edit the contents of a Text Output item or a Title item by using standard Windows text-editing features. You can also copy your output into another Windows application (for example, a word processing program) and further edit it.

### To Edit a Text Output Item

▶ Double-click the Text Output item in the contents pane.

Use the Backspace, Delete, Insert, and arrow keys as in other Windows programs.

Select text with the left mouse button.

To cut, copy, paste, search, or replace text, use the Edit menu. You can also click the right mouse button and use the pop-up context menu to cut, copy, paste, or delete text.

### Adding Items to the Output Navigator

In the Output Navigator, you can add items such as titles, new text, charts, or external text files.

### To Add a New Title or Text Item to the Output Navigator Contents

▶ Text items that are not connected to a table or chart can be added to the Output Navigator.

▶ Click the table, chart, or other object that will precede the title or text.

▶ From the menus choose:
Insert
  New Title

*or*

Insert
  New Text

▶ Double-click the new object.

▶ Enter the text you want at this location.

### To Insert a Chart in the Output Navigator

Charts from older versions of SPSS can be inserted into the Output Navigator. To insert a chart:

▶ Click the table, chart, or other object that will precede the chart.

▶ From the menus choose:
Insert
  Chart...

▶ Select a chart file.

### To Add an Existing Text File to the Output Navigator

▶ In either the outline or the contents pane of the Output Navigator, click the table, chart, or other object that will precede the text.

▶ From the menus choose:
Insert
  Text File...

▶ Select a text file.

To edit the text, double-click the new text.

# Using SPSS Output in Other Applications

SPSS pivot tables and charts can be copied and pasted into another Windows application, such as a word processing program or a spreadsheet. You can paste the pivot tables or charts in various formats, including the following:

**An embedded object (pivot tables only).** For applications that support Active-X objects, you can embed SPSS pivot tables. After you paste the table, it can be activated in place by double-clicking and then edited as if in SPSS.

**A picture (metafile).** The picture format can be resized in the other application, and sometimes a limited amount of editing can be done with the facilities of the other application. Pivot tables pasted as pictures retain all borders and font characteristics.

**BIFF.** The contents of a table can be pasted into a spreadsheet and retain numeric precision.

**Text.** The contents of a table can be copied and pasted as text. This can be useful for applications such as electronic mail, where the application can accept only text or can transmit only text.

### To Copy a Table or Chart

▶ Select the table or chart to be copied.

▶ From the menus choose:
   Edit
    Copy

### To Copy Data from a Pivot Table

▶ Activate the pivot table.

▶ Select the labels for the data you want to copy.

▶ From the menus choose:
   Edit
    Select
     Table Body *or* Data Cells *or* Data and Label Cells

▶ From the menus choose:
   Edit
    Copy

### To Copy and Paste Output Into Another Application

▶  Copy the output in SPSS.

▶  From the menus in the target application choose:
Edit
  Paste
  *or*
  Paste Special...

**Paste**. In most applications, Paste will paste SPSS output as a picture (metafile). For spreadsheet programs, Paste will paste SPSS pivot tables in BIFF format.

**Paste Special**. SPSS copies output to the clipboard in multiple formats. Paste Special allows you to select the format you want from the list of formats available to the target application.

## To Embed a Pivot Table in Another Application

SPSS can embed pivot tables in other applications in Active-X format. An embedded table can be activated in place by double-clicking and then edited and pivoted as if in SPSS.

If you have applications that support Active-X objects:

▶  Run the file *objs-on.bat*, located in the directory in which SPSS is installed. (Double-click the file to run it.)

This turns on Active-X embedding for SPSS pivot tables. The file *objs-off.bat* turns Active-X embedding off.

To embed a pivot table in another application:

▶  In SPSS, copy the table.

▶  From the menus in the target application choose:
Edit
  Paste Special...

▶  From the list choose *SPSS Pivot Table Object*.

The target application must support Active-X objects. See the application's documentation for information on Active-X support. Some applications that do not support Active-X may initially accept Active-X pivot tables but may then exhibit unstable behavior. Do not rely on embedded pivot tables until you have tested the application's stability with embedded Active-X objects.

## To Paste a Table or Chart as a Picture

▶ In SPSS, copy the table or chart.

▶ From the menus in the target application choose:
Edit
  Paste Special...

▶ From the list choose *Picture*.

The item is pasted as a metafile. Only the layer and columns that were visible when the item was copied are available in the metafile. Other layers or hidden columns are not available.

### To Paste a Pivot Table as Unformatted (ASCII) Text

▶ In SPSS, copy the table.

▶ From the menus in the target application choose:
Edit
  Paste Special...

▶ From the list choose *Unformatted Text*.

Unformatted pivot table text contains tabs between columns. You can align columns by adjusting the tab stops in the other application.

### To Copy and Paste Multiple Items into Another Application

▶ Select the tables and/or charts to be copied. (Shift-click or Ctrl-click to select multiple items.)

▶ From the menus choose:
Edit
  Copy as RTF

▶ From the menus in the target application choose:
Edit
  Paste

*Note*: Use Copy as RTF to copy multiple items from SPSS to another application only. For copying and pasting within SPSS (for example, between two Navigator windows), use Copy on the Edit menu.)

# Pasting Objects into the SPSS Output Navigator

Objects from other applications can be pasted into the Output Navigator. You can use either *Paste After* or *Paste Special*. Either type of pasting puts the new object after the currently selected object in the Output Navigator. Use *Paste Special* when you want to choose the format of the pasted object.

### Paste Special

Paste Special allows you to select the format of a copied object that is pasted into the SPSS Output Navigator. The possible file types for the object on the clipboard are listed.

The object will be inserted in the Output Navigator following the currently selected object.

**Figure 7.23   Paste Special dialog box**

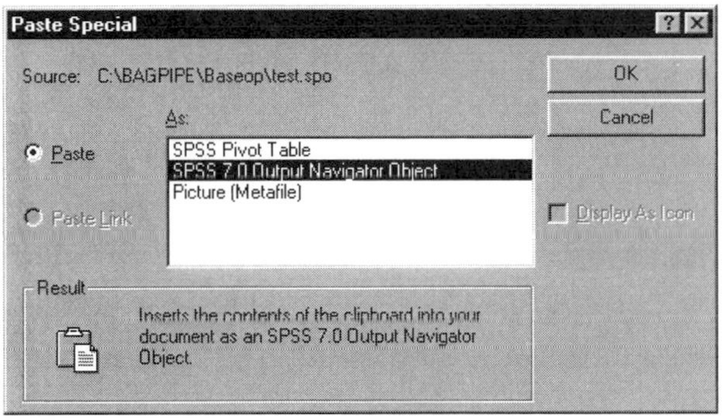

### To Paste an Object from Another Application into the Output Navigator

▶   Copy the object in the other application.

▶   In either the outline or the contents pane of the Output Navigator, click the table, chart, or other object that will precede the object.

▶ From the menus choose:
Edit
  Paste Special...

▶ From the list, select the format for the object.

# Export Output

Export Output saves SPSS pivot tables and text output in HTML and text formats, and it saves charts in a variety of common formats used by other applications.

**Output Document**. Exports any combination of pivot tables, text output, and charts. Charts are exported in the currently selected chart export format, and a separate file is created for each chart. For HTML document format, charts are embedded by reference, and you should export charts in a suitable format for inclusion in HTML documents. For text document format, a line is inserted in the text file for each chart, indicating the filename of the exported chart.

**Output Document (No Charts)**. Exports pivot tables and text output. Pivot tables can be exported as HTML tables (HTML 3.0 or later), as tab-separated text, or as space-separated text. Text output can be exported as preformatted HTML or space-separated text. A fixed-pitch (monospaced) font is required for proper alignment of space-separated text output. (By default, most Web browsers use a fixed-pitch font for preformatted text.)

**Charts Only**. Exports charts only. Charts can be exported in the following formats: Windows metafile, Windows bitmap, encapsulated PostScript, JPEG, TIFF, CGM, or Macintosh PICT.

**Export What**. You can export all objects in the Output Navigator, all visible objects, or only selected objects.

**Export Format**. For output documents, the available options are HTML and text; charts are exported in the currently selected chart format in the HTML Options or Text Options dialog box. For *Charts Only*, select a chart export format from the drop-down list.

# To Export Output

▶ Make the Output Navigator the active window (click anywhere in the window).

▶ From the menus choose:
File
  Export...

▶ Enter a filename (or prefix for charts) and select an export format.

**Figure 7.24    Export Output dialog box**

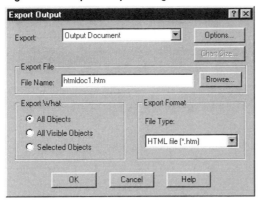

**Figure 7.25    Output exported in HTML format**

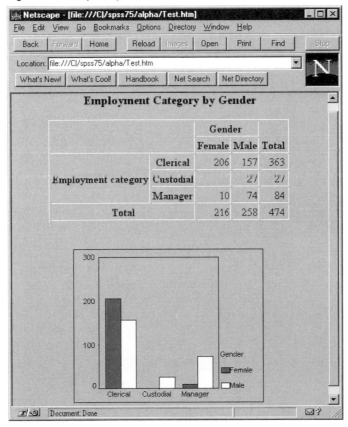

## HTML Options

HTML Options controls the chart export options and the inclusion of footnotes and captions for documents exported in HTML format.

**Figure 7.26    HTML Options dialog box**

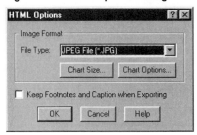

**Image Format**. Controls the chart export format and optional settings. *Chart Size* controls the size of windows metafiles and the initial image size used to create other export formats. Final chart size and other options for other export formats are controlled by *Chart Options*.

## Text Options

Text Options controls pivot table, text output, and chart format options and the inclusion of footnotes and captions for documents exported in text format.

**Figure 7.27    Text Options dialog box**

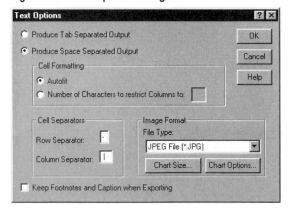

Pivot tables can be exported in tab-separated or space-separated format. For tab-separated format, if a cell is non-empty, its contents and a tab character are printed. If a cell is empty, a tab character is printed.

All text output is exported in space-separated format. All space-separated output requires a fixed-pitch (monospaced) font for proper alignment.

**Cell Formatting**. For space-separated pivot table output, by default all line wrapping is removed and each column is set to the width of the longest label or value in the column. To limit the width of columns and wrap long labels, specify a number of characters for the column width. This setting affects only pivot table output.

**Cell Separators**. For space-separated pivot table output, you can specify the characters used to create cell borders.

**Image Format**. Controls the chart export format and optional settings. *Chart Size* controls the size of windows metafiles and the initial image size used to create other export formats. Final chart size and other options for other export formats are controlled by *Chart Options*.

## Chart Size

Chart Size controls the size of windows metafiles and the initial image size used to create other export formats. You can specify a custom size in the Image Frame text box. The dimensions refer to the outer frame of the chart (even when it is invisible). The chart is then rescaled before being exported. Increasing the initial image size can enhance the quality of the final exported chart.

**Figure 7.28   Chart Size dialog box**

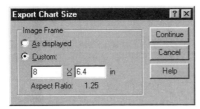

*Note*: You can specify either the width (in the first text box) or the height (in the second), but not both. Whenever you specify one dimension, the other is automatically calculated from the aspect ratio.

To control the size of charts exported in formats other than metafile format, use the Chart Options dialog box for the selected format.

# 8 Working with Command Syntax

Most SPSS commands are accessible from the SPSS menus and dialog boxes. However, some commands and options are available only by using the SPSS command language. The command language also allows you to save your jobs in a syntax file so that you can repeat your analysis at a later date or run it in an automated job with the SPSS Production Facility.

A syntax file is simply a text file that contains SPSS commands. While it is possible to open a syntax window and type in commands, it is easier if you let SPSS help you build your syntax file using one of the following methods:

- Pasting command syntax from dialog boxes
- Copying syntax from the output log
- Copying syntax from the journal file

In the online Help for a given SPSS procedure, click the *Syntax* pushbutton to find out what (if any) command language options are available for that procedure and to access the syntax diagram for the relevant SPSS command. For complete documentation of the SPSS command language, refer to the *SPSS Base Syntax Reference Guide*.

## Command Syntax Rules

Keep in mind the following simple rules when editing and writing command syntax:
- Each command must begin on a new line and end with a period (.).
- Most subcommands are separated by slashes (/). The slash before the first subcommand on a command is usually optional.
- Variable names must be spelled out fully.
- Text included within apostrophes or quotation marks must be contained on a single line.
- Each line of command syntax cannot exceed 80 characters.
- A period (.) must be used to indicate decimals, regardless of your Windows regional settings.

- Variable names ending in a period can cause errors in commands created by the dialog boxes. You cannot create such variable names in the dialog boxes, and you should generally avoid them.

SPSS command syntax is case insensitive, and three-letter abbreviations can be used for many command specifications. You can use as many lines as you want to specify a single command. You can add space or break lines at almost any point where a single blank is allowed, such as around slashes, parentheses, arithmetic operators, or between variable names. For example,

```
FREQUENCIES
  VARIABLES=JOBCAT GENDER
  /PERCENTILES=25 50 75
  /BARCHART.
```

and

```
freq var=jobcat gender /percent=25 50 75 /bar.
```

are both acceptable alternatives that generate the same results.

**Production Facility syntax files and INCLUDE files.** For SPSS command files run via the SPSS Production Facility or the INCLUDE command, the syntax rules are slightly different:

- Each command must begin in the first column of a new line.
- Continuation lines must be indented at least one space.
- The period at the end of the command is optional.

If you generate command syntax by pasting dialog box choices into a syntax window, the format of the commands is suitable for any mode of operation.

# Creating Command Syntax from Dialog Boxes

The easiest way to build a command syntax file is to make selections in SPSS dialog boxes and paste the syntax for the selections into a syntax window. By pasting the syntax at each step of a lengthy analysis, you can build a job file allowing you to repeat the analysis at a later date or run an automated job with the SPSS Production Facility.

In the syntax window, you can run the pasted syntax, edit it, and save it in a syntax file.

## To Paste Command Syntax from a Dialog Box

▶ Open the dialog box and make the selections you want.

▶ Click *Paste*.

The command syntax is pasted to the designated syntax window. If you do not have an open syntax window, SPSS opens a new syntax window and pastes the syntax there.

**Figure 8.1    Command syntax pasted from a dialog box**

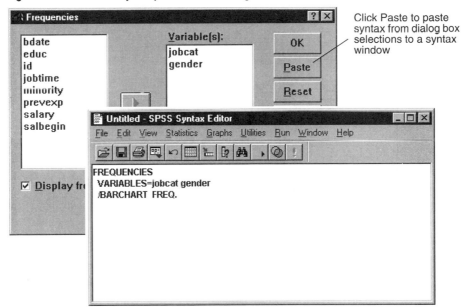

Click Paste to paste syntax from dialog box selections to a syntax window

*Note*: If you open a dialog box from the menus in a script window, code for running syntax from a script is pasted into the script window.

# Using Syntax from the Output Log

You can build a syntax file by copying command syntax from the SPSS log that appears in the Output Navigator. To use this method, you must select *Display commands in the log* on the Navigator tab in the SPSS Options dialog box before running the analysis. Each command will then appear in the Output Navigator along with the output from the analysis.

In the syntax window, you can run the pasted syntax, edit it, and save it in a syntax file.

**Figure 8.2    Command syntax in the SPSS log**

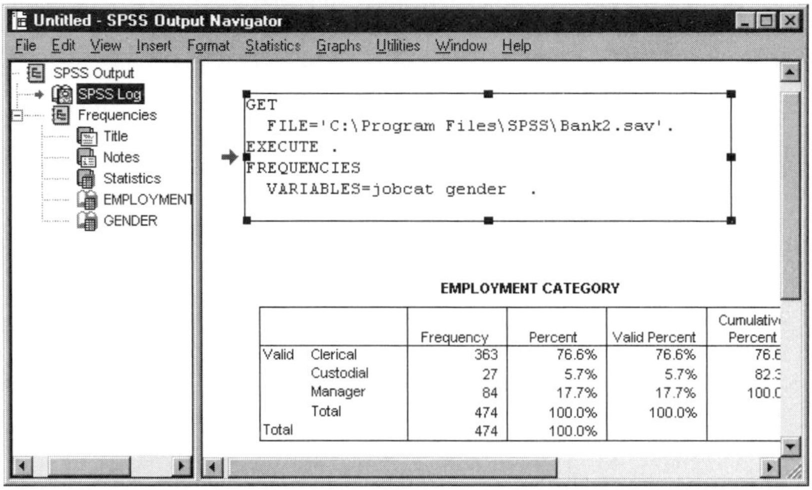

## To Copy Syntax from the Output Log

▶ Before running the analysis, from the menus choose:

Edit
  Options...

▶ On the Navigator tab, select *Display commands in the log*.

As you run analyses, the SPSS commands for your dialog box selections are recorded in the SPSS log.

▶ Open a previously saved syntax file or create a new one. To create a new syntax file, from the menus choose:

File
  New
    Syntax

▶ In the Output Navigator, double-click on an SPSS log item to activate it.

▶ Click and drag the mouse to highlight the syntax you want to copy.

▶ From the Output Navigator menus choose:

Edit
  Copy

▶ In a syntax window, from the menus choose:

Edit
  Paste

# Using Syntax from the Journal File

By default, SPSS records all commands executed during a session in a journal file named *spss.jnl* (set with Options on the Edit menu). You can edit the journal file and save it as a syntax file that you can use to repeat a previously run analysis, or you can run it in an automated job with the SPSS Production Facility.

The journal file is a text file that can be edited like any other text file. Because error messages and warnings are also recorded in the journal file along with command syntax, you must edit out any error and warning messages that appear before saving the syntax file. Note, however, that errors must be resolved or the job will not run successfully.

Save the edited journal file with a different filename. Because SPSS automatically appends or overwrites the journal file for every session, attempting to use the same filename for a syntax file and the journal file may yield unexpected results.

**Figure 8.3    Editing the journal file**

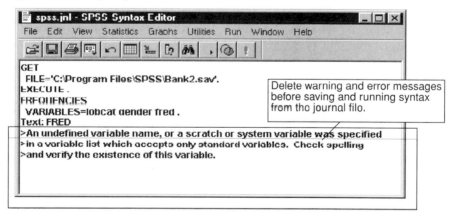

## To Edit the Journal File

▶ To open the journal file, from the menus choose:

File
  Open...

▶ Locate and open the SPSS journal file (by default, *spss.jnl* is located in the *temp* directory).

Select *All files (*.*)* for Files of type or enter **\*.jnl** in the File name text box to display journal files in the file list. If you have difficulty locating the file, use Options on the Edit menu to see where the journal is saved in your system.

▶ Edit the file to remove any error messages or warnings, indicated by the > sign.

▶ Save the edited journal file using a different filename. (We recommend that you use a filename with the extension *.sps*, the default extension for syntax files.)

## To Run Command Syntax

▶ Highlight the commands you want to run in the syntax window.

▶ Click the Run button (the right-pointing triangle) on the Syntax Editor toolbar.

*or*

▶ Select one of the choices from the Run menu:
  • **All.** Runs all commands in the syntax window.
  • **Selection.** Runs the currently selected commands. This includes any commands partially highlighted.
  • **Current.** Runs the command where the cursor is currently located.
  • **To End.** Runs all commands from the current cursor location to the end of the command syntax file.

The Run button on the Syntax Editor toolbar runs the selected commands or the command where the cursor is located if there is no selection.

**Figure 8.4   Syntax Editor toolbar**

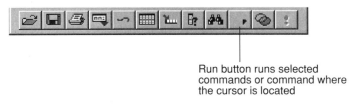

Run button runs selected
commands or command where
the cursor is located

# 9 Frequencies

The Frequencies procedure provides statistics and graphical displays that are useful for describing many types of variables. For a first look at your data, the Frequencies procedure is a good place to start.

For a frequency report and bar chart, you can arrange the distinct values in ascending or descending order or order the categories by their frequencies. The frequencies report can be suppressed when a variable has many distinct values. You can label charts with frequencies (the default) or percentages.

**Example.** A question in a customer preference survey might be: How often do you purchase Soft 'n Tuf paper towels? *Always*, *sometimes*, or *never*? From the output, you might learn that 45% respond *always*; 2.5%, *sometimes*; and 52.5%, *never*. The tabulations and percentages can also describe quantitative variables, such as *income* and *age*. From the output, you learn that the average age of your possible customers is 46 and the standard deviation is 17. From the cumulative percentages, you might find that 39% of your possible customers have an income under $25,000 per year or that 28% are over age 55.

**Statistics and plots.** Frequency counts, percentages, cumulative percentages, mean, median, mode, sum, standard deviation, variance, range, minimum and maximum values, standard error of the mean, skewness and kurtosis (both with standard errors), quartiles, user-specified percentiles, bar charts, pie charts, and histograms.

**Data.** Use numeric codes or short strings to code categorical variables (nominal or ordinal level measurements).

**Assumptions.** The tabulations and percentages provide a useful description for data from any distribution, especially for variables with ordered or unordered categories. Most of the optional summary statistics, such as the mean and standard deviation, are based on normal theory and are appropriate for quantitative variables with symmetric distributions. Robust statistics, such as the median, quartiles, and percentiles, are appropriate for quantitative variables that may or may not meet the assumption of normality.

**Related procedures.** If you want to compute summary statistics for each of several groups of cases (for example, you want separate statistics for males and females or for people living in four regions of a country), use Split File on the Data menu, or use the

Explore, Means, or Summarize procedure. For a group of histograms that all use the same scale, use the Explore procedure.

# Sample Output

### Figure 9.1    Frequencies output

**Statistics**

|  |  | Age of Respondent |
|---|---|---|
| N | Valid | 1495 |
|  | Missing | 5 |
| Mean |  | 46.23 |
| Std. Deviation |  | 17.42 |
| Percentiles | 25 | 32.00 |
|  | 50 | 43.00 |
|  | 75 | 59.00 |

Rows and columns have been transposed.

**Buy Soft 'n Tuf towels**

|  |  | Frequency | Percent | Valid Percent | Cumulative Percent |
|---|---|---|---|---|---|
| Valid | Always | 90 | 45.0 | 45.0 | 45.0 |
|  | Sometimes | 5 | 2.5 | 2.5 | 47.5 |
|  | Never | 105 | 52.5 | 52.5 | 100.0 |
|  | Total | 200 | 100.0 | 100.0 |  |
| Total |  | 200 | 100.0 |  |  |

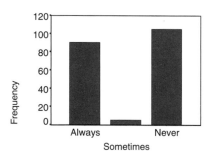

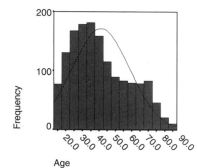

# To Obtain Frequencies and Statistics

▶   From the menus choose:

Statistics
 Summarize
  Frequencies...

**Figure 9.2    Frequencies dialog box**

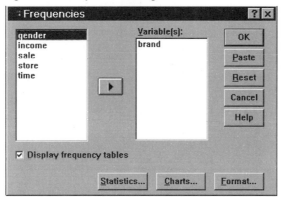

▶   Select one or more categorical or quantitative variables.

Optionally, you can:

- Click *Statistics* for descriptive statistics for quantitative variables.
- Click *Charts* for bar charts, pie charts, and histograms.
- Click *Format* for the order in which results are displayed.

## Frequencies Statistics

Figure 9.3    Frequencies Statistics dialog box

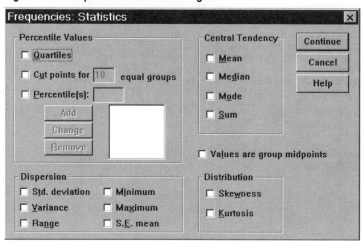

**Percentile Values.** Values of a quantitative variable that divide the ordered data into groups so that a certain percentage is above and another percentage is below. Quartiles (the 25th, 50th, and 75th percentiles) divide the observations into four groups of equal size. If you want an equal number of groups other than four, select *Cut points for n equal groups.* You can also specify individual percentiles (for example, the 95th percentile, the value below which 95% of the observations fall).

**Central Tendency.** Statistics that describe the location of the distribution include the mean, median, mode, and sum of all the values.

**Dispersion.** Statistics that measure the amount of variation or spread in the data include the standard deviation, variance, range, minimum, maximum, and standard error of the mean.

**Distribution.** Skewness and kurtosis are statistics that describe the shape and symmetry of the distribution. These statistics are displayed with their standard errors.

**Values are group midpoints.** If the values in your data are midpoints of groups (for example, ages of all people in their thirties are coded as 35), select this option to estimate the median and percentiles for the original, ungrouped data.

# Frequencies Charts

Figure 9.4    Frequencies Charts dialog box

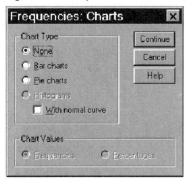

**Chart Type.** A pie chart displays the contribution of parts to a whole. Each slice of a pie chart corresponds to a group defined by a single grouping variable. A bar chart displays the count for each distinct value or category as a separate bar, allowing you to compare categories visually. A histogram also has bars, but they are plotted along an equal interval scale. The height of each bar is the count of values of a quantitative variable falling within the interval. A histogram shows the shape, center, and spread of the distribution. A normal curve superimposed on a histogram helps you judge whether the data are normally distributed.

**Chart Values.** For bar charts, the scale axis can be labeled by frequency counts or percentages.

# Frequencies Format

Figure 9.5    Frequencies Format dialog box

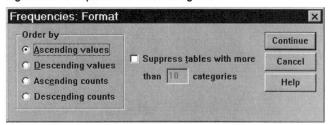

**Order by.** The frequency table can be arranged according to the actual values in the data or according to the count (frequency of occurrence) of those values, and in either ascending or descending order. However, if you request a histogram or percentiles, SPSS assumes that the variable is quantitative and displays its values in ascending order.

**Suppress tables with more than n categories.** This option prevents the display of tables with more than the specified number of values.

## FREQUENCIES Command Additional Features

The SPSS command language also allows you to:

- For bar charts, specify lower and upper data bounds and maximum scale axis value (with the BARCHART subcommand).
- For histograms, specify lower and upper data bounds, maximum vertical axis value, and interval width (with the HISTOGRAM subcommand).
- Obtain percentile-based statistics from grouped frequencies when data values are not the group midpoints (with the GROUPED subcommand).

See the *SPSS Base Syntax Reference Guide* for complete syntax information.

# 10 Descriptives

The Descriptives procedure displays univariate summary statistics for several variables in a single table and calculates standardized values ($z$ scores). Variables can be ordered by the size of their means (in ascending or descending order), alphabetically, or by the order in which you select the variables (the default).

When $z$ scores are saved, they are added to the data in the Data Editor and are available for SPSS charts, data listings, and analyses. When variables are recorded in different units (for example, gross domestic product per capita and percentage literate), a $z$-score transformation places variables on a common scale for easier visual comparison.

**Example.** If each case in your data contains the daily sales totals for each member of the sales staff (for example, one entry for Bob, one for Kim, one for Brian, etc.) collected each day for several months, the Descriptives procedure can compute the average daily sales for each staff member and order the results from highest average sales to lowest.

**Statistics.** Sample size, mean, minimum, maximum, standard deviation, variance, range, sum, standard error of the mean, and kurtosis and skewness with their standard errors.

**Data.** Use numeric variables after you have screened them graphically for recording errors, outliers, and distributional anomalies. The Descriptives procedure is very efficient for large files (thousands of cases).

**Assumptions.** Most of the available statistics (including $z$ scores) are based on normal theory and are appropriate for quantitative variables (interval- or ratio-level measurements) with symmetric distributions (avoid variables with unordered categories or skewed distributions). The distribution of $z$ scores has the same shape as that of the original data; therefore, calculating $z$ scores is not a remedy for problem data.

**Related procedures.** For the median, mode, quartiles, percentiles, and a histogram, use the Frequencies procedure. To compute summary statistics for each of several groups of cases (for example, if you want separate statistics for males and females or for people living in four regions of a country), use the Explore or the Means procedure. You can also use Split File on the Data menu.

# Sample Output

**Figure 10.1    Descriptives output**

Descriptive Statistics

| | N | Minimum | Maximum | Mean | Std. Deviation |
|---|---|---|---|---|---|
| Dave's Sales | 10 | 42.00 | 86.00 | 59.2000 | 14.2657 |
| Sharon's Sales | 10 | 23.00 | 85.00 | 56.2000 | 17.6623 |
| Brian's Sales | 10 | 45.00 | 71.00 | 56.0000 | 8.8819 |
| Mary's Sales | 10 | 34.00 | 83.00 | 52.9000 | 16.6029 |
| Bob's Sales | 10 | 28.00 | 89.00 | 52.9000 | 21.8858 |
| Kim's Sales | 10 | 23.00 | 73.00 | 52.1000 | 16.4617 |
| Juan's Sales | 10 | 25.00 | 85.00 | 50.5000 | 21.1305 |
| Valid N (listwise) | 10 | | | | |

# To Obtain Descriptive Statistics

▶ From the menus choose:

Statistics
  Summarize
    Descriptives...

**Figure 10.2    Descriptives dialog box**

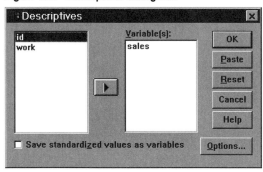

▶ Select one or more variables.

Optionally, you can:

• Click *Save standardized values as variables* to save *z* scores as new variables.

• Click *Options* for optional statistics and display order.

# Descriptives Options

Figure 10.3   Descriptives Options dialog box

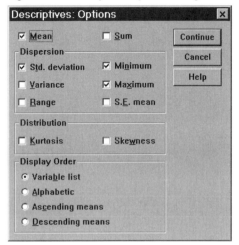

**Mean and Sum.** The mean or arithmetic average is displayed by default.

**Dispersion.** Statistics that measure the spread or variation in the data include the standard deviation, variance, range, minimum, maximum, and standard error of the mean.

**Distribution.** Kurtosis and skewness are statistics that characterize the shape and symmetry of the distribution. These are displayed with their standard errors.

**Display Order.** By default, the variables are displayed in the order in which you selected them. Optionally, you can display variables alphabetically, by ascending means, or by descending means.

# DESCRIPTIVES Command Additional Features

The SPSS command language also allows you to:

- Save standardized scores (*z* scores) for some but not all variables (with the VARIABLES subcommand).
- Specify names for new variables that contain standardized scores (with the VARIABLES subcommand).
- Exclude from the analysis cases with missing values for any variable (with the MISSING subcommand).
- Sort the variables in the display by the value of any statistic, not just the mean (with the SORT subcommand).

See the *SPSS Base Syntax Reference Guide* for complete syntax information.

# 11 Explore

The Explore procedure produces summary statistics and graphical displays, either for all of your cases or separately for groups of cases. There are many reasons for using the Explore procedure—data screening, outlier identification, description, assumption checking, and characterizing differences among subpopulations (groups of cases). Data screening may show that you have unusual values, extreme values, gaps in the data, or other peculiarities. Exploring the data can help to determine whether the statistical techniques you are considering for data analysis are appropriate. The exploration may indicate that you need to transform the data if the technique requires a normal distribution. Or, you may decide that you need nonparametric tests.

**Example.** Look at the distribution of maze-learning times for rats under four different reinforcement schedules. For each of the four groups, you can see if the distribution of times is approximately normal and whether the four variances are equal. You can also identify the cases with the five largest and five smallest times. The boxplots and stem-and-leaf plots graphically summarize the distribution of learning times for each of the groups.

**Statistics and plots.** Mean, median, 5% trimmed mean, standard error, variance, standard deviation, minimum, maximum, range, interquartile range, skewness and kurtosis and their standard errors, confidence interval for the mean (and specified confidence level), percentiles, Huber's M-estimator, Andrew's wave estimator, Hampel's redescending M-estimator, Tukey's biweight estimator, the five largest and five smallest values, the Kolmogorov-Smirnov statistic with a Lilliefors significance level for testing normality, and the Shapiro-Wilk statistic. Boxplots, stem-and-leaf plots, histograms, normality plots, and spread-versus-level plots with the Levene test and transformations.

**Data.** The Explore procedure can be used for quantitative variables (interval- or ratio-level measurements). A factor variable (used to break the data into groups of cases) should have a reasonable number of distinct values (categories). These values may be short string or numeric. The case label variable, used to label outliers in boxplots, can be short string, long string (first 15 characters), or numeric.

**Assumptions.** The distribution of your data does not have to be symmetric or normal.

**Related procedures.** If you just want a few simple summary statistics for groups of cases, use the Means procedure. To obtain counts, percentage of cases, or specific percentiles, use the Frequencies procedure. To compute $z$ scores, use the Descriptives procedure.

# Sample Output

### Figure 11.1   Explore output

**Descriptives**

| | | | Time | | | |
|---|---|---|---|---|---|---|
| | | | Schedule | | | |
| | | | 1 | 2 | 3 | 4 |
| Mean | | Statistic | 2.760 | 4.850 | 6.900 | 9.010 |
| | | Std. Error | .165 | .422 | .445 | .289 |
| 95% Confidence Interval for Mean | Lower Bound | Statistic | 2.387 | 3.895 | 5.893 | 8.357 |
| | Upper Bound | Statistic | 3.133 | 5.805 | 7.907 | 9.663 |
| 5% Trimmed Mean | | Statistic | 2.761 | 4.889 | 6.911 | 8.994 |
| Median | | Statistic | 2.850 | 4.900 | 7.050 | 9.000 |
| Variance | | Statistic | .272 | 1.783 | 1.982 | .834 |
| Std. Deviation | | Statistic | .521 | 1.335 | 1.408 | .913 |
| Minimum | | Statistic | 2.0 | 2.3 | 4.5 | 7.8 |
| Maximum | | Statistic | 3.5 | 6.7 | 9.1 | 10.5 |
| Range | | Statistic | 1.5 | 4.4 | 4.6 | 2.7 |
| Interquartile Range | | Statistic | .925 | 2.250 | 2.400 | 1.650 |
| Skewness | | Statistic | -.116 | -.559 | -.197 | .219 |
| | | Std. Error | .687 | .687 | .687 | .687 |
| Kurtosis | | Statistic | -1.210 | -.104 | -.606 | -1.350 |
| | | Std. Error | 1.334 | 1.334 | 1.334 | 1.334 |

**Extreme Values**

| | | | Case Number | Schedule | Value |
|---|---|---|---|---|---|
| Time | Highest | 1 | 31 | 4 | 10.5 |
| | | 2 | 33 | 4 | 9.9 |
| | | 3 | 39 | 4 | 9.8 |
| | | 4 | 32 | 4 | 9.5 |
| | | 5 | 36 | 4 | 9.3 |
| | Lowest | 1 | 2 | 1 | 2.0 |
| | | 2 | 7 | 1 | 2.1 |
| | | 3 | 1 | 1 | 2.3 |
| | | 4 | 11 | 2 | 2.3 |
| | | 5 | 3 | 1 | 2.5 |

```
Frequency    Stem &  Leaf

  7.00     2 . 0133589
  6.00     3 . 014577
  3.00     4 . 568
  5.00     5 . 05779
  4.00     6 . 1379
  3.00     7 . 268
  6.00     8 . 012237
  5.00     9 . 13589
  1.00    10 . 5

Stem width:     1.0
Each leaf:    1 case(s)
```

**Figure 1.1 Explore output (continued)**

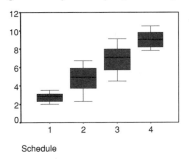

Schedule

# To Explore Your Data

▶ From the menus choose:

Statistics
  Summarize
    Explore...

**Figure 11.2   Explore dialog box**

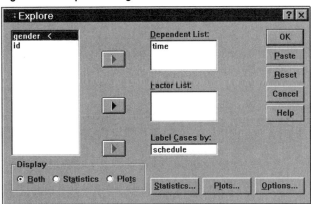

▶ Select one or more dependent variables.

Optionally, you can:

- Select one or more factor variables, whose values will define groups of cases.
- Select an identification variable to label cases.

- Click *Statistics* for robust estimators, outliers, percentiles, and frequency tables.
- Click *Plots* for histograms, normal probability plots and tests, and spread-versus-level plots with Levene's statistic.
- Click *Options* for the treatment of missing values.

## Explore Statistics

**Figure 11.3  Explore Statistics dialog box**

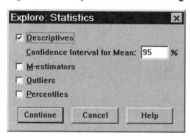

**Descriptives.** These measures of central tendency and dispersion are displayed by default. Measures of central tendency indicate the location of the distribution; they include the mean, median, and 5% trimmed mean. Measures of dispersion show the dissimilarity of the values; these include standard error, variance, standard deviation, minimum, maximum, range, and interquartile range. The descriptive statistics also include measures of the shape of the distribution; skewness and kurtosis are displayed with their standard errors. The 95% level confidence interval for the mean is also displayed; you can specify a different confidence level.

**M-estimators.** Robust alternatives to the sample mean and median for estimating the center of location. The estimators calculated differ in the weights they apply to cases. Huber's M-estimator, Andrew's wave estimator, Hampel's redescending M-estimator, and Tukey's biweight estimator are displayed.

**Outliers.** Displays the five largest and five smallest values, with case labels.

**Percentiles.** Displays the values for the 5th, 10th, 25th, 50th, 75th, 90th, and 95th percentiles.

# Explore Plots

**Figure 11.4    Explore Plots dialog box**

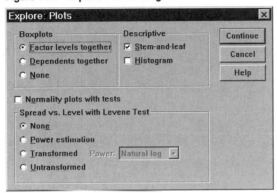

**Boxplots.** These alternatives control the display of boxplots when you have more than one dependent variable. Select *Factor levels together* to generate a separate display for each dependent variable. Within a display, boxplots are shown for each of the groups defined by a factor variable. Select *Dependents together* to generate a separate display for each group defined by a factor variable. Within a display, boxplots are shown side by side for each dependent variable. This display is particularly useful when the different variables represent a single characteristic measured at different times.

**Descriptive.** The Descriptive group allows you to choose stem-and-leaf plots and histograms.

**Normality plots with tests.** Displays normal probability and detrended normal probability plots. The Kolmogorov-Smirnov statistic, with a Lilliefors significance level for testing normality, is displayed. The Shapiro-Wilk statistic is calculated for samples with 50 or fewer observations.

**Spread vs. Level with Levene Test.** Controls data transformation for spread-versus-level plots. For all spread-versus-level plots, the slope of the regression line and Levene's test for homogeneity of variance are displayed. If you select a transformation, Levene's test is based on the transformed data. If no factor variable is selected, spread-versus-level plots are not produced. Select *Power estimation* to produce a plot of the natural logs of the interquartile ranges against the natural logs of the medians for all cells, as well as an estimate of the power transformation for achieving equal variances in the cells. A spread-versus-level plot helps determine the power for a transformation to stabilize (make more equal) variances across groups. Select *Transformed* to choose one of the power alternatives, perhaps following the recommendation from power estimation, and to produce plots of transformed data. The interquartile range and median of the transformed data are plotted. Select *Untransformed* to produce plots of the raw data. This is equivalent to a transformation with a power of 1.

### Explore Power Transformations

Following are the power transformations for spread-versus-level plots. To transform data, you must select a power for the transformation. You can choose one of the following alternatives:

- **Natural log.** Natural log transformation. This is the default.
- **1/square root.** For each data value, the reciprocal of the square root is calculated.
- **Reciprocal.** The reciprocal of each data value is calculated.
- **Square root.** The square root of each data value is calculated.
- **Square.** Each data value is squared.
- **Cube.** Each data value is cubed.

## Explore Options

**Figure 11.5   Explore Options dialog box**

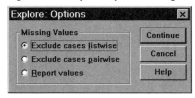

**Missing Values.** Controls the treatment of missing values.

- **Exclude cases listwise.** Cases with missing values for any dependent or factor variable are excluded from all analyses. This is the default.
- **Exclude cases pairwise.** Cases with no missing values for variables in a group (cell) are included in the analysis of that group. The case may have missing values for variables used in other groups.
- **Report values.** Missing values for factor variables are treated as a separate category. All output is produced for this additional category. Frequency tables include categories for missing values. Missing values for a factor variable are included but labeled as missing.

## EXAMINE Command Additional Features

The Explore procedure uses EXAMINE command syntax. The SPSS command language also allows you to:

- Request total output and plots in addition to output and plots for groups defined by the factor variables (with the TOTAL subcommand).
- Specify a common scale for a group of boxplots (with the SCALE subcommand).
- Specify interactions of the factor variables (with the VARIABLES subcommand).
- Specify percentiles other than the defaults (with the PERCENTILES subcommand).
- Calculate percentiles according to any of five methods (with the PERCENTILES subcommand).
- Specify any power transformation for spread-versus-level plots (with the PLOT subcommand).
- Specify the number of extreme values to be displayed (with the STATISTICS subcommand).
- Specify parameters for the M-estimators, robust estimators of location (with the MESTIMATORS subcommand).

See the *SPSS Base Syntax Reference Guide* for complete syntax information.

# 12 Crosstabs

The Crosstabs procedure forms two-way and multiway tables and provides 22 tests and measures of association for two-way tables. The structure of the table and whether categories are ordered determine what test or measure to use.

In Crosstabs, statistics and measures of association are computed for two-way tables only. If you specify a row, a column, and a layer factor (control variable), SPSS forms one panel of associated statistics and measures for each value of the layer factor (or a combination of values for two or more control variables). For example, if *gender* is a layer factor for a table of *married* (yes, no) against *life* (is life exciting, routine, or dull), the results for a two-way table for the females are computed separately from those for the males and printed as panels following one another.

**Example.** Are daughters more likely to graduate from high school if their mothers did? From a crosstabulation, you might learn that for mothers who graduated from high school, 374 (52.4%) of their daughters also graduated from high school. In fact, 230 (32.2%) daughters earned higher degrees than their mothers, and only 40 (5.6%) did not graduate from high school. The chi-square test indicates that daughters' highest degree is *not* independent of mothers' highest degree.

**Statistics and measures of association.** Pearson chi-square, likelihood-ratio chi-square, linear-by-linear association test, Fisher's exact test, Yates' corrected chi-square, Pearson's *r*, Spearman's rho, contingency coefficient, phi, Cramér's *V*, symmetric and asymmetric lambdas, Goodman and Kruskal's tau, uncertainty coefficient, gamma, Somers' *d*, Kendall's tau-*b*, Kendall's tau-*c*, eta coefficient, Cohen's kappa, relative risk estimate, odds ratio, and McNemar test.

**Data.** To define the categories of each table variable, use values of a numeric or short string (eight or fewer characters) variable. For example, for *gender*, you could code the data as 1 and 2 or as *male* and *female*.

**Assumptions.** Some statistics and measures assume ordered categories (ordinal data) or quantitative values (interval or ratio data). Others are valid when the table variables have unordered categories (nominal data). For the chi-square-based statistics (phi, Cramér's *V*, contingency coefficient), the data should be a random sample from a multinomial distribution.

**Related procedures.** To model the relationships between two or more categorical variables, use the General Loglinear procedure to fit a model to the cell frequencies. For defining intervals along a quantitative variable, use Recode on the Transform menu. For example, if you want to look at the relationship between salary and job satisfaction, and salary is recorded to the nearest dollar, use the Recode procedure to define intervals such as less than $20,000, $20,000 to $30,000, and so on.

# Sample Output

### Figure 12.1    Crosstabs output

Daughters Highest Degree * Mothers Highest Degree Crosstabulation

Count

| | | Mothers Highest Degree | | | | | Total |
|---|---|---|---|---|---|---|---|
| | | Less Than HS | High School | Junior College | Bachelor | Graduate | |
| Daughters Highest Degree | Less than HS | 169 | 40 | 2 | 3 | 2 | 216 |
| | High school | 286 | 374 | 13 | 33 | 8 | 714 |
| | Junior college | 25 | 41 | 6 | 11 | 1 | 84 |
| | Bachelor | 37 | 133 | 15 | 34 | 10 | 229 |
| | Graduate | 23 | 56 | 5 | 15 | 8 | 107 |
| Total | | 540 | 644 | 41 | 96 | 29 | 1350 |

Chi-Square Tests

| | Value | df | Asymptotic Significance (2-tailed) |
|---|---|---|---|
| Pearson Chi-Square | 263.557[1] | 16 | .000 |
| Likelihood Ratio | 260.382 | 16 | .000 |
| Linear-by-Linear Association | 168.079 | 1 | .000 |
| N of Valid Cases | 1350 | | |

[1]. 6 cells (24.0%) have expected count less than 5. The minimum expected count is 1.80

# To Obtain Crosstabulations

▶ From the menus choose:

Statistics
  Summarize
    Crosstabs...

**Figure 12.2   Crosstabs dialog box**

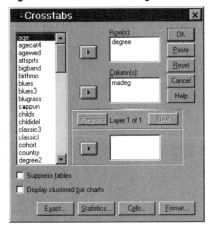

▶ Select one or more row variables and one or more column variables.

Optionally, you can:

• Select one or more control variables.

• Click *Statistics* for tests and measures of association for two-way tables or subtables.

• Click *Cells* for observed and expected values, percentages, and residuals.

• Click *Format* for controlling the order of categories.

# Crosstabs Layers

If you select one or more layer variables, a separate crosstabulation is produced for each category of each layer variable (control variable). For example, if you have one row variable, one column variable, and one layer variable with two categories, you get a two-way table for each category of the layer variable. To make another layer of control variables, click *Next*. Subtables are produced for each combination of categories for each 1st-layer variable with each 2nd-layer variable, and so on. If statistics and measures of association are requested, they apply to two-way subtables only.

# Crosstabs Clustered Bar Charts

**Display clustered bar charts.** A clustered bar chart helps summarize your data for groups of cases. There is one cluster of bars for each value of the variable you specified in the Rows list. The variable that defines the bars within each cluster is the variable you specified in the Columns list. There is one set of differently colored or patterned bars for each value of this variable. If you specify more than one variable in the Columns or the Rows list, a clustered bar chart is produced for each combination of two variables.

# Crosstabs Statistics

**Figure 12.3   Crosstabs Statistics dialog box**

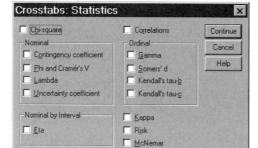

**Chi-square.** For tables with two rows and two columns, select *Chi-square* to calculate the Pearson chi-square, the likelihood-ratio chi-square, Fisher's exact test, and Yates' corrected chi-square (continuity correction). For $2 \times 2$ tables, Fisher's exact test is computed when a table that does not result from missing rows or columns in a larger table has a cell with an expected frequency of less than 5. Yates' corrected chi-square is computed for all other $2 \times 2$ tables. For tables with any number of rows and columns, select *Chi-square* to calculate the Pearson chi-square and the likelihood-ratio chi-square. When both table variables are quantitative, *Chi-square* yields the linear-by-linear association test.

**Correlations.** For tables where both row and columns contain ordered values, *Correlations* yields Spearman's correlation coefficient, rho (numeric data only). The Spearman correlation coefficient is a measure of association between rank orders. When both table variables (factors) are quantitative, *Correlations* yields the Pearson correlation coefficient, *r*, a measure of linear association between the variables.

**Nominal.** For nominal data (no intrinsic order, such as Catholic, Protestant, Jewish), you can select *Phi and Cramér's V*, *Contingency coefficient*, *Lambda* (symmetric and asymmetric lambdas and Goodman and Kruskal's tau), and *Uncertainty coefficient*.

**Ordinal.** For tables where both rows and columns contain ordered values, select *Gamma* (zero-order for 2-way tables and conditional for 3-way to 10-way tables), *Kendall's tau-b*, and *Kendall's tau-c*. For predicting column categories from row categories, select *Somers' d*.

**Nominal by Interval.** When one variables is categorical and the other is quantitative, select *Eta*. The categorical variable must be coded numerically.

**Kappa.** For tables that have the same categories in the columns as in the rows (for example, measuring agreement between two raters), select *Kappa* (Cohen's kappa).

**Risk.** For tables with two rows and two columns, select *Risk* for relative risk estimates and the odds ratio.

**McNemar.** A nonparametric test for two related dichotomous variables. Tests for changes in responses using the chi-square distribution. Useful for detecting changes in responses due to experimental intervention in *before* and *after* designs.

## Crosstabs Cell Display

Figure 12.4   Crosstabs Cell Display dialog box

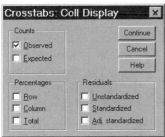

To help you uncover patterns in the data that contribute to a significant chi-square test, the Crosstabs procedure displays expected frequencies and three types of residuals (deviates) that measure the difference between observed and expected frequencies. Each cell of the table can contain any combination of counts, percentages, and residuals selected.

**Counts.** The number of cases actually observed and the number of cases expected if the row and column variables are independent of each other.

**Percentages.** The percentages can add up across the rows or down the columns. The percentages of the total number of cases represented in the table (one layer) are also available.

**Residuals.** Raw unstandardized residuals give the difference between the observed and expected values. Standardized and adjusted standardized residuals are also available.

Standardized and adjusted standardized residuals are calculated as in Haberman (1978).

## Crosstabs Table Format

Figure 12.5   Crosstabs Table Format dialog box

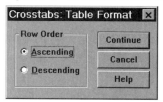

You can arrange rows in ascending or descending order of the values of the row variable.

## CROSSTABS Command Additional Features

The SPSS command language also allows you to:

- Specify value ranges for variables in integer mode (with the VARIABLES subcommand). Integer mode is not significantly faster, but it conserves memory when variables are coded as adjacent integers. An option to display rows and columns containing missing data is available in integer mode (with the MISSING subcommand).

- Write the table(s) into a formatted ASCII file for use by other software (with the WRITE subcommand). (You can also accomplish this by using Aggregate on the Data menu.)

- Use long string variables (over eight characters) in tables. Only the first eight characters are used to define categories.

See the *SPSS Base Syntax Reference Guide* for complete syntax information.

# 13 Summarize

The Summarize procedure calculates subgroup statistics for variables within categories of one or more grouping variables. All levels of the grouping variable are crosstabulated. You can choose the order in which the statistics are displayed. Summary statistics for each variable across all categories are also displayed. Data values in each category can be listed or suppressed. With large data sets, you can choose to list only the first *n* cases.

**Example.** Compute the median education level and the mean number of children for parents with different philosophies about spanking. You might learn that parents who strongly agree with spanking have a median education level of 12 years and a mean of 2.15 children. On the other hand, parents who strongly disagree with spanking have a median education level of 14 years and a mean of 1.62 children. You can also list the number of cases in each subgroup. For example, 503 of the 996 parents sampled agree that spanking is okay.

**Statistics.** Sum, number of cases, mean, median, grouped median, standard error of the mean, minimum, maximum, range, variable value of the first category of the grouping variable, variable value of the last category of the grouping variable, standard deviation, variance, kurtosis, standard error of kurtosis, skewness, standard error of skewness.

**Data.** Grouping variables are categorical variables whose values can be numeric or short string. The number of categories should be reasonably small. The other variables should be able to be ranked.

**Assumptions.** Some of the optional subgroup statistics, such as the mean and standard deviation, are based on normal theory and are appropriate for quantitative variables with symmetric distributions. Robust statistics, such as the median and the range, are appropriate for quantitative variables that may or may not meet the assumption of normality.

**Related procedures.** To obtain more extensive statistics and graphical displays for each cell, use the Split File procedure in combination with the Explore procedure. If you have a large number of subgroups and want to list cases, the Report Summaries in Rows procedure will make better use of your computer's memory.

# Sample Output

**Figure 13.1   Summarize output**

Case Summaries

|  |  |  | Number of Children | Highest Year of School Completed |
|---|---|---|---|---|
| Favor Spanking to Discipline Child | Strongly Agree | Mean | 2.15 | 12.42 |
|  |  | Median | 2.00 | 12.00 |
|  |  | N | 228 | 227 |
|  | Agree | Mean | 1.95 | 12.86 |
|  |  | Median | 2.00 | 12.00 |
|  |  | N | 503 | 503 |
|  | Disagree | Mean | 1.65 | 13.58 |
|  |  | Median | 2.00 | 13.50 |
|  |  | N | 199 | 198 |
|  | Strongly Disagree | Mean | 1.62 | 14.06 |
|  |  | Median | 2.00 | 14.00 |
|  |  | N | 66 | 67 |
|  | Total | Mean | 1.92 | 12.99 |
|  |  | Median | 2.00 | 12.00 |
|  |  | N | 996 | 995 |

# To Obtain Case Summaries

▶   From the menus choose:

Statistics
  Summarize
    Case Summaries...

**Figure 13.2  Summarize Cases dialog box**

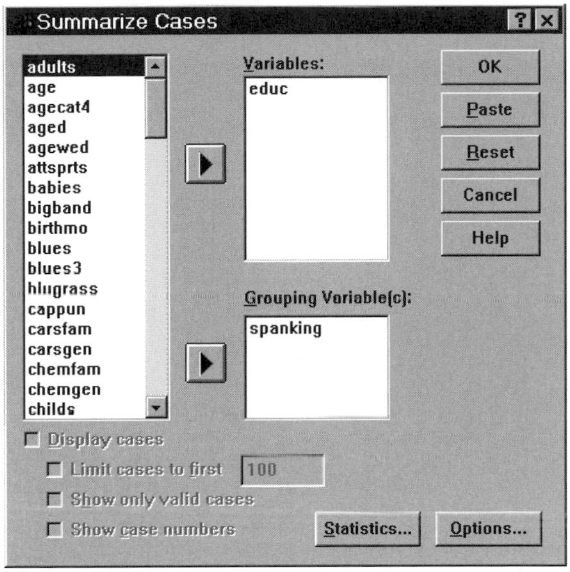

▶   Select one or more variables.

Optionally, you can:

- Select one or more grouping variables to divide your data into subgroups.
- Click *Options* to change the output title, add a caption below the output, or exclude cases with missing values.
- Click *Statistics* for optional statistics.
- Select *Display cases* to list the cases in each subgroup. By default, the system lists only the first 100 cases in your file. You can raise or lower the value for *Limit cases to first*, or deselect that item to list all cases.

# Summarize Options

**Figure 13.3    Summarize Cases Options dialog box**

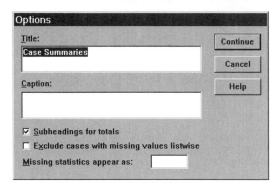

SPSS allows you to change the title of your output or add a caption that will appear be-low the output table. You can also choose to display or suppress subheadings for totals and to include or exclude cases with missing values for any of the variables used in any of the analyses. Often it is desirable to denote missing cases in output with a period or asterisk. Enter a character, phrase, or code that you would like to have appear when a value is missing; otherwise, no special treatment is applied to missing cases in the output.

# Summarize Statistics

**Figure 13.4    Summarize Cases Statistics dialog box**

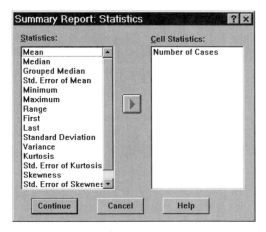

You can choose one or more of the following subgroup statistics for the variables within each category of each grouping variable: sum, number of cases, mean, median, grouped median, standard error of the mean, minimum, maximum, range, variable value of the first category of the grouping variable, variable value of the last category of the grouping variable, standard deviation, variance, kurtosis, standard error of kurtosis, skewness, standard error of skewness. The order in which the statistics appear in the Cell Statistics list is the order in which they will be displayed in the output. Summary statistics are also displayed for each variable across all categories.

## SUMMARIZE Command Additional Features

See the *SPSS Base Syntax Reference Guide* for complete syntax information.

# 14 Means

The Means procedure calculates subgroup means and related univariate statistics for dependent variables within categories of one or more independent variables. Optionally, you can obtain one-way analysis of variance, eta, and a test for linearity.

**Example.** Measure the average amount of fat absorbed by three different types of cooking oil and perform a one-way analysis of variance to see if the means differ.

**Statistics.** Sum, number of cases, mean, median, grouped median, standard error of the mean, minimum, maximum, range, variable value of the first category of the grouping variable, variable value of the last category of the grouping variable, standard deviation, variance, kurtosis, standard error of kurtosis, skewness, standard error of skewness. Analysis of variance table eta, eta squared. Tests for linearity: $R$, $R^2$.

**Data.** The dependent variables are quantitative and the independent variables are categorical. The values of categorical variables can be numeric or short string.

**Assumptions.** Some of the optional subgroup statistics, such as the mean and standard deviation, are based on normal theory and are appropriate for quantitative variables with symmetric distributions. Robust statistics, such as the median and the range, are appropriate for quantitative variables that may or may not meet the assumption of normality. Analysis of variance is robust to departures from normality, but the data in each cell should be symmetric. Analysis of variance also assumes that the groups come from populations with equal variances. To test this assumption, use Levene's homogeneity-of-variance test, available in the One-Way ANOVA procedure.

**Related procedures.** Use the One-Way ANOVA procedure to obtain a one-way analysis of variance, *a priori* contrasts, post hoc range tests, and pairwise multiple comparisons. For an analysis of variance with more than one factor, use the Simple Factorial ANOVA procedure. To list the cases in each subgroup, use the Report Summaries in Rows procedure.

# Sample Output

### Figure 14.1   Means output

Report

Absorbed Grams of Fat

| Type of Oil | Peanut Oil | Mean | 72.00 |
|---|---|---|---|
| | | N | 6 |
| | | Std. Deviation | 13.34 |
| | Lard | Mean | 85.00 |
| | | N | 6 |
| | | Std. Deviation | 7.77 |
| | Corn Oil | Mean | 62.00 |
| | | N | 6 |
| | | Std. Deviation | 8.22 |
| | Total | Mean | 73.00 |
| | | N | 18 |
| | | Std. Deviation | 13.56 |

**ANOVA Table**

| | | | Sum of Squares | df | Mean Square | F | Sig. |
|---|---|---|---|---|---|---|---|
| Absorbed Grams of Fat * Type of Oil | Between Groups | (Combined) | 1596.000 | 2 | 798.000 | 7.824 | .005 |
| | Within Groups | | 1530.000 | 15 | 102.000 | | |
| | Total | | 3126.000 | 17 | | | |

# To Obtain Means

▶ From the menus choose:

Statistics
  Compare Means
    Means...

**Figure 14.2    Means dialog box**

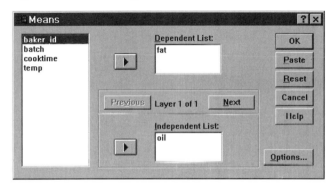

▶ Select one or more dependent variables.

▶ There are two ways to select categorical independent variables.

• Select one or more independent variables. Separate results are displayed for each independent variable.

• Select one or more layers of independent variables. Each layer further subdivides the sample. If you have one independent variable in Layer 1 and one in Layer 2, the results are displayed in one crossed table as opposed to separate tables for each independent variable.

Optionally, you can:

• Click *Options* for optional statistics, analysis-of-variance table, eta, eta squared, $R$, and $R^2$.

# Means Options

Figure 14.3   Means Options dialog box

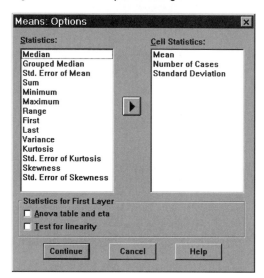

You can choose one or more of the following subgroup statistics for the variables within each category of each grouping variable: sum, number of cases, mean, median, grouped median, standard error of the mean, minimum, maximum, range, variable value of the first category of the grouping variable, variable value of the last category of the grouping variable, standard deviation, variance, kurtosis, standard error of kurtosis, skewness, standard error of skewness. You can change the order in which the subgroup statistics appear. The order the statistics appear in the Cell Statistics list is the order they are displayed in the output. Summary statistics are also displayed for each variable across all categories.

Click *ANOVA table and eta* to obtain a one-way analysis of variance, eta, and eta squared for each independent variable in the first layer. Eta and eta squared are measures of association. Eta squared is the proportion of variance in the dependent variable that is explained by differences among groups. It is the ratio of the between-groups sum of squares and the total sum of squares. *Tests for linearity* yields $R$ and $R^2$, which are appropriate measures when the categories of the independent variable are ordered. $R$ and $R^2$ measure the goodness of fit of a linear model.

# MEANS Command Additional Features

See the *SPSS Base Syntax Reference Guide* for complete syntax information.

# 15 T Tests

The Compare Means submenu of the Statistics menu provides three types of *t* tests:

**Independent-samples t test (two-sample t test).** Compares the means of one variable for two groups of cases. Descriptive statistics for each group and Levene's test for equality of variances are provided, as well as both equal- and unequal-variance *t* values and a 95% confidence interval for the difference in means.

**Paired-samples t test (dependent t test).** Compares the means of two variables for a single group. This test is also for matched pairs or case-control study designs. The output includes descriptive statistics for the test variables, the correlation between them, descriptive statistics for the paired differences, the *t* test, and a 95% confidence interval.

**One-sample t test.** Compares the mean of one variable with a known or hypothesized value. Descriptive statistics for the test variables are displayed along with the *t* test. A 95% confidence interval for the difference between the mean of the test variable and the hypothesized test value is part of the default output.

## Independent-Samples T Test

The Independent-Samples T Test procedure compares means for two groups of cases. Ideally, for this test, the subjects should be randomly assigned to two groups, so that any difference in response is due to the treatment (or lack of treatment) and not to other factors. This is not the case if you compare average income for males and females. A person is not randomly assigned to be a male or female. In such situations, you should ensure that differences in other factors are not masking or enhancing a significant difference in means. Differences in average income may be influenced by factors such as education and not by sex alone.

**Example.** Patients with high blood pressure are randomly assigned to a placebo group and a treatment group. The placebo subjects receive an inactive pill and the treatment subjects receive a new drug that is expected to lower blood pressure. After treating the subjects for two months, the two-sample *t* test is used to compare the average blood pressures for the placebo group and the treatment group. Each patient is measured once and belongs to one group.

195

**Statistics.** For each variable: sample size, mean, standard deviation, and standard error of the mean. For the difference in means: mean, standard error, and confidence interval (you can specify the confidence level). Tests: Levene's test for equality of variances, and both pooled- and separate-variances *t* tests for equality of means.

**Data.** The values of the quantitative variable of interest are in a single column in the data file. SPSS uses a grouping variable with two values to separate the cases into two groups. The grouping variable can be numeric (values such as 1 and 2, or 6.25 and 12.5) or short string (such as *yes* and *no*). As an alternative, you can use a quantitative variable, such as *age,* to split the cases into two groups by specifying a cut point (cut point 21 splits *age* into an under-21 group and a 21-and-over group).

**Assumptions.** For the equal-variance *t* test, the observations should be independent, random samples from normal distributions with the same population variance. For the unequal-variance *t* test, the observations should be independent, random samples from normal distributions. The two-sample *t* test is fairly robust to departures from normality. When checking distributions graphically, look to see that they are symmetric and have no outliers.

**Related procedures.** If you have more than two independent groups, consider the One-Way ANOVA procedure. If your groups are not independent—for example, if you measure an employee's performance before and after a training program—use the Paired-Samples T Test procedure. If the test variable is categorical (nominal or ordinal level of measurement), use the Crosstabs procedure. If the data are not normally distributed or are not quantitative, but ordered, use the Mann-Whitney *U* test (select *2 Independent Samples* from the Nonparametric Tests submenu).

# Sample Output

### Figure 15.1  Independent-Samples T Test output

Group Statistics

| | | | N | Mean | Std. Deviation | Std. Error Mean |
|---|---|---|---|---|---|---|
| Blood pressure | Treatment | placebo | 10 | 142.50 | 17.04 | 5.39 |
| | | new_drug | 10 | 116.40 | 13.62 | 4.31 |

Independent Samples Test

| | | Levene's Test for Equality of Variances | | t-test for Equality of Means | | | | | | |
| | | F | Significance | t | df | Significance (2-tailed) | Mean Difference | Std. Error Difference | 95% Confidence Interval of the Mean | |
| | | | | | | | | | Lower | Upper |
|---|---|---|---|---|---|---|---|---|---|---|
| Blood pressure | Equal variances assumed | .134 | .719 | 3.783 | 18 | .001 | 26.10 | 6.90 | 11.61 | 40.59 |
| | Equal variances not assumed | | | 3.783 | 17.163 | .001 | 26.10 | 6.90 | 11.56 | 40.64 |

# To Obtain an Independent-Samples T Test

▶ From the menus choose:

Statistics
  Compare Means
    Independent-Samples T Test...

**Figure 15.2   Independent-Samples T Test dialog box**

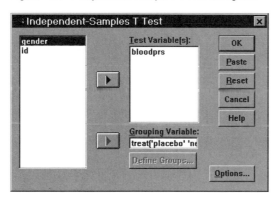

▶ Select one or more quantitative test variables. A separate *t* test is computed for each variable.

▶ Select a single grouping variable, and click *Define Groups* to specify two codes for the groups you want to compare.

Optionally, you can click *Options* to control the treatment of missing data and the level of the confidence interval.

## Independent-Samples T Test Define Groups

Figure 15.3   Define Groups dialog box for numeric variables

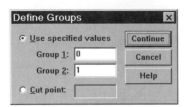

For numeric grouping variables, define the two groups for the *t* test by specifying two values or a cut point:

- **Use specified values.** Enter a value for Group 1 and another for Group 2. Cases with any other values are excluded from the analysis. Numbers need not be integers (for example, 6.25 and 12.5 are valid).

- **Cut point.** Alternatively, enter a number that splits the values of the grouping variable into two sets. All cases with values less than the cut point form one group, and cases with values greater than or equal to the cut point form the other group.

Figure 15.4   Define Groups dialog box for string variables

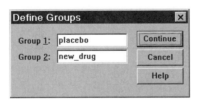

For short string grouping variables, enter a string for Group 1 and another for Group 2, such as *yes* and *no*. Cases with other strings are excluded from the analysis.

## Independent-Samples T Test Options

Figure 15.5   Independent-Samples T Test Options dialog box

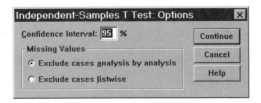

**Confidence Interval.** By default SPSS displays a 95% confidence interval for the difference in means. Enter a value between 1 and 99 to request a different confidence level.

**Missing Values.** When you test several variables and data are missing for one or more variables, you can tell SPSS which cases to include (or exclude):

- **Exclude missing data analysis by analysis.** Each *t* test uses all cases that have valid data for the variables tested. Sample sizes may vary from test to test.
- **Exclude cases listwise.** Each *t* test uses only cases that have valid data for all variables used in the requested *t* tests. The sample size is constant across tests.

# Paired-Samples T Test

The Paired-Samples T Test procedure compares the means of two variables for a single group. It computes the differences between values of the two variables for each case and tests whether the average differs from 0.

**Example.** In a study on high blood pressure, all patients are measured at the beginning of the study, given a treatment, and measured again. Thus, each subject has two measures, often called *before* and *after* measures. An alternative design for which this test is used is a matched-pairs or case-control study. Here, each record in the data file contains the response for the patient and also for his or her matched control subject. In a blood pressure study, patients and controls might be matched by age (a 75-year-old patient with a 75-year-old control group member).

**Statistics.** For each variable: mean, sample size, standard deviation, and standard error of the mean. For each pair of variables: correlation, average difference in means, *t* test, and confidence interval for mean difference (you can specify the confidence level). Standard deviation and standard error of the mean difference.

**Data.** For each paired test, specify two quantitative variables (interval- or ratio-level of measurement). For a matched-pairs or case-control study, the response for each test subject and its matched control subject must be in the same case in the data file.

**Assumptions.** Observations for each pair should be made under the same conditions. The mean differences should be normally distributed. Variances of each variable can be equal or unequal.

**Related procedures.** To test a sample mean from one group of cases against that from another group of cases, use the Independent-Samples T Test. If you want to compare a sample mean against a constant value, use the One-Sample T Test. If the data in the test variable are not quantitative, but ordered, or are not normally distributed, use the Wilcoxon signed-rank test (select *2 Related Samples* from the Nonparametric Tests submenu).

# Sample Output

**Figure 15.6   Paired-Samples T Test output**

Paired Samples Statistics

| | | Mean | N | Std. Deviation | Std. Error Mean |
|---|---|---|---|---|---|
| Pair 1 | After treatment | 116.40 | 10 | 13.62 | 4.31 |
| | Before treatment | 142.50 | 10 | 17.04 | 5.39 |

Paired Samples Test

| | | Paired Differences | | | | | | | |
|---|---|---|---|---|---|---|---|---|---|
| | | | | | 95% Confidence Interval of the Difference | | | | |
| | | Mean | Std. Deviation | Std. Error Mean | Lower | Upper | t | df | Significance (2-tailed) |
| Pair 1 | After treatment - Before treatment | -26.10 | 19.59 | 6.19 | -40.11 | -12.09 | -4.214 | 9 | .002 |

# To Obtain a Paired-Samples T Test

▶ From the menus choose:

Statistics
  Compare Means
    Paired-Samples T Test...

**Figure 15.7   Paired-Samples T Test dialog box**

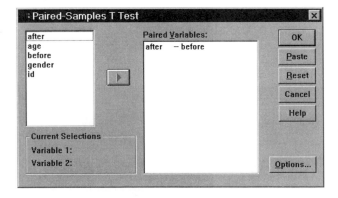

▶ Select a pair of variables, as follows:

- Click each of two variables. The first variable appears in the Current Selections group as *Variable 1*, and the second appears as *Variable 2*.

- After you have selected a pair of variables, click the arrow button to move the pair into the Paired Variables list. You may select more pairs of variables. To remove a pair of variables from the analysis, select a pair in the Paired Variables list and click the arrow button.

Optionally, you can click *Options* to control treatment of missing data and the level of the confidence interval.

## Paired-Samples T Test Options

**Figure 15.8    Paired-Samples T Test Options dialog box**

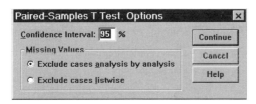

**Confidence Interval.** By default SPSS displays a 95% confidence interval for the difference in means. Enter a value between 1 and 99 to request a different confidence level.

**Missing Values.** When you test several variables and data are missing for one or more variables, you can tell SPSS which cases to include (or exclude):

- **Exclude missing data analysis by analysis.** Each *t* test uses all cases that have valid data for the pair of variables tested. Sample sizes may vary from test to test.

- **Exclude cases listwise.** Each *t* test uses only cases that have valid data for all pairs of variables tested. The sample size is constant across tests.

# One-Sample T Test

The One-Sample T Test procedure tests whether the mean of a single variable differs from a specified constant.

**Examples.** A researcher might want to test whether the average IQ score for a group of students differs from 100. Or, a cereal manufacturer can take a sample of boxes from the production line and check whether the mean weight of the samples differs from 1.3 pounds at the 95% confidence level.

**Statistics.** For each test variable: mean, standard deviation, and standard error of the mean. The average difference between each data value and the hypothesized test value, a $t$ test that tests that this difference is 0, and a confidence interval for this difference (you can specify the confidence level).

**Data.** To test the values of a quantitative variable against a hypothesized test value, choose a quantitative variable and enter a hypothesized test value.

**Assumptions.** This test assumes that the data are normally distributed; however, this test is fairly robust to departures from normality.

**Related procedures.** If you want to test a sample mean from one group of cases against that from another group of cases, use the Independent-Samples T Test procedure. To test the means of two variables estimated from the same sample, use the Paired-Samples T Test procedure.

# Sample Output

**Figure 15.9   One-Sample T Test output**

One-Sample Statistics

|  | IQ |
|---|---|
| N | 15 |
| Mean | 109.33 |
| Std. Deviation | 12.03 |
| Std. Error Mean | 3.11 |

Rows and columns have been transposed.

One-Sample Test

| | Test Value = 100 | | | | | |
|---|---|---|---|---|---|---|
| | | | | | 95% Confidence Interval of the Difference | |
| | t | df | Significance (2-tailed) | Mean Difference | Lower | Upper |
| IQ | 3.005 | 14 | .009 | 9.33 | 2.67 | 15.99 |

# To Obtain a One-Sample T Test

▶ From the menus choose:

Statistics
  Compare Means
    One-Sample T Test...

**Figure 15.10 One-Sample T Test dialog box**

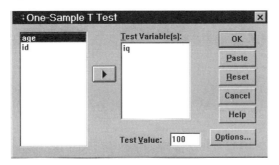

▶ Select one or more variables to be tested against the same hypothesized value.

▶ Enter a numeric test value against which each sample mean is compared.

Optionally, you can click *Options* to control the treatment of missing data and the level of the confidence interval.

## One-Sample T Test Options

**Figure 15.11 One-Sample T Test Options dialog box**

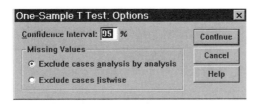

**Confidence Interval.** By default, SPSS displays a 95% confidence interval for the difference between the mean and the hypothesized test value. Enter a value between 1 and 99 to request a different confidence level.

**Missing Values.** When you test several variables and data are missing for one or more of these variables, you can tell SPSS which cases to include (or exclude).

- **Exclude missing data analysis by analysis.** Each *t* test uses all cases that have valid data for the variable tested. Sample sizes may vary from test to test.
- **Exclude cases listwise.** Each *t* test uses only cases that have valid data for all variables used in any of the *t* tests requested. The sample size is constant across tests.

## T-TEST Command Additional Features

The SPSS command language also allows you to:

- Produce both one-sample and independent-samples *t* tests by running a single command.
- Test a variable against each variable on a list, in a paired *t* test (with the PAIRS subcommand).

See the *SPSS Base Syntax Reference Guide* for complete syntax information.

# 16 One-Way Analysis of Variance

The One-Way ANOVA procedure produces a one-way analysis of variance for a quantitative dependent variable by a single factor (independent) variable. Analysis of variance is used to test the hypothesis that several means are equal. This technique is an extension of the two-sample $t$ test.

In addition to determining that differences exist among the means, you may want to know which means differ. There are two types of tests for comparing means: *a priori* contrasts and post hoc tests. Contrasts are tests set up *before* running the experiment, and post hoc tests are run *after* the experiment has been conducted. You can also test for trends across categories.

**Example.** Doughnuts absorb fat in various amounts when they are cooked. An experiment is set up involving three types of fat: peanut oil, corn oil, and lard. Peanut oil and corn oil are unsaturated fats, and lard is a saturated fat. Along with determining whether the amount of fat absorbed depends on the type of fat used, you could set up an *a priori* contrast to determine whether the amount of fat absorption differs for saturated and unsaturated fats.

**Statistics.** For each group: number of cases, mean, standard deviation, standard error of the mean, minimum, maximum, and 95% confidence interval for the mean. Levene's test for homogeneity of variance, analysis-of-variance table for each dependent variable, user-specified *a priori* contrasts, and post hoc range tests and multiple comparisons: Bonferroni, Sidak, Tukey's honestly significant difference, Hochberg's GT2, Gabriel, Dunnett, Ryan-Einot-Gabriel-Welsch $F$ test (R-E-G-W F), Ryan-Einot-Gabriel-Welsch range test (R-E-G-W Q), Tamhane's T2, Dunnett's T3, Games-Howell, Dunnett's $C$, Duncan's multiple range test, Student-Newman-Keuls (S-N-K), Tukey's $b$, Waller-Duncan, Scheffé, and least-significant difference.

**Data.** Factor variable values should be integers, and the dependent variable should be quantitative (interval level of measurement).

**Assumptions.** Each group is an independent random sample from a normal population. Analysis of variance is robust to departures from normality, although the data should be symmetric. The groups should come from populations with equal variances. To test this assumption, use Levene's homogeneity-of-variance test.

**Related procedures.** Use the Explore procedure to screen your data. Study the shape of each group's distribution, and if the groups are not normally distributed, use the

Kruskal-Wallis test in the K Independent Samples procedure, available in the Nonparametric Tests procedure. If your groups are normally distributed but two or more variables are used to form groups, use the Simple Factorial ANOVA procedure. If your groups are not independent—for example, if you observe the same person under several conditions—use the Repeated Measures procedure, available in the SPSS Advanced Statistics option.

# Sample Output

### Figure 16.1   One-Way ANOVA output

ANOVA

| | | Sum of Squares | df | Mean Square | F | Significance |
|---|---|---|---|---|---|---|
| Absorbed Grams of Fat | Between Groups | 1596.00 | 2 | 798.00 | 7.824 | .005 |
| | Within Groups | 1530.00 | 15 | 102.00 | | |
| | Total | 3126.00 | 17 | | | |

Descriptives

| | | | N | Mean | Std. Deviation | Std. Error | 95% Confidence Interval for Mean | | Minimum | Maximum |
|---|---|---|---|---|---|---|---|---|---|---|
| | | | | | | | Lower Bound | Upper Bound | | |
| Absorbed Grams of Fat | Type of Oil | Peanut Oil | 6 | 72.00 | 13.34 | 5.45 | 58.00 | 86.00 | 56 | 95 |
| | | Lard | 6 | 85.00 | 7.77 | 3.17 | 76.84 | 93.16 | 77 | 97 |
| | | Corn Oil | 6 | 62.00 | 8.22 | 3.36 | 53.37 | 70.63 | 49 | 70 |
| | | Total | 18 | 73.00 | 13.56 | 3.20 | 66.26 | 79.74 | 49 | 97 |

Contrast Coefficients

| | | Type of Oil | | |
|---|---|---|---|---|
| | | Peanut Oil | Lard | Corn Oil |
| Contrast | 1 | -.5 | 1 | -.5 |

Contrast Tests

| | | | | Value of Contrast | Std. Error | t | df | Significance (2-tailed) |
|---|---|---|---|---|---|---|---|---|
| Absorbed Grams of Fat | Assume equal variances | Contrast | 1 | 18.00 | 5.05 | 3.565 | 15 | .003 |
| | Does not assume equal variances | Contrast | 1 | 18.00 | 4.51 | 3.995 | 12.542 | .002 |

Test of Homogeneity of Variances

|  | Levene Statistic | df1 | df2 | Significance |
|---|---|---|---|---|
| Absorbed Grams of Fat | .534 | 2 | 15 | .597 |

# To Obtain a One-Way Analysis of Variance

▶ From the menus choose:

Statistics
  Compare Means
    One-Way ANOVA...

**Figure 16.2  One-Way ANOVA dialog box**

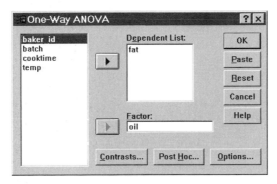

▶ Select one or more dependent variables.

▶ Select a single independent factor variable.

## One-Way ANOVA Contrasts

Figure 16.3   One-Way ANOVA Contrasts dialog box

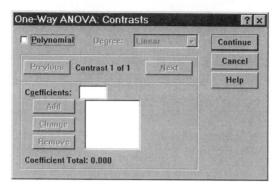

You can partition the between-groups sums of squares into trend components or specify *a priori* contrasts.

**Polynomial.** Partitions the between-groups sums of squares into trend components. You can test for a trend of the dependent variable across the ordered levels of the factor variable. For example, you could test for a linear trend (increasing or decreasing) in salary across the ordered levels of highest degree earned.

• **Degree.** You can choose a 1st, 2nd, 3rd, 4th, or 5th degree polynomial.

**Coefficients.** User-specified *a priori* contrasts to be tested by the $t$ statistic. Enter a coefficient for each group (category) of the factor variable and click *Add* after each entry. Each new value is added to the bottom of the coefficient list. To specify additional sets of contrasts, click *Next*. Use *Next* and *Previous* to move between sets of contrasts.

The order of the coefficients is important because it corresponds to the ascending order of the category values of the factor variable. The first coefficient on the list corresponds to the lowest group value of the factor variable, and the last coefficient corresponds to the highest value. For example, if there are six categories of the factor variable, the coefficients -1, 0, 0, 0, 0.5, and 0.5 contrast the first group with the fifth and sixth groups. For most applications, the coefficients should sum to 0. Sets that do not sum to 0 can also be used, but a warning message is displayed.

# One-Way ANOVA Post Hoc Tests

Figure 16.4   One-Way ANOVA Post Hoc dialog box

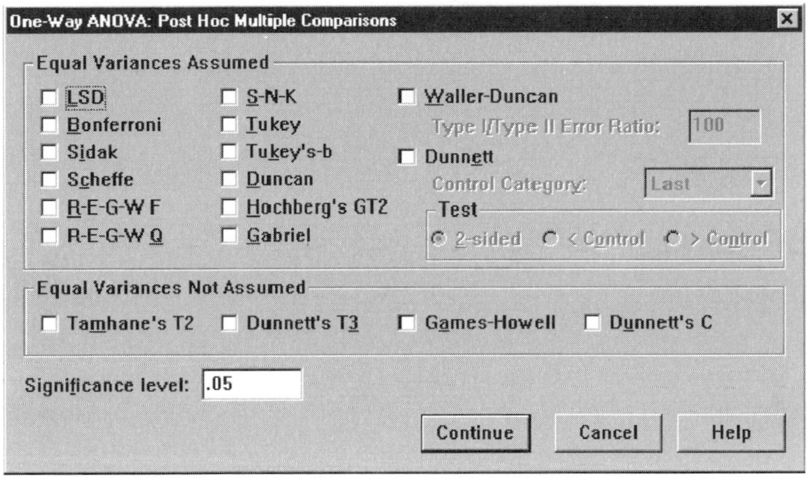

**Tests.** Once you have determined that differences exist among the means, post hoc range tests and pairwise multiple comparisons can determine which means differ. Range tests identify homogeneous subsets of means that are not different from each other. Pairwise multiple comparisons test the difference between each pair of means, and yield a matrix where asterisks indicate significantly different group means at an alpha level of 0.05.

Tukey's honestly significant difference test, Hochberg's GT2, Gabriel's test, and Scheffé's test are multiple comparison tests and range tests. Other available range tests are Tukey's *b*, S-N-K (Student-Newman-Keuls), Duncan, R-E-G-W F (Ryan-Einot-Gabriel-Welsch *F* test), R-E-G-W Q (Ryan-Einot-Gabriel-Welsch range test), and Waller-Duncan. Available multiple comparison tests are Bonferroni, Tukey's honestly significant difference test, Sidak, Gabriel, Hochberg, Dunnett, Scheffé, and LSD (least significant difference). Multiple comparison tests that do not assume equal variances are Tamhane's T2, Dunnett's T3, Games-Howell, and Dunnett's *C*.

*Note*: You may find it easier to interpret the output from post hoc tests if you deselect *Hide Empty Rows and Columns* in the Table Properties dialog box (in an activated pivot table, choose *Table Properties* on the Format menu).

## One-Way ANOVA Options

Figure 16.5 One-Way ANOVA Options dialog box

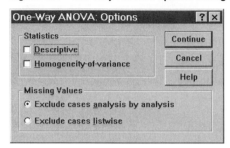

**Statistics.** Choose one or more of the following:

- **Descriptive.** Calculates the number of cases, mean, standard deviation, standard error of the mean, minimum, maximum, and 95% confidence intervals for each dependent variable for each group.

- **Homogeneity-of-variance.** Calculates the Levene statistic to test for the equality of group variances. This test is not dependent on the assumption of normality.

**Missing Values.** Controls the treatment of missing values.

- **Exclude cases analysis by analysis.** A case with a missing value for either the dependent or the factor variable for a given analysis is not used in that analysis. Also, a case outside the range specified for the factor variable is not used.

- **Exclude cases listwise.** Cases with missing values for the factor variable or for any dependent variable included on the dependent list in the main dialog box are excluded from all analyses. If you have not specified multiple dependent variables, this has no effect.

## ONEWAY Command Additional Features

The SPSS command language also allows you to:

- Obtain fixed- and random-effects statistics. Standard deviation, standard error of the mean, and 95% confidence intervals for the fixed-effects model. Standard error, 95% confidence intervals, and estimate of between-components variance for random-effects model (using STATISTICS=EFFECTS).

- Specify alpha levels for the least significance difference, Bonferroni, Duncan, and Scheffé multiple comparison tests (with the RANGES subcommand).

- Write a matrix of means, standard deviations, and frequencies, or read a matrix of means, frequencies, pooled variances, and degrees of freedom for the pooled variances. These matrices can be used in place of raw data to obtain a one-way analysis of variance (with the MATRIX subcommand).

See the *SPSS Base Syntax Reference Guide* for complete syntax information.

# 17 Simple Factorial Analysis of Variance

The Simple Factorial ANOVA procedure performs analysis of variance for factorial designs. It tests the hypothesis that the group or cell means of the dependent variable are equal. If your model contains five or fewer factors, the default model is full factorial, meaning that all factor-by-factor interaction terms up to order five are included. Although you can specify covariates, Simple Factorial ANOVA does not permit a full analysis of covariance. Three methods are available for decomposing the sums of squares. You can control the order of entry of the covariates and factor main effects and request a multiple classification analysis (MCA) table.

**Example.** An orthodontist offers three types of braces and claims that one type works best with children. Two children and two adults are randomly selected to wear each type of braces. You can use analysis of variance to determine whether there is a difference in how long each type has to be worn and whether the length of time braces must be worn by adults and children differs. An interaction between type of braces and age group (adult or child) could indicate that certain braces work better for children.

**Statistics.** Cell means, cell sample size, analysis-of-variance table, covariate coefficients, $R$, $R^2$. Multiple classification analysis table containing a listing of unadjusted category effects for each factor, category effects adjusted for other factors, category effects adjusted for all factors and covariates, and eta and beta values. Total number of cases, number and percentage of cases included and excluded from the model.

**Data.** Factor variables are categorical, the dependent variable is quantitative (interval level of measurement), and the covariates, or explanatory variables, are continuous. All variables are numeric.

**Assumptions.** The data in each cell are an independent random sample from a normal population. The cells should come from populations with equal variances.

**Related procedures.** To graphically inspect for interactions, use the multiple line plot procedure, available from the Graphs menu. Use Split File in combination with the Explore procedure to screen your data. Study the shape of each group's distribution, and if the groups are not normally distributed, use the K Independent Samples Tests procedure, available in the Nonparametric Tests procedure. If your groups are not independent—for example, if you observe the same people under several conditions—use the Repeated Measures procedure, available in the SPSS Advanced Statistics option. For multiple dependent variables, factor-by-covariate interactions in the analysis of covariance, or nested or nonfactorial designs, use the Multivariate ANOVA procedure, available in the SPSS Advanced Statistics option.

# Sample Output

### Figure 17.1   Simple Factorial ANOVA output

**ANOVA**

| | | | Unique Method | | | | |
|---|---|---|---|---|---|---|---|
| | | | Sum of Squares | df | Mean Square | F | Sig. |
| Months | Main Effects | (Combined) | 37.000 | 3 | 12.333 | 4.111 | .067 |
| | | Age | 8.333 | 1 | 8.333 | 2.778 | .147 |
| | | Type of Braces | 28.667 | 2 | 14.333 | 4.778 | .057 |
| | 2-Way Interactions | Age * Type of Braces | 60.667 | 2 | 30.333 | 10.111 | .012 |
| | Model | | 97.667 | 5 | 19.533 | 6.511 | .021 |
| | Residual | | 18.000 | 6 | 3.000 | | |
| | Total | | 115.667 | 11 | 10.515 | | |

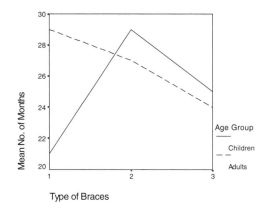

# To Obtain a Simple Factorial Analysis of Variance

▶ From the menus choose:

Statistics
  General Linear Model
    Simple Factorial...

**Figure 17.2   Simple Factorial ANOVA dialog box**

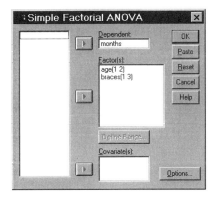

▶ Select one dependent variable.

▶ Select one or more categorical factor variables, and click *Define Range* to define ranges for these variables.

Optionally, you can select one or more continuous explanatory variables, or covariates.

## Simple Factorial ANOVA Define Range

**Figure 17.3   Simple Factorial ANOVA Define Range dialog box**

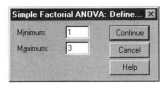

You must indicate the range of categories for each factor variable. Values for minimum and maximum correspond to the lowest and highest categories of the factor variable. Both values must be positive integers, and the minimum value must be less than the maximum value. Cases with values outside the bounds are excluded. For example, if you specify a minimum value of 1 and a maximum value of 3, only the values 1, 2, and 3 are used. Repeat this process for each factor variable.

## Simple Factorial ANOVA Options

Figure 17.4   Simple Factorial ANOVA Options dialog box

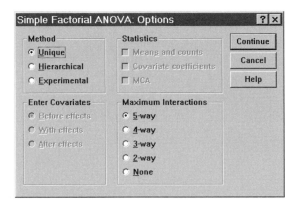

**Method.** Allows you to choose an alternate method for decomposing sums of squares. Method selection controls how the effects are assessed. Available methods are Unique, Hierarchical, and Experimental.

**Enter Covariates.** Operation of the experimental and hierarchical methods depends on the order of entry of any covariates. If you want to select a covariate entry alternative, there must be at least one covariate on the Covariate(s) list. In addition, the experimental or hierarchical method must be specified (with the unique method, covariates are always entered concurrently with all other effects). You can choose to process covariates before the main effects for factors, concurrently with the main effects, or after the main effects.

**Statistics.** Choose one or more of the following:

- **Means and counts.** Requests means and counts for each dependent variable for groups defined for each factor and each combination of factors up to the fifth level.

- **Covariate coefficients.** Regression coefficients for the covariate(s). If you want covariate coefficients, there must be at least one covariate on the Covariate(s) list.

- **MCA.** Multiple classification analysis. The MCA table includes a listing of unadjusted category effects for each factor, category effects adjusted for other factors, category effects adjusted for all factors and covariates, and eta and beta values. The MCA table is not available if you specify unique sums of squares.

**Maximum Interactions.** You can control the effects of various orders of interactions. Any interaction effects that are not computed are pooled into the residual sums of squares. You can display terms for up to five orders of interactions.

## ANOVA Command Additional Features

The SPSS command language also allows you to:

- Specify more than one dependent variable.

See the *SPSS Base Syntax Reference Guide* for complete syntax information.

# 18 Bivariate Correlations

The Bivariate Correlations procedure computes Pearson's correlation coefficient, Spearman's rho and Kendall's tau-*b* with their significance levels. Correlations measure how variables or rank orders are related. Before calculating a correlation coefficient, screen your data for outliers (which can cause misleading results) and evidence of a linear relationship. Pearson's correlation coefficient is a measure of linear association. Two variables can be perfectly related, but if the relationship is not linear, Pearson's correlation coefficient is not an appropriate statistic for measuring their association.

**Example.** Is the number of games won by a basketball team correlated with the average number of points scored per game? A scatterplot indicates that there is a linear relationship. Analyzing data from the 1994-1995 NBA season yields that Pearson's correlation coefficient (0.581) is significant at the 0.01 level. You might suspect that the more games won per season, the fewer points the opponents scored. These variables are negatively correlated (-0.401) and the correlation is significant at the 0.05 level.

**Statistics.** For each variable: number of cases with nonmissing values, mean, standard deviation. For each pair of variables: Pearson's correlation coefficient, Spearman's rho, Kendall's tau-*b*, cross-product of deviations, covariance.

**Data.** Use symmetric quantitative variables for Pearson's correlation coefficient; use quantitative variables or variables with ordered categories for Spearman's rho and Kendall's tau-*b*.

**Assumptions.** Pearson's correlation coefficient assumes that each pair of variables is bivariate normal.

**Related procedures.** Use the scatterplot procedure (available from the Graphs menu) to screen your data for evidence of a linear relationship. Use the Explore procedure to screen your data for symmetry and outliers. If the distribution of your data is not symmetric, try transforming your data or use the Spearman correlation coefficient. To obtain a correlation between two variables while controlling for the effects of one or more additional variables, use the Partial Correlations procedure.

# Sample Output

### Figure 18.1　Bivariate Correlations output

Correlations

| | | Number of Games Won | Scoring Points Per Game | Defense Points Per Game |
|---|---|---|---|---|
| Pearson Correlation | Number of Games Won | 1.000 | .581** | -.401* |
| | Scoring Points Per Game | .581** | 1.000 | .457* |
| | Defense Points Per Game | -.401* | .457* | 1.000 |
| Significance (2-tailed) | Number of Games Won | . | .001 | .038 |
| | Scoring Points Per Game | .001 | . | .017 |
| | Defense Points Per Game | .038 | .017 | . |
| N | Number of Games Won | 27 | 27 | 27 |
| | Scoring Points Per Game | 27 | 27 | 27 |
| | Defense Points Per Game | 27 | 27 | 27 |

** . Correlation at 0.01(2-tailed):...

* . Correlation at 0.05(2-tailed):...

# To Obtain Bivariate Correlations

▶ From the menus choose:

Statistics
  Correlate
    Bivariate...

**Figure 18.2    Bivariate Correlations dialog box**

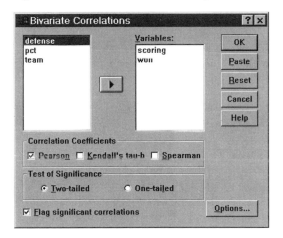

▶ Select two or more numeric variables.

The following options are also available:

- **Correlation Coefficients.** For quantitative, normally distributed variables, choose the *Pearson* correlation coefficient. If your data are not normally distributed or have ordered categories, choose *Kendall's tau-b* or *Spearman*, which measure the association between rank orders. Correlation coefficients range in value from −1 (a perfect negative relationship) and +1 (a perfect positive relationship). A value of 0 indicates no linear relationship. When interpreting your results, be careful not to draw any cause-and-effect conclusions due to a significant correlation.

- **Test of Significance.** You can choose two-tailed or one-tailed probabilities. If the direction of association is known in advance, choose *One-tailed*. Otherwise, choose *Two-tailed*.

- **Flag significant correlations.** Correlation coefficients significant at the 0.05 level are identified with a single asterisk, and those significant at the 0.01 level are identified with two asterisks.

## Bivariate Correlations Options

**Figure 18.3    Bivariate Correlations Options dialog box**

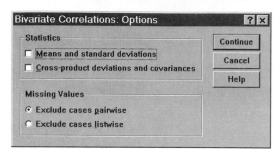

**Statistics.** For Pearson correlations, you can choose one or both of the following:

- **Means and standard deviations.** Displayed for each variable. The number of cases with nonmissing values is also shown. Missing values are handled on a variable-by-variable basis regardless of your missing values setting.

- **Cross-product deviations and covariances.** Displayed for each pair of variables. The cross-product of deviations is equal to the sum of the products of mean-corrected variables. This is the numerator of the Pearson correlation coefficient. The covariance is an unstandardized measure of the relationship between two variables, equal to the cross-product deviation divided by $N-1$.

**Missing Values.** You can choose one of the following:

- **Exclude cases pairwise.** Cases with missing values for one or both of a pair of variables for a correlation coefficient are excluded from the analysis. Since each coefficient is based on all cases that have valid codes on that particular pair of variables, the maximum information available is used in every calculation. This can result in a set of coefficients based on a varying number of cases.

- **Exclude cases listwise.** Cases with missing values for any variable are excluded from all correlations.

## CORRELATIONS and NONPAR CORR Command Additional Features

The SPSS command language also allows you to:

- Write a correlation matrix for Pearson correlations that can be used in place of raw data to obtain other analyses such as factor analysis (with the MATRIX subcommand).

- Obtain correlations of each variable on a list with each variable on a second list (using the keyword WITH on the VARIABLES subcommand).

See the *SPSS Base Syntax Reference Guide* for complete syntax information.

# 19 Partial Correlations

The Partial Correlations procedure computes partial correlation coefficients that describe the linear relationship between two variables while controlling for the effects of one or more additional variables. Correlations are measures of linear association. Two variables can be perfectly related, but if the relationship is not linear, a correlation coefficient is not an appropriate statistic for measuring their association.

**Example.** Is there a correlation between birth rate and death rate? An ordinary correlation reveals a significant correlation coefficient (0.367) at the 0.01 level. However, when you take into effect (or control for) an economic measure, birth rate and death rate are no longer significantly correlated. The correlation coefficient drops to 0.1003 (with a $p$ value of 0.304).

**Statistics.** For each variable: number of cases with nonmissing values, mean, and standard deviation. Partial and zero-order correlation matrices, with degrees of freedom and significance levels.

**Data.** Use symmetric, quantitative variables.

**Assumptions.** The Partial Correlations procedure assumes that each pair of variables is bivariate normal.

**Related procedures.** If there is reason to suspect that the variables are related in a nonlinear way, the partial correlation coefficient is not an appropriate statistic to calculate. Try transforming the data. Use the Explore procedure to screen your data for symmetry and outliers (which can cause misleading results). If your data do not appear symmetric, try transforming them.

# Sample Output

### Figure 19.1   Partial Correlations output

--- P A R T I A L   C O R R E L A T I O N   C O E F F I C I E N T S ---

Zero Order Partials

```
         BIRTH_RT   DEATH_RT   LOG_GDP

BIRTH_RT   1.0000      .3670    -.7674
           (   0)    ( 106)    ( 106)
           P= .       P= .000   P= .000


DEATH_RT    .3670     1.0000    -.4015
           ( 106)    (   0)    ( 106)
           P= .000    P= .       P= .000


LOG_GDP    -.7674     -.4015    1.0000
           ( 106)    ( 106)    (   0)
           P= .000    P= .000    P= .
```

(Coefficient / (D.F.) / 2-tailed Significance)

" . " is printed if a coefficient cannot be computed

--- P A R T I A L   C O R R E L A T I O N   C O E F F I C I E N T S ---

Controlling for..   LOG_GDP

```
         BIRTH_RT   DEATH_RT

BIRTH_RT   1.0000      .1003
           (   0)    ( 105)
           P= .       P= .304


DEATH_RT    .1003     1.0000
           ( 105)    (   0)
           P= .304    P= .
```

(Coefficient / (D.F.) / 2-tailed Significance)

" . " is printed if a coefficient cannot be computed

# To Obtain Partial Correlations

▶ From the menus choose:

Statistics
  Correlate
    Partial...

**Figure 19.2    Partial Correlations dialog box**

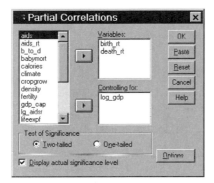

▶ Select two or more numeric variables for which partial correlations are to be computed.

▶ Select one or more numeric control variables.

The following options are also available:

- **Test of Significance.** You can choose two-tailed or one-tailed probabilities. If the direction of association is known in advance, choose *One-tailed*. Otherwise, choose *Two-tailed*.

- **Display actual significance level.** By default, the probability and degrees of freedom are shown for each correlation coefficient. If you deselect this item, coefficients significant at the 0.05 level are identified with a single asterisk, coefficients significant at the 0.01 level are identified with a double asterisk, and degrees of freedom are suppressed. This setting affects both partial and zero-order correlation matrices.

## Partial Correlations Options

**Figure 19.3    Partial Correlations Options dialog box**

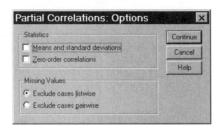

**Statistics.** You can choose one or both of the following:

- **Means and standard deviations.** Displayed for each variable. The number of cases with nonmissing values is also shown.

- **Zero-order correlations.** A matrix of simple correlations between all variables, including control variables, is displayed.

**Missing Values.** You can choose one of the following alternatives:

- **Exclude cases listwise.** Cases having missing values for any variable, including a control variable, are excluded from all computations.

- **Exclude cases pairwise.** For computation of the zero-order correlations on which the partial correlations are based, a case having missing values for both or one of a pair of variables is not used. Pairwise deletion uses as much of the data as possible. However, the number of cases may differ across coefficients. When pairwise deletion is in effect, the degrees of freedom for a particular partial coefficient are based on the smallest number of cases used in the calculation of any of the zero-order correlations.

## PARTIAL CORR Command Additional Features

The SPSS command language also allows you to:

- Read a zero-order correlation matrix or write a partial correlation matrix (with the MATRIX subcommand).

- Obtain partial correlations between two lists of variables (using the keyword WITH on the VARIABLES subcommand).

- Obtain multiple analyses (with multiple VARIABLES subcommands).

- Specify order values to request (for example, both first- and second-order partial correlations) when you have two control variables (with the VARIABLES subcommand).

- Suppress redundant coefficients (with the FORMAT subcommand).

- Display a matrix of simple correlations when some coefficients cannot be computed (with the STATISTICS subcommand).

See the *SPSS Base Syntax Reference Guide* for complete syntax information.

# 20 Distances

This procedure calculates any of a wide variety of statistics measuring either similarities or dissimilarities (distances), either between pairs of variables or between pairs of cases. These similarity or distance measures can then be used with other procedures such as factor analysis, cluster analysis, or multidimensional scaling, to help analyze complex data sets.

**Example.** Is it possible to measure similarities between pairs of automobiles based on certain characteristics such as engine size, MPG, and horsepower? By computing similarities between autos, you can gain a sense of which autos are similar to each other and which are different from one another. For a more formal analysis, you might consider applying a hierarchical cluster analysis or multidimensional scaling to the similarities to explore the underlying structure.

**Statistics.** Dissimilarity (distance) measures for interval data are Euclidean distance, squared Euclidean distance, Chebychev, block, Minkowski, or customized. For count data: chi-square or phi-square. For binary data: Euclidean distance, squared Euclidean distance, size difference, pattern difference, variance, shape, or Lance and Williams. Similarity measures for interval data are Pearson correlation or cosine. For binary data: Russel and Rao, simple matching, Jaccard, dice, Rogers and Tanimoto, Sokal and Sneath 1, Sokal and Sneath 2, Sokal and Sneath 3, Kulczynski 1, Kulczynski 2, Sokal and Sneath 4, Hamann, Lambda, Anderberg's $D$, Yule's $Y$, Yule's $Q$, Ochiai, Sokal and Sneath 5, phi 4-point correlation, or dispersion.

## To Obtain a Distance Matrix

▶ From the menus choose:

Statistics
  Correlate
    Distances...

Figure 20.1    Distances dialog box

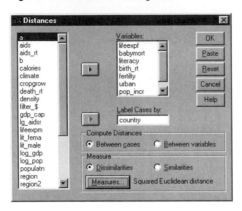

▶ Select at least one numeric variable to compute distances between cases, or select at least two numeric variables to compute distances between variables.

▶ Select an alternative in the Compute Distances group to calculate proximities either between cases or between variables.

## Distances Dissimilarity Measures

Figure 20.2    Distances Dissimilarities dialog box

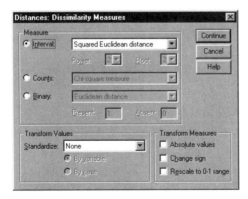

From the Measure group, select the alternative that corresponds to your type of data (interval, count, or binary); then, from the drop-down list, select one of the measures that corresponds to that type of data. Available measures, by data type, are:

- **Interval data.** Euclidean distance, squared Euclidean distance, Chebychev, block, Minkowski, or customized.
- **Count data.** Chi-square measure or phi-square measure.
- **Binary data.** Euclidean distance, squared Euclidean distance, size difference, pattern difference, variance, shape, or Lance and Williams. (Enter values for Present and Absent to specify which two values are meaningful; SPSS will ignore all other values.)

The Transform Values group allows you to standardize data values for either cases or variables *before* computing proximities. These transformations are not applicable to binary data. Available standardization methods are $z$ scores, range –1 to 1, range 0 to 1, maximum magnitude of 1, mean of 1, or standard deviation of 1.

The Transform Measures group allows you to transform the values generated by the distance measure. They are applied *after* the distance measure has been computed. Available options are absolute values, change sign, and rescale to 0–1 range.

## Distances Similarity Measures

**Figure 20.3   Distances Similarities dialog box**

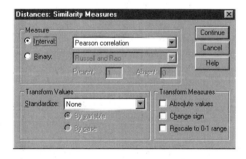

From the Measure group, select the alternative that corresponds to your type of data (interval or binary); then, from the drop-down list, select one of the measures that corresponds to that type of data. Available measures, by data type, are:

- **Interval data.** Pearson correlation or cosine.
- **Binary data.** Russell and Rao, simple matching, Jaccard, Dice, Rogers and Tanimoto, Sokal and Sneath 1, Sokal and Sneath 2, Sokal and Sneath 3, Kulczynski 1, Kulczynski 2, Sokal and Sneath 4, Hamann, Lambda, Anderberg's $D$, Yule's $Y$, Yule's $Q$, Ochiai, Sokal and Sneath 5, phi 4-point correlation, or dispersion. (Enter values for Present and Absent to specify which two values are meaningful; SPSS will ignore all other values.)

The Transform Values group allows you to standardize data values for either cases or variables *before* computing proximities. These transformations are not applicable to binary data. Available standardization methods are $z$ scores, range –1 to 1, range 0 to 1, maximum magnitude of 1, mean of 1, and standard deviation of 1.

The Transform Measures group allows you to transform the values generated by the distance measure. They are applied *after* the distance measure has been computed. Available options are absolute values, change sign, and rescale to 0–1 range.

## PROXIMITIES Command Additional Features

The SPSS command language also allows you to:

- Specify any integer as the power for the Minkowski distance measure
- Specify any integers as the power and root for a customized distance measure.

See the *SPSS Base Syntax Reference Guide* for complete syntax information.

# 21 Linear Regression

Linear Regression estimates the coefficients of the linear equation, involving one or more independent variables, that best predict the value of the dependent variable. For example, you can try to predict a salesperson's total yearly sales (the dependent variable) from independent variables such as age, education, and years of experience.

**Example.** Is the number of games won by a basketball team in a season related to the average number of points the team scores per game? A scatterplot indicates that these variables are linearly related. The number of games won and the average number of points scored by the opponent are also linearly related. These variables have a negative relationship. As the number of games won increases, the average number of points scored by the opponent decreases. With linear regression, you can model the relationship of these variables. A good model can be used to predict how many games teams will win.

**Statistics.** For each variable: number of valid cases, mean, and standard deviation. For each model: regression coefficients, correlation matrix, part and partial correlations, multiple $R$, $R^2$, adjusted $R^2$, change in $R^2$, standard error of the estimate, analysis-of-variance table, predicted values, and residuals. Also, 95% confidence intervals for each regression coefficient, variance-covariance matrix, variance inflation factor, tolerance, Durbin-Watson test, distance measures (Mahalanobis, Cook, and leverage values), DfBeta, DfFit, prediction intervals, and casewise diagnostics. Plots: scatterplots, partial plots, histograms, and normal probability plots.

**Data.** The dependent and independent variables should be quantitative. Categorical variables such as religion, major, or region of residence need to be recoded to binary (dummy) variables or other types of contrast variables.

**Assumptions.** For each value of the independent variable, the distribution of the dependent variable must be normal. The variance of the distribution of the dependent variable should be constant for all values of the independent variable. The relationship between the dependent variable and each independent variable should be linear, and all observations should be independent.

**Related procedures.** Use the Scatterplot procedure on the Graphs menu to obtain bivariate scatterplots or scatterplot matrices. Scatterplots aid in the screening of your data. The Explore procedure can also be used to screen your data. Explore provides tests for normality and homogeneity of variance, as well as graphical displays. If your data appear to violate an assumption (such as normality or constant variance), try transforming them. If your data are not related linearly and a transformation does not help, use an alternate model in the Curve Estimation procedure. If your dependent variable is dichotomous, such as whether a particular sale is completed or not or whether an item is defective or not, use the Logistic Regression procedure, available in the SPSS Advanced Statistics option. If your dependent variable is censored, such as survival time after surgery, use Life Tables, Kaplan-Meier, or Cox Regression, available in the SPSS Advanced Statistics option. If your data are not independent—for example, if you observe the same person under several conditions—use the Repeated Measures procedure, available in the SPSS Advanced Statistics option.

## Sample Output

### Figure 21.1    Linear Regression output

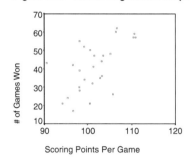
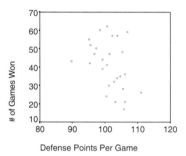

Model Summary [3,4]

| | | Variables | | | | | Std. Error of the Estimate |
| | | Entered | Removed | R | R Square | Adjusted R Square | |
|---|---|---|---|---|---|---|---|
| Model | 1 | Defense Points Per Game, Scoring Points Per Game [1,2] | . | .947 | .898 | .889 | 4.40 |

[1]. Indep. vars: (constant) Defense Points Per Game, Scoring Points Per Game...

[2]. All requested variables entered.

[3]. Dependent Variable: Number of Games Won

[4]. Method: Enter

ANOVA[2]

|  |  |  | Sum of Squares | df | Mean Square | F | Significance |
|---|---|---|---|---|---|---|---|
| Model | 1 | Regression | 4080.533 | 2 | 2040.266 | 105.198 | .000[1] |
|  |  | Residual | 465.467 | 24 | 19.394 |  |  |
|  |  | Total | 4546.000 | 26 |  |  |  |

1. Indep. vars: (constant) Defense Points Per Game, Scoring Points Per Game...

2. Dependent Variable: Number of Games Won

**Coefficients[1]**

| Model |  | Unstandardized Coefficients | | Standardized Coefficients | t | Sig. |
|---|---|---|---|---|---|---|
|  |  | B | Std. Error | Beta |  |  |
| 1 | (Constant) | 28.121 | 21.404 |  | 1.314 | .201 |
|  | Scoring Points Per Game | 2.539 | .193 | .965 | 13.145 | .000 |
|  | Defense Points Per Game | -2.412 | .211 | -.841 | -11.458 | .000 |

1. Dependent Variable: Number of Games Won

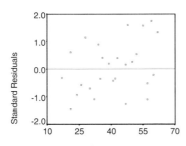

# To Obtain a Linear Regression Analysis

▶ From the menus choose:

Statistics
  Regression
    Linear...

**Figure 21.2   Linear Regression dialog box**

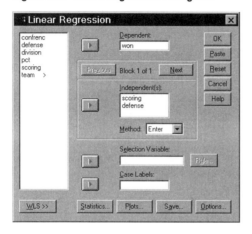

▶ In the Linear Regression dialog box, select a numeric dependent variable.

▶ Select one or more numeric independent variables.

Optionally, you can:

- Group independent variables into blocks and specify different entry methods for different subsets of variables.

- Choose a selection variable to limit the analysis to a subset of cases having a particular value(s) for this variable.

- Select a case identification variable for identifying points on plots.

- Click *WLS* for a weighted least-squares analysis and move a numeric weighting variable into the WLS Weight box.

## Linear Regression Variable Selection Methods

Method selection allows you to specify how independent variables are entered into the analysis. Using different methods, you can construct a variety of regression models from the same set of variables.

To enter the variables in the block in a single step, select *Enter*. To remove the variables in the block in a single step, select *Remove*. *Forward* variable selection enters the variables in the block one at a time based on entry criteria. *Backward* variable elimination enters all of the variables in the block in a single step and then removes them one at a time based on removal criteria. *Stepwise* variable entry and removal examines the variables in the block at each step for entry or removal. This is a forward stepwise procedure.

All variables must pass the tolerance criterion to be entered in the equation, regardless of the entry method specified. The default tolerance level is 0.0001. A variable also is not entered if it would cause the tolerance of another variable already in the model to drop below the tolerance criterion.

All independent variables selected are added to a single regression model. However, you can specify different entry methods for different subsets of variables. For example, you can enter one block of variables into the regression model using stepwise selection and a second block using forward selection. To add a second block of variables to the regression model, click *Next*.

## Linear Regression Set Rule

**Figure 21.3    Linear Regression Set Rule dialog box**

Cases defined by the selection rule are included in the analysis. For example, if you select a variable, equals, and 5 for the value, then only cases for which the selected variable has a value equal to 5 are included in the analysis. A string value is also permitted.

# Linear Regression Plots

**Figure 21.4    Linear Regression Plots dialog box**

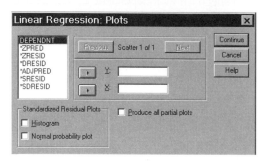

Plots can aid in the validation of the assumptions of normality, linearity, and equality of variances. Plots are also useful for detecting outliers, unusual observations, and influential cases. After saving them as new variables, predicted values, residuals, and other diagnostics are available in the Data Editor for constructing plots with the independent variables. The following plots are available:

**Scatterplots.** You can plot any two of the following: the dependent variable, standardized predicted values, standardized residuals, deleted residuals, adjusted predicted values, Studentized residuals, or Studentized deleted residuals. Plot the standardized residuals against the standardized predicted values to check for linearity and equality of variances.

**Produce all partial plots.** Displays scatterplots of residuals of each independent variable and the residuals of the dependent variable when both variables are regressed separately on the rest of the independent variables. At least two independent variables must be in the equation for a partial plot to be produced.

**Standardized Residual Plots.** You can obtain histograms of standardized residuals and normal probability plots comparing the distribution of standardized residuals to a normal distribution.

If any plots are requested, summary statistics are displayed for standardized predicted values and standardized residuals (*ZPRED* and *ZRESID*).

# Linear Regression Save

**Figure 21.5    Linear Regression Save dialog box**

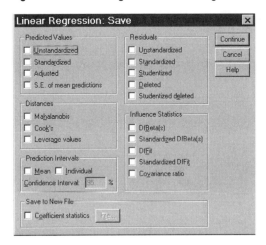

You can save predicted values, residuals, and other statistics useful for diagnostics. Each selection adds one or more new variables to your active data file.

**Predicted Values.** Values that the regression model predicts for each case.

**Distances.** Measures to identify cases with unusual combinations of values for the independent variables and cases which may have a large impact on the regression model.

**Prediction Intervals.** The upper and lower bounds for both mean and individual prediction intervals.

**Residuals.** The actual value of the dependent variable minus the value predicted by the regression equation.

**Influence Statistics.** The change in the regression coefficients (DfBeta(s)) and predicted values (DfFit) that results from the exclusion of a particular case. Standardized DfBetas and DfFit values are also available along with the covariance ratio, which is the ratio of the determinant of the covariance matrix with a particular case excluded to the determinant of the covariance matrix with all cases included.

**Save to New File.** Saves regression coefficients to a file that you specify.

## Linear Regression Statistics

**Figure 21.6   Linear Regression Statistics dialog box**

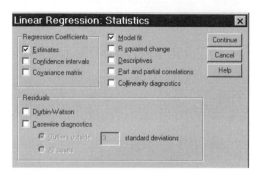

The following statistics are available:

**Regression Coefficients.** Estimates displays Regression coefficient $B$, standard error of $B$, standardized coefficient beta, $t$ value for $B$, and two-tailed significance level of $t$. Confidence intervals displays 95% confidence intervals for each regression coefficient, or a covariance matrix. Covariance matrix displays a variance-covariance matrix of regression coefficients with covariances off the diagonal and variances on the diagonal. A correlation matrix is also displayed.

**Model fit.** The variables entered and removed from the model are listed, and the following goodness-of-fit statistics are displayed: multiple $R$, $R^2$ and adjusted $R^2$, standard error of the estimate, and an analysis-of-variance table.

**R squared change.** Displays changes in $R^2$ change, $F$ change, and the significance of $F$ change.

**Descriptives.** Provides the number of valid cases, the mean, and the standard deviation for each variable in the analysis. A correlation matrix with a one-tailed significance level and the number of cases for each correlation are also displayed.

**Part and partial correlations.** Displays zero-order, part, and partial correlations.

**Collinearity diagnostics.** Eigenvalues of the scaled and uncentered cross-products matrix, condition indices, and variance-decomposition proportions are displayed along with variance inflation factors (VIF) and tolerances for individual variables.

**Residuals.** Displays the Durbin-Watson test for serial correlation of the residuals and casewise diagnostics for the cases meeting the selection criterion (outliers above n standard deviations).

# Linear Regression Options

Figure 21.7   Linear Regression Options dialog box

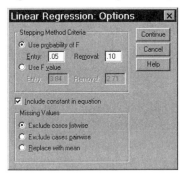

The following options are available:

**Stepping Method Criteria.** These options apply when either the forward, backward, or stepwise variable selection method has been specified. Variables can be entered or removed from the model depending on either the significance (probability) of the $F$ value, or the $F$ value itself.

**Include constant in equation.** By default, the regression model includes a constant term. Deselecting this option forces regression through the origin which is rarely done. Some results of regression through the origin are not comparable to results of regression that do include a constant. For example, $R^2$ cannot be interpreted in the usual way.

**Missing Values.** You can choose one of the following:

- **Exclude cases listwise.** Only cases with valid values for all variables are included in the analyses.

- **Exclude cases pairwise.** Cases with complete data for the pair of variables being correlated are used to compute the correlation coefficient on which the regression analysis is based. Degrees of freedom are based on the minimum pairwise N.

- **Replace with mean.** All cases are used for computations, with the mean of the variable substituted for missing observations.

## REGRESSION Command Additional Features

The SPSS command language also allows you to:

- Write a correlation matrix or read a matrix in place of raw data to obtain your regression analysis (with the MATRIX subcommand).

- Specify tolerance levels (with the CRITERIA subcommand).

- Obtain multiple models for the same or different dependent variables (with the METHOD and DEPENDENT subcommands).

- Obtain additional statistics (with the DESCRIPTIVES and STATISTICS subcommands).

See the *SPSS Base Syntax Reference Guide* for complete syntax information.

# 22 Curve Estimation

The Curve Estimation procedure produces curve estimation regression statistics and related plots for 11 different curve estimation regression models. A separate model is produced for each dependent variable. You can also save predicted values, residuals, and prediction intervals as new variables.

**Example.** A fire insurance company conducts a study to relate the amount of damage in serious residential fires to the distance between the closest fire station and the residence. A scatterplot reveals that the relationship between fire damage and distance to the fire station is linear. You might fit a linear model to the data and check the validity of assumptions and the goodness of fit of the model.

**Statistics.** For each model: regression coefficients, multiple $R$, $R^2$, adjusted $R^2$, standard error of the estimate, analysis-of-variance table, predicted values, residuals, and prediction intervals. Models: linear, logarithmic, inverse, quadratic, cubic, power, compound, S-curve, logistic, growth, and exponential.

**Data.** The dependent and independent variables should be quantitative. If you select *time* instead of a variable from the working data file as the independent variable, SPSS generates a time variable where the length of time between cases is uniform. If *Time* is selected, the dependent variable should be a time series measure. Time series analysis requires a data file structure in which each case (row) represents a set of observations at a different time and the length of time between cases is uniform.

**Assumptions.** Screen your data graphically to determine how the independent and dependent variables are related (linearly, exponentially, etc.). The residuals of a good model should be randomly distributed and normal. If a linear model is used, the following assumptions should be met. For each value of the independent variable, the distribution of the dependent variable must be normal. The variance of the distribution of the dependent variable should be constant for all values of the independent variable. The relationship between the dependent variable and the independent variable should be linear, and all observations should be independent.

**Related procedures.** To screen your data graphically, use the Scatterplot procedure on the Graphs menu. If the relationship between the dependent and the independent variable appears normal, use the Linear Regression procedure.

# Sample Output

### Figure 22.1   Curve Estimation output

```
MODEL:  MOD_1.

Dependent variable.. DAMAGE                Method.. LINEAR

Listwise Deletion of Missing Data

Multiple R            .96098
R Square              .92348
Adjusted R Square     .91759
Standard Error       2.31635

                 Analysis of Variance:

               DF     Sum of Squares      Mean Square

Regression      1         841.76636        841.76636
Residuals      13          69.75098          5.36546

F =     156.88616     Signif F =   .0000

-------------------- Variables in the Equation --------------------

Variable                B        SE B        Beta        T   Sig T

DISTANCE          4.919331     .392748     .960978    12.525   .0000
(Constant)       10.277929    1.420278                 7.237   .0000

The following new variables are being created:

   Name        Label

   ERR_1       Error for DAMAGE with DISTANCE from CURVEFIT, MOD_1 LINEAR
```

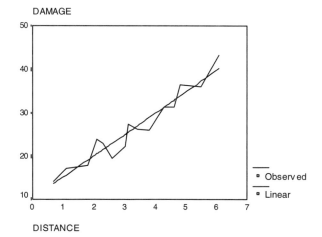

# To Obtain a Curve Estimation

▶ From the menus choose:

Statistics
  Regression
    Curve Estimation...

**Figure 22.2   Curve Estimation dialog box**

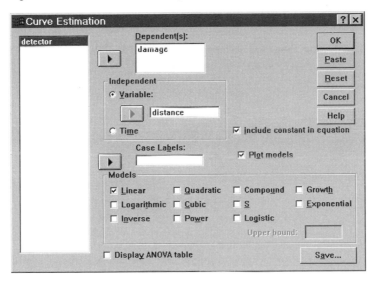

▶ Select one or more dependent variables. A separate model is produced for each dependent variable.

▶ Select an independent variable (either a variable in the working data file or *Time*).

Optionally, you can:

- Select a variable for labeling cases in scatterplots. For each point in the scatterplot, you can use the Point Selection tool to display the value of the *Case Label* variable.

- Click *Save* to save predicted values, residuals, and prediction intervals as new variables.

The following options are also available:

- **Include constant in equation.** Estimates a constant term in the regression equation. The constant is included by default.

- **Plot models.** Plots the values of the dependent variable and each selected model against the independent variable. A separate chart is produced for each dependent variable.

- **Display ANOVA table.** Displays a summary analysis-of-variance table for each selected model.

## Curve Estimation Models

You can choose one or more curve estimation regression models. To determine which model to use, plot your data. If your variables appear to be related linearly, use a simple linear regression model. When your variables are not linearly related, try transforming your data. When a transformation does not help, you may need a more complicated model. View a scatterplot of your data; if the plot resembles a mathematical function you recognize, fit your data to that type of model. For example, if your data resemble an exponential function, use an exponential model. The following models are available in the Curve Estimation procedure: linear, logarithmic, inverse, quadratic, cubic, power, compound, S-curve, logistic, growth, and exponential. If you are unsure which model best fits your data, try several models and select among them.

## Curve Estimation Save

**Figure 22.3   Curve Estimation Save dialog box**

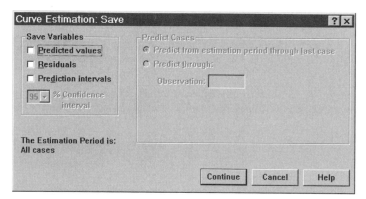

**Save Variables.** For each selected model you can save predicted values, residuals (observed value of the dependent variable minus the model predicted value), and prediction intervals (upper and lower bounds). The new variable names and descriptive labels are displayed in a table in the output window.

**Predict Cases.** If you select *Time* instead of a variable in the working data file as the independent variable, you can specify a forecast period beyond the end of the time series. You can choose one of the following alternatives:

- **Predict from estimation period through last case.** Predicts values for all cases in the file, based on the cases in the estimation period. The estimation period, displayed at the bottom of the dialog box, is defined with the Range subdialog box of the Select Cases option on the Data menu. If no estimation period has been defined, all cases are used to predict values.

- **Predict through.** Predicts values through the specified date, time, or observation number, based on the cases in the estimation period. This can be used to forecast values beyond the last case in the time series. The available text boxes for specifying the end of the prediction period are dependent on the currently defined date variables. If there are no defined date variables, you can specify the ending observation (case) number.

Use the Define Dates option on the Data menu to create date variables.

## CURVEFIT Command Additional Features

See the *SPSS Base Syntax Reference Guide* for complete syntax information.

# 23 Discriminant Analysis

Discriminant analysis is useful for situations in which you want to build a predictive model of group membership based on observed characteristics of each case. The procedure generates a discriminant function (or, for more than two groups, a set of discriminant functions) based on linear combinations of the predictor variables that provide the best discrimination between the groups. The functions are generated from a sample of cases for which group membership is known; the functions can then be applied to new cases with measurements for the predictor variables but unknown group membership.

*Note*: The grouping variable can have more than two values. The codes for the grouping variable must be integers, however, and you need to specify their minimum and maximum values. Cases with values outside these bounds are excluded from the analysis.

**Example.** On average, people in temperate-zone countries consume more calories per day than those in the tropics, and a greater proportion of the people in the temperate zones are city dwellers. A researcher wants to combine this information in a function to determine how well an individual can discriminate between the two groups of countries. The researcher thinks that population size and economic information may also be important. Discriminant analysis allows you to estimate coefficients of the linear discriminant function, which looks like the right-hand side of a multiple linear regression equation. That is, using coefficients $a$, $b$, $c$, and $d$, the function is:

$D = a *$ climate $+ b *$ urban $+ c *$ population $+ d *$ gross domestic product per capita

If these variables are useful for discriminating between the two climate zones, the values of $D$ will differ for the temperate and tropic countries. If you use a stepwise variable selection method, you may find that you do not need to include all four variables in the function.

**Statistics.** For each variable: means, standard deviations, univariate ANOVA. For each analysis: Box's M, within-groups correlation matrix, within-groups covariance matrix, separate-groups covariance matrix, total covariance matrix. For each canonical discriminant function: eigenvalue, percentage of variance, canonical correlation, Wilks' lambda, chi-square. For each step: prior probabilities, Fisher's function coefficients, unstandardized function coefficients, Wilks' lambda for each canonical function.

**Data.** The grouping variable must have a limited number of distinct categories, coded as integers. Independent variables that are nominal must be recoded to dummy or contrast variables.

**Assumptions.** Cases should be independent. Predictor variables should have a multivariate normal distribution, and within-group variance-covariance matrices should be equal across groups. Group membership is assumed to be mutually exclusive (that is, no case belongs to more than one group) and collectively exhaustive (that is, all cases are members of a group). The procedure is most effective when group membership is a truly categorical variable; if group membership is based on values of a continuous variable (for example, high IQ versus low IQ), you should consider using linear regression to take advantage of the richer information offered by the continuous variable itself.

**Related procedures.** If your grouping variable has two categories, you may want to use Logistic Regression, which depends on less stringent assumptions. If your dependent variable is continuous, consider Linear Regression. Discriminant analysis is also related to multivariate analysis of variance, in that Wilks' lambda, the same test statistic used in multivariate ANOVA, is used to test the equality of group centroids.

# Sample Output

### Figure 23.1   Discriminant Analysis output

**Eigenvalues**

| Function | Eigenvalue | % of Variance | Cumulative % | Canonical Correlation |
|---|---|---|---|---|
| 1 | 1.002 | 100.0 | 100.0 | .707 |

**Wilks' Lambda**

| Test of Function(s) | Wilks' Lambda | Chi-square | df | Sig. |
|---|---|---|---|---|
| 1 | .499 | 31.934 | 4 | .000 |

**Structure Matrix**

| | Function |
|---|---|
| | 1 |
| CALORIES | .986 |
| LOG_GDP | .790 |
| URBAN | .488 |
| LOG_POP | .082 |

**Functions at Group Centroids**

| CLIMATE | Function |
|---|---|
| | 1 |
| tropical | -.869 |
| temperate | 1.107 |

# To Obtain a Discriminant Analysis

▶ From the menus choose:

Statistics
  Classify
    Discriminant...

**Figure 23.2    Discriminant Analysis dialog box**

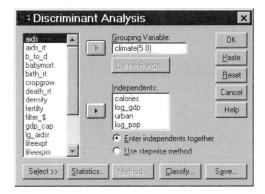

▶ Select an integer-valued grouping variable and click *Define Range* to specify the categories of interest.

▶ Select the independent or predictor variables. (If your grouping variable does not have integer values, Automatic Recode in the Transform menu will create one that does.)

Optionally, you can select cases with a selection variable.

## Discriminant Analysis Define Range

**Figure 23.3    Discriminant Analysis Define Range dialog box**

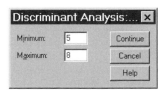

Specify the minimum and maximum value of the grouping variable for the analysis. Cases with values outside this range are not used in the analysis but are classified into one of the existing groups based on the results of the analysis.

The minimum and maximum must be integers.

## Discriminant Analysis Select Cases

**Figure 23.4   Discriminant Analysis Select Cases dialog box**

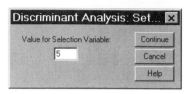

To select cases for your analysis, click *Select*, choose a selection variable, and click *Value* to enter an integer as the selection value. Only cases with that value for the selection variable are used to derive the discriminant functions.

## Discriminant Analysis Statistics

**Figure 23.5   Discriminant Analysis Statistics dialog box**

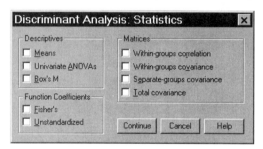

**Descriptives.** Available options are means (including standard deviations), univariate ANOVAs, and Box's M.

**Function Coefficients.** Available options are Fisher's classification coefficients and unstandardized coefficients.

**Matrices.** Available matrices of coefficients for independent variables are within-groups correlation matrix, within-groups covariance matrix, separate-groups covariance matrix, and total covariance matrix.

## Discriminant Analysis Stepwise Method

Figure 23.6   Discriminant Analysis Stepwise Method dialog box

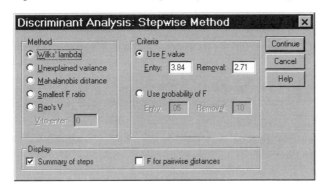

**Method.** Select the statistic to be used for entering or removing new variables. Available alternatives are Wilks' lambda, unexplained variance, Mahalanobis distance, smallest $F$ ratio, and Rao's $V$. With Rao's $V$, you can specify the minimum increase in $V$ for a variable to enter.

**Criteria.** Available alternatives are Use $F$ value and Use probability of $F$. Enter values for entering and removing variables.

**Display.** Select *Summary of steps* to display statistics for all variables after each step; select *F for pairwise distances* to display a matrix of pairwise $F$ ratios for each pair of groups.

## Discriminant Analysis Classify

Figure 23.7   Discriminant Analysis Classification dialog box

**Prior Probabilities.** These values are used in classification. You can specify equal prior probabilities for all groups, or you can let the observed group sizes in your sample determine the probabilities of group membership.

**Display.** Available display options are casewise results, summary table, and leave-one-out classification.

**Replace missing values with mean.** Select this option to substitute the mean of an independent variable for a missing value, *during the classification phase only*.

**Use Covariance Matrix.** You can choose to classify cases using a within-groups covariance matrix or a separate-groups covariance matrix.

**Plots.** Available plot options are combined-groups, separate-groups, and territorial map.

## Discriminant Analysis Save

Figure 23.8    Discriminant Analysis Save dialog box

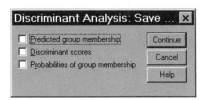

You can add new variables to your active data file. Available options are predicted group membership (a single variable), discriminant scores (one variable for each discriminant function in the solution), and probabilities of group membership given the discriminant scores (one variable for each group).

## DISCRIMINANT Command Additional Features

The SPSS command language also allows you to:

- Perform multiple discriminant analyses with one command, and control the order in which variables are entered (with the ANALYSIS subcommand).
- Specify prior probabilities for classification (with the PRIORS subcommand).
- Display rotated pattern and structure matrices (with the ROTATE subcommand).
- Limit the number of discriminant functions extracted (with the FUNCTIONS subcommand).

- Restrict classification to the cases selected (or unselected) for the analysis (with the SELECT subcommand).
- Read and analyze a correlation matrix (with the MATRIX subcommand).
- Write a correlation matrix for later analysis (with the MATRIX subcommand).

See the *SPSS Base Syntax Reference Guide* for complete syntax information.

# 24 Factor Analysis

Factor analysis attempts to identify underlying variables, or **factors**, that explain the pattern of correlations within a set of observed variables. Factor analysis is often used in data reduction, by identifying a small number of factors that explain most of the variance observed in a much larger number of manifest variables. Factor analysis can also be used to generate hypotheses regarding causal mechanisms or to screen variables for subsequent analysis (for example, to identify collinearity prior to a linear regression analysis).

The factor analysis procedure offers a high degree of flexibility:

- Seven methods of factor extraction are available.
- Five methods of rotation are available, including direct oblimin and promax for non-orthogonal rotations.
- Three methods of computing factor scores are available, and scores can be saved as variables for further analysis.

**Example.** What underlying attitudes lead people to respond to the questions on a political survey as they do? Examining the correlations among the survey items reveals that there is significant overlap among various subgroups of items—questions about taxes tend to correlate with each other, questions about military issues correlate with each other, and so on. With factor analysis, you can investigate the number of underlying factors, and, in many cases, you can identify what the factors represent conceptually. Additionally, you can compute factor scores for each respondent, which can then be used in subsequent analyses. For example, you might build a logistic regression model to predict voting behavior based on factor scores.

**Statistics.** For each variable: number of valid cases, mean, and standard deviation. For each factor analysis: correlation matrix of variables, including significance levels, determinant, inverse; reproduced correlation matrix, including anti-image; initial solution (communalities, eigenvalues, and percentage of variance explained); Kaiser-Meyer-Olkin measure of sampling adequacy and Bartlett's test of sphericity; unrotated solution, including factor loadings, communalities, and eigenvalues; rotated solution, including rotated pattern matrix and transformation matrix. For oblique rotations: rotated pattern and structure matrices; factor score coefficient matrix and factor covariance matrix. Plots: Scree plot of eigenvalues and loading plot of first two or three factors.

**Data.** The variables should be quantitative at the interval or ratio level. Categorical data (such as religion or country of origin) are not suitable for factor analysis. Data for which Pearson correlation coefficients can sensibly be calculated should be suitable for factor analysis.

**Assumptions.** The data should have a bivariate normal distribution for each pair of variables, and observations should be independent. The factor analysis model specifies that variables are determined by common factors (the factors estimated by the model) and unique factors (which do not overlap between observed variables); the computed estimates are based on the assumption that all unique factors are uncorrelated with each other and with the common factors.

**Related procedures.** Use the Scatterplot procedure on the Graphs menu to obtain bivariate scatterplots or scatterplot matrices. Scatterplots aid in the screening of your data. The Explore procedure can also be used to screen your data. If your data appear non-normally distributed, you can try transforming them. The factor analysis procedure can accept input in the form of a correlation matrix generated from another procedure, such as the Correlations procedure (you must use command syntax to read in matrix data).

# Sample Output

### Figure 24.1   Factor analysis output

**Descriptive Statistics**

|  | Mean | Std. Deviation | Analysis N |
|---|---|---|---|
| Average female life expectancy | 72.833 | 8.272 | 72 |
| Infant mortality (deaths per 1000 live births) | 35.132 | 32.222 | 72 |
| People who read (%) | 82.472 | 18.625 | 72 |
| Birth rate per 1000 people | 24.375 | 10.552 | 72 |
| Fertility: average number of kids | 3.205 | 1.593 | 72 |
| People living in cities (%) | 62.583 | 22.835 | 72 |
| Log (base 10) of GDP_CAP | 3.504 | .608 | 72 |
| Population increase (% per year)) | 1.697 | 1.156 | 72 |
| Birth to death ratio | 3.577 | 2.313 | 72 |
| Death rate per 1000 people | 8.038 | 3.174 | 72 |
| Log (base 10) of Population | 4.153 | .686 | 72 |

**Figure 24.1    Factor analysis output (Continued)**

### Communalities

|          | Initial | Extraction |
|----------|---------|------------|
| LIFEEXPF | 1.000   | .953       |
| BABYMORT | 1.000   | .949       |
| LITERACY | 1.000   | .825       |
| BIRTH_RT | 1.000   | .943       |
| FERTILTY | 1.000   | .875       |
| URBAN    | 1.000   | .604       |
| LOG_GDP  | 1.000   | .738       |
| POP_INCR | 1.000   | .945       |
| B_TO_D   | 1.000   | .925       |
| DEATH_RT | 1.000   | .689       |
| LOG_POP  | 1.000   | .292       |

Extraction Method: Principal
Component Analysis.

### Total Variance Explained

|           |    | Initial Eigenvalues | | | Extraction Sums of Squared Loadings | | | Rotation Sums of Squared Loadings | | |
|-----------|----|-------|---------------|---------------|-------|---------------|---------------|-------|---------------|---------------|
|           |    | Total | % of Variance | Cumulative %  | Total | % of Variance | Cumulative %  | Total | % of Variance | Cumulative %  |
| Component | 1  | 6.242 | 56.750        | 56.750        | 6.242 | 56.750        | 56.750        | 6.108 | 55.525        | 55.525        |
|           | 2  | 2.495 | 22.005        | 70.405        | 2.495 | 22.695        | 79.435        | 2.630 | 23.910        | 79.435        |
|           | 3  | .988  | 8.986         | 88.421        |       |               |               |       |               |               |
|           | 4  | .591  | 5.372         | 93.793        |       |               |               |       |               |               |
|           | 5  | .236  | 2.142         | 95.935        |       |               |               |       |               |               |
|           | 6  | .172  | 1.561         | 97.496        |       |               |               |       |               |               |
|           | 7  | .124  | 1.126         | 98.622        |       |               |               |       |               |               |
|           | 8  | 7.0E-02 | .633        | 99.254        |       |               |               |       |               |               |
|           | 9  | 4.5E-02 | .405        | 99.660        |       |               |               |       |               |               |
|           | 10 | 2.4E-02 | .222        | 99.882        |       |               |               |       |               |               |
|           | 11 | 1.3E-02 | .118        | 100.000       |       |               |               |       |               |               |

Extraction Method: Principal Component Analysis.

**Figure 24.1    Factor analysis output (Continued)**

**Rotated Component Matrix**

| | Component | |
|---|---|---|
| | 1 | 2 |
| BIRTH_RT | .969 | |
| FERTILTY | .931 | |
| LITERACY | -.880 | .226 |
| LIFEEXPF | -.856 | .469 |
| BABYMORT | .853 | -.469 |
| POP_INCR | .847 | .476 |
| LOG_GDP | -.794 | .327 |
| URBAN | -.561 | .539 |
| DEATH_RT | | -.827 |
| B_TO_D | .614 | .741 |
| LOG_POP | | -.520 |

Extraction Method: Principal
Component Analysis.
Rotation Method: Varimax
with Kaiser Normalization.

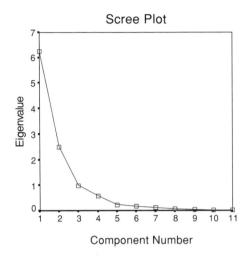

**Component Transformation Matrix**

| Component | | 1 | 2 |
|---|---|---|---|
| | 1 | .982 | -.190 |
| | 2 | .190 | .982 |

Extraction Method: Principal Component
Analysis.
Rotation Method: Varimax with Kaiser
Normalization.

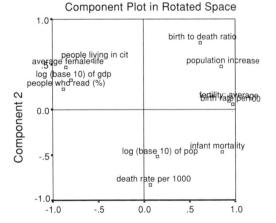

# To Obtain a Factor Analysis

▶ From the menus choose:

Statistics
  Data Reduction
    Factor...

▶ Select the variables for the factor analysis.

**Figure 24.2   Factor Analysis dialog box**

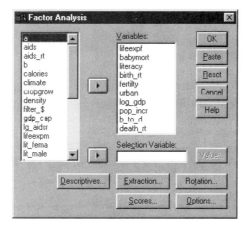

## Factor Analysis Select Cases

**Figure 24.3   Factor Analysis Select Cases dialog box**

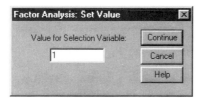

To select cases for your analysis, click *Select*, choose a selection variable, and click *Value* to enter an integer as the selection value. Only cases with that value for the selection variable are used to in the factor analysis.

## Factor Analysis Descriptives

**Figure 24.4   Factor Analysis Descriptives dialog box**

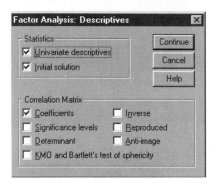

**Statistics.** Univariate statistics include the mean, standard deviation, and number of valid cases for each variable. Initial solution displays initial communalities, eigenvalues, and the percentage of variance explained.

**Correlation Matrix.** The available options are coefficients, significance levels, determinant, inverse, reproduced, anti-image, and KMO and Bartlett's test of sphericity.

# To Specify Descriptive Statistics and Correlation Coefficients

▶   From the menus choose:

Statistics
  Data Reduction
    Factor...

▶   In the Factor Analysis dialog box, click *Descriptives*.

## Factor Analysis Extraction

**Figure 24.5   Factor Analysis Extraction dialog box**

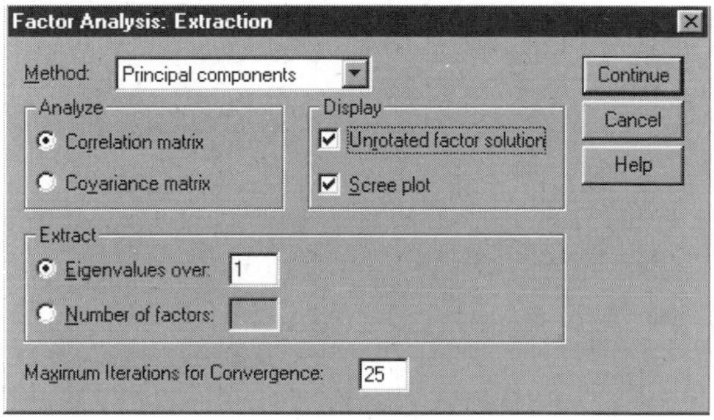

**Method.** Allows you to specify the method of factor extraction. Available methods are principal components, unweighted least squares, generalized least squares, maximum likelihood, principal axis factoring, alpha factoring, and image factoring.

**Analyze.** Allows you to specify either a correlation matrix or a covariance matrix.

**Extract.** You can either retain all factors for which eigenvalues exceed a specified value or retain a specific number of factors.

**Display.** Allows you to request the unrotated factor solution and a scree plot of the eigenvalues.

**Maximum Iterations for Convergence.** Allows you to specify the maximum number of steps the algorithm can take to estimate the solution.

# To Specify Extraction Options

▶ From the menus choose:

Statistics
  Data Reduction
    Factor...

▶ In the Factor Analysis dialog box, click *Extraction*.

## Factor Analysis Rotation

**Figure 24.6  Factor Analysis Rotation dialog box**

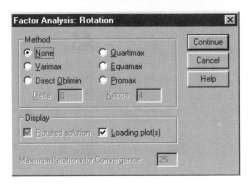

**Method.** Allows you to select the method of factor rotation. Available methods are varimax, equamax, quartimax, direct oblimin, or promax.

**Display.** Allows you to include output on the rotated solution, as well as loading plots for the first two or three factors.

**Maximum Iterations for Convergence.** Allows you to specify the maximum number of steps the algorithm can take to perform the rotation.

# To Specify Rotation Options

▶ From the menus choose:

Statistics
  Data Reduction
    Factor...

▶ In the Factor Analysis dialog box, click *Rotation*.

## Factor Analysis Scores

**Figure 24.7   Factor Analysis Scores dialog box**

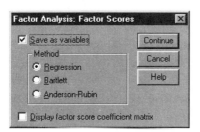

**Save as variables.** Creates one new variable for each factor in the final solution. Select one of the following alternative methods for calculating the factor scores: regression, Bartlett, or Anderson-Rubin.

**Display factor score coefficient matrix.** Shows the coefficients by which variables are multiplied to obtain factor scores.

# To Specify Factor Score Options

▶  From the menus choose:

Statistics
  Data Reduction
    Factor...

▶  In the Factor Analysis dialog box, click *Scores*.

## Factor Analysis Options

**Figure 24.8   Factor Analysis Options dialog box**

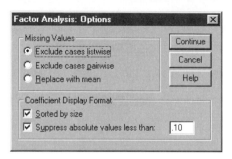

**Missing Values.** Allows you to specify how missing values are handled. The available alternatives are exclude cases listwise, exclude cases pairwise, or replace with mean.

**Coefficient Display Format.** Allows you to control aspects of the output matrices. You sort coefficients by size and suppress coefficients with absolute values less than the specified value.

# To Specify Factor Analysis Options

▶  From the menus choose:

Statistics
  Data Reduction
    Factor...

▶  In the Factor Analysis dialog box, click *Options*.

## FACTOR Command Additional Features

The SPSS command language also allows you to:

- Specify convergence criteria for iteration during extraction and rotation.
- Specify individual rotated-factor plots.
- Specify how many factor scores to save.
- Specify diagonal values for the principal axis factoring method.
- Write correlation matrices or factor loading matrices to disk for later analysis.
- Read and analyze correlation matrices or factor loading matrices.

See the *SPSS Base Syntax Reference Guide* for complete syntax information.

# 25 Hierarchical Cluster Analysis

This procedure attempts to identify relatively homogeneous groups of cases (or variables) based on selected characteristics, using an algorithm that starts with each case (or variable) in a separate cluster and combines clusters until only one is left. You can analyze raw variables or you can choose from a variety of standardizing transformations. Distance or similarity measures are generated by the Proximities procedure. Statistics are displayed at each stage to help you select the best solution.

**Example.** Are there identifiable groups of television shows which attract similar audiences within each group? With hierarchical cluster analysis, you could cluster television shows (cases) into homogeneous groups based on viewer characteristics. This can be used to identify segments for marketing. Or you can cluster cities (cases) into homogeneous groups so that comparable cities can be selected to test various marketing strategies.

**Statistics.** Agglomeration schedule, distance (or similarity) matrix, and cluster membership for a single solution or a range of solutions. Plots: dendrograms and icicle plots.

**Data.** The variables can be quantitative, binary, or count data. Scaling of variables is an important issue—differences in scaling may affect your cluster solution(s). If your variables have large differences in scaling (for example, one variable is measured in dollars and the other is measured in years), you should consider standardizing them (this can be done automatically by the Hierarchical Cluster Analysis procedure).

**Assumptions.** The distance or similarity measures used should be appropriate for the data analyzed (see the Proximities procedure for more information on choices of distance and similarity measures). Also, you should include all relevant variables in your analysis. Omission of influential variables can result in a misleading solution. Because hierarchical cluster analysis is an exploratory method, results should be treated as tentative until they are confirmed with an independent sample.

**Related procedures.** The Proximities procedure can be used independently to generate distance or similarity scores, which can then be read by the Cluster procedure using command syntax. Once you have identified groups, you can determine which variables distinguish between them using the Discriminant procedure. If you know ahead of time how many clusters to look for, use K-Means Cluster Analysis for a quicker solution.

# Sample Output

### Figure 25.1   Hierarchical Cluster Analysis output

**Agglomeration Schedule**

| | | Cluster Combined | | | Stage Cluster First Appears | | |
|---|---|---|---|---|---|---|---|
| | | Cluster 1 | Cluster 2 | Coefficients | Cluster 1 | Cluster 2 | Next Stage |
| Stage | 1 | 11 | 12 | .112 | 0 | 0 | 2 |
| | 2 | 6 | 11 | .132 | 0 | 1 | 4 |
| | 3 | 7 | 9 | .185 | 0 | 0 | 5 |
| | 4 | 6 | 8 | .227 | 2 | 0 | 7 |
| | 5 | 7 | 10 | .274 | 3 | 0 | 7 |
| | 6 | 1 | 3 | .423 | 0 | 0 | 10 |
| | 7 | 6 | 7 | .438 | 4 | 5 | 14 |
| | 8 | 13 | 14 | .484 | 0 | 0 | 15 |
| | 9 | 2 | 5 | .547 | 0 | 0 | 11 |
| | 10 | 1 | 4 | .691 | 6 | 0 | 11 |
| | 11 | 1 | 2 | 1.023 | 10 | 9 | 13 |
| | 12 | 15 | 16 | 1.370 | 0 | 0 | 13 |
| | 13 | 1 | 15 | 1.716 | 11 | 12 | 14 |
| | 14 | 1 | 6 | 2.642 | 13 | 7 | 15 |
| | 15 | 1 | 13 | 4.772 | 14 | 8 | 0 |

**Cluster Membership**

| | | Label | 4 Clusters | 3 Clusters | 2 Clusters |
|---|---|---|---|---|---|
| Case | 1 | Argentina | 1 | 1 | 1 |
| | 2 | Brazil | 1 | 1 | 1 |
| | 3 | Chile | 1 | 1 | 1 |
| | 4 | Domincan R. | 1 | 1 | 1 |
| | 5 | Indonesia | 1 | 1 | 1 |
| | 6 | Austria | 2 | 2 | 1 |
| | 7 | Canada | 2 | 2 | 1 |
| | 8 | Denmark | 2 | 2 | 1 |
| | 9 | Italy | 2 | 2 | 1 |
| | 10 | Japan | 2 | 2 | 1 |
| | 11 | Norway | 2 | 2 | 1 |
| | 12 | Switzerland | 2 | 2 | 1 |
| | 13 | Bangladesh | 3 | 3 | 2 |
| | 14 | India | 3 | 3 | 2 |
| | 15 | Bolivia | 4 | 1 | 1 |
| | 16 | Paraguay | 4 | 1 | 1 |

**Vertical Icicle**

Case

| | 14:India | 14 | 13:Banglade | 13 | 10:Japan | 10 | 9:Italy | 9 | 7:Canada | 7 | 8:Denmark | 8 | 12:Switzerlar | 12 | 11:Norway | 11 | 6:Austria | 6 | 16:Paraguay | 16 | 15:Bolivia | 15 | 5:Indonesia | 5 | 2:Brazil | 2 | 4:Domincan | 4 | 3:Chile | 3 | 1:Argentina |
|---|---|---|---|---|---|---|---|---|---|---|---|---|---|---|---|---|---|---|---|---|---|---|---|---|---|---|---|---|---|---|---|

Number of clusters

```
 1  X X X X X X X X X X X X X X X X X X X X X X X X X X X X X X X
 2  X X X   X X X X X X X X X X X X X X X X X X X X X X X X X X X
 3  X X X   X X X X X X X X X X X   X X X X X X X X X X X X
 4  X X X   X X X X X X X X X X X X   X X X   X X X X X X X X X
 5  X X X   X X X X X X X X X X X X   X   X   X X X X X X X X X
 6  X X X   X X X X X X X X X X X X   X   X   X X X   X X X X X
 7  X X X   X X X X X X X X X X X X   X   X   X X X   X   X X X
 8  X X X   X X X X X X X X X X X X   X   X   X   X   X   X X X
 9  X   X   X X X X X X X X X X X X   X   X   X   X   X   X X X
10  X   X   X X X X X   X X X X X X   X   X   X   X   X   X X X
11  X   X   X X X X X   X X X X X X   X   X   X   X   X   X   X
12  X   X   X   X X X   X X X X X X   X   X   X   X   X   X   X
13  X   X   X   X X X   X   X X X X X   X   X   X   X   X   X   X
14  X   X   X   X   X   X   X X X X X   X   X   X   X   X   X   X
15  X   X   X   X   X   X   X X X   X   X   X   X   X   X   X   X
```

```
* * * * * * H I E R A R C H I C A L   C L U S T E R    A N A L Y S I S * * * *
* *


Dendrogram using Average Linkage (Between Groups)

                      Rescaled Distance Cluster Combine

        C A S E          0         5        10        15        20        25
      Label        Num   +---------+---------+---------+---------+---------+

      Norway        11    -+
      Switzerland   12    -+
      Austria        6    -+-+
      Denmark        8    -+ +---------------------+
      Canada         7    -+ I                     I
      Italy          9    -+-+                     I
      Japan         10    -+                       +---------------------+
      Brazil         2    -----+---+               I                     I
      Indonesia      5    -----+   +-------+       I                     I
      Argentina      1    ---+---+ I       I       I                     I
      Chile          3    ---+   +-+       +---------+                   I
      Domincan R.    4    -------+         I                             I
      Bolivia       15    -------------+---+                             I
      Paraguay      16    -------------+                                 I
      Bangladesh    13    ---+-------------------------------------------+
      India         14    ---+
```

# To Obtain a Hierarchical Cluster Analysis

▶ From the menus choose:

Statistics
  Classify
    Hierarchical Cluster...

**Figure 25.2   Hierarchical Cluster Analysis dialog box**

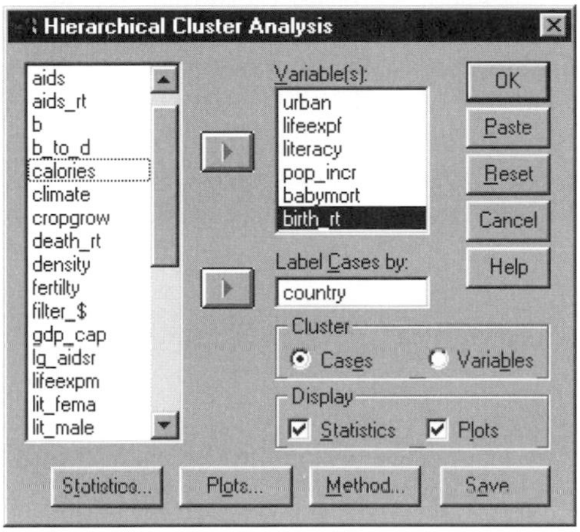

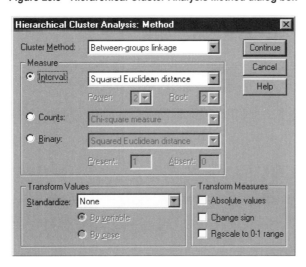

▶ If you are clustering cases, select at least one numeric variable. If you are clustering variables, select at least three numeric variables.

Optionally, you can select an identification variable to label cases.

# Hierarchical Cluster Analysis Method

**Figure 25.3   Hierarchical Cluster Analysis Method dialog box**

**Cluster Method.** Available alternatives are between-groups linkage, within-groups linkage, nearest neighbor, furthest neighbor, centroid clustering, median clustering, and Ward's method.

**Measure.** Allows you to specify the distance or similarity measure to be used in clustering. Select the type of data and the appropriate distance or similarity measure:

- **Interval.** Available alternatives are Euclidean distance, squared Euclidean distance, cosine, Pearson correlation, Chebychev, block, Minkowski, and customized.

- **Counts.** Available alternatives are chi-square measure and phi-square measure.

- **Binary.** Available alternatives are Euclidean distance, squared Euclidean distance, size difference, pattern difference, variance, dispersion, shape, simple matching, phi 4-point correlation, lambda, Anderberg's $D$, dice, Hamann, Jaccard, Kulczynski 1, Kulczynski 2, Lance and Williams, Ochiai, Rogers and Tanimoto, Russel and Rao, Sokal and Sneath 1, Sokal and Sneath 2, Sokal and Sneath 3, Sokal and Sneath 4, Sokal and Sneath 5, Yule's $Y$, and Yule's $Q$.

**Transform Values.** Allows you to standardize data values for either cases or values *before* computing proximities (not available for binary data). Available standardization methods are $z$ scores, range –1 to 1, range 0 to 1, maximum magnitude of 1, mean of 1, and standard deviation of 1.

**Transform Measures.** Allows you to transform the values generated by the distance measure. They are applied *after* the distance measure has been computed. Available alternatives are absolute values, change sign, and rescale to 0–1 range.

## Hierarchical Cluster Analysis Statistics

Figure 25.4   Hierarchical Cluster Analysis Statistics dialog box

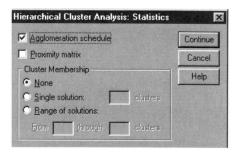

**Agglomeration schedule.** Displays the cases or clusters combined at each stage, the distances between the cases or clusters being combined, and the last cluster level at which a case (or variable) joined the cluster.

**Proximity matrix.** Gives the distances or similarities between items.

**Cluster Membership.** Displays the cluster to which each case is assigned at one or more stages in the combination of clusters. Available options are single solution and range of solutions

## Hierarchical Cluster Analysis Plots

**Figure 25.5   Hierarchical Cluster Analysis Plots dialog box**

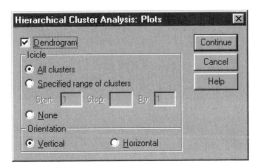

**Dendrogram.** Displays a dendrogram. Dendrograms can be used to assess the cohesiveness of the clusters formed and can provide information about the appropriate number of clusters to keep.

**Icicle.** Displays an icicle plot, including all clusters or a specified range of clusters. Icicle plots display information about how cases are combined into clusters at each iteration of the analysis. Orientation allows you to select a vertical or horizontal plot

## Hierarchical Cluster Analysis Save New Variables

**Figure 25.6   Hierarchical Cluster Analysis Save New Variables dialog box**

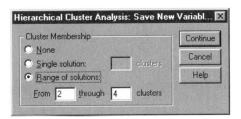

**Cluster Membership.** Allows you to save cluster memberships for a single solution or a range of solutions. Saved variables can then be used in subsequent analyses to explore other differences between groups.

## CLUSTER Command Additional Features

The SPSS command language also allows you to:

- Use several clustering methods in a single analysis.
- Read and analyze a proximity matrix.
- Write a proximity matrix to disk for later analysis.
- Specify any values for power and root in the customized (POWER) distance measure.
- Specify names for saved variables.

See the *SPSS Base Syntax Reference Guide* for complete syntax information.

# 26 K-Means Cluster Analysis

This procedure attempts to identify relatively homogeneous groups of cases based on selected characteristics, using an algorithm that can handle large numbers of cases. However, the algorithm requires you to specify the number of clusters. You can specify initial cluster centers if you know this information. You can select one of two methods for classifying cases, either updating cluster centers iteratively or classifying only (based on fixed cluster centers). You can save cluster membership, distance information, and final cluster centers. Optionally, you can specify a variable whose values are used to label casewise output. You can also request analysis of variance $F$ statistics. While these statistics are opportunistic (the procedure tries to form groups that do differ), the relative size of the statistics provides information about each variable's contribution to the separation of the groups.

**Example.** What are some identifiable groups of television shows that attract similar audiences within each group? With $k$-means cluster analysis, you could cluster television shows (cases) into $k$ homogeneous groups based on viewer characteristics. This can be used to identify segments for marketing. Or you can cluster cities (cases) into homogeneous groups so that comparable cities can be selected to test various marketing strategies.

**Statistics.** Complete solution: initial cluster centers, ANOVA table. Each case: cluster information, distance from cluster center.

**Data.** Variables should be quantitative at the interval or ratio level. If your variables are binary or counts, use the Hierarchical Cluster Analysis procedure.

**Assumptions.** Distances are computed using simple Euclidean distance. If you want to use another distance or similarity measure, use the Hierarchical Cluster Analysis procedure. Scaling of variables is an important consideration—if your variables are measured on different scales (for example, one variable is expressed in dollars and another is expressed in years), your results may be misleading. In such cases, you should consider standardizing your variables before you perform the $k$-means cluster analysis (this can be done in the Descriptives procedure). The procedure assumes that you have selected the appropriate number of clusters and that you have included all relevant variables. If you have chosen an inappropriate number of clusters or omitted important variables, your results may be misleading.

**Related procedures**. The main advantage of the K-Means Cluster Analysis procedure is that it is much faster than the Hierarchical Cluster Analysis procedure. On the other hand, the hierarchical procedure allows much more flexibility in your cluster analysis—you can use any of a number of distance or similarity measures, including options for binary and count data, and you do not need to specify the number of clusters *a priori*. Once you have identified groups, you can build a model useful for identifying new cases using the Discriminant procedure. You can also use saved cluster membership information to explore other relationships in subsequent analyses, such as Crosstabs or ANOVA.

# Sample Output

### Figure 26.1   K-Means Cluster Analysis output

**Initial Cluster Centers**

|  | Cluster | | | |
|---|---|---|---|---|
|  | 1 | 2 | 3 | 4 |
| ZURBAN | -1.88606 | -1.54314 | 1.45741 | .55724 |
| ZLIFEEXP | -3.52581 | -1.69358 | .62725 | .99370 |
| ZLITERAC | -2.89320 | -1.65146 | -.51770 | .88601 |
| ZPOP_INC | .93737 | .16291 | 3.03701 | -1.12785 |
| ZBABYMOR | 4.16813 | 1.38422 | -.69589 | -.88983 |
| ZBIRTH_R | 2.68796 | .42699 | .33278 | -1.08033 |
| ZDEATH_R | 4.41517 | .63185 | -1.89037 | .63185 |
| ZLOG_GDP | -1.99641 | -1.78455 | .53091 | 1.22118 |
| ZB_TO_D | -.52182 | -.31333 | 4.40082 | -.99285 |
| ZFERTILT | 2.24070 | .75481 | .46008 | -.76793 |
| ZLOG_POP | .24626 | 2.65246 | -1.29624 | -.74406 |

**Iteration History**

|  |  | Change in Cluster Centers | | | |
|---|---|---|---|---|---|
|  |  | 1 | 2 | 3 | 4 |
| Iteration | 1 | 1.932 | 2.724 | 3.343 | 1.596 |
|  | 2 | .000 | .471 | .466 | .314 |
|  | 3 | .861 | .414 | .172 | .195 |
|  | 4 | .604 | .337 | .000 | .150 |
|  | 5 | .000 | .253 | .237 | .167 |
|  | 6 | .000 | .199 | .287 | .071 |
|  | 7 | .623 | .160 | .000 | .000 |
|  | 8 | .000 | .084 | .000 | .074 |
|  | 9 | .000 | .080 | .000 | .077 |
|  | 10 | .000 | .097 | .185 | .000 |

**Final Cluster Centers**

|  | Cluster | | | |
| --- | --- | --- | --- | --- |
|  | 1 | 2 | 3 | 4 |
| ZURBAN | -1.70745 | -.30863 | .16816 | .62767 |
| ZLIFEEXP | -2.52826 | -.15939 | -.28417 | .80611 |
| ZLITERAC | -2.30833 | .13880 | -.81671 | .73368 |
| ZPOP_INC | .59747 | .13400 | 1.45301 | -.95175 |
| ZBABYMOR | 2.43210 | .22286 | .25622 | -.80817 |
| ZBIRTH_R | 1.52607 | .12929 | 1.13716 | -.99285 |
| ZDEATH_R | 2.10314 | -.44640 | -.71414 | .31319 |
| ZLOG_GDP | -1.77704 | -.58745 | -.16871 | .94249 |
| ZB_TO_D | -.29856 | .19154 | 1.45251 | -.84758 |
| ZFERTILT | 1.51003 | -.12150 | 1.27010 | -.87669 |
| ZLOG_POP | .83475 | .34577 | -.49499 | -.22199 |

**Distances between Final Cluster Centers**

|  |  | 1 | 2 | 3 | 4 |
| --- | --- | --- | --- | --- | --- |
| Cluster | 1 |  | 5.627 | 5.640 | 7.924 |
|  | 2 | 5.627 |  | 2.897 | 3.249 |
|  | 3 | 5.640 | 2.897 |  | 5.246 |
|  | 4 | 7.924 | 3.249 | 5.246 |  |

**ANOVA**

|  | Cluster | | Error | | | |
| --- | --- | --- | --- | --- | --- | --- |
|  | Mean Square | df | Mean Square | df | F | Sig. |
| ZURBAN | 10.409 | 3 | .541 | 68 | 19.234 | .000 |
| ZLIFEEXP | 19.410 | 3 | .210 | 68 | 92.614 | .000 |
| ZLITERAC | 18.731 | 3 | .229 | 68 | 81.655 | .000 |
| ZPOP_INC | 18.464 | 3 | .219 | 68 | 84.428 | .000 |
| ZBABYMOR | 18.621 | 3 | .239 | 68 | 77.859 | .000 |
| ZBIRTH_R | 19.599 | 3 | .167 | 68 | 117.339 | .000 |
| ZDEATH_R | 13.628 | 3 | .444 | 68 | 30.676 | .000 |
| ZLOG_GDP | 17.599 | 3 | .287 | 68 | 61.313 | .000 |
| ZB_TO_D | 16.316 | 3 | .288 | 68 | 56.682 | .000 |
| ZFERTILT | 18.829 | 3 | .168 | 68 | 112.273 | .000 |
| ZLOG_POP | 3.907 | 3 | .877 | 68 | 4.457 | .006 |

The F tests should be used only for descriptive purposes because the clusters have been chosen to maximize the differences among cases in different clusters. The observed significance levels are not corrected for this and thus cannot be interpreted as tests of the hypothesis that the cluster means are equal.

# To Obtain a K-Means Cluster Analysis

▶ From the menus choose:

Statistics
　Classify
　　K-Means Cluster...

**Figure 26.2   K-Means Cluster Analysis dialog box**

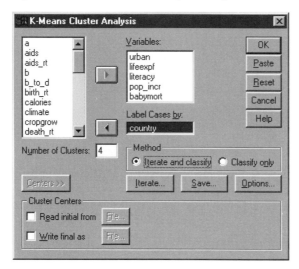

▶ Select the variables to be used in the cluster analysis.

▶ Specify the number of clusters. The number of clusters must be at least two and must not be greater than the number of cases in the data file.

▶ Select a method, either *Iterate and classify* or *Classify only*.

Optionally, you can select an identification variable to label cases.

## K-Means Cluster Analysis Efficiency

The *k*-means cluster analysis command is efficient primarily because it does not compute the distances between all pairs of cases, as do many clustering algorithms, including that used by the hierarchical clustering command in SPSS.

For maximum efficiency, take a sample of cases and use the iterative method to determine cluster centers. Click *Centers*, select *Write final as*, and click *File*. Then restore the entire data file, and select *Classify only* as the method. Click *Centers*, select *Read initial from*, and click *File* to classify the entire file using the centers estimated from the sample.

# K-Means Cluster Analysis Iterate

Figure 26.3   K-Means Cluster Analysis Iterate dialog box

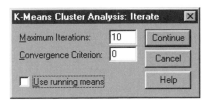

These options are available only if you select *Iterate and classify* in the main dialog box.

**Maximum Iterations.** Limits the number of iterations in the *k*-means algorithm. Iteration stops after this many iterations even if the convergence criterion is not satisfied. This number must be between 1 and 999.

To reproduce the algorithm used by the quick cluster command in SPSS prior to release 5.0, set the maximum iterations to 1.

**Convergence Criterion.** Determines when iteration ceases. It represents a proportion of the minimum distance between *initial* cluster centers, so it must be greater than 0 but not greater than 1. If the criterion equals 0.02, for example, iteration ceases when a complete iteration does not move any of the cluster centers by a distance of more than 2% of the smallest distance between any of the initial cluster centers.

**Use running means.** Allows you to request that cluster centers be updated after each case is assigned. If you do not select this option, new cluster centers are calculated after all cases have been assigned.

# K-Means Cluster Analysis Save

Figure 26.4   K-Means Cluster Save New Variables dialog box

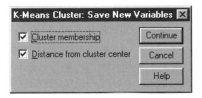

You can save information about the solution as new variables to be used in subsequent analyses:

**Cluster membership.** Creates a new variable indicating the final cluster membership of each case. Values of the new variable range from 1 to the number of clusters.

**Distance from cluster center.** Creates a new variable indicating the Euclidean distance be-tween each case and its classification center.

## K-Means Cluster Analysis Options

**Figure 26.5   K-Means Cluster Analysis Options dialog box**

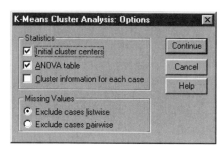

**Statistics.** You can select the following statistics: initial cluster centers, ANOVA table, and cluster information for each case.

**Missing Values.** Available options are exclude cases listwise or exclude cases pairwise.

## QUICK CLUSTER Command Additional Features

The SPSS command language also allows you to:

- Accept the first *k* cases as initial cluster centers, thereby avoiding the data pass nor-mally used to estimate them.
- Specify initial cluster centers directly as a part of the command syntax.
- Specify names for saved variables.

See the *SPSS Base Syntax Reference Guide* for complete syntax information.

# 27 Nonparametric Tests

The Nonparametric Tests procedure provides several tests that do not require assumptions about the shape of the underlying distribution:

**Chi-Square Test.** Tabulates a variable into categories and computes a chi-square statistic based on the differences between observed and expected frequencies.

**Binomial Test.** Compares the observed frequency in each category of a dichotomous variable with expected frequencies from the binomial distribution.

**Runs Test.** Tests whether the order of occurrence of two values of a variable is random.

**One-Sample Kolmogorov-Smirnov Test.** Compares the observed cumulative distribution function for a variable with a specified theoretical distribution, which may be normal, uniform, or Poisson.

**Two-Independent-Samples Tests.** Compares two groups of cases on one variable. The Mann-Whitney $U$ test, the two-sample Kolmogorov-Smirnov test, Moses test of extreme reactions, and the Wald-Wolfowitz runs test are available.

**Tests for Several Independent Samples.** Compares two or more groups of cases on one variable. The Kruskal-Wallis test, the median test, and the Jonckheere-Terpstra test are available.

**Two-Related-Samples Tests.** Compares the distributions of two variables. The Wilcoxon signed-rank test, the sign test, and the McNemar test are available.

**Tests for Several Related Samples.** Compares the distributions of two or more variables. Friedman's test, Kendall's $W$, and Cochran's $Q$ are available.

Quartiles and the mean, standard deviation, minimum, maximum, and number of nonmissing cases are available for all of the above tests.

# Chi-Square Test

The Chi-Square Test procedure tabulates a variable into categories and computes a chi-square statistic. This goodness-of-fit test compares the observed and expected frequencies in each category to test either that all categories contain the same proportion of values or that each category contains a user-specified proportion of values.

**Examples.** The chi-square test could be used to determine if a bag of jelly beans contains equal proportions of blue, brown, green, orange, red, and yellow candies. You could also test to see if a bag of jelly beans contains 5% blue, 30% brown, 10% green, 20% orange, 15% red, and 15% yellow candies.

**Statistics.** Mean, standard deviation, minimum, maximum, and quartiles. The number and the percentage of nonmissing and missing cases, the number of cases observed and expected for each category, residuals, and the chi-square statistic.

**Data.** Use ordered or unordered numeric categorical variables (ordinal or nominal levels of measurement). To convert string variables to numeric variables, use the Automatic Recode procedure, available on the Transform menu.

**Assumptions.** Nonparametric tests do not require assumptions about the shape of the underlying distribution. The data are assumed to be a random sample. The expected frequencies for each category should be at least 1. No more than 20% of the categories should have expected frequencies of less than 5.

**Related procedures.** To obtain chi-square tests of the relationship between two or more variables, use the Crosstabs procedure.

# Sample Output

**Figure 27.1 Chi-Square Test output**

Color of Jelly Bean

| | Observed N | Expected N | Residual |
|---|---|---|---|
| Blue | 6 | 18.8 | -12.8 |
| Brown | 33 | 18.8 | 14.2 |
| Green | 9 | 18.8 | -9.8 |
| Yellow | 17 | 18.8 | -1.8 |
| Orange | 22 | 18.8 | 3.2 |
| Red | 26 | 18.8 | 7.2 |
| Total | 113 | | |

**Figure 27.1 Chi-Square Test output (continued)**

Test Statistics

|  | Color of Jelly Bean |
|---|---|
| Chi-Square [1] | 27.973 |
| df | 5 |
| Asymptotic Significance | .000 |

[1] 0 Cells .0% low freqs 18.8
expected low...

Color of Jelly Bean

|  | Observed N | Expected N | Residual |
|---|---|---|---|
| Blue | 6 | 5.7 | .3 |
| Brown | 33 | 33.9 | -.9 |
| Green | 9 | 11.3 | -2.3 |
| Yellow | 17 | 17.0 | .0 |
| Orange | 22 | 22.6 | -.6 |
| Red | 26 | 22.6 | 3.4 |
| Total | 113 |  |  |

Test Statistics

|  | Color of Jelly Bean |
|---|---|
| Chi-Square [1] | 1.041 |
| df | 5 |
| Asymptotic Significance | .959 |

[1] 0 Cells .0% low freqs 5.7
expected low...

# To Obtain a Chi-Square Test

▶ From the menus choose:

Statistics
  Nonparametric Tests
    Chi-Square...

**Figure 27.2   Chi-Square Test dialog box**

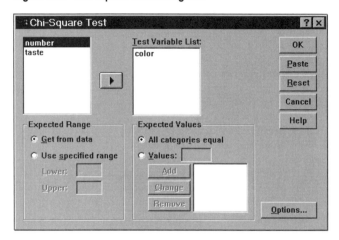

▶ Select one or more test variables. Each variable produces a separate test.

Optionally, you can click *Options* for descriptive statistics, quartiles, and control of the treatment of missing data.

## Chi-Square Test Expected Range and Expected Values

**Expected Range.** By default, each distinct value of the variable is defined as a category. To establish categories within a specific range, click *Use specified range* and enter integer values for lower and upper bounds. Categories are established for each integer value within the inclusive range, and cases with values outside of the bounds are excluded. For example, if you specify a lowerbound value of 1 and an upperbound value of 4, only the integer values of 1 through 4 are used for the chi-square test.

**Expected Values.** By default, all categories have equal expected values. Categories can have user-specified expected proportions. Select *Values*, enter a value greater than 0 for each category of the test variable, and click *Add*. Each time you add a value, it appears at the bottom of the value list. The order of the values is important; it corresponds to the ascending order of the category values of the test variable. The first value on the list corresponds to the lowest group value of the test variable, and the last value corresponds to the highest value. Elements of the value list are summed, and then each value is divided by this sum to calculate the proportion of cases expected in the corresponding category. For example, a value list of 3, 4, 5, 4 specifies expected proportions of 3/16, 4/16, 5/16, and 4/16.

## Chi-Square Test Options

**Figure 27.3   Chi-Square Test Options dialog box**

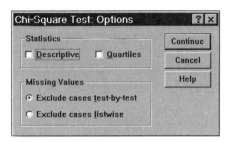

**Statistics.** You can choose one or both of the following summary statistics:

- **Descriptive.** Displays the mean, standard deviation, minimum, maximum, and number of nonmissing cases.
- **Quartiles.** Displays values corresponding to the 25th, 50th, and 75th percentiles.

**Missing Values.** Controls the treatment of missing values.

- **Exclude cases test-by-test.** When several tests are specified, each test is evaluated separately for missing values.
- **Exclude cases listwise.** Cases with missing values for any variable are excluded from all analyses.

## NPAR TESTS Command Additional Features (Chi-Square Test)

The SPSS command language also allows you to:

- Specify different minimum and maximum values or expected frequencies for different variables (with the CHISQUARE subcommand).
- Test the same variable against different expected frequencies or use different ranges (with the EXPECTED subcommand).

See the *SPSS Base Syntax Reference Guide* for complete syntax information.

# Binomial Test

The Binomial Test procedure compares the observed frequencies of the two categories of a dichotomous variable to the frequencies expected under a binomial distribution with a specified probability parameter. By default, the probability parameter for both groups is 0.5. To change the probabilities, you can enter a test proportion for the first group. The probability for the second group will be 1 minus the specified probability for the first group.

**Example.** When you toss a dime, the probability of a head equals 1/2. Based on this hypothesis, a dime is tossed 40 times, and the outcomes are recorded (heads or tails). From the binomial test, you might find that 3/4 of the tosses were heads and that the observed significance level is small (0.0027). These results indicate that it is not likely that the probability of a head equals 1/2; the coin is probably biased.

**Statistics.** Mean, standard deviation, minimum, maximum, number of nonmissing cases, and quartiles.

**Data.** The variables tested should be numeric and dichotomous. To convert string variables to numeric variables, use the Automatic Recode procedure, available on the Transform menu. A dichotomous variable is a variable that can take on only two possible values: *yes* or *no*, *true* or *false*, 0 or 1, etc. If the variables are not dichotomous, you must specify a cut point. The cut point assigns cases with values less than the cut point to one group and the rest of the cases to another group.

**Assumptions.** Nonparametric tests do not require assumptions about the shape of the underlying distribution. The data are assumed to be a random sample.

**Related procedures.** If the test variable is not dichotomous and you want to specify more than two categories, use the Chi-Square Test procedure.

# Sample Output

**Figure 27.4   Binomial Test output**

Binomial Test

| | | Category | N | Observed Proportion | Test Proportion | Asymptotic Significance (2-tailed) |
|---|---|---|---|---|---|---|
| Coin | Group 1 | Head | 30 | .75 | .50 | .003[1] |
| | Group 2 | Tail | 10 | .25 | | |
| | Total | | 40 | 1.00 | | |

[1] Based on Z Approximation

# To Obtain a Binomial Test

▶ From the menus choose:

Statistics
  Nonparametric Tests
    Binomial...

**Figure 27.5   Binomial Test dialog box**

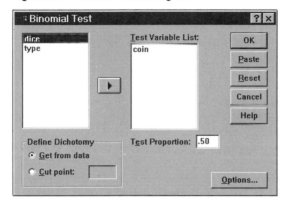

▶ Select one or more numeric test variables.

Optionally, you can click *Options* for descriptive statistics, quartiles, and control of the treatment of missing data.

# Binomial Test Options

**Figure 27.6   Binomial Test Options dialog box**

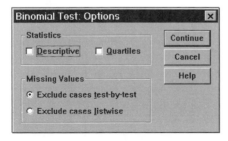

**Statistics.** You can choose one or both of the following summary statistics:

- **Descriptive.** Displays the mean, standard deviation, minimum, maximum, and number of nonmissing cases.
- **Quartiles.** Displays values corresponding to the 25th, 50th, and 75th percentiles.

**Missing Values.** Controls the treatment of missing values.

- **Exclude cases test-by-test.** When several tests are specified, each test is evaluated separately for missing values.
- **Exclude cases listwise.** Cases with missing values for any variable tested are excluded from all analyses.

## NPAR TESTS Command Additional Features (Binomial Test)

The SPSS command language also allows you to:

- Select specific groups (and exclude others) when a variable has more than two categories (with the BINOMIAL subcommand).
- Specify different cut points or probabilities for different variables (with the BINOMIAL subcommand).
- Test the same variable against different cut points or probabilities (with the EXPECTED subcommand).

See the *SPSS Base Syntax Reference Guide* for complete syntax information.

# Runs Test

The Runs Test procedure tests whether the order of occurrence of two values of a variable is random. A run is a sequence of like observations. A sample with too many or too few runs suggests that the sample is not random.

**Examples.** Suppose that 20 people are polled to find out if they would purchase a product. The assumed randomness of the sample would be seriously questioned if all 20 people were of the same gender. The runs test can be used to determine if the sample was drawn at random.

**Statistics.** Mean, standard deviation, minimum, maximum, number of nonmissing cases, and quartiles.

**Data.** The variables must be numeric. To convert string variables to numeric variables, use the Automatic Recode procedure, available on the Transform menu.

**Assumptions.** Nonparametric tests do not require assumptions about the shape of the underlying distribution. Use samples from continuous probability distributions.

**Related procedures.** To test that two samples come from populations with the same distributions, use the Wald-Wolfowitz runs test, available in the Two-Independent-Samples procedure.

# Sample Output

**Figure 27.7    Runs Test output**

Runs Test

|  | Gender |
|---|---|
| Test Value [1] | 1.00 |
| Cases < Test Value | 7 |
| Cases >= Test Value | 13 |
| Total Cases | 20 |
| Number of Runs | 15 |
| Z | 2.234 |
| Asymptotic Significance (2-tailed) | .025 |

[1]. Median

# To Obtain a Runs Test

▶ From the menus choose:

Statistics
  Nonparametric Tests
    Runs...

**Figure 27.8   Runs Test dialog box**

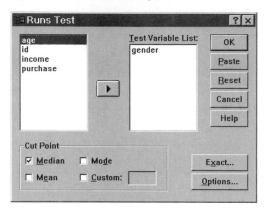

▶   Select one or more numeric test variables.

Optionally, you can click *Options* for descriptive statistics, quartiles, and control of the treatment of missing data.

## Runs Test Cut Point

**Cut Point.** Specifies a cut point to dichotomize the variables you have chosen. You can use either the observed mean, median, or mode or a specified value as a cut point. Cases with values less than the cut point are assigned to one group, and cases with values greater than or equal to the cut point are assigned to another group. One test is performed for each cut point chosen.

## Runs Test Options

**Figure 27.9   Runs Test Options dialog box**

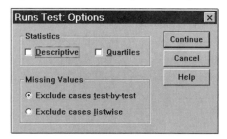

**Statistics.** You can choose one or both of the following summary statistics:

- **Descriptive.** Displays the mean, standard deviation, minimum, maximum, and number of nonmissing cases.
- **Quartiles.** Displays values corresponding to the 25th, 50th, and 75th percentiles.

**Missing Values.** Controls the treatment of missing values.

- **Exclude cases test-by-test.** When several tests are specified, each test is evaluated separately for missing values.
- **Exclude cases listwise.** Cases with missing values for any variable are excluded from all analyses.

## NPAR TESTS Command Additional Features (Runs Test)

The SPSS command language also allows you to:

- Specify different cut points for different variables (with the RUNS subcommand).
- Test the same variable against different custom cut points (with the RUNS subcommand).

See the *SPSS Base Syntax Reference Guide* for complete syntax information.

# One-Sample Kolmogorov-Smirnov Test

The One-Sample Kolmogorov-Smirnov Test procedure compares the observed cumulative distribution function for a variable with a specified theoretical distribution, which may be normal, uniform, or Poisson. The Kolmogorov-Smirnov Z is computed from the largest difference (in absolute value) between the observed and theoretical cumulative distribution functions. This goodness-of-fit test tests whether the observations could reasonably have come from the specified distribution.

**Example.** Many parametric tests require normally distributed variables. The one-sample Kolmogorov-Smirnov test can be used to test that a variable, such as *income,* is normally distributed.

**Statistics.** Mean, standard deviation, minimum, maximum, number of nonmissing cases, and quartiles.

**Data.** Use quantitative variables (interval or ratio level of measurement).

**Assumptions.** The Kolmogorov-Smirnov test assumes that the parameters of the test distribution are specified in advance. This procedure estimates the parameters from the sample. The sample mean and sample standard deviation are the parameters for a normal distribution, the sample minimum and maximum values define the range of the uniform distribution, and the sample mean is the parameter for the Poisson distribution.

**Related procedures.** When the parameters of the test distribution are estimated from the sample, the distribution of the test statistic changes. Tests for normality that make this correction are available using the Explore procedure. Also, see "NPAR TESTS Command Additional Features (One-Sample Kolmogorov-Smirnov Test)" on p. 290.

# Sample Output

**Figure 27.10    One-Sample Kolmogorov-Smirnov Test output**

One-Sample Kolmogorov-Smirnov Test

|  |  | Income |
|---|---|---|
| N |  | 20 |
| Normal Parameters [1,2] | Mean | 56250.00 |
|  | Std. Deviation | 45146.40 |
| Most Extreme Differences | Absolute | .170 |
|  | Positive | .170 |
|  | Negative | -.164 |
| Kolmogorov-Smirnov Z |  | .760 |
| Asymptotic Significance (2-tailed) |  | .611 |

[1.] Test Distribution is Normal

[2.] Calculated from data

# To Obtain a One-Sample Kolmogorov-Smirnov Test

▶    From the menus choose:

Statistics
  Nonparametric Tests
    1-Sample K-S...

**Figure 27.11   One-Sample Kolmogorov-Smirnov Test dialog box**

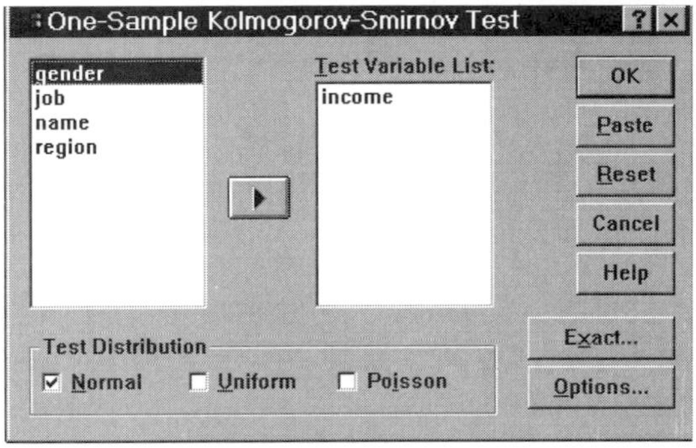

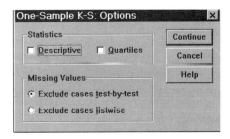

▶   Select one or more numeric test variables. Each variable produces a separate test.

Optionally, you can click *Options* for descriptive statistics, quartiles, and control of the treatment of missing data.

# One-Sample Kolmogorov-Smirnov Test Options

**Figure 27.12   One-Sample K-S Options dialog box**

**Statistics.** You can choose one or both of the following summary statistics:

- **Descriptive.** Displays the mean, standard deviation, minimum, maximum, and number of nonmissing cases.
- **Quartiles.** Displays values corresponding to the 25th, 50th, and 75th percentiles.

**Missing Values.** Controls the treatment of missing values.

- **Exclude cases test-by-test.** When several tests are specified, each test is evaluated separately for missing values.
- **Exclude cases listwise.** Cases with missing values for any variable are excluded from all analyses.

### NPAR TESTS Command Additional Features (One-Sample Kolmogorov-Smirnov Test)

The SPSS command language also allows you to:

- Specify the parameters of the test distribution (with the K-S subcommand).

See the *SPSS Base System Syntax Reference Guide* for complete syntax information.

# Two-Independent-Samples Tests

The Two-Independent-Samples Tests procedure compares two groups of cases on one variable.

**Example.** New dental braces have been developed that are intended to be more comfortable, to look better, and to provide more rapid progress in realigning teeth. To find out if the new braces have to be worn as long as the old braces, 10 children are randomly chosen to wear the old braces, and another 10 are chosen to wear the new braces. From the Mann-Whitney *U* test, you might find that, on average, those with the new braces did not have to wear the braces as long as those with the old braces.

**Statistics.** Mean, standard deviation, minimum, maximum, number of nonmissing cases, and quartiles. Tests: Mann-Whitney *U*, Moses extreme reactions, Kolmogorov-Smirnov *Z*, Wald-Wolfowitz runs.

**Data.** Use numeric variables that can be ordered.

**Assumptions.** Use independent, random samples. The Mann-Whitney *U* test requires that the two samples tested are similar in shape.

**Related procedures.** If you are performing a Mann-Whitney *U* test, use the Explore procedure to verify that the samples are similar in shape. If you have more than two samples, use the K Independent Samples Tests procedure. If the samples come from normal distributions with equal population variances, use the Independent-Samples T Test procedure.

# Sample Output

**Figure 27.13   Two-Independent-Samples output**

Ranks

| | | | N | Mean Rank | Sum of Ranks |
|---|---|---|---|---|---|
| Time Worn in Days | Type of Braces | Old Braces | 10 | 14.10 | 141.00 |
| | | New Braces | 10 | 6.90 | 69.00 |
| | | Total | 20 | | |

Test Statistics [2]

| | Time Worn in Days |
|---|---|
| Mann-Whitney U | 14.000 |
| Wilcoxon W | 69.000 |
| Z | -2.721 |
| Asymptotic Significance (2-tailed) | .007 |
| Exact Significance [2*(1-tailed Sig.)] | .005 [1] |

[1.] Not corrected for ties.

[2.] Grouping Variable: Type of Braces

# To Obtain Two-Independent-Samples Tests

From the menus choose:

Statistics
  Nonparametric Tests
    2 Independent Samples...

Figure 27.14   Two-Independent-Samples Tests dialog box

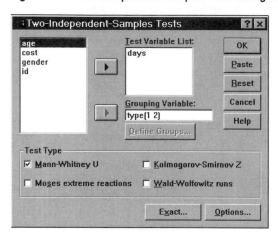

▶    Select one or more numeric variables.

▶    Select a grouping variable and click *Define Groups* to split the file into two groups or samples.

## Two-Independent-Samples Test Types

**Test Type.** Four tests are available to test whether two independent samples (groups) come from the same population.

The **Mann-Whitney *U* test** is the most popular of the two-independent-samples tests. It is equivalent to the Wilcoxon rank sum test and the Kruskal-Wallis test for two groups. Mann-Whitney tests that two sampled populations are equivalent in location. The observations from both groups are combined and ranked, with the average rank assigned in the case of ties. The number of ties should be small relative to the total number of observations. If the populations are identical in location, the ranks should be randomly mixed between the two samples. The number of times a score from group 1 precedes a score from group 2 and the number of times a score from group 2 precedes a score from group 1 are calculated. The Mann-Whitney *U* statistic is the smaller of these two numbers. The Wilcoxon rank sum *W* statistic, also displayed, is the rank sum of the smaller sample. If both samples have the same number of observations, *W* is the rank sum of the group named first in the Two-Independent-Samples Define Groups dialog box.

The **Kolmogorov-Smirnov *Z* test** and the **Wald-Wolfowitz runs test** are more general tests that detect differences in both the locations and the shapes of the distributions. The Kolmogorov-Smirnov test is based on the maximum absolute difference between the observed cumulative distribution functions for both samples. When this difference is significantly large, the two distributions are considered different. The Wald-Wolfowitz runs test combines and ranks the observations from both groups. If the two samples are from the same population, the two groups should be randomly scattered throughout the ranking.

The **Moses extreme reactions test** assumes that the experimental variable will affect some subjects in one direction and other subjects in the opposite direction. It tests for extreme responses compared to a control group. This test focuses on the span of the control group and is a measure of how much extreme values in the experimental group influence the span when combined with the control group. The control group is defined by the group 1 value in the Two-Independent-Samples Define Groups dialog box. Observations from both groups are combined and ranked. The span of the control group is computed as the difference between the ranks of the largest and smallest values in the control group plus 1. Because chance outliers can easily distort the range of the span, 5% of the control cases are trimmed automatically from each end.

## Two-Independent-Samples Tests Define Groups

Figure 27.15    Two-Independent-Samples Define Groups dialog box

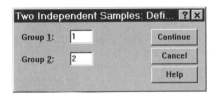

To split the file into two groups or samples, enter an integer value for group 1 and another for group 2. Cases with other values are excluded from the analysis.

## Two-Independent-Samples Tests Options

Figure 27.16    Two-Independent-Samples Options dialog box

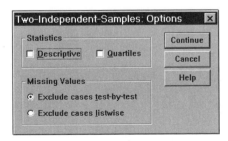

**Statistics.** You can choose one or both of the following summary statistics:

- **Descriptive.** Displays the mean, standard deviation, minimum, maximum, and the number of nonmissing cases.
- **Quartiles.** Displays values corresponding to the 25th, 50th, and 75th percentiles.

**Missing Values.** Controls the treatment of missing values.

- **Exclude cases test-by-test.** When several tests are specified, each test is evaluated separately for missing values.
- **Exclude cases listwise.** Cases with missing values for any variable are excluded from all analyses.

## NPAR TESTS Command Additional Features (Two Independent Samples)

The SPSS command language also allows you to:

- Specify the number of cases to be trimmed for the Moses test (with the MOSES sub-command).

See the *SPSS Base Syntax Reference Guide* for complete syntax information.

# Tests for Several Independent Samples

The Tests for Several Independent Samples procedure compares two or more groups of cases on one variable.

**Example.** Do three brands of 100-watt lightbulbs differ in the average time the bulbs will burn? From the Kruskal-Wallis one-way analysis of variance, you might learn that the three brands do differ in average lifetime.

**Statistics.** Mean, standard deviation, minimum, maximum, number of nonmissing cases, and quartiles. Tests: Kruskal-Wallis $H$, median.

**Data.** Use numeric variables that can be ordered.

**Assumptions.** Use independent, random samples. The Kruskal-Wallis $H$ test requires that the samples tested be similar in shape.

**Related procedures.** If you are performing a Kruskal-Wallis $H$ test, use the Explore procedure to verify that the samples are similar in shape. If the samples come from normal distributions with equal population variances, use the One-Way ANOVA procedure.

# Sample Output

**Figure 27.17  Tests for Several Independent Samples output**

Ranks

|  |  |  | N | Mean Rank |
|---|---|---|---|---|
| Hours | Brand | Brand A | 10 | 15.20 |
|  |  | Brand B | 10 | 25.50 |
|  |  | Brand C | 10 | 5.80 |
|  |  | Total | 30 |  |

Test Statistics [1,2]

|  | Hours |
|---|---|
| Chi-Square | 25.061 |
| df | 2 |
| Asymptotic Significance | .000 |

[1.] Kruskal Wallis Test

[2.] Grouping Variable: Brand

# To Obtain Tests for Several Independent Samples

▶  From the menus choose:

Statistics
  Nonparametric Tests
    K Independent Samples...

**Figure 27.18   Tests for Several Independent Samples dialog box**

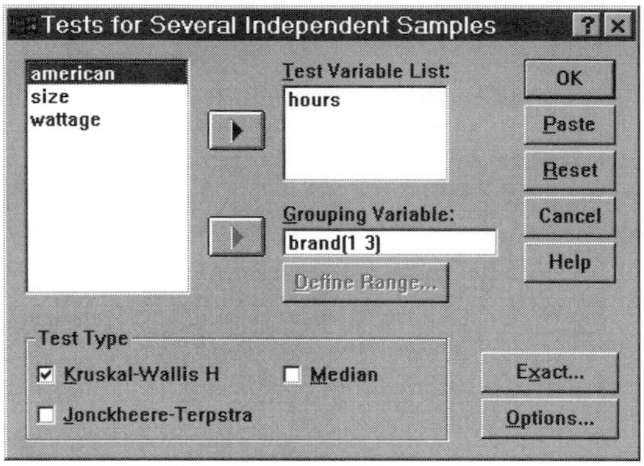

▶  Select one or more numeric variables.

▶  Select a grouping variable and click *Define Range* to specify minimum and maximum integer values for the grouping variable.

## Several Independent Samples Test Types

**Test Type.** Three tests are available to determine if several independent samples come from the same population.

The Kruskal-Wallis *H* test, the median test, and the Jonckheere-Terpstra test all test whether several independent samples are from the same population. The **Kruskal-Wallis *H* test**, an extension of the Mann-Whitney *U* test, is the nonparametric analog of one-way analysis of variance and detects differences in distribution location. The **median test**, which is a more general test but not as powerful, detects distributional differences in location and shape. The Kruskal-Wallis *H* test and the median test assume that there is no *a priori* ordering of the *k* populations from which the samples are drawn. When there *is* a natural *a priori* ordering (ascending or descending) of the *k* populations, the **Jonckheere-Terpstra test** is more powerful. For example, the *k* populations might represent *k* increasing temperatures. The hypothesis that different temperatures produce the same response distribution is tested against the alternative that as the temperature increases, the magnitude of the response increases. Here the alternative hypothesis is ordered; therefore, Jonckheere-Terpstra is the most appropriate test to use. The Jonckheere-Terpstra test is available only if you have installed SPSS Exact Tests.

## Tests for Several Independent Samples Define Range

Figure 27.19   Several Independent Samples Define dialog box

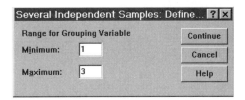

To define the range, enter integer values for minimum and maximum that correspond to the lowest and highest categories of the grouping variable. Cases with values outside of the bounds are excluded. For example, if you specify a minimum value of 1 and a maximum value of 3, only the integer values of 1 through 3 are used. The minimum value must be less than the maximum value, and both values must be specified.

## Tests for Several Independent Samples Options

Figure 27.20   Several Independent Samples Options dialog box

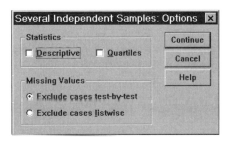

**Statistics.** You can choose one or both of the following summary statistics:

- **Descriptive.** Displays the mean, standard deviation, minimum, maximum, and the number of nonmissing cases.
- **Quartiles.** Displays values corresponding to the 25th, 50th, and 75th percentiles.

**Missing Values.** Controls the treatment of missing values.

- **Exclude cases test-by-test.** When several tests are specified, each test is evaluated separately for missing values.
- **Exclude cases listwise.** Cases with missing values for any variable are excluded from all analyses.

## NPAR TESTS Command Additional Features (K Independent Samples)

The SPSS command language also allows you to:

- Specify a value other than the observed median for the median test (with the MEDIAN subcommand).

See the *SPSS Base Syntax Reference Guide* for complete syntax information.

# Two-Related-Samples Tests

The Two-Related-Samples Tests procedure compares the distributions of two variables.

**Example.** In general, do families receive the asking price when they sell their homes? By applying the Wilcoxon signed-rank test to data for 10 homes, you might learn that seven families receive less than the asking price, one family receives more than the asking price, and two families receive the asking price.

**Statistics.** Mean, standard deviation, minimum, maximum, number of nonmissing cases, and quartiles. Tests: Wilcoxon signed-rank, sign, McNemar.

**Data.** Use numeric variables that can be ordered.

**Assumptions.** Although no particular distributions are assumed for the two variables, the population distribution of the paired differences is assumed to be symmetric.

**Related procedures.** If the samples come from normal distributions, use the Paired-Samples T Test procedure.

# Sample Output

**Figure 27.21   Two-Related-Samples output**

Ranks

|  |  | N | Mean Rank | Sum of Ranks |
|---|---|---|---|---|
| Asking Price - Sale Price | Negative Ranks | 7[1] | 4.93 | 34.50 |
|  | Positive Ranks | 1[2] | 1.50 | 1.50 |
|  | Ties | 2[3] |  |  |
|  | Total | 10 |  |  |

[1]. Asking Price < Sale Price

[2]. Asking Price > Sale Price

[3]. Asking Price = Sale Price

**Figure 27.21 Two-Related Samples output (continued)**

Test Statistics [2]

|  | Asking Price<br>- Sale Price |
|---|---|
| Z | -2.313[1] |
| Asymptotic<br>Significance<br>(2-tailed) | .021 |

[1.] Based on positive ranks

[2.] Wilcoxon Signed Ranks
Test

# To Obtain Two-Related-Samples Tests

▶ From the menus choose:

Statistics
  Nonparametric Tests
    2 Related Samples...

**Figure 27.22   Two-Related-Samples Tests dialog box**

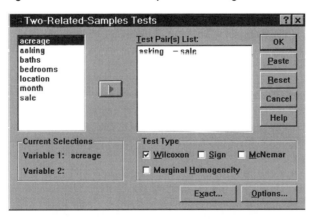

▶ Select one or more pairs of variables, as follows:

• Click each of two variables. The first variable appears in the Current Selections group as *Variable 1*, and the second appears as *Variable 2*.

• After you have selected a pair of variables, click the arrow button to move the pair into the Test Pair(s) list. You may select more pairs of variables. To remove a pair of variables from the analysis, select a pair in the Test Pair(s) list and click the arrow button.

## Two-Related-Samples Test Types

**Test Type.** The tests in this section compare the distributions of two related variables. The appropriate test to use depends on the type of data.

If your data are continuous, use the sign test or the Wilcoxon signed-rank test. The **sign test** computes the differences between the two variables for all cases and classifies the differences as either positive, negative, or tied. If the two variables are similarly distributed, the number of positive and negative differences will not differ significantly. The **Wilcoxon signed-rank test** considers information about both the sign of the differences and the magnitude of the differences between pairs. Because the Wilcoxon signed-rank test incorporates more information about the data, it is more powerful than the sign test.

If your data are binary, use the **McNemar test**. This test is typically used in a repeated measures situation, in which each subject's response is elicited twice, once before and once after a specified event occurs. The McNemar test determines whether the initial response rate (before the event) equals the final response rate (after the event). This test is useful for detecting changes in responses due to experimental intervention in before-and-after designs.

If your data are categorical, use the **marginal homogeneity test**. This is an extension of the McNemar test from binary response to multinomial response. It tests for changes in response using the chi-square distribution and is useful for detecting response changes due to experimental intervention in before-and-after designs. The marginal homogeneity test is available only if you have installed SPSS Exact Tests.

## Two-Related-Samples Tests Options

Figure 27.23    Two-Related-Samples Options dialog box

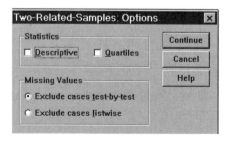

**Statistics.** You can choose one or both of the following summary statistics:

- **Descriptive.** Displays the mean, standard deviation, minimum, maximum, and the number of nonmissing cases.
- **Quartiles.** Displays values corresponding to the 25th, 50th, and 75th percentiles.

**Missing Values.** Controls the treatment of missing values.

- **Exclude cases test-by-test.** When several tests are specified, each test is evaluated separately for missing values.
- **Exclude cases listwise.** Cases with missing values for any variable are excluded from all analyses.

## NPAR TESTS Command Additional Features (Two Related Samples)

The SPSS command language also allows you to:

- Test a variable with each variable on a list.

See the *SPSS Base Syntax Reference Guide* for complete syntax information.

# Tests for Several Related Samples

The Tests for Several Related Samples procedure compares the distributions of two or more variables.

**Example.** Does the public associate different amounts of prestige with a doctor, a lawyer, a police officer, and a teacher? Ten people are asked to rank these four occupations in order of prestige. Friedman's test indicates that the public does in fact associate different amounts of prestige with these four professions.

**Statistics.** Mean, standard deviation, minimum, maximum, number of nonmissing cases, and quartiles. Tests: Friedman, Kendall's $W$, and Cochran's $Q$.

**Data.** Use numeric variables that can be ordered.

**Assumptions.** Nonparametric tests do not require assumptions about the shape of the underlying distribution. Use dependent, random samples.

**Related procedures.** If the variances of all of your variables are equal and their covariances are 0, use the Repeated Measures ANOVA procedure, available in the SPSS Advanced Statistics option.

# Sample Output

**Figure 27.24   Tests for Several Related Samples output**

Ranks

|  | Mean Rank |
|---|---|
| Doctor | 1.50 |
| Lawyer | 2.50 |
| Police | 3.40 |
| Teacher | 2.60 |

Test Statistics [1]

| N | 10 |
|---|---|
| Chi-Square | 10.920 |
| df | 3 |
| Asymptotic Significance | .012 |

[1.] Friedman Test

# To Obtain Tests for Several Related Samples

From the menus choose:

Statistics
  Nonparametric Tests
    K Related Samples...

**Figure 27.25   Tests for Several Related Samples dialog box**

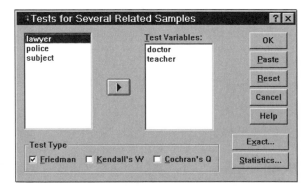

▶   Select two or more numeric test variables.

## Tests for Several Related Samples Test Types

**Test Type.** Three tests are available to compare the distributions of several related variables.

The **Friedman test** is the nonparametric equivalent of a one-sample repeated measures design or a two-way analysis of variance with one observation per cell. Friedman tests the null hypothesis that $k$ related variables come from the same population. For each case, the $k$ variables are ranked from 1 to $k$. The test statistic is based on these ranks. **Kendall's $W$** is a normalization of the Friedman statistic. Kendall's $W$ is interpretable as the coefficient of concordance, which is a measure of agreement among raters. Each case is a judge or rater and each variable is an item or person being judged. For each variable, the sum of ranks is computed. Kendall's $W$ ranges between 0 (no agreement) and 1 (complete agreement). **Cochran's $Q$** is identical to the Friedman test but is applicable when all responses are binary. It is an extension of the McNemar test to the $k$-sample situation. Cochran's $Q$ tests the hypothesis that several related dichotomous variables have the same mean. The variables are measured on the same individual or on matched individuals.

## Tests for Several Related Samples Statistics

**Figure 27.26    Several Related Samples Statistics dialog box**

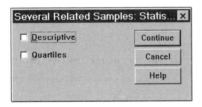

- **Descriptive.** Displays the mean, standard deviation, minimum, maximum, and the number of nonmissing cases.
- **Quartiles.** Displays values corresponding to the 25th, 50th, and 75th percentiles.

## NPAR TESTS Command Additional Features (K Related Samples)

See the *SPSS Base Syntax Reference Guide* for complete syntax information.

# 28 Multiple Response Analysis

Two procedures are available for analyzing multiple dichotomy and multiple category sets. The Multiple Response Frequencies procedure displays frequency tables. The Multiple Response Crosstabs procedure displays two- and three-dimensional crosstabulations. Before using either procedure, you must define multiple response sets.

**Example.** This example illustrates the use of multiple response items in a market research survey. The data are fictitious and should not be interpreted as real. An airline might survey passengers flying a particular route to evaluate competing carriers. In this example, American Airlines wants to know about its passengers' use of other airlines on the Chicago–New York route and the relative importance of schedule and service in selecting an airline. The flight attendant hands each passenger a brief questionnaire upon boarding. The first question reads: Circle all airlines you have flown at least once in the last six months on this route—American, United, TWA, USAir, Other. This is a multiple response question, since the passenger can circle more than one response. However, this question cannot be coded directly because an SPSS variable can have only one value for each case. You must use several variables to map responses to each question. There are two ways to do this. One is to define a variable corresponding to each of the choices (for example, American, United, TWA, USAir, and Other). If the passenger circles United, the variable *united* is assigned a code of 1, otherwise 0. This is the **multiple dichotomy method** of mapping variables. The other way to map responses is the **multiple category method**, in which you estimate the maximum number of possible responses to the question and set up the same number of variables, with codes used to specify the airline flown. By perusing a sample of questionnaires, you might discover that no user has flown more than three different airlines on this route in the last six months. Further, you find that due to the deregulation of airlines, 10 other airlines are named in the Other category. Using the multiple category method, you would define three variables, each coded as 1 = *american*, 2 = *united*, 3 = *twa*, 4 = *usair*, 5 = *delta*, and so on. If a given passenger circles American and TWA, the first variable has a code of 1, the second has a code of 3, and the third has a missing-value code. Another passenger might have circled American and entered Delta. Thus, the first variable has a code of 1, the second has a code of 5, and the third has a missing-value code. If you use the multiple dichotomy method, on the other hand, you end up with 14 separate variables. Although either method of mapping is feasible for this survey, the method you choose depends on the distribution of responses.

# Multiple Response Define Sets

The Define Multiple Response Sets procedure groups elementary variables into multiple dichotomy and multiple category sets, for which you can obtain frequency tables and crosstabulations. You can define up to 20 multiple response sets. Each set must have a unique name. To remove a set, highlight it on the list of multiple response sets and click *Remove*. To change a set, highlight it on the list, modify any set definition characteristics, and click *Change*.

You can code your elementary variables as dichotomies or categories. To use dichotomous variables, select *Dichotomies* to create a multiple dichotomy set. Enter an integer value for Counted value. Each variable having at least one occurrence of the counted value becomes a category of the multiple dichotomy set. Select *Categories* to create a multiple category set having the same range of values as the component variables. Enter integer values for the minimum and maximum values of the range for categories of the multiple category set. SPSS totals each distinct integer value in the inclusive range across all component variables. Empty categories are not tabulated.

Each multiple response set must be assigned a unique name of up to seven characters. SPSS prefixes a dollar sign ($) to the name you assign. You cannot use the following reserved names: *casenum*, *sysmis*, *jdate*, *date*, *time*, *length*, and *width*. The name of the multiple response set exists only for use in multiple response procedures. You cannot refer to multiple response set names in other procedures. Optionally, you can enter a descriptive variable label for the multiple response set. The label can be up to 40 characters long.

## To Define Multiple Response Sets

▶ From the menus choose:

Statistics
  Multiple Response
    Define Sets...

**Figure 28.1    Define Multiple Response Sets dialog box**

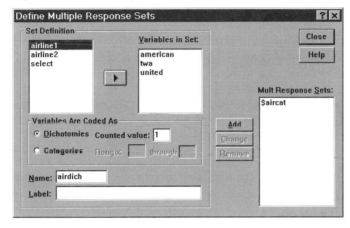

▶ Select two or more variables.

▶ If your variables are coded as dichotomies, indicate which value you want to have counted. If your variables are coded as categories, define the range of the categories.

▶ Enter a unique name for each multiple response set.

▶ Click *Add* to add the multiple response set to the list of defined sets.

# Multiple Response Frequencies

The Multiple Response Frequencies procedure produces frequency tables for multiple response sets. You must first define one or more multiple response sets (see "Multiple Response Define Sets" on p. 306).

For multiple dichotomy sets, category names shown in the output come from variable labels defined for elementary variables in the group. If the variable labels are not defined, variable names are used as labels. For multiple category sets, category labels come from the value labels of the first variable in the group. If categories missing for the first variable are present for other variables in the group, define a value label for the missing categories.

**Missing Values.** Cases with missing values are excluded on a table-by-table basis. Alternatively, you can choose one or both of the following:

- **Exclude cases listwise within dichotomies.** Excludes cases with missing values for any variable from the tabulation of the multiple dichotomy set. This applies only to multiple response sets defined as dichotomy sets. By default, a case is considered missing for a multiple dichotomy set if none of its component variables contains the counted value. Cases with missing values for some, but not all, variables are included in the tabulations of the group if at least one variable contains the counted value.

- **Exclude cases listwise within categories.** Excludes cases with missing values for any variable from tabulation of the multiple category set. This applies only to multiple response sets defined as category sets. By default, a case is considered missing for a multiple category set only if none of its components has valid values within the defined range.

**Example.** Each SPSS variable created from a survey question is an elementary variable. To analyze a multiple response item, you must combine the variables into one of two types of multiple response sets: a multiple dichotomy set or a multiple category set. For example, if an airline survey asked which of three airlines (American, United, TWA) you have flown in the last six months and you used dichotomous variables and defined a **multiple dichotomy set**, each of the three variables in the set would become a category of the group variable. The counts and percentages for the three airlines are displayed in one frequency table. If you discover that no respondent mentioned more than two airlines, you could create two variables, each having three codes, one for each airline. If you define a **multiple category set**, the values are tabulated by adding the same codes in the elementary variables together. The resulting set of values is the same as those for each of the elementary variables. For example, 30 responses for United are the sum of the 5 United responses for airline 1 and the 25 United responses for airline 2. The counts and percentages for the three airlines are displayed in one frequency table.

**Statistics.** Frequency tables displaying counts, percentages of responses, percentages of cases, number of valid cases, and number of missing cases.

**Data.** Use multiple response sets.

**Assumptions.** The counts and percentages provide a useful description for data from any distribution.

**Related procedures.** The Define Multiple Response Sets procedure allows you to define multiple response sets.

## Sample Output

**Figure 28.2  Multiple Response Frequencies output**

```
Group $AIRDICH
     (Value tabulated = 1)

                                                      Pct of  Pct of
Dichotomy label                    Name     Count  Responses  Cases

American                           AMERICAN    75     67.6     92.6
TWA                                TWA          6      5.4      7.4
United                             UNITED      30     27.0     37.0
                                           -------   -----    -----
                   Total responses            111    100.0    137.0

19 missing cases;   81 valid cases
```

## To Obtain Multiple Response Frequencies

▶  From the menus choose:

Statistics
  Multiple Response
    Frequencies...

**Figure 28.3  Multiple Response Frequencies dialog box**

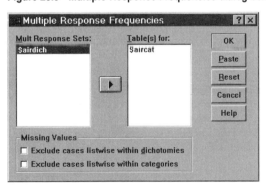

▶  Select one or more multiple response sets.

# Multiple Response Crosstabs

The Multiple Response Crosstabs procedure crosstabulates defined multiple response sets, elementary variables, or a combination. You can also obtain cell percentages based on cases or responses, modify the handling of missing values, or get paired crosstabulations. You must first define one or more multiple response sets (see "To Define Multiple Response Sets" on p. 307).

For multiple dichotomy sets, category names shown in the output come from variable labels defined for elementary variables in the group. If the variable labels are not defined, variable names are used as labels. For multiple category sets, category labels come from the value labels of the first variable in the group. If categories missing for the first variable are present for other variables in the group, define a value label for the missing categories. SPSS displays category labels for columns on three lines, with up to eight characters per line. To avoid splitting words, you can reverse row and column items or redefine labels.

**Example.** Both multiple dichotomy and multiple category sets can be crosstabulated with other variables in this procedure. An airline passenger survey asks passengers for the following information: Circle all of the following airlines you have flown at least once in the last six months (American, United, TWA). Which is more important in selecting a flight—schedule or service? Select only one. After entering the data as dichotomies or multiple categories and combining them into a set, you can crosstabulate the airline choices with the question involving service or schedule.

**Statistics.** Crosstabulation with cell, row, column, and total counts, and cell, row, column, and total percentages. The cell percentages can be based on cases or responses.

**Data.** Use multiple response sets or numeric categorical variables.

**Assumptions.** The counts and percentages provide a useful description of data from any distribution.

**Related procedures.** The Define Multiple Response Sets procedure allows you to define multiple response sets.

# Sample Output

**Figure 28.4    Multiple Response Crosstabs output**

```
                        SELECT

                 Count   |Schedule Service
                         |                     Row
                         |                     Total
                         |    0  |    1  |
       $AIRCAT   --------+--------+--------+
                    1  |    41  |    34  |    75
         American       |       |       |    92.6
                        +--------+--------+
                    2  |    27  |     3  |    30
         United         |       |       |    37.0
                        +--------+--------+
                    3  |     3  |     3  |     6
         TWA            |       |       |    7.4
                        +--------+--------+
                 Column     44      37      01
                 Total     54.3    45.7   100.0

Percents and totals based on respondents

81 valid cases;  19 missing cases
```

# To Obtain Multiple Response Crosstabs

▶ From the menus choose:

Statistics
  Multiple Response
    Crosstabs...

**Figure 28.5    Multiple Response Crosstabs dialog box**

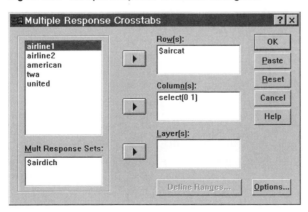

▶ Select one or more numeric variables or multiple response sets for each dimension of the crosstabulation.

▶ Define the range of each elementary variable.

Optionally, you can obtain a two-way crosstabulation for each category of a control variable or multiple response set. Select one or more items for the Layer(s) list.

### Multiple Response Crosstabs Define Variable Ranges

Figure 28.6    Multiple Response Crosstabs Define Variable Range dialog box

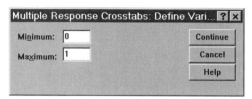

Value ranges must be defined for any elementary variable in the crosstabulation. Enter the integer minimum and maximum category values that you want to tabulate. Categories outside the range are excluded from analysis. Values within the inclusive range are assumed to be integers (non-integers are truncated).

### Multiple Response Crosstabs Options

Figure 28.7    Multiple Response Crosstabs Options dialog box

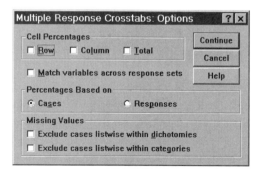

**Cell Percentages.** Cell counts are always displayed. You can choose to display row percentages, column percentages, and two-way table (total) percentages.

**Percentages Based on.** You can base cell percentages on cases (or respondents). This is not available if you select *Match variables across response sets*. You can also base cell percentages on responses. For multiple dichotomy sets, the number of responses is equal to the number of counted values across cases. For multiple category sets, the number of responses is the number of values in the defined range.

**Missing Values.** You can choose one or both of the following:

- **Exclude cases listwise within dichotomies.** Excludes cases with missing values for any variable from the tabulation of the multiple dichotomy set. This applies only to multiple response sets defined as dichotomy sets. By default, a case is considered missing for a multiple dichotomy set if none of its component variables contains the counted value. Cases with missing values for some, but not all, variables are included in the tabulations of the group if at least one variable contains the counted value.

- **Exclude cases listwise within categories.** Excludes cases with missing values for any variable from tabulation of the multiple category set. This applies only to multiple response sets defined as category sets. By default, a case is considered missing for a multiple category set only if none of its components has valid values within the defined range.

By default, when crosstabulating two multiple category sets, SPSS tabulates each variable in the first group with each variable in the second group and sums the counts for each cell; therefore, some responses can appear more than once in a table. You can choose the following option:

**Match variables across response sets.** Pairs the first variable in the first group with the first variable in the second group, and so on. If you select this option, SPSS bases cell percentages on responses rather than respondents. Pairing is not available for multiple dichotomy sets or elementary variables.

## MULT RESPONSE Command Additional Features

The SPSS command language also allows you to:

- Obtain crosstabulation tables with up to five dimensions (with the BY subcommand).
- Change output formatting options, including suppression of value labels (with the FORMAT subcommand).

See the *SPSS Base Syntax Reference Guide* for complete syntax information.

# 29 Reporting Results

Case listings and descriptive statistics are basic tools for studying and presenting data. You can obtain case listings with the Data Editor or the Summarize procedure, frequency counts and descriptive statistics with the Frequencies procedure, and subpopulation statistics with the Means procedure. Each of these uses a format designed to make information clear. If you want to display the information in a different format, Report Summaries in Rows and Report Summaries in Columns give you the control you need over data presentation.

## Report Summaries in Rows

Report Summaries in Rows produces reports in which different summary statistics are laid out in rows. Case listings are also available, with or without summary statistics.

**Example.** A company with a chain of retail stores keeps records of employee information, including salary, job tenure, and the store and division where each employee works. You could generate a report that provides individual employee information (listing) broken down by store and division (break variables), with summary statistics (for example, mean salary) for each store, division, and division within each store.

**Data Columns.** Lists the report variables for which you want case listings or summary statistics and controls the display format of data columns.

**Break Columns.** Lists optional break variables that divide the report into groups and controls the summary statistics and display formats of break columns. For multiple break variables, there will be a separate group for each category of each break variable within categories of the preceding break variable in the list. Break variables should be discrete categorical variables that divide cases into a limited number of meaningful categories. Individual values of each break variable appear, sorted, in a separate column to the left of all data columns.

**Report.** Controls overall report characteristics, including overall summary statistics, display of missing values, page numbering, and titles.

**Display cases**. Displays the actual values (or value labels) of the data column variables for every case. This produces a listing report, which can be much longer than a summary report.

**Preview**. Displays only the first page of the report. This option is useful for previewing the format of your report without processing the whole report.

**Data are already sorted**. For reports with break variables, the data file must be sorted by break variable values before generating the report. If your data file is already sorted by values of the break variables, you can save processing time by selecting this option. This option is particularly useful after running a preview report.

## Sample Output

**Figure 29.1   Combined report with case listings and summary statistics**

| Division | Age | Tenure in Company | Tenure in Grade | Salary--Annual |
|----------|-----|---------|-------|----------------|
| Carpeting | 27.00 | 3.67 | 2.17 | $9,200 |
| | 22.00 | 3.92 | 3.08 | $10,900 |
| | 23.00 | 3.92 | 3.08 | $10,900 |
| | 24.00 | 4.00 | 3.25 | $10,000 |
| | 30.00 | 4.08 | 3.08 | $10,000 |
| | 27.00 | 4.33 | 3.17 | $10,000 |
| | 33.00 | 2.67 | 2.67 | $9,335 |
| | 33.00 | 3.75 | 3.25 | $10,000 |
| | 44.00 | 4.83 | 4.33 | $15,690 |
| | 36.00 | 3.83 | 3.25 | $10,000 |
| | 35.00 | 3.50 | 3.00 | $15,520 |
| | 35.00 | 6.00 | 5.33 | $19,500 |
| Mean | 30.75 | 4.04 | 3.31 | $11,754 |
| Appliances | 21.00 | 2.67 | 2.67 | $8,700 |
| | 26.00 | 2.92 | 2.08 | $8,000 |
| | 32.00 | 2.92 | 2.92 | $8,900 |
| | 33.00 | 3.42 | 2.92 | $8,900 |
| | 34.00 | 5.08 | 4.50 | $15,300 |
| | 24.00 | 3.17 | 3.17 | $8,975 |
| | 42.00 | 6.50 | 6.50 | $18,000 |
| | 30.00 | 2.67 | 2.67 | $7,500 |
| | 38.00 | 5.00 | 4.42 | $28,300 |
| Mean | 31.11 | 3.81 | 3.54 | $12,508 |

## To Obtain a Summary Report: Summaries in Rows

▶ From the menus choose:

Statistics
 Summarize
  Report Summaries in Rows...

**Figure 29.2   Report Summaries in Rows dialog box**

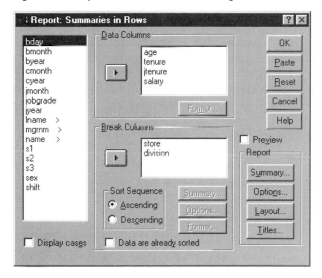

▶ Select one or more variables for Data Columns. One column in the report is generated for each variable selected.

▶ For reports sorted and displayed by subgroups, select one or more variables for Break Columns.

▶ For reports with summary statistics for subgroups defined by break variables, select the break variable in the Break Columns list and click *Summary* in the Break Columns group to specify the summary measure(s).

▶ For reports with overall summary statistics, click *Summary* in the Report group to specify the summary measure(s).

## Report Column Format

The Format dialog boxes control column titles, column width, text alignment, and the display of data values or value labels. Data Column Format controls the format of data columns on the right side of the report page. Break Format controls the format of break columns on the left side.

**Figure 29.3   Report Data Column Format dialog box**

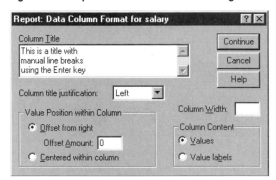

**Column Title**. For the selected variable, controls the column title. Long titles are automatically wrapped within the column. Use the Enter key to manually insert line breaks where you want titles to wrap.

**Value Position within Column**. For the selected variable, controls the alignment of data values or value labels within the column. Alignment of values or labels does not affect alignment of column headings. You can either indent the column contents by a specified number of characters or center the contents.

**Column Content**. For the selected variable, controls the display of either data values or defined value labels. Data values are always displayed for any values that do not have defined value labels. (Not available for data columns in column summary reports.)

## Report Summary Lines

The two Summary Lines dialog boxes control the display of summary statistics for break groups and for the entire report. Summary Lines controls subgroup statistics for each category defined by the break variable(s). Final Summary Lines controls overall statistics, displayed at the end of the report.

Figure 29.4   Report Summary Lines dialog box

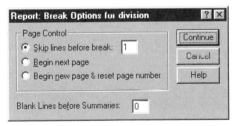

Available summary statistics are sum, mean, minimum, maximum, number of cases, percentage of cases above or below a specified value, percentage of cases within a specified range of values, standard deviation, kurtosis, variance, and skewness.

# Report Break Options

Break Options controls spacing and pagination of break category information.

Figure 29.5   Report Break Options

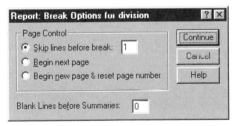

**Page Control**. Controls spacing and pagination for categories of the selected break variable. You can specify a number of blank lines between break categories or start each break category on a new page.

**Blank Lines before Summaries**. Controls the number of blank lines between break category labels or data and summary statistics. This is particularly useful for combined reports that include both individual case listings and summary statistics for break categories; in these reports, you can insert space between the case listings and the summary statistics.

# Report Options

Report Options controls the treatment and display of missing values and report page numbering.

**Figure 29.6    Report Options dialog box**

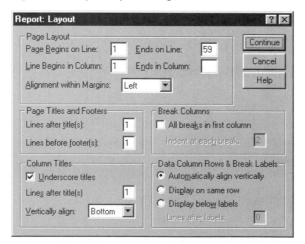

**Exclude cases with missing values listwise.** Eliminates (from the report) any case with missing values for any of the report variables.

**Missing Values Appear as.** Allows you to specify the symbol that represents missing values in the data file. The symbol can be only one character and is used to represent both system-missing and user-missing values.

**Number Pages from.** Allows you to specify a page number for the first page of the report.

# Report Layout

Report Layout controls the width and length of each report page, placement of the report on the page, and the insertion of blank lines and labels.

**Figure 29.7    Report Layout dialog box**

**Page Layout**. Controls the page margins expressed in lines (top and bottom) and characters (left and right) and report alignment within the margins.

**Page Titles and Footers**. Controls the number of lines that separate page titles and footers from the body of the report.

**Break Columns**. Controls the display of break columns. If multiple break variables are specified, they can be in separate columns or in the first column. Placing all break variables in the first column produces a narrower report.

**Column Titles**. Controls the display of column titles, including title underlining, space between titles and the body of the report, and vertical alignment of column titles.

**Data Column Rows & Break Labels.** Controls the placement of data column information (data values and/or summary statistics) in relation to the break labels at the start of each break category. The first row of data column information can start either on the same line as break category label or on a specified number of lines after the break category label. (Not available for column summary reports.)

## Report Titles

Report Titles controls the content and placement of report titles and footers. You can specify up to 10 lines of page titles and up to 10 lines of page footers, with left-justified, centered, and right-justified components on each line.

**Figure 29.8   Report Titles dialog box**

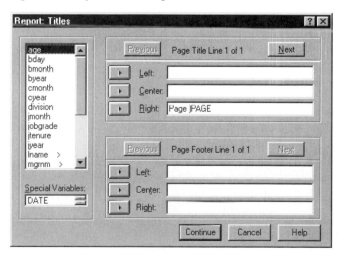

If you insert variables into titles or footers, the current value label or value of the variable is displayed in the title or footer. In titles, the value label corresponding to the value of the variable at the beginning of the page is displayed. In footers, the value label corresponding to the value of the variable at the end of the page is displayed. If there is no value label, the actual value is displayed.

**Special Variables**. The special variables *DATE* and *PAGE* allow you to insert the current date or the page number into any line of a report header or footer. If your data file contains variables named *DATE* or *PAGE*, you cannot use these variables in report titles or footers.

# Report Summaries in Columns

Report Summaries in Columns produces summary reports in which different summary statistics appear in separate columns.

**Example.** A company with a chain of retail stores keeps records of employee information, including salary, job tenure, and the division where each employee works. You could generate a report that provides summary salary statistics (for example, mean, minimum, maximum) for each division.

**Data Columns**. Lists the report variables for which you want summary statistics and controls the display format and summary statistics displayed for each variable.

**Break Columns**. Lists optional break variables that divide the report into groups and controls the display formats of break columns. For multiple break variables, there will be a separate group for each category of each break variable within categories of the preceding break variable in the list. Break variables should be discrete categorical variables that divide cases into a limited number of meaningful categories.

**Report**. Controls overall report characteristics, including display of missing values, page numbering, and titles.

**Preview**. Displays only the first page of the report. This option is useful for previewing the format of your report without processing the whole report.

**Data are already sorted**. For reports with break variables, the data file must be sorted by break variable values before generating the report. If your data file is already sorted by values of the break variables, you can save processing time by selecting this option. This option is particularly useful after running a preview report.

## Sample Output

**Figure 29.9    Summary report with summary statistics in columns**

| Division | Mean Age | Mean Annual Salary | Minimum Annual Salary | Maximum Annual Salary |
|----------|----------|--------------------|-----------------------|------------------------|
| Carpeting | 30.75 | $11,754 | $9,200 | $19,500 |
| Appliances | 31.11 | $12,508 | $7,500 | $28,300 |
| Furniture | 36.87 | $13,255 | $8,975 | $17,050 |
| Hardware | 36.20 | $17,580 | $7,450 | $22,500 |

## To Obtain a Summary Report: Summaries in Columns

▶  From the menus choose:

Statistics
  Summarize
    Report Summaries in Columns...

**Figure 29.10    Report Summaries in Columns dialog box**

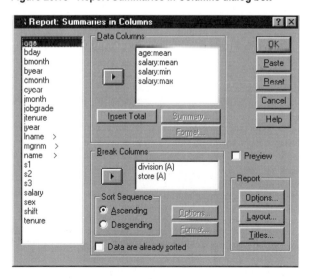

▶ Select one or more variables for Data Columns. One column in the report is generated for each variable selected.

▶ To change the summary measure for a variable, select the variable in the Data Columns list and click *Summary*.

▶ To obtain more than one summary measure for a variable, select the variable in the source list and move it into the Data Columns list multiple times, one for each summary measure you want.

▶ To display a column containing the sum, mean, ratio, or other function of existing columns, click *Insert Total*. This places a variable called *total* into the Data Columns list.

▶ For reports sorted and displayed by subgroups, select one or more variables for Break Columns.

## Report Summary Lines

Summary Lines controls the summary statistic displayed for the selected data column variable.

**Figure 29.11    Report Summary Lines dialog box**

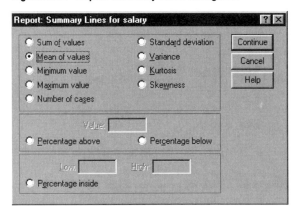

Available summary statistics are sum, mean, minimum, maximum, number of cases, percentage of cases above or below a specified value, percentage of cases within a specified range of values, standard deviation, variance, kurtosis, and skewness.

## Total Summary Column

Summary Column controls the total summary statistics that summarize two or more data columns.

Available total summary statistics are sum of columns, mean of columns, minimum, maximum, difference between values in two columns, quotient of values in one column divided by values in another column, and product of columns values multiplied together.

**Figure 29.12   Report Summary Column dialog box**

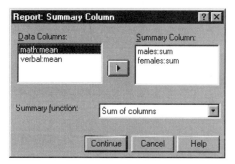

**Sum of columns.** The *total* column is the sum of the columns in the Summary Column list.

**Mean of columns**. The *total* column is the average of the columns in the Summary Column list.

**Minimum of columns**. The *total* column is the minimum of the columns in the Summary Column list.

**Maximum of columns**. The *total* column is the maximum of the columns in the Summary Column list.

**1st column - 2nd column**. The *total* column is the difference of the columns in the Summary Column list. The Summary Column list must contain exactly two columns.

**1st column / 2nd column**. The *total* column is the quotient of the columns in the Summary Column list. The Summary Column list must contain exactly two columns.

**% 1st column / 2nd column**. The *total* column is the first column's percentage of the second column in the Summary Column list. The Summary Column list must contain exactly two columns.

**Product of columns**. The *total* column is the product of the columns in the Summary Column list.

## Report Column Format

Data and break column formatting options for Report Summaries in Columns are the same as those described for Report Summaries in Rows.

## Report Break Options for Summaries in Columns

Break Options controls subtotal display, spacing, and pagination for break categories.

**Figure 29.13    Report Break Options dialog box**

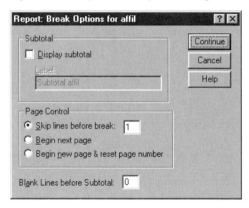

**Subtotal**. Controls the display subtotals for break categories.

**Page Control**. Controls spacing and pagination for categories of the selected break variable. You can specify a number of blank lines between break categories or start each break category on a new page.

**Blank Lines before Subtotal**. Controls the number of blank lines between break category data and subtotals.

## Report Options for Summaries in Columns

Report Options controls the display of grand totals, the display of missing values, and pagination in column summary reports.

**Figure 29.14   Report Options dialog box**

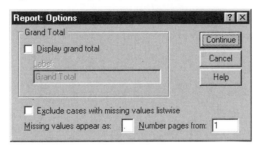

**Grand Total**. Displays and labels a grand total for each column; displayed at the bottom of the column.

**Missing values appear as.** You can exclude missing values from the report or select a single character to indicate missing values in the report.

## Report Layout for Summaries in Columns

Report layout options for Report Summaries in Columns are the same as those described for Report Summaries in Rows.

## REPORT Command Additional Features

The SPSS command language also allows you to:

- Display different summary functions in the columns of a single summary line.
- Insert summary lines into data columns for variables other than the data column variable, or for various combinations (composite functions) of summary functions.
- Use MEDIAN, MODE, FREQUENCY, and PERCENT as summary functions.
- Control more precisely the display format of summary statistics.
- Insert blank lines at various points in reports.
- Insert blank lines after every $n$th case in listing reports.

Because of the complexity of the REPORT syntax, you may find it useful, when building a new report with syntax, to approximate the report generated from the dialog boxes, copy and paste the corresponding syntax, and refine that syntax to yield the exact report that you want.

See the *SPSS Base Syntax Reference Guide* for complete syntax information.

# 30 Overview of the SPSS Chart Facility

High-resolution charts and plots are created by the procedures on the Graphs menu and by many of the procedures on the Statistics menu. This chapter provides an overview of the SPSS chart facility.

## How to Create and Modify a Chart

Before you can create a chart, you need to get your data into SPSS. You can enter the data in the Data Editor, open a previously saved SPSS data file, or read a spreadsheet, tab-delimited data file, or database file. The SPSS Tutorial has online examples of creating and modifying a chart.

### Creating the Chart

After you get your data into SPSS, you can create a chart by selecting a chart type from the Graphs menu. This opens a chart dialog box, as shown in Figure 30.1.

Figure 30.1 Chart dialog box

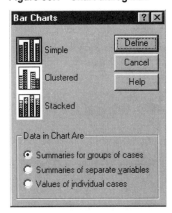

329

The dialog box contains icons for various types of charts and a list of data structures. Click *Define* to open a chart definition dialog box such as the following one.

**Figure 30.2   Chart definition dialog box**

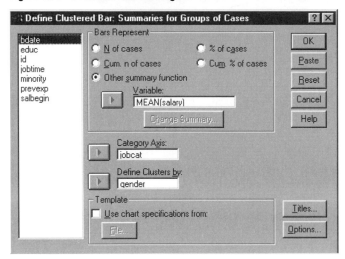

In this dialog box, you can select the variables appropriate for the chart and choose options you want. For information about the various choices, click *Help*.

The chart is displayed in the Output Navigator, as shown in Figure 30.3.

**Figure 30.3   Chart in Output Navigator**

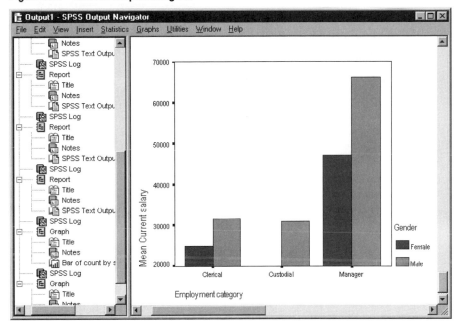

## Modifying the Chart

To modify a chart, double-click anywhere on the chart. This displays the chart in a chart window, as shown in Figure 30.4.

**Figure 30.4   Original chart in chart window**

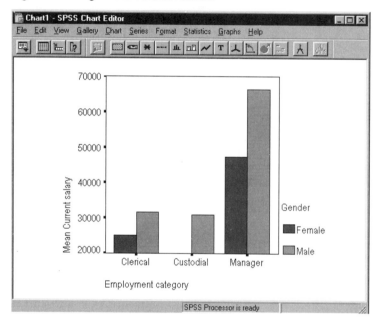

You can modify any part of the chart or use the gallery to change to another type of chart illustrating the same data. Chart modification and the Chart Editor menus are described in the next several chapters. Some typical modifications include the following:

- Edit axis titles and labels.
- Edit the legend, which identifies the colors or patterns of the bars.
- Add a title.
- Change the location of the bar origin line.
- Add annotation.
- Add an outer frame.

Figure 30.5 shows a modified chart.

**Figure 30.5    Modified chart**

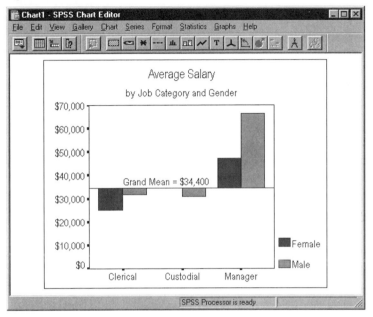

Chart modifications are saved when you close the chart window, and the modified chart is displayed in the Output Navigator.

# Exporting Charts

You can export charts in formats that can be read by other applications from a chart window. You can also export charts when running in production mode, where SPSS runs unattended.

To export a chart:

▶ From the chart window menus choose:
File
  Export Chart

▶ Select an export format.

▶ Enter a name for the chart and click *Save*.

## Specifying a File Type

Before you export a chart file, you must specify a file type.

**Save File as Type.** You can choose one of the following file types:

- **Windows Metafile (*.wmf).** This is the default format.
- **CGM Metafile (*.cgm)**
- **PostScript (*.eps)**
- **Windows Bitmap (*.bmp)**
- **Tagged Image File (*.tif)**
- **Macintosh PICT (*.pct)**
- **JPEG (*.jpg)**

## Specifying File Type Options

You can click *Options* in the Export Chart dialog box to change the selected character-istics of the file type. Available options are dependent on the selected export format.

## Chart Definition Global Options

When you are defining a chart, the specific chart definition dialog box usually contains the pushbuttons *Titles* and *Options*, and a Template group, as shown in Figure 30.6. These global options are available for most charts, regardless of type. They are not avail-able for P-P plots, Q-Q plots, sequence charts, or time series charts.

**Figure 30.6    A chart definition dialog box**

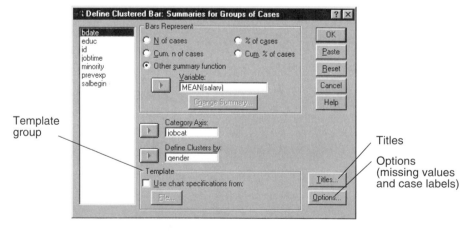

The Titles dialog box allows you to specify titles, subtitles, and footnotes. You can click *Options* to control the treatment of missing values for most charts and case labels for scatterplots. You can apply a template of previously selected attributes either when you are defining the chart or after the chart has been created. The next few sections describe how to define these characteristics at the time you define the chart.

## Titles, Subtitles, and Footnotes

In any chart, you can define two title lines, one subtitle line, and two footnote lines as part of your original chart definition. To specify titles or footnotes while defining a chart, click *Titles* in the chart definition dialog box (see Figure 30.6). This opens the Titles dialog box, as shown in Figure 30.7.

**Figure 30.7   Titles dialog box**

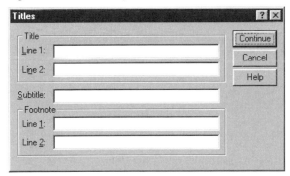

Each line can be up to 72 characters long. The number of characters that will actually fit in the chart depends upon the font and size. Most titles are left justified by default and, if too long, are cropped on the right. Pie chart titles, by default, are center justified and, if too long, are cropped at both ends.

You can also add, delete, or revise text lines, as well as change their font, size, and justification, within the Chart Editor.

# Options

The Options dialog box provides options for treatment of missing values and display of case labels, as shown in Figure 30.8. This dialog box is available from the chart definition dialog box (see Figure 30.6).

**Figure 30.8   Options dialog box**

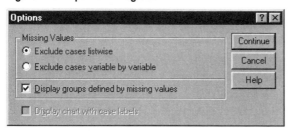

The availability of each option depends on your previous choices. Missing-value options are not available for charts using values of individual cases or for histograms. The case-labels display option is available only for a scatterplot that has a variable selected for case labels.

**Missing Values.** If you selected summaries of separate variables for a categorical chart or if you are creating a scatterplot, you can choose one of the following alternatives for exclusion of cases having missing values:

- **Exclude cases listwise.** If any of the variables in the chart has a missing value for a given case, the whole case is excluded from the chart.

- **Exclude cases variable by variable.** If a selected variable has any missing values, the cases having those missing values are excluded when the variable is analyzed.

The following option is also available for missing values:

- **Display groups defined by missing values.** If there are missing values in the data for variables used to define categories or subgroups, user-missing values (values identified as missing by the user) and system-missing values are included together in a category labeled *Missing*. The "missing" category is displayed on the category axis or in the legend, adding, for example, an extra bar, a slice to a pie chart, or an extra box to a boxplot. In a scatterplot, missing values add a "missing" category to the set of markers. If there are no missing values, the "missing" category is not displayed.

   This option is selected by default. If you want to suppress display after the chart is drawn, select *Displayed* from the Series menu and move the categories you want suppressed to the Omit group.

   This option is not available for an overlay scatterplot or for single-series charts in which the data are summarized by separate variables.

To see the difference between listwise and variable-by-variable exclusion of missing values, consider Figure 30.9, which shows a bar chart for each of the two options. The charts were created from a version of the *bank.sav* employee data file that was edited to have some system-missing (blank) values in the variables for current salary and job category. In some other cases of the job category variable, the value 9 was entered and defined as missing. For both charts, the option *Display groups defined by missing values* is selected, which adds the category *Missing* to the other job categories displayed. In each chart, the values of the summary function, *Number of cases*, are displayed in the bar labels.

**Figure 30.9   Examples of missing-data treatment in charts**

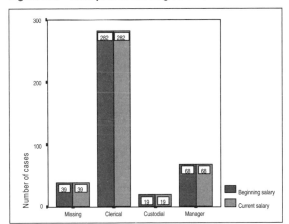

Listwise exclusion of missing values

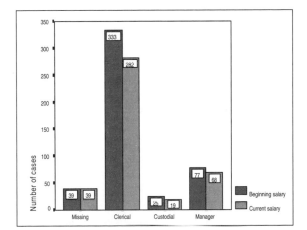

Variable-by-variable exclusion of missing values

In both charts, 26 cases have a system-missing value for the job category and 13 cases have the user-missing value (9). In the listwise chart, the number of cases is the same for both variables in each bar cluster because whenever a value was missing, the case was excluded for all variables. In the variable-by-variable chart, the number of nonmissing cases for each variable in a category is plotted without regard to missing values in other variables.

The final selection in the Options dialog box controls the status of case labels when a scatterplot is first displayed.

- **Display chart with case labels.** When this option is selected, all case labels are displayed when a scatterplot is created. By default, it is deselected—that is, the default scatterplot is displayed without labels. If you select this option, case labels may overlap.

## Chart Templates

You can apply many of the attributes and text elements from one chart to another. This allows you to modify one chart, save that chart, and then use it as a template to create a number of other similar charts.

To use a template when creating a chart, select *Use chart specifications from* (in the Template group in the chart definition dialog box shown in Figure 30.6) and click *File*. This opens a standard file selection dialog box.

To apply a template to a chart already in a chart window, from the menus choose:

File
  Apply Chart Template...

This opens a standard file selection dialog box. Select a file to use as a template. If you are creating a new chart, the filename you select is displayed in the Template group when you return to the chart definition dialog box.

A template is used to borrow the format from one chart and apply it to the new chart you are generating. In general, any formatting information from the old chart that can apply to the new chart will automatically apply. For example, if the old chart is a clustered bar chart with bar colors modified to yellow and green and the new chart is a multiple line chart, the lines will be yellow and green. If the old chart is a simple bar chart with drop shadows and the new chart is a simple line chart, the lines will not have drop shadows because drop shadows don't apply to line charts. If there are titles in the template chart but not in the new chart, you will get the titles from the template chart. If there are titles defined in the new chart, they will override the titles in the template chart.

- **Apply title and footnote text.** Applies the text of the title and footnotes of the template to the current chart, overriding any text defined in the Titles dialog box in the current chart. The attributes of the title and footnotes (font, size, and color) are applied whether or not this item is selected. This check box appears only if you are applying the template in a chart window, not when creating a new chart.

## Creating Chart Templates

To create a chart template:

▶ Create a chart.

▶ Edit the chart to contain the attributes you want to save in a template.

▶ From the chart window menus, choose:

File
  Save Chart Template

# 31 Bar, Line, Area, and Pie Charts

Bar, line, area, and pie charts all present summary statistics for one or more variables, most often within groups defined by one or two grouping variables. For example, a bar chart could give you a bar for each of three job categories (defined by *jobcat*), or a bar for each sex within each job category. The height of each bar could represent a count of cases in each subgroup. Or it could represent a mean, a maximum, or one of many summary measures computed on another variable—such as the median age for the employees in each job category. Depending on the arrangement of your data, a bar chart might also represent a set of variables; it might contain a bar for each of three separate test scores (*score1, score2, score3*), with or without a further breakdown by *jobcat*.

Line charts have the same structure as bar charts, except that a point is plotted instead of a bar drawn for each summary measure, and the points are connected by lines. Line charts usually make most sense when the category axis is defined by a series, although they can be used for any set of categories. In the following chart, the same function is plotted twice, once as bars and once as a line.

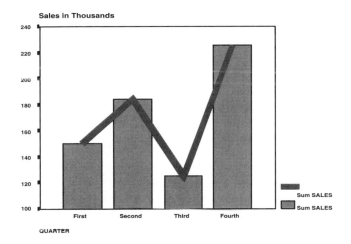

Area charts are line charts with the space below each line shaded. With multiple series, the series are stacked and are exactly analogous to stacked bar charts, emphasizing the proportion each series contributes to a whole.

Pie charts demonstrate the contribution of parts to a whole. Each slice corresponds to a group defined by a single grouping variable or to a separate variable. Although you can choose almost any summary statistic, pie charts make sense most commonly for counts and sums.

# How to Obtain Bar, Line, Area, and Pie Charts

To obtain bar, line, area, or pie charts, choose the appropriate chart type from the Graphs menu, as shown in Figure 31.1.

**Figure 31.1   Graphs Menu**

This opens a chart dialog box for the selected chart type, as shown in Figure 31.2 (chart dialog boxes for line, area, and pie charts are shown in Figure 31.14, Figure 31.26, and Figure 31.35, respectively).

**Figure 31.2   Bar Charts dialog box**

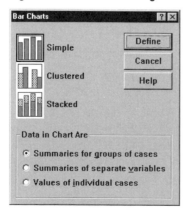

From the chart dialog box, choose the type of chart you want. Your choices depend upon the type of chart you selected on the Graphs menu. For bar charts, the choices are *simple*, *clustered*, or *stacked*.

**Data in Chart Are.** Select the choice that describes the structure of your data organization.

- **Summaries for groups of cases.** Cases are counted, or one variable is summarized, in subgroups. The subgroups are determined by one variable for simple charts or by two variables for complex charts.
- **Summaries of separate variables.** More than one variable is summarized. Simple charts summarize each variable over all cases in the file. Complex charts summarize each variable within categories determined by another variable.
- **Values of individual cases.** Individual values of one variable are plotted in simple charts. Values of more than one variable are plotted in complex charts.

Examples of these choices, shown with data organization structures and the charts they produce, are presented in the tables at the beginning of each section.

## Bar Charts

To obtain a bar chart, from the menus choose:

Graphs
  Bar...

This opens the Bar Charts dialog box, as shown in Figure 31.2.

Each combination of chart type and data organization structure produces a different definition box. Each is discussed briefly below. The icon and section title indicate the choices that have to be made in the chart dialog box to open that chart definition dialog box. The discussion for each chart type describes the selections required to enable the *OK* pushbutton. Optional selections are discussed only with the first chart using each data structure. For a detailed description of optional statistics, see "Summary Functions" on p. 370.

All chart definition dialog boxes have a *Titles* pushbutton and Template group. These are discussed in "Titles, Subtitles, and Footnotes" on p. 335 and "Chart Templates" on p. 338, both in Chapter 30. Chart definition dialog boxes for summaries for groups of cases and for summaries of separate variables also have an *Options* pushbutton. The *Options* pushbutton brings up a dialog box that controls missing-value options, discussed in "Options" on p. 336 in Chapter 30.

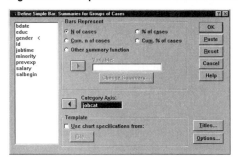

**Simple:
Summaries for groups of cases**

Figure 31.3 shows a chart definition dialog box and the resulting simple bar chart with summaries for groups of cases.

**Figure 31.3    Simple bar chart with summaries for groups of cases**

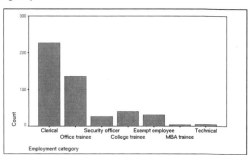

The numeric, short string, and long string variables in your data file are displayed on the source variable list. Select a variable to define the category axis. To get a simple chart showing number of cases for groups of cases in default format, click *OK*.

Optionally, you can select a different summary statistic, use a template to control the format of the chart, or add a title, subtitle, or footnote. Optional summary statistics are discussed in "Summary Functions" on p. 370. The other options are discussed in detail in Chapter 30.

**Category Axis.** Select a variable to define the categories shown in the chart. There is one bar for each value of the variable.

If you select *Other summary function* in the Define Simple Bar Summaries for Groups of Cases dialog box, you must also select a variable to be summarized. Figure 31.4

shows the chart definition dialog box with a variable to be summarized and the resulting simple bar chart with a summarized variable.

**Figure 31.4    Simple bar chart with summary of a variable**

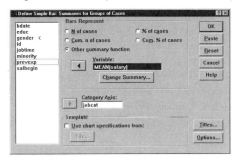
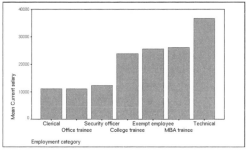

The default chart shows the mean of the selected variable within each category (determined by the category axis variable).

**Clustered:**
**Summaries for groups of cases**

Figure 31.5 shows a chart definition dialog box and the resulting clustered bar chart with summaries for groups of cases.

**Figure 31.5    Clustered bar chart with summaries for groups of cases**

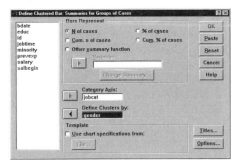
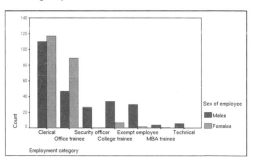

**Category Axis.** Select a variable to define the categories shown in the chart. There is one cluster of bars for each value of the variable.

**Define Clusters by.** Select a variable to define the bars within each cluster. There is one set of differently colored or patterned bars for each value of the variable.

## Stacked:
## Summaries for groups of cases

Figure 31.6 shows a chart definition dialog box and the resulting stacked bar chart with summaries for groups of cases.

**Figure 31.6    Stacked bar chart with summaries for groups of cases**

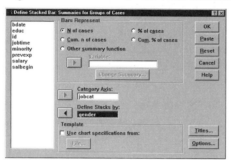 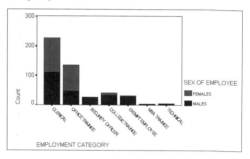

**Category Axis.** Select a variable to define the categories shown on the chart. There is one stack of bars for each value of the variable.

**Define Stacks by.** Select a variable to define the bar segments within each stack. There is one bar segment within each stack for each value of the variable.

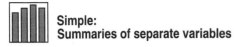

## Simple:
## Summaries of separate variables

Figure 31.7 shows a chart definition dialog box and the resulting simple bar chart with summaries of separate variables.

**Figure 31.7    Simple bar chart with summaries of separate variables**

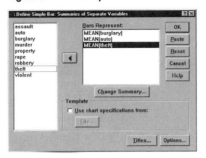 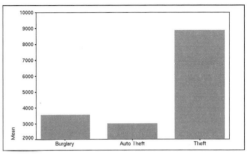

The numeric variables in your data file are displayed on the source variable list. Select the variables you want to define the bars. To get a simple bar chart showing the mean value of each variable in default format, click *OK*.

Optionally, you can select a different summary statistic, use a template to control the format of the chart, or add a title, subtitle, or footnote. Summary statistics are discussed in "Summary Functions" on p. 370. The other options are discussed in detail in Chapter 30.

**Bars Represent.** Select two or more variables to define the categories shown in the chart. There is one bar for each variable. By default, the bar shows the mean of the selected variables.

## Clustered:
## Summaries of separate variables

Figure 31.8 shows a chart definition dialog box and the resulting clustered bar chart with summaries of separate variables.

**Figure 31.8    Clustered bar chart with summaries of separate variables**

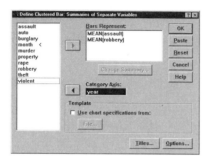 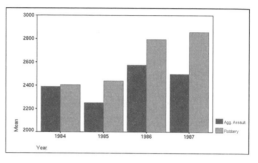

**Bars Represent.** Select two or more variables. There is one bar within each group for each variable. By default, the bars show the mean of the selected variables.

**Category Axis.** Select a variable to define the categories shown in the chart. There is one cluster of bars for each value of the variable.

## Stacked:
## Summaries of separate variables

Figure 31.9 shows a chart definition dialog box and the resulting stacked bar chart with summaries of separate variables.

**Figure 31.9    Stacked bar chart with summaries of separate variables**

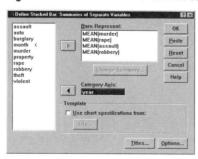 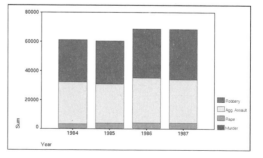

**Bars Represent.** Select two or more variables. There is one bar within each stack for each variable. By default, the bars show the sum of the selected variables.

**Category Axis.** Select a variable to define the categories shown in the chart. There is one stack of bars for each value of the variable.

## Simple:
## Values of individual cases

Figure 31.10 shows a chart definition dialog box and the resulting simple bar chart with values of individual cases.

**Figure 31.10    Simple bar chart with values of individual cases**

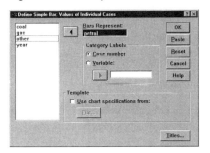 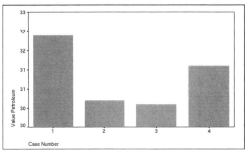

The numeric, short string, and long string variables in your data file are displayed on the source variable list. Select the numeric variable you want to define the bars. To get a simple bar chart showing the value of each case in default format, click *OK*.

Optionally, you can change the value labels shown in the chart, use a template to control the format of the chart, or add a title, subtitle, or footnote. These options are discussed in detail in Chapter 30.

**Bars Represent.** Select a numeric variable to define the bars. Each case is represented by a separate bar.

**Category Labels.** Determines how the bars are labeled. You can choose one of the following category label sources:

- **Case number.** Each category is labeled with the case number. This is the default.

- **Variable.** Each category is labeled with the current value label of the selected variable.

Figure 31.11 shows a chart definition dialog box with a label variable selected and the resulting bar chart.

**Figure 31.11    Bar chart with category labels from the variable year**

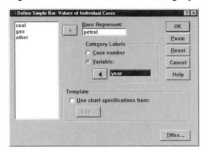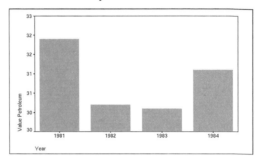

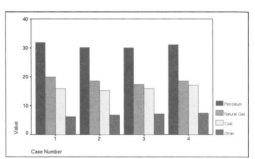
**Clustered:**
**Values of individual cases**

Figure 31.12 shows a chart definition dialog box and the resulting clustered bar chart with values of individual cases.

**Figure 31.12    Clustered bar chart with bars as values of individual cases**

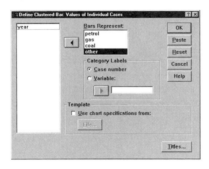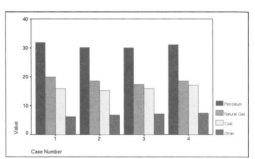

**Bars Represent.** Select two or more numeric variables. There is one separately colored or patterned set of bars for each variable. Each case is represented by a separate cluster of bars. The height of each bar represents the value of the variable.

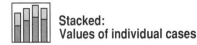

## Stacked:
## Values of individual cases

Figure 31.13 shows a chart definition dialog box and the resulting stacked bar chart with values of individual cases.

**Figure 31.13    Stacked bar chart with values of individual cases**

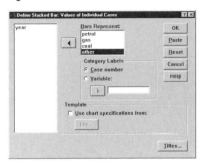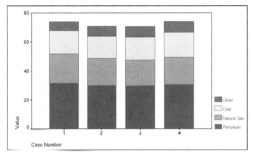

**Bars Represent.** Select two or more numeric variables. Each case is represented by a separate stack. Each variable is represented by a separate bar within each stack.

# Line Charts

To obtain a line chart, from the menus choose:

Graphs
　Line...

This opens the Line Charts dialog box, as shown in Figure 31.14.

**Figure 31.14 Line Charts dialog box**

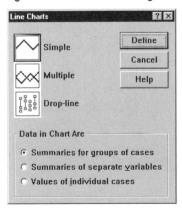

Select the type of line chart you want, and select the choice that describes the structure of your data organization. Click *Define* to open a dialog box specific to your selections.

## Simple:
## Summaries for groups of cases

Figure 31.15 shows a chart definition dialog box and the resulting simple line chart with summaries for groups of cases.

**Figure 31.15    Simple line chart with summaries for groups of cases**

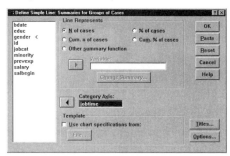 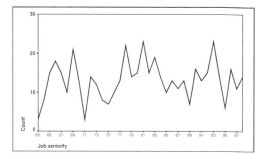

The numeric, short string, and long string variables in your data file are displayed on the source variable list. Select a variable to define the category axis. To get a simple line chart showing the number of cases in each category, click *OK*.

Optionally, you can select a different summary statistic, use a template to control the format of the chart, or add a title, subtitle, or footnote. Summary statistics are discussed in "Summary Functions" on p. 370. The other options are discussed in detail in Chapter 30.

**Category Axis.** Select a variable to define the categories shown in the chart. There is one point for each value of the variable.

If you select *Other summary function* in the Define Simple Line Summaries for Groups of Cases dialog box, you must also select a variable to be summarized. Figure 31.16

shows the chart definition dialog box with a variable to be summarized and the resulting chart.

**Figure 31.16    Simple line chart with summary of a variable**

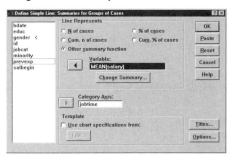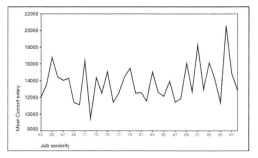

The chart generated by default shows the mean of the selected variable within each category (determined by the category axis variable).

## Multiple:
## Summaries for groups of cases

Figure 31.17 shows a chart definition dialog box and the resulting multiple line chart with summaries for groups of cases.

**Figure 31.17    Multiple line chart with summaries for groups of cases**

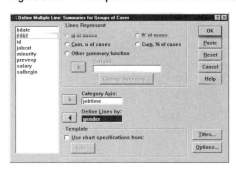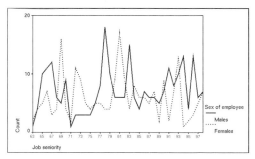

**Category Axis.** Select a variable to define the categories shown in the chart. There is one point on each line for each value of the variable.

**Define Lines by.** Select a variable to define the lines. There is one line for each value of the variable.

## Drop-line:
## Summaries for groups of cases

Figure 31.18 shows a chart definition dialog box and the resulting drop-line chart with summaries for groups of cases.

**Figure 31.18    Drop-line chart with summaries for groups of cases**

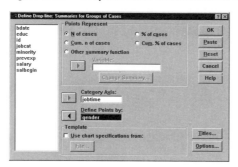 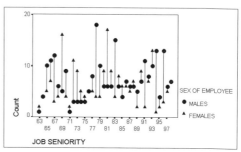

**Category Axis.** Select a variable to define the categories shown in the chart. There is one vertical line for each value of the variable.

**Define Points by.** Select a variable to define the points. There is one sequence of differently colored, patterned, or shaped points for each value of the variable.

**Simple:**
**Summaries of separate variables**

Figure 31.19 shows a chart definition dialog box and the resulting simple line chart with summaries of separate variables.

**Figure 31.19    Simple line chart with summaries of separate variables**

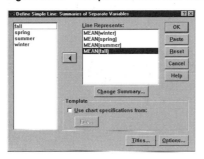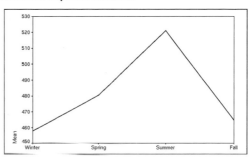

The numeric variables in your data file are displayed on the source variable list. Select the variables you want the line to represent. To get a simple line chart showing the mean value of each variable in default format, click *OK*.

Optionally, you can select a different summary statistic, use a template to control the format of the chart, or add a title, subtitle, or footnote. Summary statistics are discussed in "Summary Functions" on p. 370. The other options are discussed in detail in Chapter 30.

**Line Represents.** Select two or more variables to define the categories shown in the chart. There is one point on the line for each variable. By default, the points show the mean of the selected variables.

## Multiple:
## Summaries of separate variables

Figure 31.20 shows a chart definition dialog box and the resulting multiple line chart with summaries of separate variables.

**Figure 31.20    Multiple line chart with summaries of separate variables**

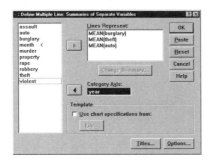
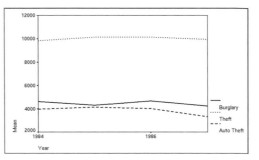

**Lines Represent.** Select two or more variables to define the lines. There is one line for each variable. By default, the lines show the mean of the selected variables.

**Category Axis.** Select a variable to define the categories shown in the chart. There is one point on each line for each value of the variable.

## Drop-line:
## Summaries of separate variables

Figure 31.21 shows a chart definition dialog box and the resulting drop-line chart with summaries of separate variables.

**Figure 31.21  Drop-line chart with summaries of separate variables**

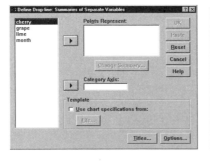
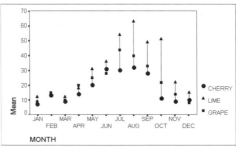

**Points Represent.** Select two or more variables to define the points. There is one sequence of differently colored, patterned, or shaped points for each variable. By default, the points show the mean of the selected variables.

**Category Axis.** Select a variable to define the categories shown in the chart. There is one vertical line for each value of the variable.

### Simple:
### Values of individual cases

Figure 31.22 shows a chart definition dialog box and the resulting simple line chart with values of individual cases.

**Figure 31.22 Simple line chart with values of individual cases**

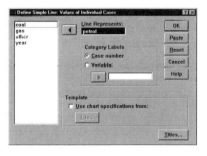 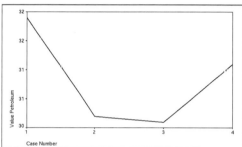

The numeric, short string, and long string variables in your data file are displayed on the source variable list. Select the numeric variable you want to define the line. To get a simple line chart showing the value of each case in default format, click *OK*.

Optionally, you can change the value labels shown in the chart, use a template to control the format of the chart, or add a title, subtitle, or footnote. These options are discussed in detail in Chapter 30.

**Line Represents.** Select a numeric variable to define the line. Each case will be displayed as a point.

**Category Labels.** Determines how the categories are labeled. You can choose one of the following category label sources:

• **Case number.** Each category is labeled with the case number. This is the default.

• **Variable.** Each category is labeled with the current value label of the selected variable.

Figure 31.23 shows a chart definition dialog box with a label variable selected and the resulting simple line chart with category labels.

**Figure 31.23    Line chart with category labels from the variable year**

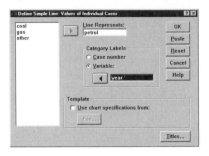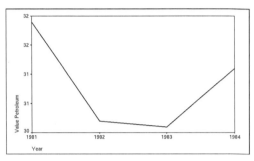

### Multiple:
### Values of individual cases

Figure 31.24 shows a chart definition dialog box and the resulting multiple line chart with values of individual cases.

**Figure 31.24    Multiple line chart with values of individual cases**

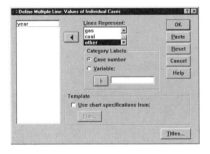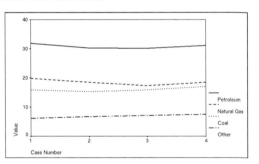

**Lines Represent.** Select two or more numeric variables to define the lines. There is one line for each variable. There is one point on each line for each case.

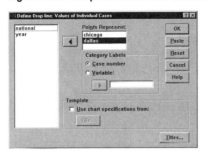

### Drop-line:
### Values of individual cases

Figure 31.25 shows a chart definition dialog box and the resulting drop-line chart with values of individual cases.

**Figure 31.25  Drop-line chart with values of individual cases**

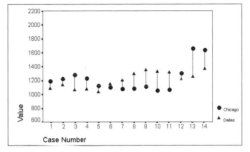

**Points Represent.** Select two or more numeric variables to define the points. There is one sequence of differently colored, patterned, or shaped points for each variable. There is one vertical line for each case.

## Area Charts

To obtain an area chart, from the menus choose:

Graphs
  Area...

This opens the Area Charts dialog box, as shown in Figure 31.26.

**Figure 31.26    Area Charts dialog box**

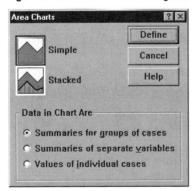

Select the type of area chart you want, and select the choice that describes the structure of your data organization. Click *Define* to open a dialog box specific to your selections.

## Simple:
## Summaries for groups of cases

Figure 31.27 shows a chart definition dialog box and the resulting simple area chart with summaries for groups of cases.

**Figure 31.27    Simple area chart with summaries for groups of cases**

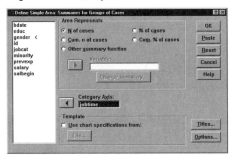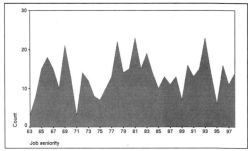

The numeric, short string, and long string variables in your data file are displayed on the source variable list. Select the variable you want to define the category axis. To get a simple area chart showing the number of cases in each category, click *OK*.

Optionally, you can select a different summary statistic, use a template to control the format of the chart, or add a title, subtitle, or footnote. Summary statistics are discussed in "Summary Functions" on p. 370. The other options are discussed in detail in Chapter 30.

**Category Axis.** Select a variable to define the categories shown in the chart. There is one point on the boundary of the area for each value of the variable.

If you select *Other summary function* in the chart definition dialog box, you must also select a variable to be summarized. Figure 31.28 shows the dialog box with a variable to be summarized and the resulting chart.

**Figure 31.28    Summary of a variable in a simple area chart**

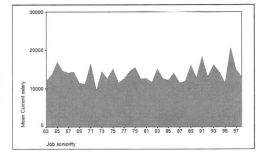

The chart generated by default shows the mean of the selected variable within each category (determined by the category axis variable). For a detailed description of optional statistics, see "Summary Functions" on p. 370.

### Stacked:
### Summaries for groups of cases

Figure 31.29 shows a chart definition dialog box and the resulting stacked area chart with summaries for groups of cases.

**Figure 31.29    Stacked area chart with summaries for groups of cases**

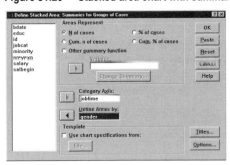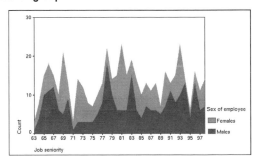

**Category Axis.** Select a variable to define the categories shown in the chart. There is one point on the boundary of each area for each value of the variable.

**Define Areas by.** Select a variable to define the areas. There is one differently colored or patterned area for each value of the variable.

## Simple:
## Summaries of separate variables

Figure 31.30 shows a chart definition dialog box and the resulting simple area chart with summaries of separate variables.

**Figure 31.30    Simple area chart with summaries of separate variables**

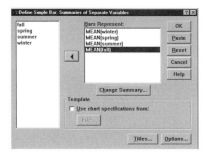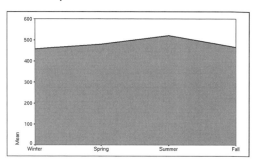

The numeric variables in your data file are displayed on the source variable list. Select the variables you want to define points on the boundary of the area. To get a simple area chart showing the mean value of each variable in default format, click *OK*.

Optionally, you can select a different summary statistic, use a template to control the format of the chart, or add a title, subtitle, or footnote. Summary statistics are discussed in "Summary Functions" on p. 370. The other options are discussed in detail in Chapter 30.

**Area Represents.** Select two or more variables to define the categories shown in the chart. There is one point on the boundary of the area for each variable. By default, the points show the mean of the selected variables.

**Stacked:**
**Summaries of separate variables**

Figure 31.31 shows a chart definition dialog box and the resulting stacked area chart with summaries of separate variables.

**Figure 31.31    Stacked area chart with summaries of separate variables**

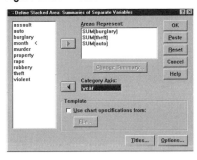　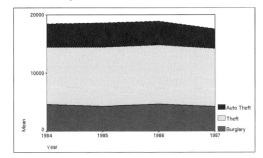

**Areas Represent.** Select two or more variables to define the areas. There is one area for each variable. By default, the value axis shows the sum of the selected variables.

**Category Axis.** Select a variable to define the categories shown in the chart. There is one point on the boundary of each area for each value of the variable.

 **Simple:**
**Values of individual cases**

Figure 31.32 shows a chart definition dialog box and the resulting simple area chart with values of individual cases.

**Figure 31.32    Simple area chart with values of individual cases**

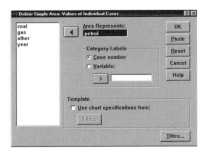　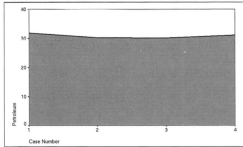

The numeric, short string, and long string variables in your data file are displayed on the source variable list. Select the numeric variable you want to define the area. To get a simple area chart showing the value of each case in default format, click *OK*.

Optionally, you can change the value labels shown in the chart, use a template to control the format of the chart, or add a title, subtitle, or footnote. These options are discussed in detail in Chapter 30.

**Area Represents.** Select a numeric variable to define the area. Each case will be displayed as a category.

**Category Labels.** Determines how the categories are labeled. You can choose one of the following category label sources:

- **Case number**. Each category is labeled with the case number. This is the default.
- **Variable.** Each category is labeled with the current value label of the selected variable.

Figure 31.33 shows the chart definition dialog box with a label variable selected and the resulting area chart.

**Figure 31.33    Area chart with category labels from the variable year**

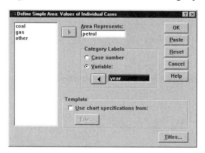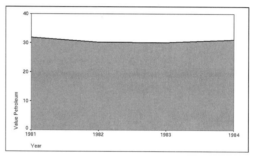

**Stacked:**
**Values of individual cases**

Figure 31.34 shows the chart definition dialog box and the resulting stacked area chart with values of individual cases.

**Figure 31.34    Stacked area chart with values of individual cases**

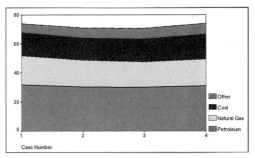

**Areas Represent.** Select two or more numeric variables. There is one area for each variable. There is one point on the boundary of each area for each case.

# Pie Charts

To obtain a pie chart, from the menus choose:

Graphs
  Pie...

This open the Pie Charts dialog box, as shown in Figure 31.35.

**Figure 31.35    Pie Charts dialog box**

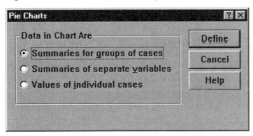

Select the choice that describes the structure of your data organization, and click *Define* to open a dialog box specific to your selection.

## Summaries for Groups of Cases

Figure 31.36 shows a chart definition dialog box and the resulting simple pie chart with summaries for groups of cases.

**Figure 31.36    Pie chart with summaries for groups of cases**

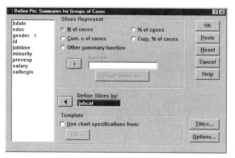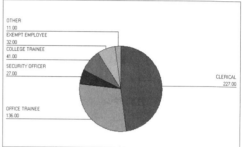

The numeric, short string, and long string variables in your data file are displayed on the source variable list. Select the variable you want to define the categories or slices. To get a simple pie chart showing the number of cases in each category, click *OK*.

Optionally, you can select a different summary statistic, use a template to control the format of the chart, or add a title, subtitle, or footnote. Summary statistics are discussed in "Summary Functions" on p. 370. The other options are discussed in detail in Chapter 30.

**Define Slices by.** Select a variable to define the pie slices shown in the chart. There is one slice for each value of the variable. A slice definition variable must be selected to enable the *OK* pushbutton.

If you select *Other summary function* in the Define Pie Summaries for Groups of Cases dialog box, you must also select a variable to be summarized. Figure 31.37 shows the chart definition dialog box with a variable to be summarized and the resulting simple pie chart.

**Figure 31.37    Simple pie chart with summary of a variable**

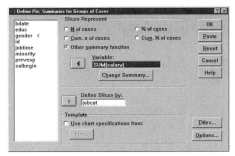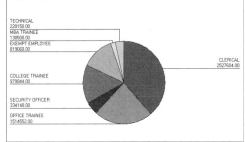

The chart generated by default shows the sum of the selected variable within each category (determined by the slice variable).

## Summaries of Separate Variables

Figure 31.38 shows a chart definition dialog box and the resulting simple pie chart with summaries of separate variables.

**Figure 31.38    Pie chart with summaries of separate variables**

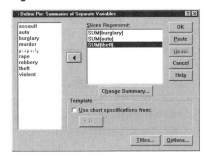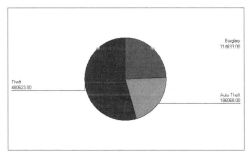

The numeric variables in your data file are displayed on the source variable list. Select the variables you want to define the pie slices. To get a simple pie chart showing the sum of each variable in default format, click *OK*.

Optionally, you can select a different summary statistic, use a template to control the format of the chart, or add a title, subtitle, or footnote. Summary statistics are discussed in "Summary Functions" on p. 370. The other options are discussed in detail in Chapter 30.

**Slices Represent.** Select two or more variables to define the slices shown in the chart. There is one slice for each variable. By default, the slices show the sum of the selected variables. Two or more slice variables must be selected to enable the *OK* pushbutton.

## Values of Individual Cases

Figure 31.39 shows a chart definition dialog box and the resulting simple pie chart with values of individual cases.

**Figure 31.39    Pie chart with values of individual cases**

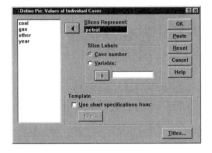 

The numeric, short string, and long string variables in your data file are displayed on the source variable list. Select the numeric variable you want slices to represent. To get a simple pie chart showing the value of each case in default format, click *OK*.

Optionally, you can change the value labels shown in the chart, use a template to control the format of the chart, or add a title, subtitle, or footnote. These options are discussed in detail in Chapter 30.

**Slices Represent.** Select a numeric variable to define the slices. Each case will be displayed as a separate pie slice. A variable must be selected to enable the *OK* pushbutton.

**Slice Labels.** Determines how the slices are labeled. You can choose one of the following sector label sources:

- **Case number.** Each slice is labeled with the case number. This is the default.
- **Variable.** Each slice is labeled with the current value label of the selected variable.

Figure 31.40 shows the chart definition dialog box with a label variable selected and the resulting pie chart.

**Figure 31.40    Pie chart with category labels from the variable petrol**

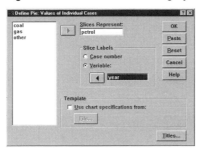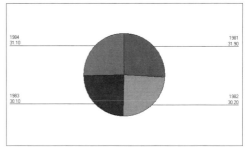

# Transposed Charts

Sometimes, especially with inventory or accounting time series data, the categories you want are defined as separate cases or values while each date is a separate variable. For example, the inventory data in Figure 31.41 are defined this way.

**Figure 31.41    Inventory data**

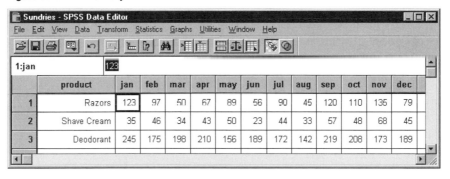

If you draw a line chart of these data, you get the chart in Figure 31.42.

To flip this chart so that each line is a separate product and each month is a separate category, edit the chart. From the menu of the chart window choose:

Series
  Transpose Data

This produces the chart shown in Figure 31.43.

**Figure 31.42    Chart of inventory data**

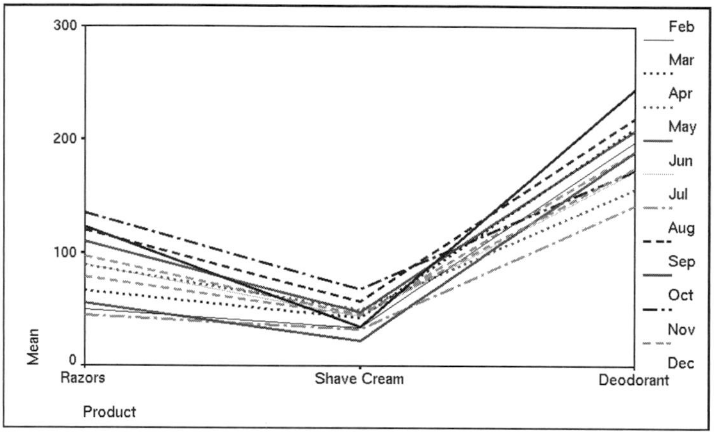

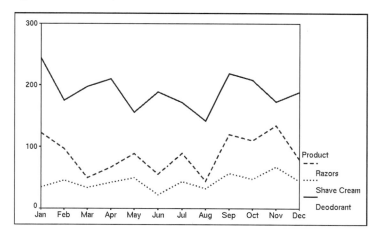

**Figure 31.43    Transposed chart**

You can transpose other multiple-series categorical charts, such as clustered bar charts (see "Transposing Data" on p. 469 in Chapter 39).

## Summary Functions

Data can be summarized by counting the number of cases in each category or subcategory, or by calculating a statistic summarizing the values in each category or subcategory.

## Count Functions

For simple summaries of groups of cases, the dialog box in Figure 31.44 shows the general layout of the chart definition dialog boxes for bar, line, area, and pie charts. For complex summaries of groups of cases, the summaries in the dialog box are similar, as shown in Figure 31.45.

**Figure 31.44     Define simple summaries for groups of cases dialog box**

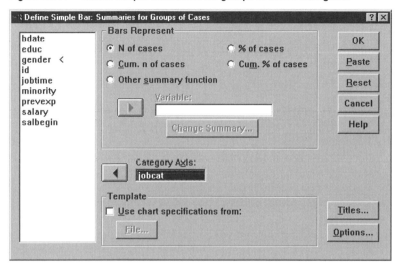

**Figuro 31.45     Dofino multioorioo oummarioo for groupo of oaooo dialog box**

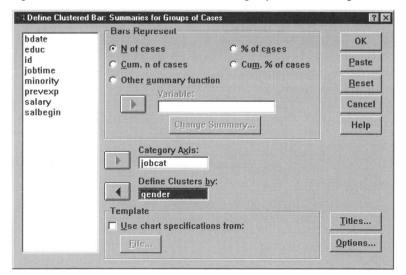

**Bars/Lines/Areas/Slices Represent.** Determines the summary statistic used to generate the data series illustrated by the chart. You can choose one of the following alternatives:

- **N of cases.** Each bar, point on a line, point on the boundary of an area, or pie slice represents the number of cases in a category. This is the default.

- **% of cases.** Each bar, point on a line, point on the boundary of an area, or pie slice represents the percentage of cases in a category.

- **Cum. n of cases.** Cumulative number of cases. Each bar, point on a line, point on the boundary of an area, or pie slice represents the number of cases in the current category plus all cases in previous categories. This function is not appropriate for some charts; see "Cumulative Functions" on p. 374.

- **Cum. % of cases.** Cumulative percentage of cases. Each bar, point on a line, or point on the boundary of an area represents the cumulative number of cases as a percentage of the total number of cases. This function is not appropriate for some charts; see "Cumulative Functions" on p. 374.

- **Other summary function.** The values in a series are calculated from a summary measure of a variable. In most cases, the mean of the variable is the default. For stacked bar, stacked area, and pie charts, the sum of the variable is the default.

## Other Summary Functions

You can request statistical summary functions for any chart where values are summarized. When values are summarized for *groups of cases*, select *Other summary function*; then select a variable to summarize and click on ▶. The Variable box indicates the default summary function (mean or sum). If you want a summary function other than the default, click *Change Summary*. This opens the Summary Function dialog box, as shown in Figure 31.46.

When values are summarized for *separate variables*, first move the variables to the box for bars, lines, areas, or slices, as shown in Figure 31.7 and Figure 31.38. The default measure (mean or sum) is indicated for each variable on the list. If you want a summary function other than the default, select a variable on the list and click *Change Summary*. This opens the Summary Function dialog box, as shown in Figure 31.46. If you want the same summary function to apply to more than one variable, you can select several variables by dragging over them and then clicking *Change Summary*.

**Figure 31.46    Summary Function dialog box**

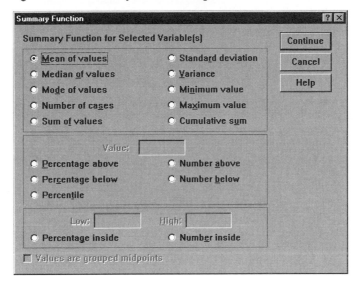

You can choose one of the following summary functions:

- **Mean of values.** The arithmetic average within the category. This is the default in most cases.

- **Median of values.** The value below which half the cases fall.

- **Mode of values.** The most frequently occurring value.

- **Number of cases.** The number of cases having a nonmissing value of the selected variable. If there are no missing values, this is the same as *N of cases* in the previous dialog box.

- **Sum of values**. The default for stacked bar charts, stacked area charts, or pie charts.

- **Standard deviation.** A measure of how much observations vary from the mean, expressed in the same units as the data.

- **Variance.** A measure of how much observations vary from the mean, expressed in squared units.

- **Minimum value.** The smallest value.
- **Maximum value.** The largest value.
- **Cumulative sum.** The sum of all values in the current category plus all values in previous categories. This function is not appropriate for some charts; see "Cumulative Functions" in the next section.
- **Percentage above.** The percentage of cases above the indicated value.
- **Percentage below.** The percentage of cases below the indicated value.
- **Percentile.** The data value below which the specified percentage of values fall.
- **Number above.** The number of cases above the specified value.
- **Number below.** The number of cases below the specified value.
- **Percentage inside.** The percentage of cases with values between the specified high and low value, including the high and low values. Select this item, then type in the high and low values.
- **Number inside.** The number of cases with values between the specified high and low values, including the high and low values. Select this item, then type in the high and low values.

## Cumulative Functions

*Cum. N of cases*, *Cum. % of cases*, and *Cumulative sum* are inappropriate in pie charts. These functions are also inappropriate in stacked bar charts and area charts that have been transposed so that the cumulative function is along the scale axis. Because the Chart Editor does not recalculate summary functions, many Displayed Data operations (from the Series menu) will invalidate cumulative functions, particularly if scaled to 100%.

# 32 High-Low Charts

High-low and high-low-close charts are most familiar in stock market data, where they display the highest, lowest, and closing price for each day. They are particularly useful whenever you want to show both the overall trend in a series and the short-term fluctuations. Range bar charts display high and low values in bars. The bars can be clustered to show, for example, the high and low scores for each of three regions on a weekly performance test. The category axis for a high-low or range bar chart is most often a variable that defines a series, but there is no reason that it needs to be a series. Difference line charts display two series, shading the area between the series with a different color or pattern, depending upon which is higher; you might expect to see one used to display the relative sales by month of two competing products.

## How to Obtain High-Low Charts

To obtain a high-low chart, from the menus choose:

Graphs
  High-Low...

This opens the High-Low Charts dialog box, as shown in Figure 32.1.

**Figure 32.1   High-Low Charts dialog box**

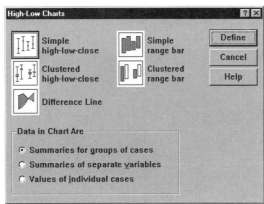

From the High-Low Charts dialog box, choose one of the chart types, and then select the choice that describes the structure of your data organization.

**Data in Chart Are.** Select the choice that describes the structure of your data organization.

- **Summaries for groups of cases.** There is one bar, point on a line, or cluster of bars for each category of the category axis variable. In simple charts (simple high-low-close, simple range bar, and difference line), a variable with two values defines the high and low points for each category. In a simple high-low-close chart, a variable with three values may be used instead to define high, low, and closing values. In clustered charts, two variables determine the high and low values, and a third variable defines the bars within each cluster. In a clustered high-low-close chart, another variable may also be used to determine a closing value for each bar.

- **Summaries of separate variables.** More than one variable is summarized. Simple high-low charts summarize each variable over all cases in the file. Clustered high-low charts summarize each variable within categories determined by another variable.

- **Values of individual cases.** Each case in the data is a separate category in the chart.

Each combination of chart type and data organization structure produces a different definition box. Each is discussed briefly in this chapter. The icon and section title indicate the choices that have to be made in the chart dialog box to open that chart definition dialog box. Optional selections are discussed only with the first chart using each data structure. For a detailed description of optional statistics, see "Summary Functions" on p. 370 in Chapter 31.

### Simple high-low-close:
### Summaries for groups of cases

Figure 32.2 shows a chart definition dialog box and the resulting simple high-low-close chart with summaries for groups of cases.

**Figure 32.2    Simple high-low-close chart with summaries for groups of cases**

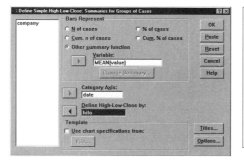
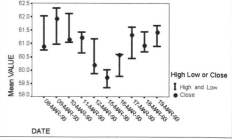

The numeric, short string, and long string variables in your data file are displayed on the source variable list. Select the variable you want to define the category axis and select the variable you want to define the high-low-close bars. The high-low-close variable must have either two or three values. To get a simple high-low-close chart showing high-low-close bars for each category, click *OK*.

Optionally, you can select a different summary statistic, use a template to control the format of the chart, or add a title, subtitle, or footnote. Summary statistics are discussed in "Other Summary Functions" on p. 372 in Chapter 31.

**Bars Represent.** If *Other summary function* in the chart definition dialog box is selected, you must select a variable to be summarized. The chart generated by default shows the mean of the selected variable within each category (determined by the category axis variable). For a detailed description of optional statistics, see "Summary Functions" on p. 370 in Chapter 31.

**Category Axis.** Select a variable to define the categories shown in the chart. There is one high-low-close bar for each value of the variable.

**Define High-Low-Close by.** Select a variable with two or three values. If there are two values, they are shown as high-low-close bars without close points. If there are three values, the first and second define the high and low ends of the bars and the third value determines the position of the close points. If your data are coded in the wrong order and all the close points appear above or below the high-low bars, you can edit the displayed series in the chart so that the close points appear between the high and low points. Figure 32.3 shows a high-low-close chart for a variable with two categories.

**Figure 32.3    Simple high-low-close chart without close points**

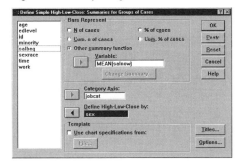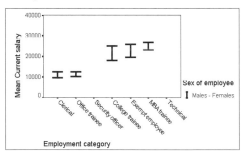

If *Other summary function* is not selected, you do not need to specify a variable. Figure 32.4 shows a high-low-close chart that shows number of cases.

**Figure 32.4   High-low-close chart with number of cases**

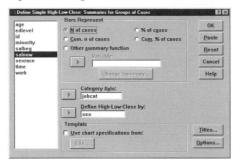
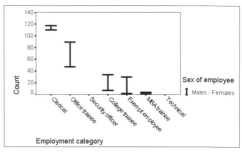

## Simple range bar:
## Summaries for groups of cases

Figure 32.5 shows a chart definition dialog box and the resulting simple range bar chart with summaries for groups of cases.

**Figure 32.5   Simple range bar chart with summaries for groups of cases**

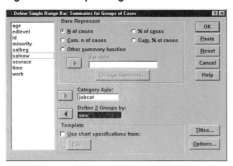
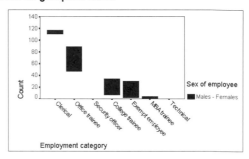

**Category Axis.** Select a variable to define the categories shown in the chart. There is one range bar for each value of the variable.

**Define 2 Groups by.** Select a variable with two values. The top of each range bar is determined by cases with one value; the bottom of each range bar is determined by cases with the other value.

### Difference line:
### Summaries for groups of cases

Figure 32.6 shows a chart definition dialog box and the resulting difference line chart with summaries for groups of cases.

**Figure 32.6    Difference line chart with summaries for groups of cases**

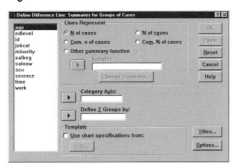 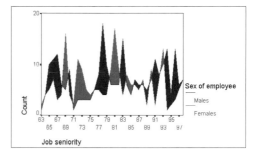

**Category Axis.** Select a variable to define the categories shown in the chart. There is one point on each line for each value of the variable.

**Define 2 Groups by.** Select a variable to define the lines. The variable must have two values. There are two differently colored or patterned lines in the chart, one for each value of this variable.

### Clustered high-low-close:
### Summaries for groups of cases

Figure 32.7 shows a chart definition dialog box and the resulting clustered high-low-close chart with summaries for groups of cases.

**Figure 32.7    Clustered high-low-close chart with summaries for groups of cases**

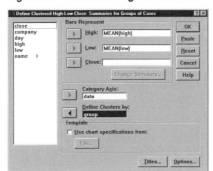 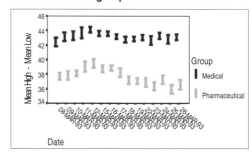

**High.** Select a variable to determine one end of each high-low-close bar. By default, the bars show the mean of the selected value.

**Low.** Select a variable to determine the other end of each high-low-close bar. By default, the bars show the mean of the selected value.

**Close.** You may optionally select a variable to determine the position of close points. By default, the close points show the mean of the selected value. Close points are connected by a line.

**Category Axis.** Select a variable to define the categories shown in the chart. There is one cluster of high-low-close bars for each value of the category axis variable.

**Define Clusters by.** Select a variable to define the bars within each cluster. There is a differently colored or patterned series of high-low-close bars for each value of the cluster variable.

### Clustered range bar:
### Summaries for groups of cases

Figure 32.8 shows a chart definition dialog box and the resulting clustered range bar chart with summaries for groups of cases.

**Figure 32.8   Clustered range bar chart with summaries for groups of cases**

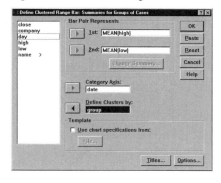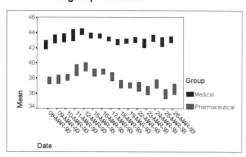

**1st.** Select a variable to determine one end of each range bar. By default, each bar shows the mean of the selected value.

**2nd.** Select a variable to determine the other end of each range bar. By default, each bar shows the mean of the selected value.

**Category Axis.** Select a variable to define the categories shown in the chart. There is one cluster of range bars for each value of the category axis variable.

**Define Clusters by.** Select a variable to define the bars within each cluster. There is a differently colored or patterned series of range bars for each value of the cluster variable.

## Simple high-low-close:
## Summaries of separate variables

Figure 32.9 shows a chart definition dialog box and the resulting simple high-low-close chart with summaries for groups of cases.

**Figure 32.9   Simple high-low-close chart with summaries of separate variables**

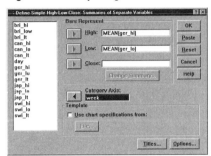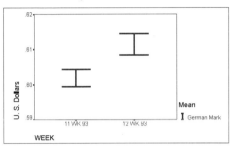

The numeric, short string, and long string variables in your data file are displayed on the source variable list. Select the variable you want to define the high end of each bar, the variable you want to define the low end of each bar, and a category axis variable. The high and low variables must be numeric. To get a simple high-low-close chart showing means for each category, click *OK*.

Optionally, you can add close points, select a different summary statistic, use a template to control the format of the chart, or add a title, subtitle, or footnote. Summary statistics are discussed in "Other Summary Functions" on p. 372 in Chapter 31.

**High.** Select a variable to determine one end of each high-low-close bar. By default, the bars show the mean of the selected variable.

**Low.** Select a variable to determine the other end of each high-low-close bar. By default, the bars show the mean of the selected variable.

**Close.** You may optionally select a variable to determine the position of close points. By default, the close points show the mean of the selected variable. Figure 32.10 shows a high-low-close chart with close points.

**Figure 32.10 Simple high-low-close chart with close points**

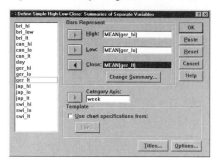
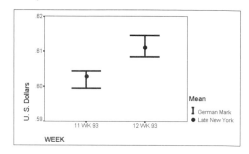

**Category Axis.** Select a variable to define the categories shown in the chart. There is one high-low-close bar for each value of the variable.

### Simple range bar:
### Summaries of separate variables

Figure 32.11 shows a chart definition dialog box and the resulting simple range bar chart with summaries of separate variables.

**Figure 32.11 Simple range bar chart with summaries of separate variables**

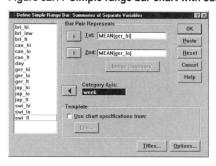
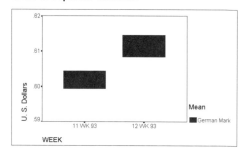

**1st.** Select a variable to determine one end of each range bar. By default, each bar shows the mean of the selected variable.

**2nd.** Select a variable to determine the other end of each range bar. By default, each bar shows the mean of the selected variable.

**Category Axis.** Select a variable to define the categories shown in the chart. There is one range bar for each value of the variable.

## Difference line:
## Summaries of separate variables

Figure 32.12 shows a chart definition dialog box and the resulting difference line chart with summaries of separate variables.

**Figure 32.12 Difference line chart with summaries of separate variables**

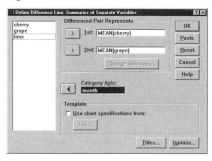
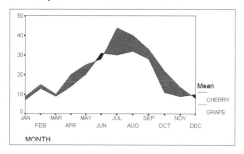

**1st.** Select a variable to determine one line in the set. By default, the line shows the mean of the selected value.

**2nd.** Select a variable to determine the other line in the set. By default, the line shows the mean of the selected value.

**Category Axis.** Select a variable to define the categories shown in the chart. There is one point on each line for each value of the category axis variable.

## Clustered high-low-close:
## Summaries of separate variables

Figure 32.13 shows a chart definition dialog box and the resulting clustered high-low-close chart with summaries of separate variables.

**Figure 32.13 Clustered high-low-close chart with summaries of separate variables**

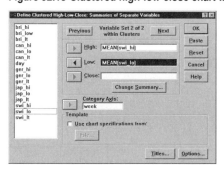
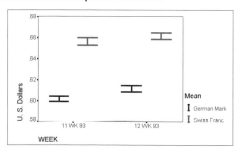

**High.** Select a variable to determine one end of each high-low-close bar in the set. By default, the bars show the mean of the selected variable. To edit a different set of high, low, and close values, press *Previous* or *Next*.

**Low.** Select a variable to determine the other end of each high-low-close bar in the set. By default, the bars show the mean of the selected variable. To edit a different set of high, low, and close values, press *Previous* or *Next*.

**Close.** You may optionally select a variable to determine the position of close points in the set. By default, the close points show the mean of the selected variable. To edit a different set of high, low, and close values, press *Previous* or *Next*.

**Category Axis.** Select a variable to define the categories shown in the chart. There is one cluster of high-low-close bars for each value of the category axis variable.

### Clustered range bar:
### Summaries of separate variables

Figure 32.14 shows a chart definition dialog box and the resulting clustered range bar chart with summaries of separate variables.

**Figure 32.14 Clustered range bar chart with summaries of separate variables**

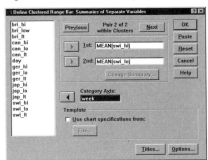 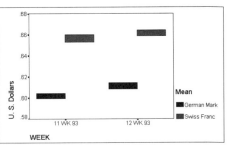

**1st.** Select a variable to determine one end of each range bar in the set. By default, the bars show the mean of the selected variable. To edit a different set of 1st and 2nd values, press *Previous* or *Next*.

**2nd.** Select a variable to determine the other end of each range bar in the set. By default, the bars show the mean of the selected variable. To edit a different set of 1st and 2nd values, press *Previous* or *Next*.

**Category Axis.** Select a variable to define the categories shown in the chart. There is one cluster of high-low-close bars for each value of the category axis variable.

 **Simple high-low-close:
Values of individual cases**

Figure 32.15 shows a chart definition dialog box and the resulting simple high-low-close chart with values of individual cases.

**Figure 32.15 Simple high-low-close chart with values of individual cases**

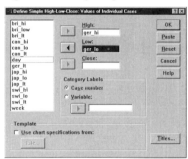 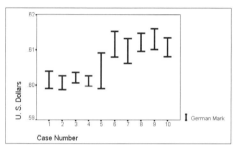

The numeric, short string, and long string variables in your data file are displayed on the source variable list. Select the numeric variable you want to define the high end of each bar and the numeric variable you want to define the low end of each bar. To get a simple high-low-close chart showing the value for each case, click *OK*.

Optionally, you can add close points, add category labels, use a template to control the format of the chart, or add a title, subtitle, or footnote. Summary statistics are discussed in "Other Summary Functions" on p. 372 in Chapter 31.

**High.** Select a variable to determine one end of each high-low-close bar. Each case is represented by a separate bar.

**Low.** Select a variable to determine the other end of each high-low-close bar. Each case is represented by a separate bar.

**Close.** You may optionally select a variable to determine the position of close points. Figure 32.16 shows a high-low-close chart with close points.

**Figure 32.16 Simple high-low-close chart with close points**

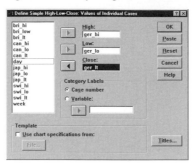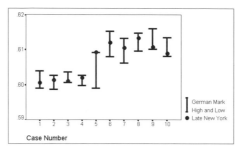

**Category Labels.** Determines how the bars are labeled. You can choose one of the following category label sources:

- **Case number.** Each category is labeled with the case number.
- **Variable.** Each category is labeled with the current value label of the selected variable.

Figure 32.17 shows a chart definition dialog box with a label variable selected and the resulting high-low-close chart.

**Figure 32.17 High-low-close chart with category labels from variable day**

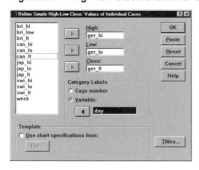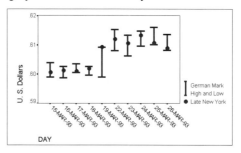

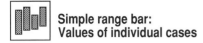

## Simple range bar:
## Values of individual cases

Figure 32.18 shows a chart definition dialog box and the resulting simple range bar chart with values of individual cases.

**Figure 32.18 Simple range bar chart with values of individual cases**

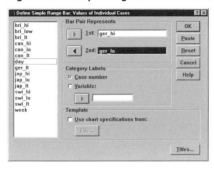 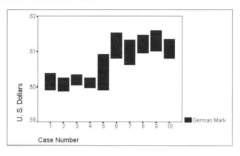

**1st.** Select a variable to determine one end of each range bar. Each case is represented by a separate bar.

**2nd.** Select a variable to determine the other end of each range bar. Each case is represented by a separate bar.

## Difference line:
## Values of individual cases

Figure 32.19 shows a chart definition dialog box and the resulting difference line chart with values of individual cases.

**Figure 32.19 Difference line chart with values of individual cases**

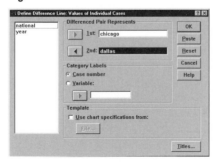 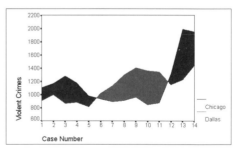

**1st.** Select a variable to determine one line in the set. Each case is represented by a separate point on the line.

**2nd.** Select a variable to determine the other line in the set. Each case is represented by a separate point on the line.

### Clustered high-low-close:
### Values of individual cases

Figure 32.20 shows a chart definition dialog box and the resulting clustered high-low-close chart with values of individual cases.

**Figure 32.20 Clustered high-low-close chart with values of individual cases**

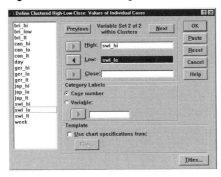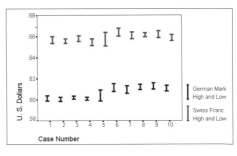

**High.** Select a variable to determine one end of each high-low-close bar in the set. Each case is represented by a separate bar. To edit a different set of high, low, and close values, press *Previous* or *Next*.

**Low.** Select a variable to determine the other end of each high-low-close bar in the set. Each case is represented by a separate bar. To edit a different set of high, low, and close values, press *Previous* or *Next*.

**Close.** You may optionally select a variable to determine the position of close points in the set. Each case is represented by a separate close point. Close points are connected by a line. To edit a different set of high, low, and close values, press *Previous* or *Next*.

### Clustered range bar:
### Values of individual cases

Figure 32.21 shows a chart definition dialog box and the resulting clustered range bar chart with values of individual cases.

**Figure 32.21 Clustered range bar chart with values of individual cases**

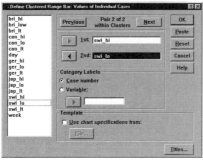 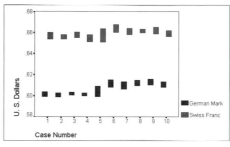

**1st.** Select a variable to determine one end of each range bar in the set. Each case is represented by a separate bar. To edit a different set of 1st and 2nd values, press *Previous* or *Next*.

**2nd.** Select a variable to determine the other end of each range bar in the set. Each case is represented by a separate bar. To edit a different set of 1st and 2nd values, press *Previous* or *Next*.

# 33 Boxplots and Error Bar Charts

Boxplots and error bar charts help you visualize distributions and dispersion. Boxplots characterize the distribution of a variable, displaying its median and quartiles. Special symbols identify the position of outliers, if any. Error bar charts display means with confidence intervals or standard errors. Simple boxplots and error bar charts display boxes (or means with error bars) for one or more quantitative variables, or for a single quantitative variable for cases grouped by the values of one categorical variable. Clustered boxplots and error bar charts display a cluster of boxes or error bars for each value of a categorical variable. The clusters can represent multiple variables or a single variable grouped by a second categorical variable. You can, for example, show the distribution of *age* within groups defined by *life* (as in whether you find life exciting, routine, or dull).

## How to Obtain a Boxplot

To obtain a boxplot, from the menus choose:

Graphs
  Boxplot...

This opens the Boxplot dialog box, as shown in Figure 33.1.

**Figure 33.1   Boxplot dialog box**

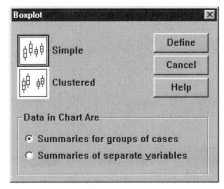

From the Boxplot dialog box, choose either simple or clustered boxplots, and then select the choice that describes the structure of your data organization.

**Data in Chart Are.** Select the choice that describes the structure of your data organization.

- **Summaries for groups of cases.** One variable is summarized in subgroups. The subgroups are determined by one variable for simple boxplots or two variables for clustered boxplots.
- **Summaries of separate variables.** More than one variable is summarized. Simple boxplots summarize each variable over all cases in the file. Clustered boxplots summarize each variable within categories determined by another variable.

## Defining Boxplots

Each combination of boxplot type and data structure produces a different definition dialog box. Each is briefly discussed below. The icon and section title indicate the choices that have to be made in the Boxplot dialog box to open that chart definition dialog box. The discussion for each boxplot type describes the selection required to enable the *OK* pushbutton. Optional selections are discussed only with the first chart using each data structure.

**Simple:**
**Summaries for groups of cases**

Figure 33.2 shows a simple boxplot with summaries for groups of cases. The specifications are on the left and the resulting chart is on the right.

**Figure 33.2   Simple boxplot of groups of cases**

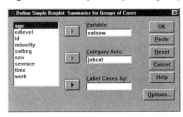 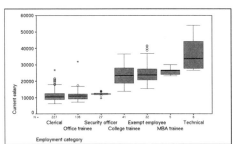

The numeric, short string, and long string variables in your data file are displayed on the source variable list. Select the numeric variable you want summarized and the variable you want to use to define the categories. To get a simple boxplot showing the distribution of cases in each category, click *OK*.

**Variable.** Select a numeric variable to be summarized.

**Category Axis.** Select a variable to define the categories shown in the boxplot. There is one boxplot for each value of the variable.

**Label Cases by.** Select a variable whose value labels are to be used to label outliers and extremes. For instance, if the boxplot variable is *salnow* and cases are labeled by *sex* and the third case is an outlier, the boxplot will indicate the sex of the person with that outlier salary. If this field is left blank, case numbers are used to label outliers and extremes. If two outliers or extremes have the same value, but different case labels, no label is displayed. In the Chart Editor, you can turn off labels altogether, as was done in Figure 33.2.

## Clustered:
## Summaries for groups of cases

Figure 33.3 shows a clustered boxplot with summaries for groups of cases. The specifications are on the left and the resulting boxplot is on the right.

**Figure 33.3  Clustered boxplot of groups of cases**

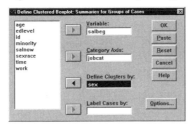 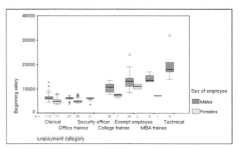

**Variable.** Select a numeric variable to be summarized.

**Category Axis.** Select a variable to define the categories shown in the boxplot. There is one boxplot for each value of the variable.

**Define Clusters by.** Select a variable to define the boxplots within each cluster. In each cluster, there is one boxplot for each value of the variable. A cluster variable must be selected to enable the *OK* pushbutton.

## Simple:
## Summaries of separate variables

Figure 33.4 shows a simple boxplot with summaries of separate variables. The specifications are on the left and the resulting boxplot is on the right.

**Figure 33.4    Simple boxplot of separate variables**

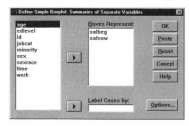 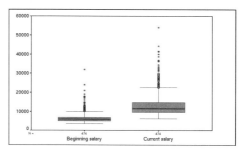

The numeric, short string, and long string variables in your data file are displayed on the source variable list. Select the numeric variables you want to define the boxplots. To get a simple boxplot showing the distribution of each variable in default format, click *OK*.

**Boxes Represent.** Select one or more variables to define the boxplots shown in the chart. There is one boxplot for each variable.

## Clustered:
## Summaries of separate variables

Figure 33.5 shows a clustered boxplot of separate variables. The specifications are on the left and the resulting boxplot is on the right.

**Figure 33.5    Clustered boxplot of separate variables**

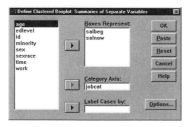 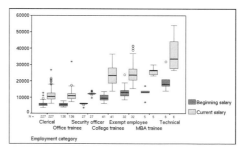

**Boxes Represent.** Select two or more variables to define the boxplots shown in the chart. There is one boxplot for each variable. Two or more box variables must be selected to enable the *OK* pushbutton.

**Category Axis.** Select a variable to define the categories shown in the boxplot. There is one cluster of boxplots for each value of the variable. A category axis variable must be selected to enable the *OK* pushbutton.

# How to Obtain an Error Bar Chart

To obtain an error bar chart, from the menus choose:

Graphs
  Error Bar...

This opens the Error Bar dialog box, as shown in Figure 33.6.

**Figure 33.6   Error Bar dialog box**

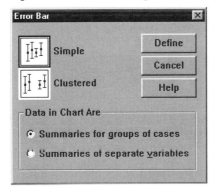

From the Error Bar dialog box, choose either simple or clustered error bars, and then select the choice that describes the structure of your data organization.

**Data in Chart Are.** Select the choice that describes the structure of your data organization.

- **Summaries for groups of cases.** One variable is summarized in subgroups. The subgroups are determined by one variable for simple error bars or two variables for clustered error bars.

- **Summaries of separate variables.** More than one variable is summarized. Simple error bars summarize each variable over all cases in the file. Clustered error bars summarize each variable within categories determined by another variable.

## Defining Error Bar Charts

Each combination of error bar type and data structure produces a different definition dialog box. Each is briefly discussed below. The icon and section title indicate the choices that have to be made in the Error Bar dialog box to open that chart definition dialog box. The discussion for each error bar type always describes the selection required to enable the *OK* pushbutton. Optional selections are discussed only with the first chart using each data structure.

### Simple:
### Summaries for groups of cases

Figure 33.7 shows a simple error bar chart with summaries for groups of cases. The specifications are on the left and the resulting chart is on the right.

**Figure 33.7   Simple error bar chart of groups of cases**

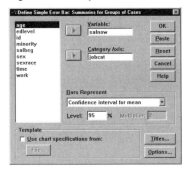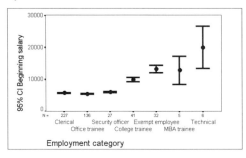

The numeric, short string, and long string variables in your data file are displayed on the source variable list. Select the numeric variable you want summarized and the variable you want to use to define the categories. To get a simple error bar chart showing the 95% confidence interval in each category, click *OK*.

**Variable.** Select a numeric variable to be summarized.

**Category Axis.** Select a variable to define the categories shown in the error bar chart. There is one error bar for each value of the variable.

**Bars Represent.** Select the statistic used to determine the length of the error bars.

- **Confidence interval for mean.** Bars represent confidence intervals. Enter the confidence level.

- **Standard error of mean.** The multiplier indicates the number of standard errors each bar represents.

- **Standard deviation.** The multiplier indicates the number of standard deviations each bar represents.

**Clustered:**
**Summaries for groups of cases**

Figure 33.8 shows a clustered error bar chart with summaries for groups of cases. The specifications are on the left and the resulting error bar chart is on the right.

**Figure 33.8  Clustered error bar chart of groups of cases**

 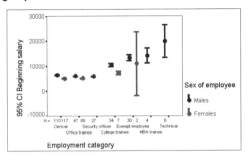

**Variable.** Select a numeric variable to be summarized.

**Category Axis.** Select a variable to define the categories shown in the error bar chart. There is one error bar for each value of the variable.

**Define Clusters by.** Select a variable to define the error bars within each cluster. In each cluster, there is one error bar for each value of the variable. A cluster variable must be selected to enable the *OK* pushbutton.

 **Simple:**
**Summaries of separate variables**

Figure 33.9 shows a simple error bar chart with summaries of separate variables. The specifications are on the left and the resulting error bar chart is on the right.

**Figure 33.9  Simple error bar chart of separate variables**

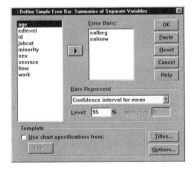 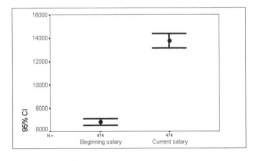

The numeric, short string, and long string variables in your data file are displayed on the source variable list. Select the numeric variables you want to define the error bars. To get a simple error bar chart showing the confidence interval of each variable in default format, click *OK*.

**Error Bars.** Select one or more numeric variables to define the error bars shown in the chart. There is one error bar for each variable.

## Clustered:
## Summaries of separate variables

Figure 33.10 shows a clustered error bar chart of separate variables. The specifications are on the left and the resulting error bar chart is on the right.

**Figure 33.10 Clustered error bar of separate variables**

 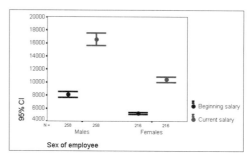

**Variables.** Select two or more variables to define the error bars shown in the chart. There is one error bar in each category for each variable. Two or more variables must be selected to enable the *OK* pushbutton.

**Category Axis.** Select a variable to define the categories shown in the error bar chart. There is one cluster of error bars for each value of the variable. A category axis variable must be selected to enable the *OK* pushbutton.

# 34 Scatterplots and Histograms

Scatterplots highlight the relationship between two quantitative variables by plotting the actual values along two axes. They often allow you to see relationships, such as a curvilinear pattern, that descriptive statistics do not reveal, and they can uncover bivariate outliers such as an 18-year-old with eight children. To help visualize the relationship, you can add a simple linear or quadratic regression line or a lowess smoother. Scatterplot matrices are useful when you want to look at a number of relationships together. 3-D scatterplots add a third variable to the relationship; you can rotate the two-dimensional projection of the three dimensions to uncover patterns.

Histograms show the distribution of values in a quantitative variable by dividing the range into equally-spaced intervals and plotting the count of cases in each interval as a bar. A histogram will show outliers and deviations from symmetry that make a variable unsuitable for analysis by a procedure that assumes a normal distribution.

## How to Obtain a Scatterplot

To obtain a scatterplot, from the menus choose:

Graph
  Scatter...

This opens the Scatterplot dialog box, as shown in Figure 34.1.

**Figure 34.1   Scatterplot dialog box**

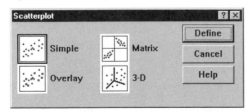

You can choose one of the following scatterplot types:

**Simple.** Each point represents the values of two variables for each case.

**Matrix.** Defines a square matrix of simple scatterplots, two for each combination of variables specified.

**Overlay.** Plots multiple scatterplots in the same frame.

**3-D.** Each point represents the value of three variables for each case. The points are plotted in a 3-D coordinate system which can be rotated.

# Defining Simple Scatterplots

To obtain a simple scatterplot, select the *Simple* picture button in the Scatterplot dialog box and click *Define*. This opens the Simple Scatterplot dialog box, as shown in Figure 34.2. The specifications are on the left and the resulting scatterplot is on the right.

**Figure 34.2    Simple Scatterplot dialog box and chart**

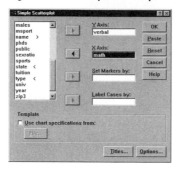
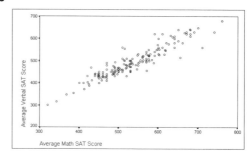

The numeric, short string, and long string variables in your data file are displayed on the source variable list. Select the numeric variables you want to define the *x* and *y* axes. To get a simple scatterplot in default format, click *OK*.

Optionally, you can divide the scatterplot points into groups; label each point; use a template to control the format of the scatterplot; add a title, subtitle, or footnote; or change the missing value options.

**Y Axis.** Select the variable that will determine the vertical position of each point.

**X Axis.** Select the variable that will determine the horizontal position of each point.

**Set Markers by.** Select a variable to determine the categories that will be shown on the chart. Each value of the variable is a different color or marker symbol on the scatterplot.

**Label Cases by.** Select a variable to provide labels for each marker. The value label of each case is placed above the point on the scatterplot. If there is no value label, the actual value will be placed above the point. The value label displayed is truncated after the 20th character.

**Template.** You can use another file to define the format of your charts (see "Chart Templates" on p. 338 in Chapter 30).

**Titles.** You can add titles, subtitles, and footnotes to your charts (see "Titles, Subtitles, and Footnotes" on p. 335 in Chapter 30).

**Options.** You can exclude cases with missing values listwise or by variable. You can also display groups defined by missing values. For more details, see "Options" on p. 336 in Chapter 30.

## Defining Scatterplot Matrices

To obtain a scatterplot matrix, select *Matrix* in the Scatterplot dialog box and click *Define*. This opens the Scatterplot Matrix dialog box, as shown in Figure 34.3. The specifications are on the left and the resulting scatterplot is on the right.

**Figure 34.3    Scatterplot Matrix dialog box and chart**

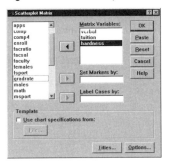
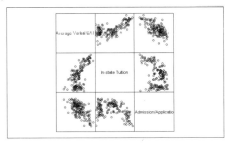

The numeric, short string, and long string variables in your data file are displayed on the source variable list. Select two or more numeric variables to define the cells of the matrix. To get a scatterplot matrix in the default format, click *OK*.

Optionally, you can show different markers for different categories; use a template to control the format of the scatterplot; or add a title, subtitle, or footnote.

**Matrix Variables.** Select two or more variables to define the cells of the matrix. There is one row and one column for each variable. Each cell contains a simple scatterplot of the row variable and the column variable.

**Set Markers by.** Select a variable to determine the categories that will be shown on the chart. Each value of the variable is a different marker symbol on the scatterplot matrix.

**Label Cases by.** Select a variable to provide labels for each marker. The value label of each case is placed above the point on the scatterplot. If there is no value label, the actual value will be placed above the point. The value label displayed is truncated after the 20th character.

**Template.** You can use another file to define the format of your charts (see "Chart Templates" on p. 338 in Chapter 30).

**Titles.** You can add titles, subtitles, and footnotes to your charts (see "Titles, Subtitles, and Footnotes" on p. 335 in Chapter 30).

**Options.** You can exclude cases with missing values listwise or by variable. You can also display groups defined by missing values. For more details, see "Options" on p. 336 in Chapter 30.

## Defining Overlay Scatterplots

To obtain an overlay scatterplot, select *Overlay* in the Scatterplot dialog box and click *Define*. This opens the Overlay Scatterplot dialog box, as shown in Figure 34.4. The specifications are on the left and the resulting overlay scatterplot is on the right.

**Figure 34.4    Overlay Scatterplot dialog box and chart**

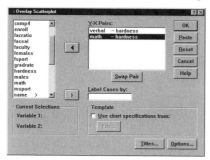
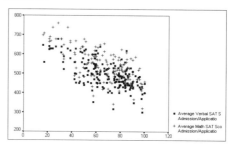

The numeric, short string, and long string variables in your data file are displayed on the source variable list. Select two or more numeric *y-x* variable pairs. To get an overlay scatterplot in default format, click *OK*.

Optionally, you can label the scatterplot points; use a template to control the format of the scatterplot; or add a title, subtitle, or footnote.

**Y-X Pairs.** Select two or more variable pairs. Each pair of variables is plotted on the same scatterplot with a separate marker symbol. To select a variable pair, highlight two variables on the source variable list by clicking on each one. The selected variables are indicated on the Current Selections list. Click the ▶ pushbutton. This copies the variables from the Current Selection list to the *y-x* pairs list. The same variable may be selected in multiple variable pairs. To swap the *y* and *x* variables in a *y-x* pair, highlight the pair and click *Swap Pair*.

**Label Cases by.** Select a variable to provide labels for each marker. The value label of each case is placed beside the point on the scatterplot. If there is no value label, the actual value will be placed beside the point. The value label displayed is truncated after the 20th character.

**Template.** You can use another file to define the format of your charts (see "Chart Templates" on p. 338 in Chapter 30).

**Titles.** You can add titles, subtitles, and footnotes to your charts (see "Titles, Subtitles, and Footnotes" on p. 335 in Chapter 30).

**Options.** You can exclude cases with missing values listwise or by variable. You can also display groups defined by missing values. For more details, see "Options" on p. 336 in Chapter 30.

## Defining 3-D Scatterplots

To obtain a 3-D scatterplot, select *3-D* in the Scatterplot dialog box and click *Define*. This opens the 3-D Scatterplot dialog box, as shown in Figure 34.5. The specifications are on the left and the resulting 3-D scatterplot is on the right.

**Figure 34.5    3-D Scatterplot dialog box and chart**

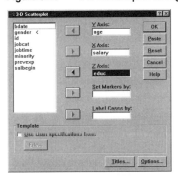
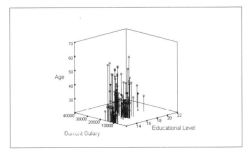

The numeric, short string, and long string variables in your data file are displayed on the source variable list. Select the numeric variables you want to define the *z*, *y*, and *x* axes. To get a 3-D scatterplot in default format, click *OK*.

Optionally, you can show different markers for different categories; label each point; use a template to control the format of the scatterplot; and add a title, subtitle, and footnote.

**Y Axis.** Select the variable that will determine the height of each point.

**X Axis.** Select the variable that will determine the horizontal position of each point.

**Z Axis.** Select the variable that will determine the depth of each point.

**Set Markers by.** Select a variable to determine the categories that will be shown on the chart. Each value of the variable is a different marker symbol on the scatterplot.

**Label Cases by.** Select a variable to provide labels for each marker. The value label of each case is placed beside the point on the scatterplot. If there is no value label, the actual value will be placed beside the point. The value label displayed is truncated after the 20th character.

**Template.** You can use another file to define the format of your charts (see "Chart Templates" on p. 338 in Chapter 30).

**Titles.** You can add titles, subtitles, and footnotes to your charts (see "Titles, Subtitles, and Footnotes" on p. 335 in Chapter 30).

**Options.** You can exclude cases with missing values listwise or by variable. You can also display groups defined by missing values. For more details, see "Options" on p. 336 in Chapter 30.

# How to Obtain a Histogram

For a discussion of how to interpret histograms, see Chapter 9. To obtain a histogram, from the menus choose:

Graphs
  Histogram...

This opens the Histogram dialog box, as shown in Figure 34.6.

**Figure 34.6     Histogram dialog box and chart**

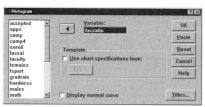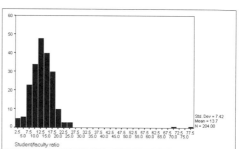

The numeric variables in your data file are displayed on the source variable list. Select the variable for which you want a histogram. To get a histogram in the default format, as shown in Figure 34.6, click *OK*.

Optionally, you can use a template to control the format of the histogram; add a title, subtitle, or footnote; or superimpose a normal curve on the histogram.

**Variable.** Select the variable for which you want a histogram. By default, you get bars showing the data divided into several evenly spaced intervals. The height of each bar shows the number of cases in each interval. The data series used to create the bar chart contains the individual values of each case. This means you can alter the intervals shown on the bar chart from the chart editor.

**Template.** You can use another file to define the format of your charts (see "Chart Templates" on p. 338 in Chapter 30).

**Display normal curve.** Select this to superimpose over the histogram a normal curve with the same mean and variance as your data.

**Titles.** You can add titles, subtitles, and footnotes to your charts (see "Titles, Subtitles, and Footnotes" on p. 335 in Chapter 30).

# 35 Pareto and Control Charts

Pareto and control charts are tools used to analyze and improve the quality of an on-going process. Pareto charts focus attention on the most important category out of a wide variety of possibilities. Control charts help differentiate between random variations in a process and variations that are meaningful. Pareto and control charts can be used in manufacturing processes, where the things being measured are physical and are usually produced on an assembly line. Or, these charts can be used in service processes, where the things being measured—such as opinions, budgetary flows, or the effect of a medical treatment—are more abstract.

## How to Obtain a Pareto Chart

To obtain a Pareto chart, from the menus choose:

Graphs
　Pareto...

This opens the Pareto Charts dialog box, as shown in Figure 35.1.

**Figure 35.1　Pareto Charts dialog box**

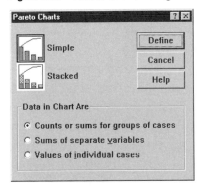

From the Pareto Charts dialog box, choose one of the chart types, and then select the choice that describes the structure of your data organization.

**Data in Chart Are.** Select the choice that describes the organization of your data.

- **Counts or sums for groups of cases.** One variable is counted or summed in subgroups. The subgroups are determined by one variable for simple Pareto charts or two variables for stacked Pareto charts.

- **Sums of separate variables.** More than one variable is summed. Simple Pareto charts sum each variable over all cases in the file. Stacked Pareto charts sum each variable within categories determined by another variable.

- **Values of individual cases.** Each case in the data is a separate category in the chart.

Each combination of chart type and data organization structure produces a different definition box. Each is discussed briefly below. The icon and section title indicate the choices that have to be made in the chart dialog box to open that chart definition dialog box. The discussion for each chart type always describes the selections required to enable the *OK* pushbutton. Optional selections are discussed only with the first chart using each data structure.

### Simple:
### Counts or sums for groups of cases

Figure 35.2 shows a chart definition dialog box and the resulting simple Pareto chart with counts for groups of cases.

**Figure 35.2   Simple Pareto chart with counts for groups of cases**

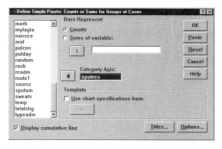 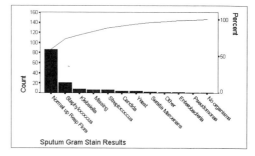

The numeric, short string, and long string variables in your data file are displayed on the source variable list. Select a variable to define the category axis. To get a simple chart showing number of cases for groups of cases in default format, click *OK*.

Optionally, you can select sums of a variable rather than counts, use a template to control the format of the chart, turn off the cumulative line, or add a title, subtitle, or footnote. Templates, titles, subtitles, and footnotes are discussed in detail in Chapter 30.

**Bars Represent.** Determines what the scale axis of the Pareto chart represents. Choose one of the following:

- **Counts.** The number of cases in each category determines the height of each bar.
- **Sum of variable.** The height of each bar is calculated from the sum of the specified variable. If you select *Sum of variable*, you must specify a numeric variable to be summed. Figure 35.3 shows the chart definition dialog box with a variable to be summed and the resulting simple Pareto chart.

**Category Axis.** Select a variable to define the categories shown in the chart. There is one bar for each value of the variable. The bars are sorted in descending order.

**Display cumulative line.** By default, a line will be drawn in the Pareto chart. This line indicates the cumulative sum of the values shown by the bars. Deselect this option to get a Pareto chart without the line.

**Figure 35.3   Simple Pareto chart with sums of a variable**

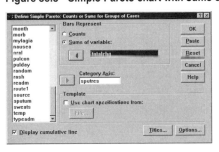 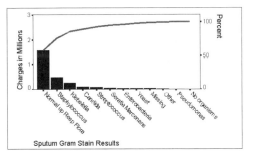

### Stacked:
### Counts or sums for groups of cases

Figure 35.4 shows a chart definition dialog box and the resulting clustered bar chart with summaries for groups of cases.

**Figure 35.4    Stacked Pareto chart with counts for groups of cases**

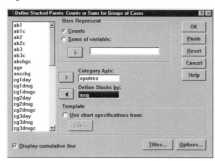
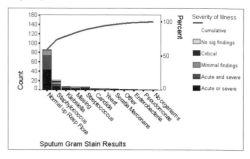

**Category Axis.** Select a variable to define the categories shown in the chart. There is one stack of bars for each value of the variable.

**Define Stacks by.** Select a variable to define the bar segments within each stack. There is one bar segment within each stack for each value of the variable.

### Simple:
### Sums of separate variables

Figure 35.5 shows a chart definition dialog box and the resulting simple bar chart with sums of separate variables.

**Figure 35.5    Simple Pareto chart with sums of separate variables**

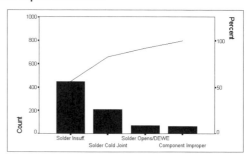

The numeric variables in your data file are displayed on the source variable list. Select the variables you want to define the bars. To get a simple Pareto chart showing the sum of each variable in default format, click *OK*.

Optionally, use a template to control the format of the chart, or add a title, subtitle, or footnote. These options are discussed in detail in Chapter 30.

**Variables.** Select two or more variables to define the categories shown in the chart. There is one bar for each variable. The bars show the sum of each variable and are sorted in descending order.

## Stacked:
## Sums of separate variables

Figure 35.6 shows a chart definition dialog box and the resulting stacked Pareto chart with sums of separate variables.

**Figure 35.6   Stacked Pareto chart with summaries of separate variables**

 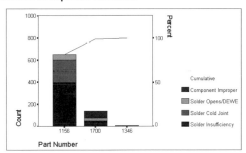

**Variables.** Select two or more variables. There is one bar within each stack for each variable. The bars show the sum of the selected variables.

**Category Axis.** Select a variable to define the categories shown in the chart. There is one stack of bars for each value of the variable.

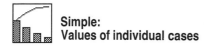

### Simple:
### Values of individual cases

Figure 35.7 shows a chart definition dialog box and the resulting simple Pareto chart with values of individual cases.

**Figure 35.7   Simple Pareto chart with values of individual cases**

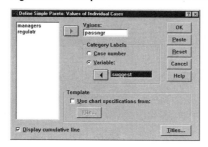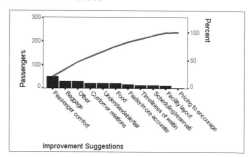

The numeric, short string, and long string variables in your data file are displayed on the source variable list. Select the numeric variable you want to define the bars. To get a simple Pareto chart showing the value of each case in default format, click *OK*.

Optionally, you can change the value labels shown in the chart, use a template to control the format of the chart, disable the cumulative line, or add a title, subtitle, or footnote. Templates, titles, subtitles, and footnotes are discussed in detail in Chapter 30.

**Values.** Select a numeric variable to define the bars. Each case will be displayed as a separate bar.

**Category Labels.** Determines how the bars are labeled. You can choose one of the following category label sources:

- **Case number.** Each category is labeled with the case number.
- **Variable.** Each category is labeled with the current value of the selected variable.

**Stacked:**
**Values of individual cases**

Figure 35.8 shows a chart definition dialog box and the resulting stacked Pareto chart with values of individual cases.

**Figure 35.8   Stacked Pareto chart with values of individual cases**

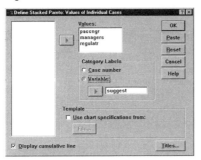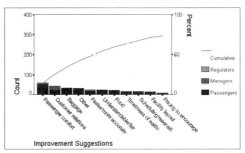

**Values.** Select two or more numeric variables. There is one bar within each stack for each variable. The bars show the value of each case. If there is a cumulative line, there is one point on the line for each case.

# How to Obtain a Control Chart

To obtain a control chart, from the menus choose:

Graphs
  Control...

This opens the Control Charts dialog box, as shown in Figure 35.9.

**Figure 35.9    Control Charts dialog box**

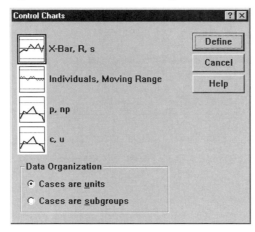

From the Control Charts dialog box, choose one of the chart types, and then select the choice that describes the structure of your data organization.

**Data Organization.** Select the choice that describes the organization of your data.

- **Cases are units.** Each unit is a separate case (row of data). One variable identifies the subgroup to which the unit belongs. Another variable records the value being measured. Each point in the control chart shows a different subgroup. The number of units can vary from subgroup to subgroup.

- **Cases are subgroups.** All units within a subgroup are recorded in a single case. Each unit is a separate variable. Like the previous organization, each point in the control chart shows a different subgroup. The number of samples per subgroup should be the same.

Each combination of chart type and data organization structure produces a different definition box. Each is discussed briefly in this chapter. The icon and section title indicate the choices that have to be made in the chart dialog box to open that chart definition dialog box.

## X-Bar, R, s:
## Cases are units

Figure 35.10 shows a chart definition dialog box and the resulting X-bar and R charts with cases as units. To plot this type of chart, your data file must contain one variable (column) that measures the process in question and one variable that breaks the process into subgroups. A subgroup can contain one or more rows from the data file. Each subgroup is plotted as a single point.

**Figure 35.10 X-Bar and R charts with cases as units**

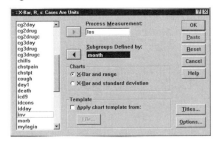
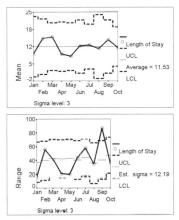

All variables are shown on the source variable list. Select a variable that measures the process of interest and select a variable that breaks the process into subgroups. To get a chart that shows the mean value for each subgroup and a chart that shows the range within each subgroup, click *OK*.

Optionally, you can select standard deviation rather than range, change the number of sigmas used for control limits, specify an upper or a lower limit, alter the minimum subgroup sample size, display subgroups defined by missing values, use a template to control the format of the chart, or add a title, subtitle, or footnote. Templates, titles, subtitles, and footnotes are discussed in detail in Chapter 30. The number of sigmas in the calculated control limits, specified control limits, minimum subgroup sample size, and missing values are described in "Control Chart Options" on p. 428.

If you don't have a subgroup variable but know that cases are sorted by subgroup within the file, it is easy to compute a subgroup variable. For Target Variable in the Compute Variable dialog box (choose *Compute* on the Transform menu), type the name of your new subgroup variable. For the Numeric Expression, enter

```
trunc(($CASENUM-1)/n)+1
```

where *n* is the number of cases in each subgroup.

**Process Measurement.** Select a numeric variable that measures the process of interest. The charts show the mean and range or standard deviation of this variable within each subgroup (see Figure 35.11).

**Subgroups Defined by.** Select a variable that divides the process into subgroups. There is one point on the process line for each value of this variable. Usually the variable represents a unit of time.

**Charts.** Two charts are produced. The first is an X-Bar chart. The second can be either a range chart (an R chart) or a standard deviation chart (an s chart).

An X-Bar chart shows the mean of the process for each subgroup. The center line is the mean of the process over the entire data set and the control limits are a number of standard deviations above and below the center line for each category. The number of standard deviations is shown as the sigma level.

- **X-Bar and range.** A range chart shows the range of the process within each subgroup. The center line shows the mean of the subgroup ranges (which is different for subgroups of different size). The upper and lower limits show three sigma levels above and below the center line for each category.

- **X-Bar and standard deviation.** A standard deviation chart shows the standard deviation of the process within each subgroup. The center line shows the mean of the subgroup standard deviations. The upper and lower limits show three sigma levels above and below the center line for each category.

**Figure 35.11 X-Bar and s charts with cases as units**

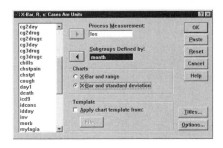

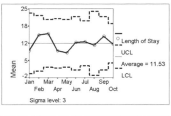

## Individuals, moving range:
## Cases are units

Figure 35.12 shows a chart definition dialog box and the resulting control charts for individuals with cases as units. To plot this type of chart, your data file must contain a variable (column) that measures the process in question; each row in the data file is plotted as a single point.

**Figure 35.12 Control charts for Individuals with cases as units**

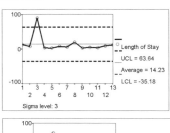

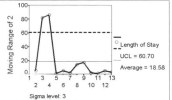

All variables are shown on the source variable list. Select a numeric variable that measures the process of interest. To obtain control charts that show the value of each case and the moving range in default format, click *OK*.

Optionally, you can select a subgroup label variable, suppress the moving range chart, select a different span, change the number of sigmas used for control limits, specify an upper or a lower limit, use a template to control the format of the chart, or add a title, subtitle, or footnote. Templates, titles, subtitles, and footnotes are discussed in detail in Chapter 30. The number of sigmas in the calculated control limits and specified control limits are described in "Control Chart Options" on p. 428.

**Process Measurement.** Select a numeric variable that measures the process of interest. The charts show the value of the variable for each case and the moving range.

**Subgroups Labeled by.** When a subgroup label variable is used, each category is labeled with the current value label of the selected variable. Figure 35.13 shows a control chart for individuals with a subgroup labels variable.

**Figure 35.13 Control chart for individuals with category labels from variable ab1**

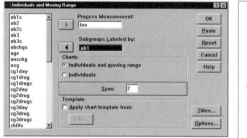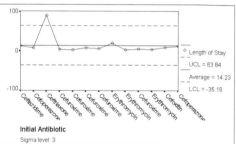

**Charts.** Determines the types of charts generated. You can choose from the following options:

- **Individuals and moving range.** Both an individuals and a moving range chart are generated.

- **Individuals.** Only an individuals chart is generated.

  **Span.** Indicate the number of cases used for calculating the control limits in both charts and for calculating the moving range. For example, if the span is 3, the current case and the previous two cases are used in the calculations.

## p, np:
## Cases are units

Figure 35.14 shows a chart definition dialog box and the resulting p chart with cases as units. To plot this type of chart, your data file must contain a variable (column) that indicates the presence of a nonconforming characteristic and a variable that divides the data into subgroups. A subgroup can contain one or more rows from the data file. Each subgroup is plotted as a single point.

**Figure 35.14  p chart with cases as units**

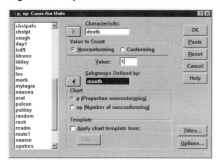 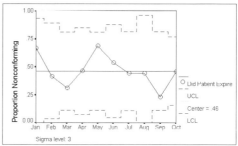

All variables are shown on the source variable list. Select a variable that indicates the presence of the characteristic of interest and a variable that divides the data into subgroups. Then, enter the value to count. To obtain a control chart that shows the proportion of nonconforming cases in default format, click *OK*.

Optionally, you can change the value to be counted, get an np chart rather than a p chart, change the number of sigmas used for control limits, display subgroups defined by missing values, use a template to control the format of the chart, or add a title, subtitle, or footnote. Templates, titles, subtitles, and footnotes are discussed in detail in Chapter 30. The number of sigmas in the calculated control limits and missing values are described in "Control Chart Options" on p. 428.

**Characteristic.** Select a variable that indicates the presence of the characteristic to be measured.

**Value to Count.** Either nonconforming or conforming cases can be counted. In both instances, the chart shows the proportion or number of nonconforming cases.

- **Nonconforming.** The indicated value is a nonconforming value. The chart shows the proportion or number of cases with this value.

- **Conforming.** The indicated value is a conforming value. The chart shows the proportion or number of cases that do not have this value.

**Value.** Indicate the value to be counted. The value must be of the same type as the characteristic variable. (For example, if the characteristic variable is numeric, the value must be a number.)

**Subgroups Defined by.** Select a variable that divides the process into subgroups. There is one point on the process line for each value of this variable. Usually the variable represents a unit of time.

**Chart.** Determines the type of chart generated. You can choose one of the following chart types:

- **p (Proportion nonconforming).** The chart shows the proportion of nonconformities within each subgroup. Use this chart type if the number of cases varies between subgroups.

- **np (Number of nonconforming).** The chart show the number of nonconformities within each subgroup. Use this chart type if all subgroups have the same number of cases. Figure 35.15 shows a chart definition dialog box and the resulting np chart.

**Figure 35.15 np chart with cases as units**

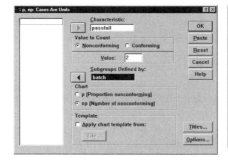 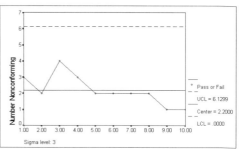

**c, u:**
**Cases are units**

Figure 35.16 shows a chart definition dialog box and the resulting u chart with cases as units. To plot this type of chart, your data file must contain one variable (column) that counts the number of nonconformities and one variable that divides the data into subgroups. A subgroup can contain one or more rows from the data file. Each subgroup is plotted as a single point.

**Figure 35.16 u chart with cases as units**

 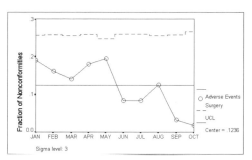

All variables are shown on the source variable list. Select a numeric variable that counts the characteristic of interest and select a variable that divides the data into subgroups. To get a control chart that shows the number of nonconformities per unit for each subgroup in default format, click *OK*.

Optionally, you can get a c chart rather than a u chart, change the number of sigmas used for control limits, display subgroups defined by missing values, use a template to control the format of the chart, or add a title, subtitle, or footnote. Templates, titles, subtitles, and footnotes are discussed in detail in Chapter 30. The number of sigmas in the calculated control limits and missing values are described in "Control Chart Options" on p. 428.

**Characteristic.** Select a numeric variable that indicates the number of times the characteristic to be measured is found.

**Subgroups Defined by.** Select a variable that divides the process into subgroups. There is one point on the process line for each value of this variable. Usually the variable represents a unit of time.

**Chart.** Determines the type of chart generated. You can choose one of the following chart types:

- **u (Nonconformities per unit).** The chart shows the proportion of nonconformities per case within each subgroup. Use this chart type if each subgroup does not have the same number of items.

- **c (Number of nonconformities).** The chart shows the total number of nonconformities per subgroup. Use this chart type if each subgroup has the same number of items. Figure 35.17 shows a chart definition dialog box and the resulting c chart.

**Figure 35.17 c chart with cases as units**

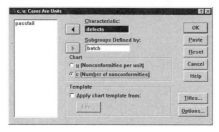 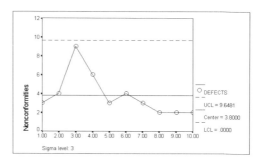

 **X-Bar, R, s:
Cases are subgroups**

Figure 35.18 shows a chart definition dialog box and the resulting X-bar and R charts with cases as subgroups. To plot this type of chart, your data file must contain two or more variables (columns) that measure the process in question; each row in the data file is plotted as a single point.

**Figure 35.18 X-Bar and R charts with cases as subgroups**

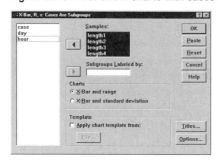 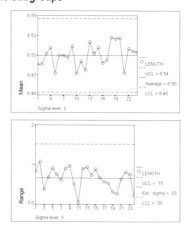

All variables are shown on the source variable list. Select two or more numeric sample variables. To get a chart that shows the mean value for each subgroup and a chart that shows the range within each subgroup, click *OK*.

Optionally, you can show standard deviation rather than the range, specify a variable to be used for subgroup labels, change the number of sigmas used for control limits, specify an upper or a lower limit, alter the minimum subgroup sample size, display subgroups defined by missing values, use a template to control the format of the chart, or add a title, subtitle, or footnote. Templates, titles, subtitles, and footnotes are discussed in detail in Chapter 30. The number of sigmas in the calculated control limits, specified control limits, minimum subgroup sample size, and missing values are described in "Control Chart Options" on p. 428.

**Samples.** Select two or more numeric variables. A single value from each selected variable is incorporated into each point. The charts show the mean and range or standard deviation for each row of data.

**Subgroups Labeled by.** Select a variable to use for labels. Each subgroup is labeled with the value label from the selected variable. If there is no value label, the actual value is used. Figure 35.19 shows an X-Bar chart using the variable *day* for labels.

**Figure 35.19 X-Bar chart using variable day for labels**

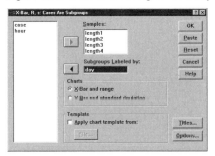 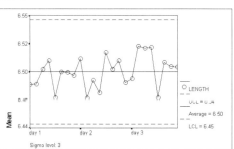

**Charts.** Two charts are produced. The first is an X-Bar chart. The second can be either a range chart (an R chart) or a standard deviation chart (an s chart).

An X-Bar chart shows the mean of the process for each subgroup. A subgroup contains all the values of the sample variables from a single row of data. The center line is the mean of the process and the control limits are a number of standard deviations above and below the center line for each category. The number of standard deviations is shown as the sigma level.

- **X-Bar and range.** A range chart shows the range of the process within each subgroup. The center line shows the mean of the subgroup ranges. The upper and lower limits show three sigma levels above and below the center line for each category.

- **X-Bar and standard deviation.** A standard deviation chart shows the standard deviation of the process for each subgroup. The center line shows the mean of the subgroup standard deviations. The upper and lower limits show three sigma levels above and below the center line for each category. Figure 35.20 shows X-Bar and s charts with cases as subgroups.

**Figure 35.20 X-Bar and s charts with cases as subgroups**

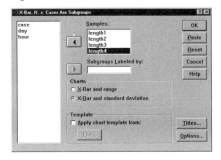
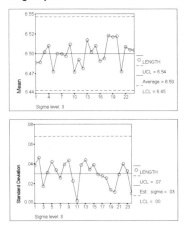

## p, np:
## Cases are subgroups

Figure 35.21 shows a chart definition dialog box and the resulting p chart with cases as subgroups. To plot this type of chart, your data file must contain a variable (column) that counts the number of nonconformities; each row in the data file is plotted as a single point.

**Figure 35.21 p chart with cases as subgroups**

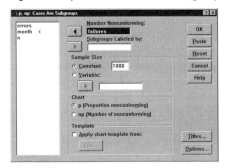
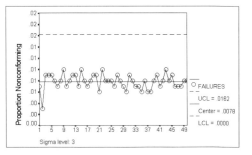

All variables in your data file are displayed on the source variable list. Select a numeric variable that indicates the number of nonconforming cases in each sample and enter the sample size. To see a control chart that shows the proportion of nonconforming cases in default format, click *OK*.

Optionally, you can specify a variable sample size, specify the name of a variable to be used for labels, generate an np chart rather than a p chart, change the number of sigmas used for control limits, display subgroups defined by missing values, use a template to control the format of the chart, or add a title, subtitle, or footnote. Templates, titles, subtitles, and footnotes are discussed in detail in Chapter 30. The number of sigmas in the calculated control limits and missing values are described in "Control Chart Options" on p. 428.

**Number Nonconforming.** Select a numeric variable indicating the number of nonconforming units in each sample. The chart shows the number or proportion of nonconforming units for each sample.

**Subgroups Labeled by**. Select a variable to use for labels. Each subgroup is labeled with the value label from the selected variable (if the variable has not been labeled, the value of the variable will be displayed). Figure 35.22 shows a p chart using the variable *month* for labels.

**Figure 35.22 p chart using variable month for labels and sample size**

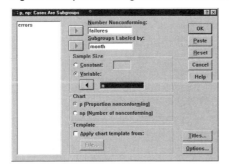 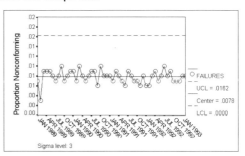

**Sample Size.** The number of units per sample can be constant or variable.

- **Constant.** Enter the number of units per sample.
- **Variable.** Select a variable that indicates the number of units in each sample.

**Chart.** Determines the type of chart generated. You can choose one of the following chart types:

- **p (Proportion nonconforming).** The chart shows the proportion of nonconformities out of the total sample. Use this chart type if the sample size varies between cases.

- **np (Number of nonconforming).** The chart shows the total number of nonconformities for each subgroup. Use this chart type if the sample size is constant. Figure 35.23 shows a chart definition dialog box and the resulting np chart.

**Figure 35.23 np chart with cases as subgroups**

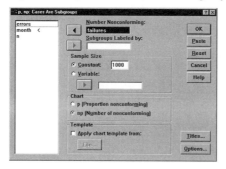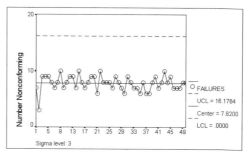

 **c, u:**
## Cases are subgroups

Figure 35.24 shows a chart definition dialog box and the resulting u chart with cases as subgroups. To plot this type of chart, your data file must contain a variable (column) that counts the number of nonconformities; each row in the data file is plotted as a single point.

**Figure 35.24 u chart with cases as subgroups**

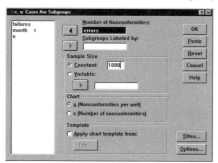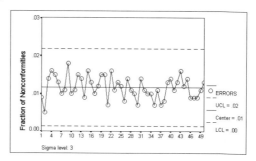

All variables in the working data file are displayed on the source variable list. Select a numeric variable that specifies the number of nonconformities for each case and enter the sample size. To generate a control chart that shows the number of nonconformities per unit for each subgroup in default format, click *OK*.

Optionally, you can specify a variable sample size, specify a variable to use for labels, generate a c chart rather than a u chart, change the number of sigmas used for control limits, display subgroups defined by missing values, use a template to control the format of the chart, or add a title, subtitle, or footnote. Templates, titles, subtitles, and footnotes are discussed in detail in Chapter 30. The number of sigmas in the calculated control limits and missing values are described in "Control Chart Options" on p. 428.

**Number of Nonconformities.** Select a variable indicating the number of nonconformities in each sample. The chart shows the number or proportion of nonconformities for each row of data.

**Subgroups Labeled by.** Select a variable to use for labels. Each subgroup is labeled with the value label from the selected variable. If there is no value label, the value of the variable will be displayed. Figure 35.25 shows a u chart using the variable *month* for labels.

**Figure 35.25 u chart using variable month for labels and sample size**

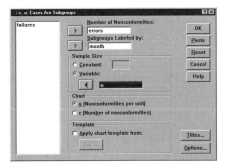 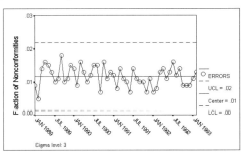

**Sample Size.** The number of units per sample can be constant or variable.

- **Constant.** Enter the number of units per sample.
- **Variable.** Select a variable that indicates the number of units in each sample.

**Chart.** Determines the type of chart generated. You can choose one of the following chart types:

- **u (Nonconformities per unit).** The chart shows the proportion of nonconformities per unit within each subgroup. Use this chart type if the sample size differs between cases.

- **c (Number of nonconformities).** The chart shows the total number of nonconformities per subgroup. Use this chart type if the sample size does not vary between cases. Figure 35.26 shows a c chart with cases as subgroups.

**Figure 35.26 c chart with cases as subgroups**

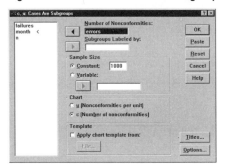
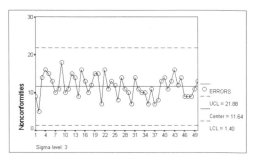

# Control Chart Options

Figure 35.27 shows the Options dialog box for X-Bar, R, and s charts, which includes all of the options found in other control chart Options dialog boxes.

**Figure 35.27 Options dialog box for X-Bar, R, and s charts**

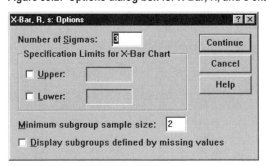

**Number of Sigmas.** Determines the number of standard deviations above and below the center line for the calculated upper and lower control limits.

**Specification Limits for X-Bar Chart.** You may specify upper and lower control limits in addition to the calculated limits for X-Bar and individuals charts. This is useful if you want to see if the process falls within predetermined tolerances.

- **Upper.** Displays the specified upper control limit.
- **Lower.** Displays the specified lower control limit.

**Minimum subgroup sample size.** In X-Bar, R, and s charts, you can change the minimum subgroup sample size. Subgroups with fewer units than the specified size are not shown in the chart.

- **Display subgroups defined by missing values.** In all control charts except individuals and moving range charts, you can display subgroups defined by missing values.

# 36 Probability Plots

SPSS offers thirteen distributions against which you can plot values of a variable, of which the normal distribution is the most familiar and commonly used. The Q-Q procedure provides traditional probability plots; the P-P procedure plots the observed cumulative proportion against the cumulatitve proportion expected under the chosen distribution. If, for Q-Q plot, you select the normal distribution, the resulting display can be used to screen data or residuals for non-normality or for the presence of outliers. The observed data values are plotted along the horizontal axis. The expected value under normality for each observation is plotted on the vertical axis. If the data are from a normal distribution, the plot points cluster around a straight line. The normal probability plot usually provides a better assessment of normality than a histogram. To help you better characterize departures from normality (or your chosen distribution), SPSS also displays a detrended probability plot. Both the P-P and Q-Q procedures have options for transforming the data to log units, standardized scores (z-scores), or differences. Alternative methods are available for estimating proportions and handling ties in the data values.

## How to Obtain Probability Plots

To obtain P-P or Q-Q probability plots and detrended probability plots, from the menus choose:

Graphs
  P-P...

*or*

Graphs
  Q-Q...

The P-P Plots and Q-Q Plots dialog boxes are identical. The P-P Plots dialog box is shown in Figure 36.1.

**Figure 36.1   P-P Plots dialog box**

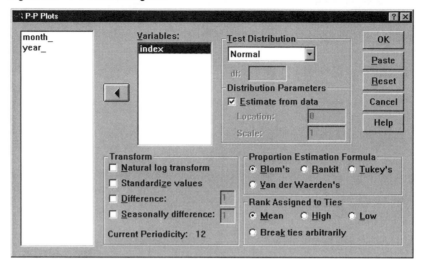

The numeric variables in the working data file are displayed on the source variable list. A probability plot and a detrended probability chart are produced for each variable.

**Test Distribution.** specifies the distribution type of your data. The parameters of the distribution type (either specified or estimated from the sample mean and standard deviation) are displayed with the plots.

- **Normal.** *Location* and *Scale* are estimated from the sample mean and sample standard deviation if *Estimate from data* is selected.

- **Exponential.** *Scale* is estimated from the sample mean if *Estimate from data* is selected. *Scale* must be positive. If an observation in the sample is negative, no chart is produced.

- **Weibull.** *Scale* and *shape* are estimated using the least square method if *Estimate from data* is selected. *Location* and *Scale* must be positive. If an observation in the sample is negative, no chart is produced.

- **Pareto.** *Threshold* is estimated with the minimum observations and *Shape* is estimated by the maximum likelihood method assuming *Threshold* is a known constant if *Estimate from data* is selected. *Threshold* and *Shape* must be positive. If an observation in the sample is not positive, no chart is produced.

- **Lognormal.** *Scale* and *Shape* are estimated from the sample mean and sample standard deviation if they are not specified. *Scale* and *Shape* must be positive. If an observation in the sample is negative, no chart is produced.

- **Beta.** *Shape* and *Shape2* are estimated from the sample mean and sample standard deviation if *Estimate from data* is selected. If an observation in the sample is negative or greater than 1, no chart is produced.

- **Gamma.** *Shape* and *Scale* are estimated from the sample mean and sample standard deviation if *Estimate from data* is selected. *Shape* and *Scale* must be positive. If an observation in the sample is negative, no chart is produced.

- **Logistic.** *Location* and *Scale* are estimated from the sample mean and sample standard deviation if *Estimate from data* is selected. *Scale* must be positive.

- **Laplace.** *Location* and *Scale* are estimated from the sample mean and sample standard deviation if *Estimate from data* is selected. *Scale* must be positive.

- **Uniform.** *Minimum* and *Maximum* are estimated from the minimum and maximum of $x_1$ to $x_n$ if *Estimate from data* is selected.

- **Half-Normal.** Data are assumed to be location free or centralized (Location = 0). *Scale* is estimated using the maximum likelihood method if *Estimate from data* is selected. *Scale* must be positive.

- **Chi-square.** You must specify *df*.

- **Student t.** You must specify *df*.

**Transform**. You can produce probability plots for transformed values using any combination of the following transformation options:

- **Natural log transform.** Transforms the variable using the natural logarithm (base *e*) of the variable. This is useful for removing varying amplitude over time in time series data. If a variable contains any values that are less than or equal to 0, the probability plot for that variable will not be produced because non-positive values cannot be log transformed.

- **Standardize values.** Transforms the variable into a sample with a mean of 0 and a standard deviation of 1.

- **Difference.** Transforms the variable by calculating the difference between successive values of the variable. Enter a positive integer to specify the degree of differencing (the number of previous values used to calculate the difference). The number of values used in the calculations decreases by 1 for each degree of differencing. Differencing a time series converts a nonstationary series to a stationary one with a constant mean and variance.

- **Seasonally difference.** Transforms time series data by calculating the difference between series values a constant span apart. The span is based on the currently defined periodicity. Enter a positive integer to specify the degree of differencing (the number of previous seasonal periods used to calculate the difference). To compute seasonal differences, you must have defined date variables that include a periodic component (such as months of the year).

**Current Periodicity**. Indicates the currently defined period used to calculate seasonal differences for time series data. If the current periodicity is *None*, seasonal differencing is not available. To create a date variable with a periodic component used to define periodicity, select the *Define Dates* option on the Data menu (see Chapter 5).

These transformations affect only the probability plot and do not alter the values of the variables. For time series data, you can create new time series variables based on transformed values of existing time series with the *Create Time Series* option on the Transform menu (see Chapter 5).

**Proportion Estimation Formula.** Choose one of the following alternatives:

- **Blom's**. Uses Blom's transformation, defined by the formula

$$(r - (3/8))/(n + (1/4))$$

where $n$ is the number of observations and $r$ is the rank, ranging from 1 to $n$. This is the default.

- **Rankit**. Uses the formula

$$(r - (1/2))/n$$

where $n$ is the number of observations and $r$ is the rank, ranging from 1 to $n$.

- **Tukey's.** Uses Tukey's transformation, defined by the formula

$$(r - (1/3))/(n + (1/3))$$

where $n$ is the number of observations and $r$ is the rank, ranging from 1 to $n$.

- **Van der Waerden's**. Uses Van der Waerden's transformation, defined by the formula

$$r/(n + 1)$$

where $n$ is the number of observations and $r$ is the rank, ranging from 1 to $n$.

**Rank Assigned to Ties.** Select an option to use in resolving **ties**, or multiple observations with the same value:

- **Mean.** Assigns rank using the mean rank of the tied values. (This is the default.)
- **Low.** Applies the lowest rank of the tied values.
- **High**. Applies the highest rank of the tied values.
- **Break ties arbitrarily.** Plots each of the tied cases, ignoring any case weights that are in effect.

## Weighted Data

The P-P Plots and Q-Q Plots procedures do not use case weights. If weighting is in effect, case weights are ignored for these plots. To obtain Q-Q plots for weighted data, use the Explore procedure (Statistics menu, Summarize submenu) and select *Normality plots with tests* from the Explore Plots dialog box. See Chapter 11 for more information on the Explore procedure.

# 37 Sequence Charts

The sequence of data values is not a consideration in most statistical tests performed by SPSS. Typically, when you look at measures of central tendency or distributions, observations are independent, and the order in which you observe the values is irrelevant. When sequence is important, as in time series data, a sequence chart is used to plot one or more series. Individual values are plotted in the order of the cases in the file. You can select a variable—often, but not necessarily, a date variable—to label the cases along the base (time) axis. You may find both seasonal and overall trends in a single series, and you may want to use differencing to see whether those trends can be removed (called making the data stationary). For more options to transform time series, see Create Time Series on the Transform menu of the Data Editor. Plotting multiple series may show how they vary in parallel or provide other clues to guide further analysis. If the series are measured on very different scales, you may need to multiply or divide one by a constant before plotting them together.

## How to Obtain Sequence Charts

To obtain sequence charts, from the menus choose:

Graphs
  Sequence...

This opens the Sequence Charts dialog box, as shown in Figure 37.1.

**Figure 37.1   Sequence Charts dialog box**

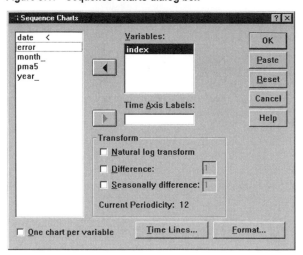

The numeric variables in the working data file are displayed on the source variable list. Sequence charts require a data file structure in which cases (rows) are sorted in a sequential order or represent observations at regular time intervals.

**Time Axis Labels**. You can use a numeric or string variable to label the time (sequence) axis of the chart. By default, the time axis is simply labeled 1 to *n*, or it is labeled with the values of the string variable *date_* if you have defined date variables (see Chapter 5).

**Transform**. You can plot transformed data values using any combination of the following transformation options:

- **Natural log transform**. Transforms data values using the natural logarithm (base *e*) of the values. This is useful for removing varying amplitude over time. If a variable contains values that are less than or equal to 0, no chart will be created for the variable because non-positive values cannot be log transformed.

- **Difference**. Transforms the data values by calculating the difference between successive values of the variable. Enter a positive integer to specify the degree of differencing (the number of previous values used to calculate the difference). The number of values used in the calculations decreases by one for each degree of differencing. Differencing a time series converts a nonstationary series to a stationary one with a constant mean and variance.

- **Seasonally difference**. Transforms the data values by calculating the difference between values a constant span apart. The span is based on the currently defined periodicity. Enter a positive integer to specify the degree of differencing (the number of previous seasonal periods used to calculate the difference). To compute seasonal differences, you must have defined date variables that include a periodic component (such as months of the year).

**Current Periodicity**. Indicates the currently defined period used to calculate seasonal differences. If the current periodicity is *None*, seasonal differencing is not available. To create a date variable with a periodic component used to define periodicity, use the Define Dates option on the Data menu (see Chapter 5).

These transformations affect only the plotted values in the sequence chart and do not alter the values of the actual variables. To create new time series variables based on transformed values of existing time series, use the Create Time Series option on the Transform menu (see Chapter 5).

The following option is also available:

- **One chart per variable**. Creates a separate sequence chart for each selected variable. By default, all selected variables are plotted in a single chart.

## Time Axis Reference Lines

To display reference lines on the time (sequence) axis at each change in a reference variable or at a specific date or time, click *Time Lines* in the Sequence Charts dialog box. This opens the Time Axis Reference Lines dialog box, similar to the one shown in Figure 37.2.

**Figure 37.2   Time Axis Reference Lines dialog box**

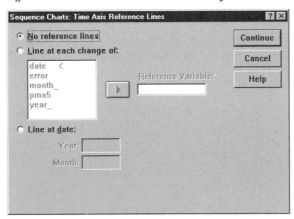

You can choose one of the following alternatives:

- **No reference lines**. This is the default.
- **Line at each change of**. Displays a reference line each time the value of the selected reference variable changes. For example, you could use the date variable *year_* to display a reference line at the beginning of each year. (Do *not* use the date variable *date_*, since that would display a reference line at each case.)
- **Line at date**. You can display a single reference line at the value of a specific date, time or observation number. The available text boxes for specifying the date and/or time are dependent on the currently defined date variables. If there are no defined date variables, you can specify an observation (case) number.

If you enter a value for a lower-order date variable, you must also enter a value for all higher-order date variables above it. For example, in Figure 37.2, you cannot specify a *Month* value without a *Year* value. If you enter a value for a higher-order date variable without entering any values for lower-order date variables, the reference line will be drawn at the first occurrence of the value.

Use the Define Dates option on the Data menu to create date variables. See Chapter 5 for more information, including valid ranges for each date variable.

## Formatting Options

To change formatting options, such as switching the axis used as the time (sequence) axis or displaying area charts instead of line charts, click *Format* in the Sequence Charts dialog box. This opens the Sequence Charts Format dialog box, as shown in Figure 37.3.

**Figure 37.3   Sequence Charts Format dialog box**

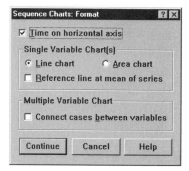

The following formatting options are available:

- **Time on horizontal axis**. Uses the horizontal axis as the time (sequence) axis. This is the default. Deselect this item to use the vertical axis as the time axis.

**Single Variable Chart(s)**. If only a single variable is plotted in each chart, you can choose one of the following alternatives:

- **Line chart**. Displays a line chart for each variable. This is the default.
- **Area chart**. Displays an area chart for each variable, with the area between the line and the time (sequence) axis filled in with a color or pattern.

The following option is also available for single variable charts:

- **Reference line at mean of series**. Displays a reference line on the scale axis at the mean value of the variable.

**Multiple Variable Chart**. If more than one variable is plotted in a chart, the following formatting option is available:

- **Connect cases between variables**. Draws a line at each case between values of the plotted variables.

# 38

# Autocorrelation and Cross-Correlation

In time series data, adjacent values are often highly correlated. Values can also be correlated with those from fixed time intervals, such as December sales with sales for previous Decembers. A first-order **autocorrelation** reveals how correlated adjacent values are. This statistic is the Pearson correlation of a series of numbers with the same series shifted by one observation $(y_2,y_1; y_3,y_2;...; y_n,y_{n-1})$. This is called "lag 1." For lag 2, shift the series down two time points; for lag 3, three time points; and so on. The **partial autocorrelation** also measures correlations among observations $j$ lags apart, except that all intervening lags are "partialed out." Plots of autocorrelations and partial autocorrelations for a wide range of lags are used to select parameters for time series models and to evaluate the residuals from the fit.

**Cross-correlations** identify relations between two different series when one series lags the other series—when one is a "leading indicator" of the other.

SPSS provides options for:

- Log transforming the data to make the variance across time more stable. It is unwise to fit a model when the spread of the series increases over time.

- Differencing the series by one or more lags in order to make the mean of the series constant across time. Differencing replaces each value by the difference between it and the previous value (or the previous $j$th lag).

## How to Obtain Autocorrelation and Partial Autocorrelation Charts

To obtain autocorrelation charts, partial autocorrelation charts, and related statistics for time series data, from the menus choose:

Graphs
  Time Series ▶
    Autocorrelations...

This opens the Autocorrelations dialog box, as shown in Figure 38.1.

**Figure 38.1   Autocorrelations dialog box**

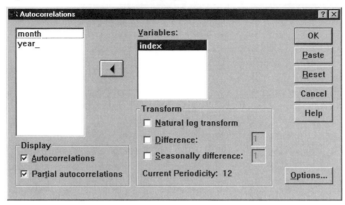

The numeric variables in the working data file are displayed on the source variable list. Time Series analysis requires a data file structure in which each case (row) represents a set of observations at a different time, and the length of time between cases is uniform.

**Display**. You can choose one or both of the following display options:

- **Autocorrelations**. Displays a chart of autocorrelation coefficients and confidence intervals (two standard errors). Autocorrelation coefficient values, standard errors, the Box-Ljung statistic, and probabilities for each lag are displayed in the output window.

- **Partial autocorrelations**. Displays a chart of partial autocorrelation coefficients and confidence intervals (two standard errors). Partial autocorrelation coefficient values and standard errors for each lag are displayed in the output window.

**Transform**. You can calculate autocorrelations for transformed time series values using any combination of the following transformation options:

- **Natural log transform**. Transforms the time series using the natural logarithm (base $e$) of the series. This is useful for removing varying amplitude over time. If a series contains values that are less than or equal to 0, autocorrelations will not be calculated for that series because non-positive values cannot be log transformed.

- **Difference**. Transforms the time series by calculating the difference between successive values in the series. Enter a positive integer to specify the degree of differencing (the number of previous values used to calculate the difference). The number of values used in the calculations decreases by one for each degree of differencing. Differencing the series converts a nonstationary series to a stationary one with a constant mean and variance.

- **Seasonally difference**. Transforms the time series by calculating the difference between series values a constant span apart. The span is based on the currently defined periodicity. Enter a positive integer to specify the degree of differencing (the number of previous seasonal periods used to calculate the difference). To compute seasonal differences, you must have defined date variables that include a periodic component (such as months of the year).

**Current Periodicity**. Indicates the currently defined period used to calculate seasonal differences. If the current periodicity is *None*, seasonal differencing is not available. To create a date variable with a periodic component used to define periodicity, use the Define Dates option on the Data menu (see Chapter 5).

These transformations affect only the calculation of the autocorrelations and do not alter the values of the time series variables. To create new time series variables based on transformed values of existing time series, use the Create Time Series option on the Transform menu (see Chapter 5).

# Options

To change the maximum number of lags plotted, or change the method used to calculate the standard error, or display autocorrelations of periodic lags, click *Options* in the Autocorrelations dialog box. This opens the Autocorrelations Options dialog box, as shown in Figure 38.2.

**Figure 38.2    Autocorrelations Options dialog box**

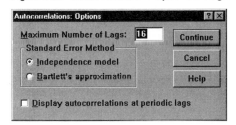

**Maximum number of lags**. Controls the maximum number of lags plotted. The default is 16.

**Standard Error Method**. For autocorrelations, you can change the method used to calculate the standard error. (This option is not available for partial autocorrelations.) You can choose one of the following methods:

- **Independence model**. Assumes the underlying process is white noise. This is the default.

- **Bartlett's approximation**. Standard errors grow at increased lags. Appropriate where the order of the moving average process is $k$-1.

The following option is also available for time series data with defined periodicity:

- **Display autocorrelations at periodic lags**. Displays autocorrelations *only* for periodic intervals, based on the currently defined periodicity.

# How to Obtain Cross-Correlation Charts

To obtain cross-correlation charts and related statistics, from the menus choose:

Graphs
  Time Series ▶
    Cross-Correlations...

This opens the Cross-Correlations dialog box, as shown in Figure 38.3.

**Figure 38.3   Cross-Correlations dialog box**

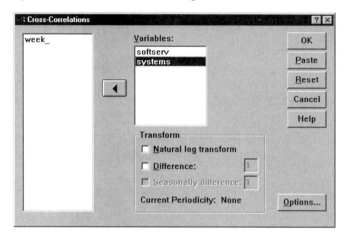

The numeric variables in the working data file are displayed on the source variable list. A separate cross-correlation chart is created for each possible pair of variables. Time Series analysis requires a data file structure in which each case (row) represents a set of observations at a different time, and the length of time between cases is uniform.

**Transform**. You can calculate cross-correlations for transformed time series values using any combination of the following transformation options:

- **Natural log transform**. Transforms the time series using the natural logarithm (base *e*) of the series. This is useful for removing varying amplitude over time. If any values in a pair of series are less than or equal to 0, cross-correlations will not be calculated for that pair because non-positive values cannot be log transformed.

- **Difference**. Transforms the time series by calculating the difference between successive values in the series. Enter a positive integer to specify the degree of differencing (the number of previous values used to calculate the difference). The number of values used in the calculations decreases by 1 for each degree of differencing. Differencing the series converts a nonstationary series to a stationary one with a constant mean and variance.

- **Seasonally difference**. Transforms the time series by calculating the difference between series values a constant span apart. The span is based on the currently defined periodicity. Enter a positive integer to specify the degree of differencing (the number of previous seasonal periods used to calculate the difference). To compute seasonal differences, you must have defined date variables that include a periodic component (such as months of the year).

**Current Periodicity**. Indicates the currently defined period used to calculate seasonal differences. If the current periodicity is *None*, seasonal differencing is not available. To create a date variable with a periodic component used to define periodicity, use the *Define Dates* option on the Data menu (see Chapter 5).

These transformations affect only the calculation of the cross-correlations and do not alter the values of the time series variables. To create new time series variables based on transformed values of existing time series, use the *Create Time Series* option on the Transform menu (see Chapter 5).

## Options

To change the maximum number of lags plotted or display cross-correlations of periodic lags, click *Options* in the Cross-Correlations dialog box. This opens the Cross-Correlations Options dialog box, as shown in Figure 38.4.

**Figure 38.4    Cross-Correlations Options dialog box**

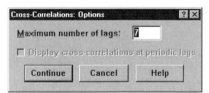

**Maximum number of lags**. Controls the maximum number of lags plotted. The default is 7.

The following option is also available for time series data with defined periodicity:

- **Display cross-correlations at periodic lags**. Displays cross-correlations *only* for periodic intervals, based on the currently defined periodicity.

# 39 Modifying Charts

After creating a chart, you may wish to modify it, either to obtain more information about the data or to enhance the chart for presentation. The chart modification capabilities of SPSS allow you to select data, change chart types, add information, and alter chart appearance to accomplish both of those goals.

Two brief examples are given in this chapter. The first example illustrates a process for exploring data relationships graphically; the second, enhancing a bar chart for presentation.

## Exploring Data with the Chart Editor

Figure 39.1 shows a preliminary scatterplot matrix of graduation rate, verbal SAT score, and student-faculty ratio in 250 colleges and universities.

Figure 39.1  Scatterplot matrix of gradrate, verbal, and facratio

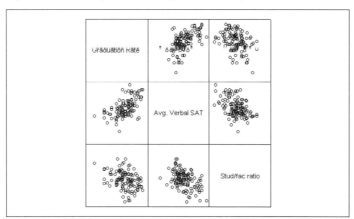

Two of the available options for scatterplots, adding axis labels and linear regression lines, help make relationships more apparent. In Figure 39.2, labels and regression lines have been added.

**Figure 39.2    Scatterplot matrix with labels and regression lines**

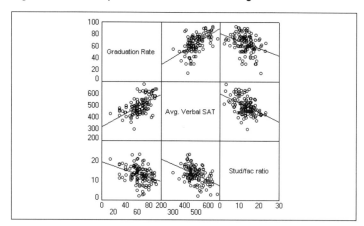

For a closer look at the relationship between schools' graduation rates and the average SAT verbal test scores of their students, we can turn to the Gallery menu and select a bivariate (simple) scatterplot of those variables. In the bivariate scatterplot, we can see more detail (see Figure 39.3).

**Figure 39.3    Scatterplot of gradrate and verbal**

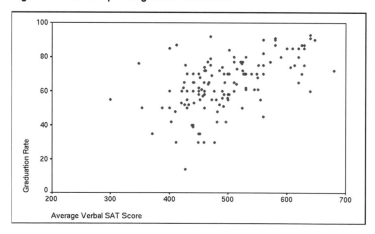

We might want to look more closely at the univariate distribution of the two variables, which we can do by returning to the Gallery menu and selecting histogram (see Figure 39.4).

**Figure 39.4   Histograms of verbal and gradrate**

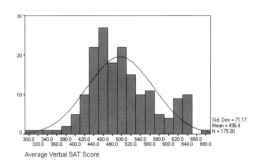
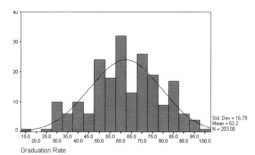

# Enhancing Charts for Presentation

Although charts as originally generated by SPSS contain the requested information in a logical format, they may require some changes to make the presentation clearer or more dramatic. Figure 39.5 is the unedited clustered bar chart of *verbal* and *math* (the average verbal and math SAT scores for each university) by *comp* (level of competitiveness).

**Figure 39.5   Default bar chart of verbal and math by comp**

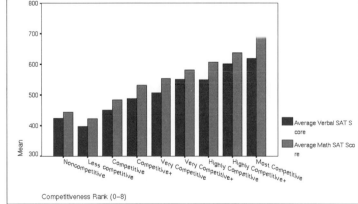

While the information is clear, at least some changes are desirable to prepare the chart for presentation. The following modifications create the chart shown in Figure 39.6:

- A title and subtitle are added.
- 3-D effect is selected for the bars.

- The cluster spacing is widened.
- Both axis titles are removed, since the information they contain appears elsewhere in the chart. This allows more room for the chart itself and the chart enlarges itself automatically.
- The noncompetitive category is removed.
- Several labels are removed from the category axis and the orientation of the remaining labels is changed. This makes the labels easier to read, yet still conveys the essential information.
- The legend labels are edited to remove unnecessary information.
- The range of the scale axis is enlarged to start at 200, the lowest possible SAT score, in order to give a better representation of the relative differences between schools in each competitiveness level.
- Annotations are added to indicate the overall averages for the two SAT tests. (These averages are easily obtained by leaving the chart window for a moment to run descriptive statistics from the Statistics menu.)

**Figure 39.6  Enhanced bar chart**

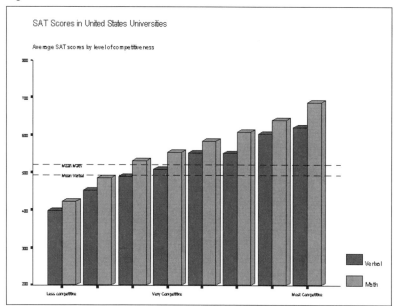

Figure 39.7 shows further bar chart variations.

- The axes and tick marks have been removed.
- The sides and tops of the bars have been shaded a different color to enhance the 3-D effect.

- Inter-cluster spacing has been increased.
- The annotation indicating overall averages has been refined.

**Figure 39.7   Another bar chart variation**

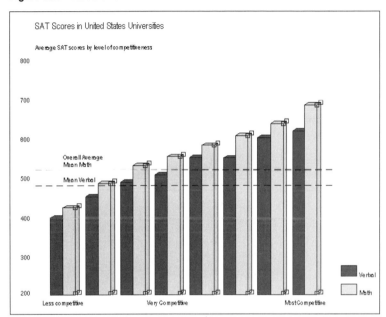

# Editing in a Chart Window

All modifications to charts are done in a chart window. You open a chart window by double-clicking, on a chart in the Output Navigator. Closing a chart window saves any changes and displays the modified chart in the Output Navigator.

Several chart windows can be open at the same time, each containing a single chart. The exact number depends on your system and on how many other windows are open at the time. If you see a message telling you that there are not enough system resources, you can close some windows to free resources.

## Chart Menus

When a chart window is active, the Chart Editor menu bar, shown in Figure 39.8, replaces the main menu bar.

**Figure 39.8   Chart Editor menu bar**

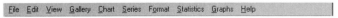

The Chart Editor menu bar contains ten menus:

**File.** From the File menu, you can save the chart template and export the chart in several different file formats.

**Edit.** From the Edit menu, you can copy the chart to the Clipboard. You can paste a chart into other applications as an embedded OLE 2 object, a metafile, or a bitmap.

You can also choose *Options* to open the Options dialog box. Charts options include global chart characteristics such as preferred type font, use of color versus pattern in lines and areas, and use of grid lines.

The Edit menu does not include items for modifying charts

**View.** From the View menu, you can control the appearance of the status bar, the standard toolbar, and the formatting toolbar.

**Gallery.** From the Gallery menu, you can select another compatible chart type to display the data in your chart. After selecting a new chart type, you can click *Replace* to replace the current chart or click *New* to create another chart in a new window. See "Changing Chart Types (Gallery Menu)" on p. 456 for more information.

**Chart.** From the Chart menu, you can modify many of the layout and labeling characteristics of your chart, such as the scaling and labeling of axes, all titles and labels, inner and outer frames, and whether the chart should expand to fill areas where titles are not assigned. See Chapter 40 for more information.

**Series.** From the Series menu, you can select data series and categories to display or omit. Only data elements present in the original chart can be included. For bar, line, and area charts, you can select whether each series should be displayed as a line, an area, or a set of bars. You can also transpose data from the Series menu. See "Selecting and Arranging Data (Series Menu)" on p. 459 for more information.

**Format.** From the Format menu, you can open a set of palettes from which you can select fill patterns, colors, line style, bar style, bar label style (for displaying values within bars), interpolation type, and text fonts and sizes. You can also swap axes of plots, explode one or more slices of a pie chart, change the treatment of missing values in lines, and rotate 3-D scatterplots. The Format menu options are duplicated on the chart window toolbar so you can select them quickly with the mouse. See "Modifying Attributes (Format Menu)" on p. 523 in Chapter 41 for more information.

**Statistics.** From the Statistics menu, you can run SPSS statistical procedures.

**Graphs.** From the Graphs menu, you can create new charts and graphs from the current data set.

**Help.** The Help menu provides the same access to Help as it does throughout the system.

## Selecting Objects to Modify

The objects that make up a chart fall into two general categories:

- **Series objects** are the bars, lines, and markers that represent the data. They are always selected and manipulated as a series.
- **Chart objects** are the layout and labeling components of the chart—everything other than the series objects.

To modify one of these objects, double-click on it in the chart. If you double-click on a series object, the Displayed Data dialog box for the current chart type is opened. If you double-click on a chart object, one of the dialog boxes from the Chart menu is opened: Axis if you have selected an axis, Title if you have selected a title, and so on (see Chapter 40). If you double-click on an object for which a specific dialog box does not exist, or if you double-click away from any object, the Options dialog box for the current chart type is opened.

Instead of double-clicking on objects, you can open the series dialog boxes from the Series and Chart menus. Both series and chart objects have **attributes** such as color and pattern. To modify the attributes of an object, select the object with a single mouse click. There is no keyboard mechanism for selecting objects. If the object is within the chart itself, **handles** (small, solid-black rectangles) indicate which object is selected. For objects outside the chart axes, such as titles or labels, a **selection rectangle** indicates that an object is selected. Selection of an inner or outer frame is indicated by handles.

### Applying Attributes

After an object is selected, select a palette from the Format menu or from the toolbar. Figure 39.9 shows handles and the Colors palette. Select the quality (color, pattern, style, etc.) you want to apply to the selected object, and click *Apply*. You can apply attributes from as many palettes as you choose; the object stays selected until you select another or click somewhere away from any object. Palettes remain open until you close them.

You can leave a palette open while you select and modify different objects. See "Modifying Attributes (Format Menu)" on p. 523 in Chapter 41 for more details.

**Figure 39.9    Bar chart showing selection handles and Colors palette**

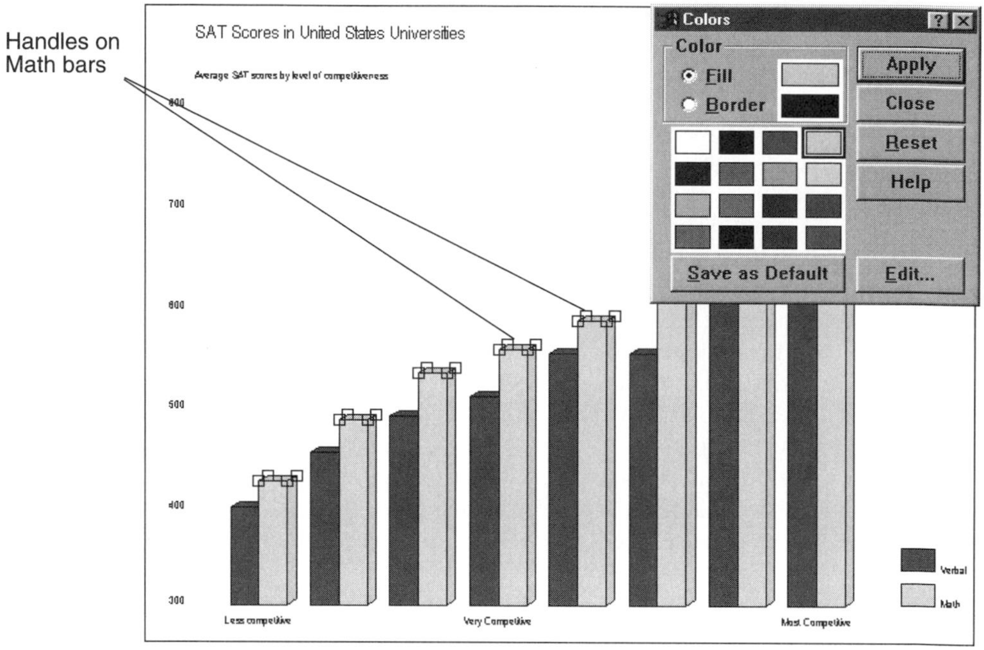

# Changing Chart Types (Gallery Menu)

The Gallery menu allows you to change from one chart type to another. The choices are primarily the same as those available from the Graph menu, with a few additions. (See Chapter 31 to Chapter 38 for detailed descriptions of chart types.)

## Additional Chart Types

Some types of charts are available only after you have created a chart. These include mixed charts, drop-line charts, and exploded pie charts.

**Mixed Charts.** Mixed charts are available on the Gallery menu. You can have bars, lines, and areas, all in the same chart, after defining a bar, line, or area multiple series chart. Figure 39.10 is an example of a mixed chart with both bars and lines.

**Figure 39.10 Mixed chart**

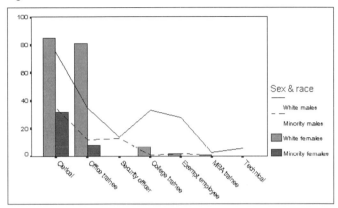

You can also define a mixed chart by choosing:

Series
  Displayed...

from the menus. For more information on mixed charts, see "Selecting and Arranging Data (Series Menu)" on p. 459.

**Exploded Pie Chart.** Exploded pie charts can be generated from the Pie Charts dialog box. To explode all slices of a pie chart at once, from the menus choose:

Gallery
  Pie...

This opens the Pie Charts dialog box. click *Exploded* and then click *Replace* or *New*. Each slice of the pie is moved outward from the center, along a radius, as shown in Figure 39.11.

**Figure 39.11 Exploded pie chart**

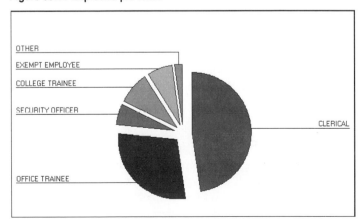

## Changing Types

You can change freely among chart types, with the following restrictions:

- You must have enough data to draw the selected chart. Thus, you cannot change from a simple bar chart to a clustered bar chart if you have only one data series defined. However, if your original chart had more than one series, and you omitted all but one of those series to obtain the simple bar, you can change to a chart that requires multiple series. See "Selecting and Arranging Data (Series Menu)" on p. 459 for information on selecting series.

- You cannot change in either direction between categorical charts (bar, line, area, pie, and high-low charts) and plots based on casewise data (scatterplots and histograms).

- You cannot change from or into a boxplot. Thus, boxplot is not on the Gallery menu.

- You cannot change into an error bar chart, but you can change from an error bar chart into another categorical chart if there are enough data series for the type of chart selected.

If there is an obvious transition between the display of series in the current chart and the display of series in the selected chart, the new chart is drawn automatically. If not, the Displayed Data dialog box for the new chart opens for you to indicate how to display the series.

You can change among bar, line, and area charts and create mixed charts within the Bar/Line/Area Displayed Data dialog box without using the Gallery menu (see "Bar, Line, and Area Chart Displayed Data" on p. 460). You can create simple bar, line, or area charts from multiple versions of the charts by omitting all but one series. You can also change between stacked bars and clustered bars in the Bar/Line/Areas Options dialog box (see "Bar/Line/Area Options" on p. 479 in Chapter 40). To change to a pie chart, however, you must use the Gallery menu.

You cannot change among scatterplot types by adding or deleting series; you must use the Gallery menu. For example, if you omit all but two series in a matrix scatterplot, you are left with a $2 \times 2$ matrix. To make a simple scatterplot from the same data, from the menus choose:

Gallery
  Scatter...
    Simple

Each type of scatterplot has its own Displayed Data dialog box. See "Bar, Line, and Area Chart Displayed Data" on p. 460 through "Histogram Displayed Data" on p. 469 for more information.

## Inheritance of Attributes and Other Chart Elements

When you change from one chart type to another, if an attribute in the current chart is applicable to the new chart, it is preserved. For example, if you change from clustered bars to multiple lines, the series represented by red bars is now represented by a red line and the green bars translate to a green line.

If a change in displayed data or in chart type makes a current chart specification invalid, that specification is set to the default. For example, suppose you are changing a clustered bar chart to a stacked bar chart. The range and increment on the scale axis are no longer valid and the stacked bar defaults are used.

## Selecting and Arranging Data (Series Menu)

The Series menu allows you to modify your chart by selecting data and reassigning data elements within the chart. All of the data must exist within the original chart; you cannot add new data in the Chart Editor. You also cannot change values within the data. The options available vary by chart type:

- For bar, line, and area charts, you can omit data series and categories as long as enough data remain to generate the chart, and change the order of series and categories. You can specify for each series individually whether it is to be displayed as a bar, line, or area. You can also transpose the data so that series become categories and categories become series.

- For pie charts, you can omit categories (slices). If the original chart defined more than one data series, you can select the series to be displayed.

- For boxplots, series operations are not available.

- For scatterplots, you can reassign series to axes, omitting those not needed in the plot. You cannot omit individual values within a series. Since the assignment of series to axes differs for each type of scatterplot, there are different Displayed Data dialog boxes for each type of scatterplot.

- For histograms, if the original chart was a scatterplot with more than one series, you can select which one of the series is to be displayed.

All of these options, except transposing data, are specified in Displayed Data dialog boxes, which are specific to the chart type and are discussed in the following sections. When you choose:

Series
  Transpose Data

data transposition takes place without further query.

### Cumulative Distributions in Charts

Data distributions are never recalculated in the Chart Editor. Thus, removing categories from a cumulative distribution, for example, will not change the values of the remaining categories. Cumulative distributions in pie charts, or in the scale dimension of stacked bar and area charts, will yield charts whose interpretation is unclear.

## Bar, Line, and Area Chart Displayed Data

To arrange the data in a bar, line, area, or mixed chart, from the menus choose:

Series
 Displayed...

This opens a Displayed Data dialog box. Figure 39.12 shows the Displayed Data dialog box for the bar chart in Figure 39.6.

**Figure 39.12 Bar/Line/Area Displayed Data dialog box**

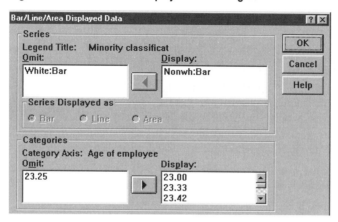

The controls in the Bar/Line/Area Displayed Data dialog box fall into two groups: those having to do with series and those having to do with categories.

**Series.** The legend title, if any, is listed (to change it, see "Legends" on p. 514 in Chapter 40). The series are displayed in two list boxes: those omitted from the chart and those displayed in the chart. To move a series from one list box to the other, select it and click on ▶ or ◀ . You must have at least one series displayed for the *OK* pushbutton to be enabled.

The order of series on the Display list controls the order of bars within clusters, the order of segments within stacked bars, the order of stacked areas, and the order of legend items for all bar, area, and line charts. In mixed charts, lines appear in the legend above areas and areas above bars.

**Series Displayed as.** On the list of series, each series name is followed by a colon and the word *Bar*, *Line*, or *Area* to indicate how it will be displayed when the chart is next drawn. To change the display for a series, select the series and then select one of the *Series Displayed As* alternatives. The chart in Figure 39.13 was derived from the chart in Figure 39.10 by changing the lines to areas and stacking the bars.

**Categories.** You can select categories to omit or display in the same way you select series. Displayed categories form the category axis in the order listed. You can reorder the Display list by selecting a category and using the system menu (see Chapter 42).

**Figure 39.13 Mixed chart with bars and areas**

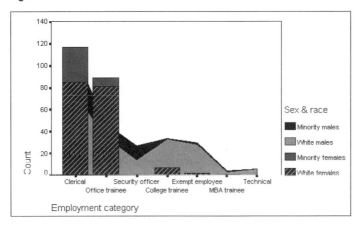

## Pie Chart Displayed Data

To adjust the display of series and categories in a pie chart, from the menus choose:

Series
  Displayed...

This opens the Pie Displayed Data dialog box, as shown in Figure 39.14.

**Figure 39.14 Pie Displayed Data dialog box**

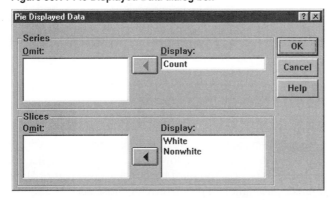

**Series.** If you created the chart as a pie chart, there is only one series listed. If you selected *Pie* from the Gallery menu with a multiple series chart, there are several series in the Omit group and one under Display. If you don't want the selected series, first move the series to the Omit group. Then select the series you want.

**Slices.** You can reorder the Display list by selecting a category and using the system menu to move your selection up or down (see Chapter 42). You can delete categories from the display by moving them to the Omit list in the Slices group. If you omit any categories, the size of each slice is recalculated, using only the categories to be displayed.

## High-Low-Close Displayed Data

To adjust the display of data series in a high-low-close chart, from the menus choose:

Series
 Displayed...

This opens the High-Low-Close Displayed Data dialog box, as shown in Figure 39.15.

**Figure 39.15 High-Low-Close Displayed Data dialog box**

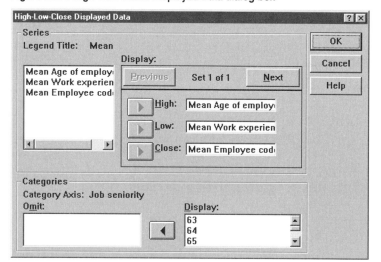

**Series.** The legend title, if any, is listed (to change it, see "Legends" on p. 514 in Chapter 40). The series available are displayed in the list box on the left. The series displayed in the chart are grouped in sets of a pair of high and low series along with an optional close series. To move a series between a high, low, or close box and the list of available series, select it and click on ▶ or ◀. You must have at least one pair of High and Low specifications for the *OK* pushbutton to be enabled. A Close specification is optional.

To view additional high-low pairs or to specify a new set, click *Next* or *Previous*. Duplicate sets of high-low-close specifications are not allowed. You can, however, use a series in more than one set, although you should be careful to select meaningful pairs.

**Categories.** The category axis title is listed. You can select categories to omit or display. To move a category from one list box to the other, select it and click on [▸] or [◂]. Displayed categories form the category axis in the order listed. You can reorder the Display list by selecting a category and using the system menu (see Chapter 42).

## Range Bar Displayed Data

To adjust the display of data series in a range bar chart, from the menus choose:

Series
  Displayed...

This opens the Range Bar Displayed Data dialog box, as shown in Figure 39.16.

**Figure 39.16 Range Bar Displayed Data dialog box**

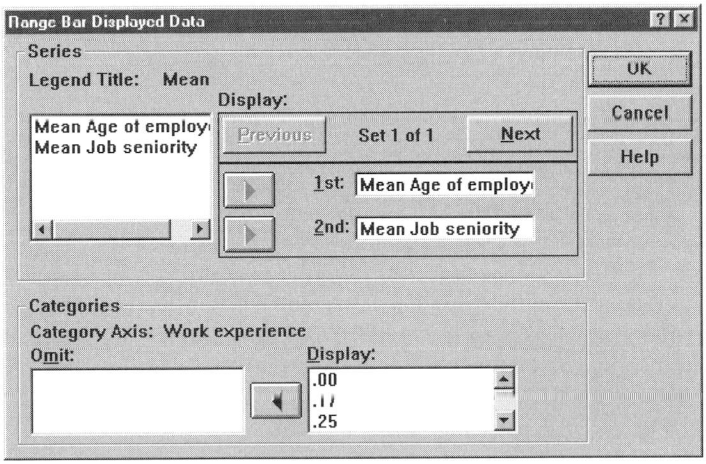

**Series.** The legend title, if any, is listed (to change the legend title, see "Legends" on p. 514 in Chapter 40). The series available are displayed in the list box on the left. The series displayed in the chart are grouped in pairs of series. To copy a series between a pair box and the list of available series, select it and click on [▸] or [◂]. You must have at least one pair of specifications for the *OK* pushbutton to be enabled.

To view additional pairs or to specify a new pair, click *Next* or *Previous*. Duplicate sets of pair specifications are not allowed. You can, however, use a series in more than one pair, although you should be careful to select meaningful pairs.

**Categories.** The category axis title is listed. You can select categories to omit or display. To move a category from one list box to the other, select it and click on [▸] or [◂]. Displayed categories form the category axis in the order listed. You can reorder the Display list by selecting a category and using the system menu (see Chapter 42).

## Difference Line Displayed Data

To adjust the display of data series in a difference line chart, from the menus choose:

Series
  Displayed...

This opens the Difference Line Displayed Data dialog box, as shown in Figure 39.17.

**Figure 39.17 Difference Line Displayed Data dialog box**

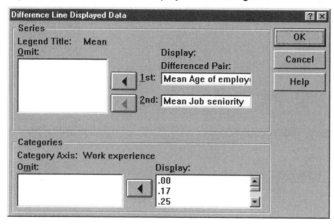

**Series.** The legend title, if any, is listed (to change it, see "Legends" on p. 514 in Chapter 40). The series are displayed in two boxes: those omitted from the chart and those displayed in the chart. To move a series between the Omit list box and one of the Differenced Pair boxes, select it and click on ▶ or ◀. You must have two series displayed for the *OK* pushbutton to be enabled.

**Categories.** You can select categories to omit or display in the same way you select series. Displayed categories form the category axis in the order listed. You can reorder the Display list by selecting a category and using the system menu (see Chapter 42).

## Error Bar Displayed Data

To adjust the display of data series in an error bar chart, from the menus choose:

Series
  Displayed...

This opens the Error Bar Displayed Data dialog box, as shown in Figure 39.18.

**Figure 39.18 Error Bar Displayed Data dialog box**

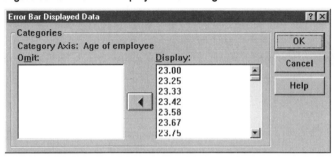

**Categories.** The category axis title is listed. You can select categories to omit or display. To move a category from one list box to the other, select it and click on ▶ or ◀. Displayed categories form the category axis in the order listed. You can reorder the Display list by selecting a category and using the system menu (see Chapter 42).

## Simple Scatterplot Displayed Data

To adjust the display of data series on a simple scatterplot, from the menus choose:

Series
  Displayed...

This opens the Simple Scatterplot Displayed Data dialog box, which controls the assignment of data series to the axes. You can use it to swap axes in a simple scatterplot. In changing to a simple scatterplot from a chart that includes more than two series, you can select the series you want to display on each axis. For example, suppose you have produced the overlay scatterplot shown in Figure 39.19, and you want to plot the verbal score against the math score.

**Figure 39.19 Overlay scatterplot of SAT scores**

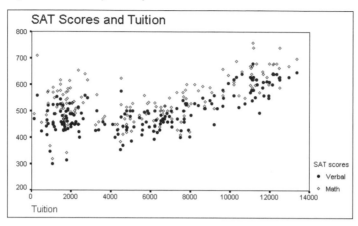

From the menus choose:

Gallery
  Scatter...

Then click *Simple* and *New.* The Simple Scatterplot Displayed Data dialog box appears, as shown in Figure 39.20.

**Figure 39.20 Simple Scatterplot Displayed Data dialog box**

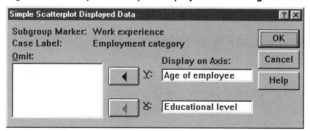

The variable that determines subgroup markers and the variable that supplies case labels (if either is assigned) are listed. (The display of subgroup markers and case labels is controlled in Scatterplot Options. See "Overlay Scatterplot Displayed Data" on p. 467.)

To create a simple scatterplot where average verbal SAT is on the *x* axis and average math SAT is on the *y* axis, first select *In-state Tuition* in Display on Axis for X and click-click on ◀ to move it to the Omit list box. Then select *Average Verbal SAT* and click on ▶ to move it to Display on Axis for Y. Both Y and X must be specified for the *OK* pushbutton to be enabled.

If the current chart data is limited to two variables, you can use this dialog box to swap the *x* and *y* axes by first moving the variables to the Omit box and then back to the appropriate Y and X boxes. When you have finished specifying variables, click *OK* to display the new chart.

## Overlay Scatterplot Displayed Data

To manipulate the display of series in an overlay scatterplot, from the menus choose:

Series
  Displayed...

This opens a dialog box similar to the one in Figure 39.21.

**Figure 39.21 Overlay Scatterplot Displayed Data dialog box**

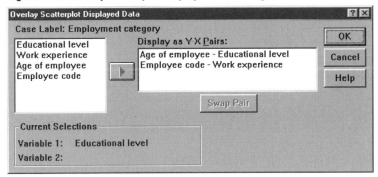

The case label variable, if any, is listed. Underneath it is a box containing a list of the variables available for the chart. You cannot add any other variables. In the box labeled Display as Y-X Pairs are the pairs of variables plotted in the current chart. To remove a pair, select it and click on ◄.

You can add pairs selected from the available variables. When you select one variable, it appears in the Current Selections group in the first position. The next variable you select appears in the second position. To deselect a variable, click on it again. When a pair of variables is in the Current Selections group and you click on ►, the pair appears in the Display box. For example, you might add the pair *Average Math SAT-Average Verbal SAT*. However, if you want the plots overlaid, you should consider the range on each axis. In the example just considered, the first two pairs listed have Tuition, which ranges into the thousands. SAT scores are in the hundreds, and the plot will look like a narrow line on the scale of thousands.

Clicking on *Swap Pair* reverses the axis assignments of a selected pair.

## Scatterplot Matrix Displayed Data

If your chart is a scatterplot matrix, to change which series and categories are displayed, from the menus choose:

Series
  Displayed...

This opens a dialog box similar to the one shown in Figure 39.22.

**Figure 39.22 Scatterplot Matrix Displayed Data dialog box**

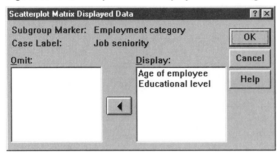

The subgroup marker and case label variable, if any, are listed. The Display list box shows a list of available variables. To remove a variable from this list, select it and click on ◀ so that it moves to the Omit box. There must be at least two variables in the Display list box for the *OK* button to be enabled.

You can reorder the Display list by selecting a variable and using the system menu to move your selection up or down (see Chapter 42).

## 3-D Scatterplot Displayed Data

To change the series displayed on a 3-D scatterplot, from the menus choose:

Series
  Displayed...

This opens the dialog box shown in Figure 39.23. This box is also displayed if you change to a 3-D scatterplot from the Gallery menu.

**Figure 39.23 3-D Scatterplot Displayed Data dialog box**

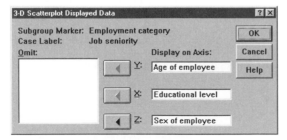

The subgroup marker and case label are listed. The variable for each axis is listed under Display on Axis. To move a variable to the Omit list box, select it and click on ◀. You can swap the axes by moving the variables to the Omit list box and then moving them back to the axes you want. In the default position, the *y* axis is vertical and perpendicular to the plane formed by the *x* and *z* axes.

## Histogram Displayed Data

If a scatterplot is displayed (as in Figure 39.1), to obtain a histogram of one of the variables, from the menus choose:

Gallery
  Histogram...

This opens the Histogram Displayed Data dialog box, as shown in Figure 39.24. It can also be opened when a histogram is displayed by choosing:

Series
  Displayed...

**Figure 39.24 Histogram Displayed Data dialog box**

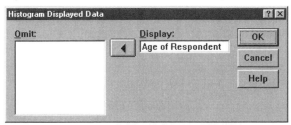

If you want to change the variable selected for display in the histogram, first select the variable in the Display box and move it to the Omit list box. Then select another variable in the Omit list box and move it to the Display box.

## Transposing Data

In a multiple bar, line, or area chart, you can transpose series and categories. You can also transpose data in a high-low-close, range bar, or difference line chart. For example, in a clustered bar chart, the categories (designated on the category axis) become series (designated in the legend) and the series become categories. To do this, from the menus choose:

Series
  Transpose Data

The system redraws the chart if possible. If there is too much data or assignment is ambiguous, the appropriate Displayed Data dialog box is displayed.

An example is shown in Figure 39.25. The difference between transposing data and swapping axes is illustrated in "Swapping Axes in Two-dimensional Charts" on p. 534 in Chapter 41. Data transposition is not available for boxplots, scatterplots, or histograms.

**Figure 39.25 Example of transposing data**

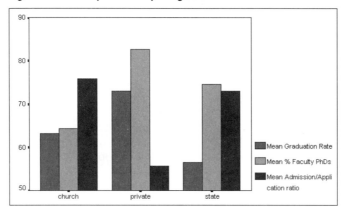

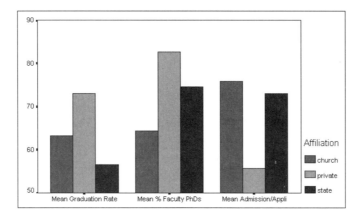

# Case Identification in Scatterplots and Boxplots

While editing a scatterplot or boxplot, you can display all case labels or selected case labels for any of the points. You can also go directly from a point to its associated case in the Data Editor.

## Point Selection

While editing a scatterplot or boxplot, you can change to **point selection mode** and click on a point to see its label. In this mode, when the original working data file that created the chart is still active, clicking on a point also selects the corresponding case in the Data Editor. In a boxplot, point selection applies only to outliers and extremes.

To change to point selection mode, click the Point Selection tool (🔲) on the toolbar, as shown in Figure 39.26.

**Figure 39.26 Point selection in a scatterplot**

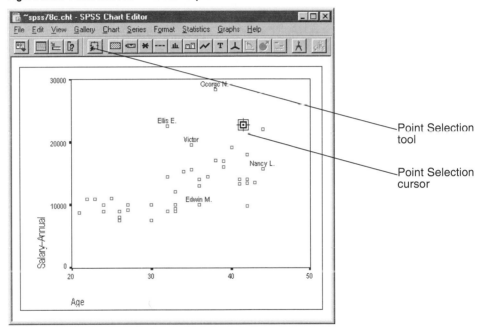

The cursor changes shape to show that the system is in point selection mode. The Point Selection tool is a toggle that turns the mode on or off.

In point selection mode, if you click on a point in the chart, the point is selected (highlighted) and a label is displayed. To turn off the label of a point, click on it again. If you click in an area away from all points, the selected point is deselected.

If you want to label a point without changing to point selection mode, you can click on a point while pressing the Ctrl key.

## Multiple Points in an Area

If there are multiple points close together in the area where you click, a drop-down list is displayed. You can select one label for display from the drop-down list. This selection also determines which case is highlighted in the Data Editor.

## Labels

The type of label displayed depends on previous specifications. The value of the ID label is displayed if an ID or case label variable was specified when the chart was defined. In Figure 39.26, the labels are from the case label variable, *name*. It was specified when the scatterplot was defined, as shown in Figure 39.27.

**Figure 39.27 Simple Scatterplot dialog box**

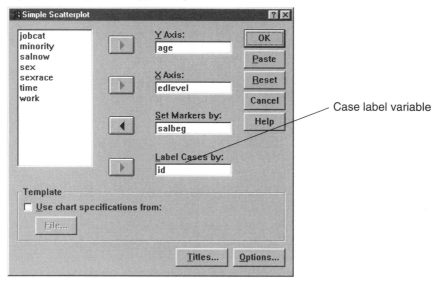

Case label variable

The case number is displayed if there is no ID or case label variable, as shown in Figure 39.28. Case numbers are also displayed if you have selected *Case number* in the Scatterplot Options dialog box (see "Scatterplot Options: Simple and Matrix" on p. 486 in Chapter 40).

**Figure 39.28 Case numbers in a scatterplot**

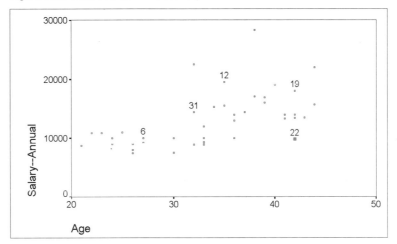

## Locating a Case

If you select a point and then click the Data Editor tool on the toolbar, the Data Editor becomes the active window, and the case that corresponds to the point selected on the chart is highlighted. Figure 39.29 shows a selected point, and Figure 39.30 shows the corresponding case highlighted in the Data Editor.

**Figure 39.29 Scatterplot with a point selected**

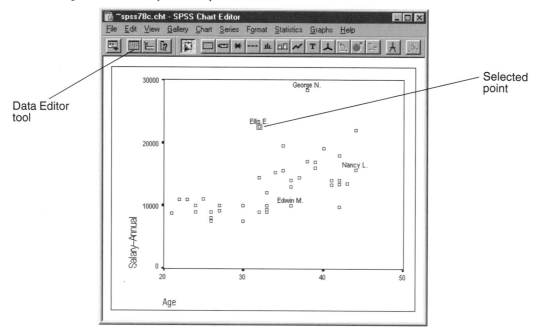

**Figure 39.30 Case highlighted in the Data Editor**

| | s1 | s2 | s3 | lname | name | sex | jobgrade | store | salary |
|---|---|---|---|---|---|---|---|---|---|
| 33 | 620 | 78 | 3762 | Totman | Ora O. | 1 | 1.00 | 2 | $13,300 |
| 34 | 625 | 25 | 8862 | Golden | Paulette S. | 1 | 1.00 | 2 | $13,400 |
| 35 | 630 | 26 | 4263 | Logan | Helga L. | 1 | 1.00 | 2 | $13,500 |
| 36 | 641 | 88 | 6426 | Baker | Ronald N. | 2 | 1.00 | 2 | $14,000 |
| 37 | 378 | 79 | 3363 | Rosen | Margaret H. | 1 | 1.00 | 2 | $7,450 |
| 38 | 228 | 27 | 8279 | Cochran | Harvey S. | 2 | 1.00 | 2 | $16,900 |
| 39 | 492 | 55 | 4519 | Carlyle | Theresa S. | 1 | 1.00 | 2 | $19,050 |
| 40 | 701 | 0 | 2337 | Syms | Ellis E. | 2 | 2.00 | 1 | $22,500 |

If you click on another unlabeled point in the scatterplot while in point selection mode, its label is turned on and the highlight in the Data Editor moves to the newly selected case.

## Links between the Chart and the Data Editor

If you change the case structure of the data file or alter it in other ways, the link between the data file and the Data Editor is broken. The link is permanently broken when you do any of the following:

- Open a new file or a saved file.
- Transpose, merge, or aggregate the file.
- Read a matrix data file.
- Sort cases, using the options available in the Sort Cases dialog box and in several others, including the Split File dialog box.
- Insert a case anywhere but at the end of the working data file.
- Delete any case other than the last from the working data file. You can delete a case by cutting it or by running *Select Cases* from the Data menu.
- Replace or add variables.
- Open a saved chart.

If the link between the chart and the Data Editor is broken, any case selected is no longer highlighted in the Data Editor, and case numbers displayed as point labels refer to the case numbers in the original data file, as it was when the chart was created.

The Point Selection cursor has two shapes, depending on whether the link between the chart and the Data Editor is on or off. The shapes are shown in Figure 39.31.

**Figure 39.31 Shapes of the Point Selection cursor**

Links on                                   Links off

## Finding a Case

If the link between the chart and the data file that created it has not been broken, you can click on a point in the chart (in point selection mode), and the corresponding case will be highlighted in the Data Editor.

If there is no link, you can label the point on the chart. If it is labeled with an ID or case label variable, you can go to the Data Editor, click in the column of the variable, and choose *Search for Data* from the Edit menu.

# 40

# Modifying Chart Elements: Chart Menu

This chapter explains how to modify the layout and annotation of your chart by accessing dialog boxes available from the Chart menu (see Figure 40.1).

From the Chart menu, you can:

- Alter the arrangement of the display or connect data points.
- Fit a variety of curves.
- Alter the scale, range, appearance, and labels of either axis, if appropriate.
- Adjust spacing between bars and between clusters of bars.
- Move the origin line in a bar chart to show how data values fall above and below the new origin line.
- Outside the chart itself, add or remove a one- or two-line title, a subtitle, and footnotes, any of which can be left- or right-justified or centered.
- Suppress or edit the legend.
- Add annotation text, at any position in the plot area, framed or unframed.
- Add horizontal and vertical reference lines.

- Add or remove the inner frame or outer frame.

**Figure 40.1   Chart menu**

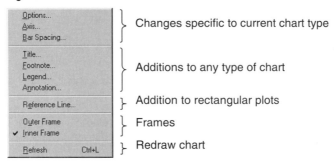

The three menu choices at the top of the Chart menu help you to modify the objects in the chart itself. For example, if you choose *Options* when a line chart is displayed, the Bar/Line/Area Options dialog box opens, but if you choose *Options* when a scatterplot is displayed, the Scatterplot Options dialog box opens.

The next four menu choices—Title, Footnote, Legend, and Annotation—are used to add information to many types of charts. Reference Line (the next choice) can be added to most rectangular charts.

The next two choices control the display of frames, and the last choice allows you to redraw the current chart.

## Accessing Chart Options

The Options dialog box appropriate to the type of chart is determined by the system. You can access options in one of two ways:

▶ From the menus choose:

Chart
  Options...

*or*

▶ Double-click in an area of the chart away from the chart objects.

## Bar/Line/Area Options

To change options for a bar, line, or area chart, double-click away from the chart objects, or from the menus choose:

Chart
  Options...

This opens the Bar/Line/Area Options dialog box, as shown in Figure 40.2.

**Figure 40.2    Bar/Line/Area Options dialog box (bar chart active)**

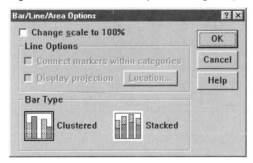

For bar or area charts, you can change the scale axis to percentage representation.

• **Change scale to 100%.** In a bar chart, this option automatically stacks the bars and changes each resulting bar to the same total length, representing 100% for the category (see Figure 40.3). In an area chart, the total distance from the axis, representing 100%, is the same for each category. This feature is useful for comparing the relative percentages of different categories.

**Figure 40.3    Stacked and 100% bar charts**

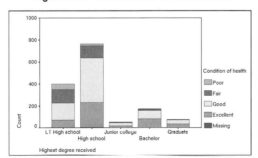 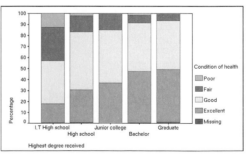

**Line Options.** Line options are available for line charts. You can choose one or both of the following options:

- **Connect markers within categories.** Applies to charts with more than one line. If this option is selected, vertical lines are drawn connecting the data points in the same category on different lines (different series). This option does not affect the current state of interpolation or line markers.

- **Display projection.** Select this option to differentiate visually between values to the left and values to the right in a line chart. To specify the category at which the projection begins, click *Location* in the Bar/Line/Area Options dialog box. This opens the Projection dialog box, as shown in Figure 40.4.

**Figure 40.4    Bar/Line/Area Options Projection dialog box**

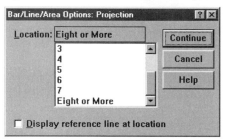

Choose the category where you want the projection line to start. The projection line will be displayed with a weight or style different from the original line. To make the projection stand out, you can select each part of the line individually and change its attributes. For example, the left part of the data line could be red and heavy while the right part of the data line, representing the projection, could be blue, thin, and dotted. An example is shown in Figure 40.5.

- **Display reference line at location.** Displays a line perpendicular to the category axis at the selected location

**Figure 40.5  Projection line chart**

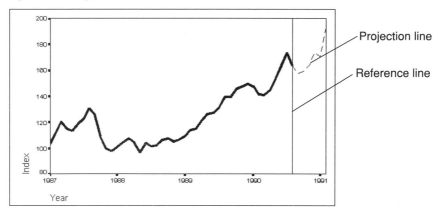

**Bar Type.** If two or more series are displayed on a bar chart, two bar types are available. You can choose one of the following options:

 **Clustered.** Bars are grouped in clusters by category. Each series has a different color or pattern, identified in the legend.

 **Stacked.** Bar segments, representing the series, are stacked one on top of the other for each category.

## Pie Options

To change options for a pie chart, double-click away from the chart objects, or from the menus choose:

Chart
  Options...

This opens the Pie Options dialog box, as shown in Figure 40.6.

**Figure 40.6   Pie Options dialog box**

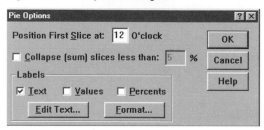 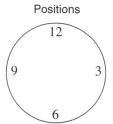

**Position First Slice at n O'clock.** Enter an integer from 1 to 12 to determine the position of the first sector or "slice" of the pie. The integers represent the positions of the hours on a clock face. The default position is 12.

To combine the smallest slices into one slice labeled *Other*, select the following option:

- **Collapse (sum) slices less than n%.** Adds the values of the summary functions of the smallest slices and displays the sum as one slice labeled *Other*. This formatting option does not recalculate any statistics and is appropriate only for functions that have a meaningful sum—that is, if you defined the summary function as N of cases, % of cases, Number of cases, Sum of values, Number above, Number below, or Number within.

   If you select this option, each category for which the summary function has a value less than the specified percentage of the whole pie becomes part of the slice labeled *Other*. You can enter an integer from 0 to 100. If you create another chart type from the Gallery menu, all of the original categories are available.

**Labels.** You can choose one or more of the following label options. You can also control the format of labels. See "Label Format" on p. 483.

- **Text.** Displays a text label for each slice. To edit the labels, see "Edit Text Labels" on p. 483.
- **Values.** Displays the value of the summary function for each slice.
- **Percents.** Displays the percentage of the whole pie that each slice represents.

### Edit Text Labels

To edit text labels, click *Edit Text* in the Pie Options dialog box. This opens the Edit Text Labels dialog box, as shown in Figure 40.7.

**Figure 40.7    Edit Text Labels dialog box**

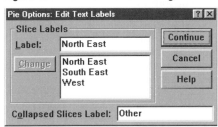

**Slice Labels**. To change the text of a slice label, select the label from the scroll list, edit it in the Label text box, and click *Change*. Text labels can be up to 20 characters long.

**Collapsed Slices Label.** To change the text of collapsed slices label, edit it directly. (This label is available only if *Collapse (sum) slices less than n%* is selected in the Pie Options dialog box.)

When you have finished editing, click *Continue*.

### Label Format

To control the format of labels, click *Format* in the Pie Options dialog box. This opens the Label Format dialog box, as shown in Figure 40.8. (You can also select the labels in the chart and change the color, font, and size attributes.)

**Figure 40.8    Label Format dialog box**

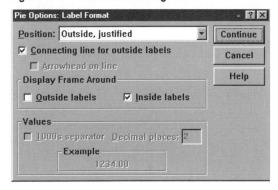

**Position.** Places labels in relation to the pie. You can choose one of the following alternatives:

- **Outside, justified.** Labels are placed outside the pie slices. Labels to the left of the pie are left-justified; labels to the right of the pie are right-justified.
- **Outside.** Labels are placed outside the pie slices.
- **Inside.** Labels are placed inside the pie slices.
- **Best fit.** Labels are placed in the space available.
- **Numbers inside, text outside.** Values and percentages are placed inside of the slices; their labels are placed outside of the slices.

**Display Frame Around.** Both inside and outside labels can have frames around them. You can select one or both sets of frames.

- **Outside labels.** Displays a frame around each label outside the pie.
- **Inside labels.** Displays a frame around each label within the pie.

**Values.** This group controls the format of displayed numbers. Your selections are displayed in the Example box.

- **1000s separator.** Displays values greater than 1000 with the separator (period or comma) currently in effect.
- **Decimal places.** You can specify any number of decimal places from 0 to 19 for values. However, the number of decimal places will be truncated to fit within the 20-character limit for values. If you specify 0, percentages, if selected, will also have no decimal places. If you specify an integer from 1 to 19, percentages will be shown with one decimal place.

You can also choose the following options:

- **Connecting line for outside labels.** Displays a line connecting each outside label with the slice of the pie to which it applies.
- **Arrowhead on line.** Places arrowheads on connecting lines pointing to the slices. Arrowheads are not available if the position selected is *Outside, justified.*

# Boxplot Options

To change options for a boxplot, double-click away from the chart objects, double-click on one of the *n* values on the category axis, or from the menus choose:

Chart
  Options...

This opens the Boxplot Options dialog box, as shown in Figure 40.9.

**Figure 40.9   Boxplot Options dialog box**

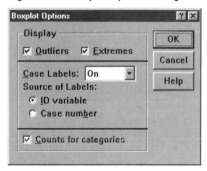

**Display.** Options in this group control whether outliers and extremes are shown in the chart. The height of the box is the interquartile range (IQR) computed from Tukey's hinges. You can choose one or more of the following alternatives:

- **Outliers.** Displays values that are more than 1.5 IQR's, but less than 3 IQR's, from the end of a box.

- **Extremes.** Displays values that are more than 3 IQR's from the end of a box.

**Case Labels.** Controls whether or not labels are displayed. You can choose one of the following alternatives:

- **Off.** No labels are displayed.

- **On.** All points on the chart are labeled.

- **As is.** Some points are labeled, as selected on the chart with the Point Selection tool. If you select *As is* after a previous selection of *Off* or *On*, no labels will be changed.

**Source of Labels.** When a boxplot is created, each point is associated with a case number in the working data file. A boxplot can also have a case label variable selected in the dialog box used to create the chart. If the chart has a case label variable, you can choose one of the following alternatives:

- **ID variable.** Each label is the value of the case label variable for the case. This is the default if a case label variable was specified.

- **Case number.** Each label is the value of the case number in the Data Editor.

You can also choose the following option:

- **Counts for categories.** Displays the number of cases under each category.

## Error Bar Options

To change options for an error bar chart, double-click away from the chart objects, double-click on one of the *n* values on the category axis, or from the menus choose:

Chart
  Options...

This opens the Error Bar Options dialog box, as shown in Figure 40.10.

**Figure 40.10 Error Bar Options dialog box**

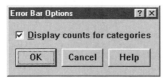

You can choose the following option:

- **Display counts for categories.** Displays the number of cases under each category. This option is selected by default.

## Scatterplot Options: Simple and Matrix

The options for a scatterplot vary according to the type of scatterplot—simple and matrix, overlay, or 3-D. To change options for a simple or matrix scatterplot, double-click away from the chart objects, or from the menus choose:

Chart
  Options...

This opens the Scatterplot Options dialog box for simple and matrix scatterplots, as shown in Figure 40.11.

**Figure 40.11 Scatterplot Options dialog box for simple and matrix scatterplots**

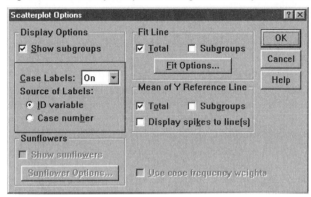

**Display Options.** Selected display options control how the groups and cases are differentiated. You can choose one or both of the following alternatives:

- **Show subgroups**. If a control variable was defined using *Set markers by*, this option is selected and markers of different colors or styles are used to differentiate the groups defined by the control variable. This option must be selected for subgroup options in other dialog boxes to be enabled.

**Case Labels.** Controls whether or not labels are displayed. You can choose one of the following alternatives:

- **Off.** No labels are displayed.
- **On.** All points on the chart are labeled.
- **As is.** Some points are labeled, as selected on the chart with the Point Selection tool. If you select *As is* after a previous selection of *Off* or *On*, no labels are changed.

**Source of Labels.** When scatterplots are created, each point is associated with a case number in the working data file. Many scatterplots also show an ID variable or a case label variable that was selected in the dialog box used to create the chart. If there is such a variable, you can choose one of the following alternatives:

- **ID variable.** Each label is the value of the case label variable for the case. This is the default if a case label variable was specified.
- **Case number.** Each label is the case number. Case numbers refer to the working data file at the time the chart was created.

**Fit Line.** Fit Line options add one or more lines or curves to the chart, showing the best fit according to the method you select for Fit Options (see "Fit Options" on p. 489). You can choose one or both of the following alternatives:

- **Total.** Fits the total set of data points.
- **Subgroups.** Fits the selected type of curve to each subgroup. This option is enabled only if subgroups are defined and shown.

**Sunflowers.** The Sunflowers option allows you to group the data points into two-dimensional cells in the chart, with a **sunflower** in each cell. The process is similar to grouping the values for one variable into bars on a histogram. The number of cases in a cell is represented by the number of petals on the sunflower. You can also customize the display of sunflowers (see "Sunflower Options" on p. 491).

- **Show sunflowers.** To represent the data as sunflowers, select this option.

**Mean of Y Reference Line.** You can draw a reference line through the $y$ axis at the mean of all the $y$ values and reference lines at the means of defined subgroups. If you have a scatterplot matrix, any items apply to each part of the matrix. You can choose one or more of the following alternatives:

- **Total.** Produces one line at the mean $y$ value for all the data points.
- **Subgroups.** Controls whether a line is shown for the mean of each subgroup. This option is available only if you specified a control variable to define subgroups and if *Show subgroups* is selected for Display Options.
- **Display spikes to line(s).** Produces a spike from each point to the appropriate mean reference line. If both *Total* and *Subgroups* are selected, spikes are drawn to the subgroup lines.

If you have defined a weight variable by selecting *Weight Cases* from the Data menu, the weights are automatically applied to a simple or overlay plot.

- **Use case frequency weights.** Selected by default if a weight variable was previously defined. (The SPSS status bar indicates *Weight On*.) When weight is on, a message appears in a footnote below the chart. Weighted values are used to compute fit lines, mean of $y$ reference lines, confidence limits, intercept, $R^2$, and sunflowers. Deselecting this option does not restore cases that were excluded from the chart because of missing or non-positive weights.

**Fit Options**

To select a method for fitting the points to a line, click *Fit Options* in the Scatterplot Options dialog box. This opens the Fit Line dialog box, as shown in Figure 40.12.

**Figure 40.12 Fit Line dialog box**

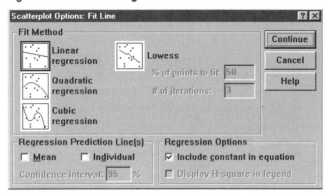

**Fit Method.** The picture buttons illustrate three regression types and another method for fitting the data points in a scatterplot. Examples of curves drawn by the fit methods are shown in Figure 40.13. You can choose one of the following options:

 **Linear regression.** Produces a linear regression line that best fits the data points on a scatterplot according to the least-squares principle. This is the default fit method.

 **Quadratic regression.** Produces a quadratic regression curve that best fits the data points on a scatterplot according to the least-squares principle.

 **Cubic regression.** Produces a cubic regression curve that best fits the data points on a scatterplot according to the least-squares principle.

 **Lowess.** Produces the locally weighted regression scatterplot smoothing method (Cleveland, 1979; Chambers et al., 1983). Lowess uses an iterative weighted least-squares method to fit a line to a set of points. At least 13 data points are needed. This method fits a specified percentage of the data points. The default is 50%. It also uses a specified number of iterations. The default is 3.

**Regression Prediction Line(s).** Produces lines illustrating the confidence level that you specify. The default confidence level is 95%. These prediction lines are available only if one of the regression types is selected. You can choose one or both of the following alternatives:

- **Mean.** Plots the prediction intervals of the mean predicted responses.
- **Individual.** Plots the prediction intervals for single observations.

**Confidence Interval.** Specify a confidence level between 10.0 and 99.9. The default value is 95.

**Regression Options.** Available only if one of the regression types is selected. You can choose one or both of the following alternatives:

- **Include constant in equation.** Displays a regression line passing through the $y$ intercept. If this option is deselected, the regression line passes through the origin.
- **Display R-squared in legend.** Displays the value of $R^2$ for each regression line in the legend, if it is displayed. This option is not available on matrix scatterplots. To display the legend, from the menus choose:

Chart
  Legend...

and select *Display legend.*

**Figure 40.13 Examples of fit methods**

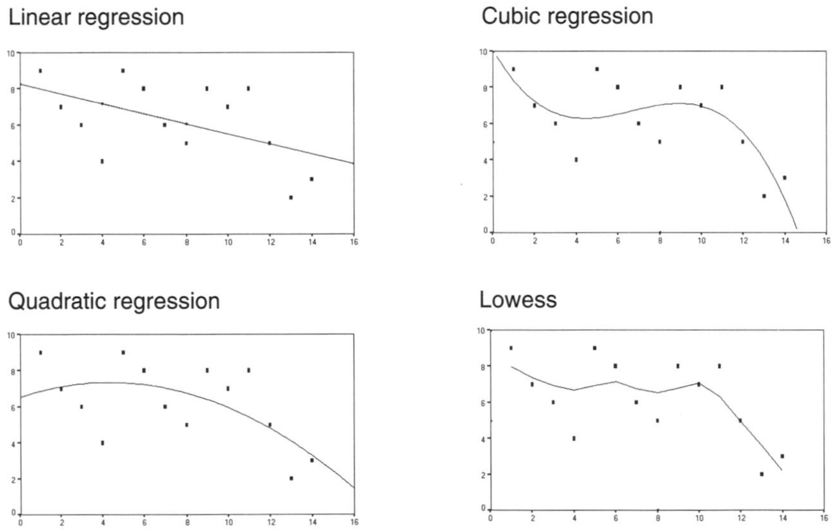

Linear regression

Cubic regression

Quadratic regression

Lowess

To access other methods of connecting the points in a scatterplot, from the menus choose:

Format
  Interpolation...

See "Line Interpolation" on p. 531 in Chapter 41 for more information.

### Sunflower Options

To customize the display of sunflowers, click *Sunflower Options* in the Scatterplot Options dialog box. This opens the Sunflowers dialog box, as shown in Figure 40.14.

**Figure 40.14 Sunflowers dialog box**

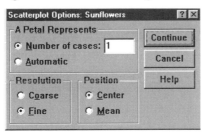

**A Petal Represents.** The petal number is equal to the number of cases in the cell (weighted or not) divided by the number of cases specified per petal. If the petal number is between 0 and 1.5, the center of the sunflower is displayed in the cell. If the petal number is 1.5 or greater, it is rounded, and the rounded number of petals is displayed. For example, in a nonweighted situation where each petal represents one case, a cell containing one case has only a sunflower center. A cell containing two cases has a sunflower with two petals, a cell with three cases has three petals, and so on.

You can choose one of the following alternatives:

- **Number of cases.** Enter the number of cases per petal.

- **Automatic.** The system determines the number of cases per petal automatically.

**Resolution.** Controls the size of the cells. You can choose one of the following alternatives:

- **Coarse.** Plots cases from a large area on one sunflower. Each dimension of a sunflower cell is 1/8 of the appropriate range.

- **Fine.** Plots cases from a small area on one sunflower. Each dimension of a sunflower cell is 1/15 of the appropriate range.

**Position.** Controls the placement of the sunflower within the cell. You can choose one of the following alternatives:

- **Center.** Positions each sunflower in the center of its cell.
- **Mean.** Positions each sunflower at the intersection of the means for the points in the cell.

Figure 40.15 contains examples of data plotted as a simple scatterplot and the same data displayed with sunflowers.

**Figure 40.15 Sunflowers**

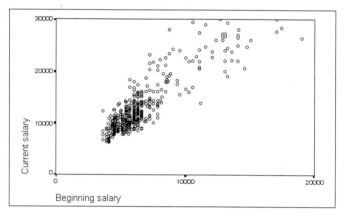

No sunflowers

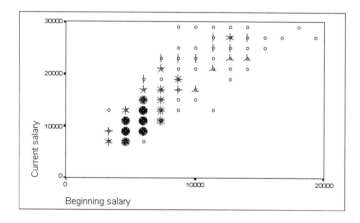

Sunflowers
(fine, center)

## Overlay Scatterplot Options

To change options for an overlay scatterplot, double-click away from the chart objects, or from the menus choose:

Chart
  Options...

This opens the Overlay Scatterplot Options dialog box, as shown in Figure 40.16.

**Figure 40.16 Overlay Scatterplot Options dialog box**

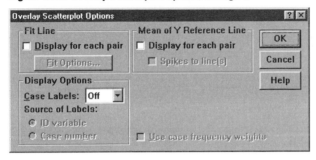

**Fit Line.** You can add lines or curves to the chart, showing the best fit.

- **Display for each pair**. If this item is selected, a line or curve is fitted for each pair of variables. To choose the type of line or curve, click *Fit Options* to open the Fit Line dialog box, shown in Figure 40.12. Available options are described in "Fit Options" on p. 489.

**Mean of Y Reference Line.** You can request a line drawn at the mean of the *y* values.

- **Display for each pair.** Draws a separate reference line for each pair of variables.
- **Spikes to line(s).** Produces a spike from each point to the appropriate mean reference line. Spikes are available only if the reference lines are displayed for each pair.

**Display Options.** The following options apply to case labels.

- **Case Labels.** Controls whether or not labels are displayed. You can choose one of the following alternatives:
  - **Off.** No labels are displayed.
  - **On.** All points on the chart are labeled.
  - **As is.** Some points are labeled, as selected on the chart with the Point Selection tool. If you select *As is* after a previous selection of *Off* or *On*, no labels are changed.

- **Source of Labels.** When scatterplots are created, each point is associated with a case number in the working data file. Many scatterplots also show an ID variable or a case label variable that was selected in the dialog box used to create the chart. If there is such a variable, you can choose one of the following alternatives:

  - **ID variable.** Each label is the value of the case label variable for the case. This is the default if a case label variable was specified.

  - **Case number.** Each label is a case number. Case numbers refer to the working data file at the time the chart was created.

You can also choose one or both of the following case options for overlay scatterplots:

- **Use case frequency weights**. Selected by default if a weight variable was previously defined by selecting *Weight Cases* from the Data menu. (The status bar indicates *Weight On*.) When weighting is on, a message appears in a footnote below the chart. Weighted values are used to compute fit lines, mean of *y* reference lines, confidence limits, and intercepts. Deselecting this option does not restore cases that were excluded from the chart because of missing or non-positive weights.

## 3-D Scatterplot Options

To change options for a 3-D scatterplot, double-click away from the chart objects, or from the menus choose:

Chart
  Options...

This opens the 3-D Scatterplot Options dialog box, as shown in Figure 40.17.

**Figure 40.17 3-D Scatterplot Options dialog box**

You can choose one or more of the following alternatives:

**Show subgroups**. If a control variable was defined using *Set markers by* in the 3-D Scatterplot dialog box, markers of different colors or styles are used to differentiate the subgroups defined by the control variable.

**Case Labels** Controls whether or not labels are displayed. You can choose one of the following alternatives:

- **Off**. No labels are displayed.
- **On**. All points on the chart are labeled.
- **As is**. Some points are labeled, as selected on the chart with the Point Selection tool. If you select *As is* after a previous selection of *Off* or *On*, no labels are changed.

**Source of Labels**. When scatterplots are created, each point is associated with a case number in the working data file. Many scatterplots also show an ID variable or a case label variable that was selected in the dialog box used to create the chart. If there is such a variable, you can choose one of the following alternatives:

- **ID variable**. Each label is the value of the case label variable for the case. This is the default if a case label variable was specified.
- **Case number**. Each label is the case number. Case numbers refer to the working data file at the time the chart was created.

You can also choose the following options:

**Use case frequency weights**. Selected by default if a weight variable was previously defined by selecting *Weight Cases* from the Data menu. (The status bar indicates *Weight On*.) When weighting is turned on, a message appears in a footnote below the chart Weighted values are used to calculate the centroid. Deselecting this option does not restore cases that were excluded from the chart because of missing or non-positive weights.

**Spikes**. Displays a line from each data point to the location that you specify. Spikes are especially useful when printing a 3-D scatterplot. You can choose one of the following alternatives:

- **None**. No spikes are displayed.
- **Floor**. Spikes are dropped to the plane of the $x$ and $z$ axes of a 3-D scatterplot.
- **Origin**. Spikes end at the origin (0,0,0). The origin may be outside of the display.
- **Centroid**. Spikes are displayed from each point to the centroid of all the points. The coordinates of the centroid are the weighted means of the three variables. A missing value in any one of the three variables excludes the case from the calculation. Changing the scale does not affect the calculation of the centroid.

**Wireframe.** The wireframe option draws a frame around the 3-D scatterplot to help you interpret it. You can choose one of the following alternatives:

 The full frame shows all of the edges of a cube surrounding the data points.

 The half frame shows the orientation of the three axes and their planes. This is the default wireframe.

 The cloud button allows you to suppress the wireframe entirely. You may want to use this view when rotating the cloud of points while looking for a pattern.

If you selected *Spikes*, the spikes are shown with or without a wireframe.

## Histogram Options

To change options for a histogram, double-click away from the chart objects, or from the menus choose:

Chart
  Options...

This opens the Histogram Options dialog box, as shown in Figure 40.18.

**Figure 40.18 Histogram Options dialog box**

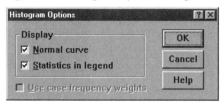

**Display.** You can choose one or both of the following display options:

- **Normal curve.** Superimposes a normal curve centered on the mean. The default histogram does not have a normal curve.
- **Statistics in legend.** Displays in the legend the standard deviation, the mean, and the number of cases. This item is selected by default. If you deselect the legend (see "Legends" on p. 514), the statistics display is also turned off.

The following option is also available:

- **Use case frequency weights.** Selected by default if a weight variable was previously defined by selecting *Weight Cases* from the Data menu. (The SPSS status bar indicates *Weight On*.) When weighting is on, a message appears in a footnote below the chart. Weighting affects the height of the bars and the computation of statistics. Deselecting this option does not restore cases that were excluded from the chart because of missing or non-positive weights. If the histogram was generated from the Frequencies procedure, the case weights cannot be turned off.

## Axis Characteristics

You can modify, create, and change the orientation of axes in a chart. Axis dialog boxes can be opened in one of the following ways:

▶ Double-click near the axis.

*or*

▶ Select an axis or axis label and from the menus choose:

Chart
  Axis...

to open the appropriate (scale, category, or interval) axis dialog box.

*or*

▶ Without an axis selected, from the menus choose:

Chart
  Axis...

to open an Axis Selection dialog box, similar to the one shown in Figure 40.19. The types of axes represented in the current chart are listed in the dialog box. Select the type of axis you want to modify and click *OK*.

**Figure 40.19 Axis Selection dialog box showing scale and category axes**

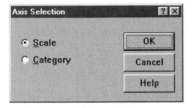

## Scale Axis

If you select a scale axis, the Scale Axis dialog box appears, as shown in Figure 40.20.

**Figure 40.20 Scale Axis dialog box**

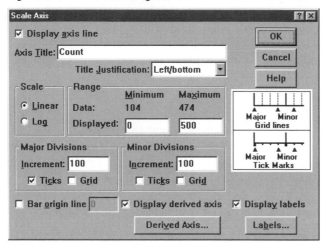

To display the axis line, select the following item:

- **Display axis line.** Controls the display of the axis line. Since it coincides with the inner frame, if you want no line displayed, you must also turn off the inner frame (see "Inner Frame" on p. 520). This item is not available for 3-D scatterplots.

**Axis Title.** You can type up to 72 characters for the axis title. To delete the title, delete all of the characters.

**Title Justification.** Controls the position of the title relative to the axis. You can select one of the following alternatives:

- **Left/bottom.** Axis title aligns to the left for horizontal axes and at the bottom for vertical axes.
- **Center.** Axis title is centered (applies to both horizontal and vertical axes).
- **Right/top.** Axis title aligns to the right for horizontal axes and at the top for vertical axes.

**Title Orientation.** Available for 3-D scatterplots only. Controls the orientation of the title. You can select one of the following alternatives:

- **Horizontal.** A horizontal title has one end near the center of the axis.
- **Parallel.** A parallel title is parallel to the axis.

**Scale.** Controls whether the scale is linear or logarithmic. You can choose one of the following alternatives:

- **Linear.** Displays a linear scale. This is the default.
- **Log.** Displays a base 10 logarithmic scale. If you select this item, you can type new values for the range or you can click *OK* and then click *Yes* when the program asks if you want the default range. Logarithmic is not available for boxplots.

**Range.** Controls the displayed range of values. The minimum and maximum actual data values are listed. If you change the range, you may also want to change the increments in Major Divisions and Minor Divisions.

If the scale is logarithmic, the range values are specified in the same units as the data values. The minimum must be greater than 0 and both values must be even logarithmic values (base 10)—that is, each must be an integer from 1 to 9 times a power of 10. For example, the range might be 9000 to 30000. If you enter unacceptable values, when you click *OK*, the system asks if you want them adjusted.

**Major Divisions/Minor Divisions.** Allows you to control the marked increments along the axis. The number you enter for the increment must be positive and the range must be a multiple of the increment. The major increment must be a multiple of the minor increment. If the scale is logarithmic, you cannot change the increment.

- **Ticks.** If you do not want tick marks displayed, deselect this item.
- **Grid.** If you want grid lines displayed perpendicular to the axis, select this item.

The following option is available for bar charts:

- **Bar origin line.** Allows you to specify a location for the origin line from which bars will hang (vertical bars) or extend (horizontal bars). The specified value must fall within the current range. For example, two versions of a bar chart are shown in Figure 40.21, one with the origin line at 0 and the other with the origin line at 12,000. The second version emphasizes the differences in current salary for employees who have 16 or more years of education.

**Figure 40.21 Bar origin lines**

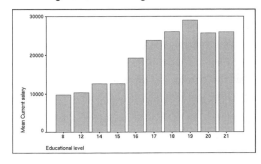 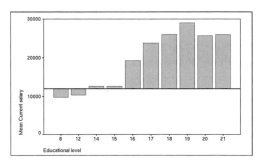

The following option allows you to display another scale opposite the original scale axis. It is selected by default in Pareto charts.

- **Display derived axis.** Allows you to specify an axis on the opposite side of the chart that has a different scale. In a Pareto chart, this axis commonly shows percentages. To specify the scale, title, increments, and labels, click *Derived Axis*. This option is not available for histograms or scatterplots.

The following option is also available for most charts:

- **Display labels.** Allows you to suppress or display the labels on the original scale axis. To modify the labels, click *Labels*.

## Derived Scale Axis

The derived axis is opposite the original scale axis. To specify or change the details of the derived axis, click *Derived Axis* in the Scale Axis dialog box. This opens the Scale Axis Derived Axis dialog box, as shown in Figure 40.22.

**Figure 40.22 Scale Axis Derived Axis dialog box**

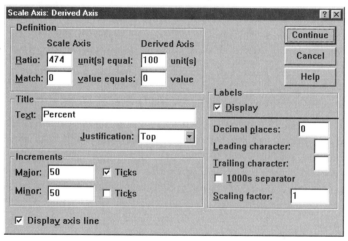

**Definition.** This group defines the derived axis in relation to the scale axis. The scale axis is not affected by these specifications.

- **Ratio: n unit(s) equal: n unit(s).** The size of a unit on the derived axis is defined by its ratio to the size of a unit on the scale axis. In Figure 40.22, 100 units on the derived axis are the same size as 41 units on the scale axis. The numbers specified must be positive. When you have specified a ratio here, be sure to consider the size of increments near the bottom of this dialog box.

- **Match: n value equals: n value.** Relates a specific position on the scale axis to a specific position on the derived axis. In Figure 40.22, the position of 0 on the scale axis matches the position of 0 on the derived axis. The match points do not have to be visible in the chart.

**Title.** The title is arranged so that it reads from top to bottom.

- **Text.** The text of the title can be up to 72 characters. To delete the title, delete all of the characters.
- **Justification.** Controls the position of the title relative to the axis: top, center, or bottom. You can select one of the following alternatives:
  - **Top.** The derived axis title is aligned with the top of the axis. This is the default for a Pareto chart.
  - **Center.** The title is centered with respect to the axis.
  - **Bottom.** The end of the title is at the bottom of the axis.

**Increments.** Controls the definition and marking of increments along the derived axis. Increments should be considered in conjunction with the range displayed on this axis, which is determined by the definition of the ratio.

- **Major.** These increments have labels if *Display* is selected in the Labels group in this dialog box. Major tick marks are emphasized when selected.
- **Minor.** These increments do not have labels. If minor ticks are selected, the minor increment must divide evenly into the major increment.

The following option is available for the derived axis:

- **Display axis line.** Controls whether or not the axis line is displayed for the derived axis. If you want no line at this position, you must deselect the inner frame on the Chart menu.

**Labels.** The following options control the labels of the derived axis:

- **Display.** Controls the display of labels at major increments.
- **Decimal Places.** Enter the number of digits you want displayed to the right of the decimal point. The number of decimal places is also applied to bar labels, if present.
- **Leading Character.** Adds the specified character at the beginning of each axis label automatically. The most commonly used leading character is a currency symbol, such as the dollar sign ($).
- **Trailing Character.** Adds the specified character to the end of each axis label automatically. The most commonly used trailing character is the percent sign (%).

To insert a thousands-digit separator in numeric axis labels, select the following option:

- **1000s separator.** Displays values greater than 1000 with the separator (period or comma) currently in effect.

- **Scaling Factor.** Computes each label on the derived axis by dividing the original value by the scaling factor. For example, the labels 1,000,000, 2,000,000, etc., can be scaled to 1, 2, etc., and the word *millions* added to the axis title. The default value is 1. Bar labels, if present, are not affected.

### Scale Axis Labels

To modify axis labels, click *Labels* in the Scale Axis dialog box. This opens the Scale Axis Labels dialog box, as shown in Figure 40.23. Any changes you make are reflected in the *Example* box.

**Figure 40.23 Scale Axis Labels dialog box**

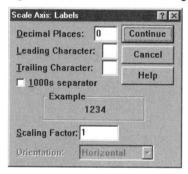

**Decimal Places.** Enter the number of digits you want displayed to the right of the decimal point. The number of decimal places is also applied to bar labels, if present.

**Leading Character.** Adds the specified character at the beginning of each axis label automatically. The most commonly used leading character is a currency symbol, such as the dollar sign ($).

**Trailing Character.** Adds the specified character to the end of each axis label automatically. The most commonly used trailing character is the percent sign (%).

To insert a thousands-digit separator in numeric axis labels, select the following option:

- **1000s separator.** Displays values greater than 1000 with the separator (period or comma) currently in effect.

**Scaling Factor.** Computes each label on the scale axis by dividing the original value by the scaling factor. For example, the labels 1,000,000, 2,000,000, etc., can be scaled to 1, 2, etc., and the word *millions* added to the axis title. The default value is 1. Bar labels, if present, are not affected.

**Orientation.** Controls the orientation of axis labels. Available only for a horizontal scale axis. Not available for 3-D scatterplots. You can select one of the following alternatives:

- **Automatic.** Selects the orientation that will give the best fit.
- **Horizontal.** Prints axis labels horizontally.
- **Vertical.** Prints axis labels vertically.
- **Staggered.** Prints axis labels horizontally but staggers them vertically.
- **Diagonal.** Prints axis labels diagonally.

### Scatterplot Matrix Scale Axes

The dialog box for scatterplot matrix scale axes is shown in Figure 40.24. You can open the dialog box in one of the following ways:

▶ From the menus, choose:

Chart
  Axis...

*or*

▶ Double-click on an axis.

*or*

▶ Double-click on one of the titles on the diagonal.

**Figure 40.24 Scatterplot Matrix Scale Axes dialog box**

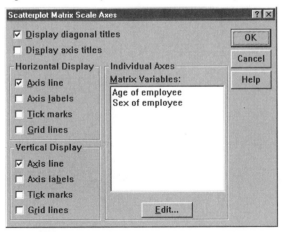

The options at the left in the dialog box apply to all of the plots in the matrix.

To display diagonal and axis titles, choose one or both of the following alternatives:

- **Display diagonal titles.** Displays titles on the diagonal of the matrix. Displayed by default.
- **Display axis titles.** Displays titles on the outer rim of the matrix.

**Horizontal Display/Vertical Display.** Items apply globally to all plots. Axis lines are displayed by default.

**Individual Axes.** Select one variable at a time and click *Edit* to edit the selected axis (see the next section, "Edit Selected Axis").

## Edit Selected Axis

To edit individual Scatterplot Matrix axes, click *Edit* in the Scale Axes dialog box. This opens the Edit Selected Axis dialog box, as shown in Figure 40.25.

**Figure 40.25 Edit Selected Axis dialog box**

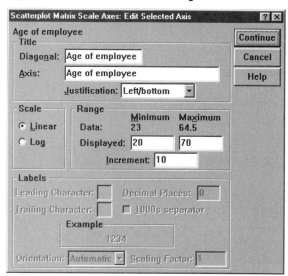

**Title.** Changes made to titles will be displayed only if you select the title display options in the Scale Axes dialog box. To fit titles into the space available, you can edit the text in the dialog box or select the text in the chart and change the size (see "Text" on p. 534 in Chapter 41).

- **Diagonal.** Allows you to edit the title that appears on the matrix diagonal.
- **Axis.** Allows you to edit the text of the axis title. With several plots in the matrix, the title for the axis often needs shortening.
- **Justification.** Controls the position of the title relative to the axis. You can select one of the following alternatives: *Left/bottom*, *Center*, or *Right/top*. Top and bottom apply to vertical axes. Left and right apply to horizontal axes. See "Axis Title" under "Scale Axis" on p. 498 for more information.

**Scale.** You can change the type of scale used for the axis.

- **Linear.** Displays a linear scale. This is the default.
- **Log.** Displays a logarithmic scale (base 10).

**Range.** Controls the displayed range of values.

- **Data.** The minimum and maximum actual data values are displayed.
- **Displayed.** You can change the displayed range by typing the new minimum and maximum. The range must be an even multiple of the increment. If the scale is logarithmic, the range values are specified in the same units as the data values. The minimum must be greater than 0 and both values must be even logarithmic values (base 10)—that is, the values of minimum and maximum must each be an integer from 1 to 9 times a power of 10. For example, a range could be 9000 to 30000. If you enter an unacceptable value, when you click *OK*, the system asks if you want the values adjusted.
- **Increment.** The value of the increment must divide evenly into the range.

**Labels.** The Labels group is available only if you selected *Axis labels* in either Horizontal Display or Vertical Display in the Scale Axes dialog box. Any changes you make are illustrated in the Example box.

- **Leading Character.** Adds the specified character at the start of each axis label automatically. The most common leading character is a currency symbol, such as the dollar sign ($).

- **Trailing Character.** Adds the specified character to the end of each axis label automatically. The most commonly used trailing character is the percent sign (%).
- **Decimal Places.** Enter the number of digits you want displayed to the right of the decimal point.
- **1000s separator.** Displays values greater than 1000 with the separator (period or comma) currently in effect.
- **Orientation.** Controls the orientation of axis labels. Available only for a horizontal axis.You can select one of the following alternatives: *Automatic*, *Horizontal*, *Vertical*, *Staggered*, or *Diagonal*.
- **Scaling Factor.** You can enter up to 20 characters in the box. The system divides each label by the factor. For example, the labels 1,000,000, 2,000,000, etc., can be scaled to 1, 2, etc., and the word *millions* added to the axis title. The default value is 1.

## Category Axis

Selecting a category axis opens the Category Axis dialog box, as shown in Figure 40.26.

**Figure 40.26 Category Axis dialog box**

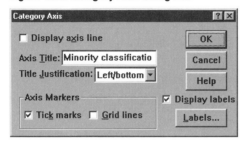

To display the category axis, select this option:

- **Display axis line.** Controls display of the axis line. Since it coincides with the inner frame, if you want no line displayed, you must also turn off the inner frame (see "Inner Frame" on p. 520).

**Axis Title.** You can type up to 72 characters for the axis title. To omit the title, delete all of the characters.

**Title Justification.** Controls the position of the title relative to the axis. You can select one of the following alternatives: *Left/bottom*, *Center*, or *Right/top*. Top and bottom apply to vertical axes. Left and right apply to horizontal axes. See "Axis Title" under "Scale Axis" on p. 498 for more information.

**Axis Markers.** Controls whether tick marks and grid lines are turned on or off.

- **Tick marks.** Controls the display of the tick marks for all categories.
- **Grid lines.** Controls the display of grid lines.

The following option is also available:

- **Display labels.** To display axis labels, select this item.

## Category Axis Labels

To modify axis labels, click *Labels* in the Category Axis dialog box. This opens the Category Axis Labels dialog box, as shown in Figure 40.27.

**Figure 40.27 Category Axis Labels dialog box**

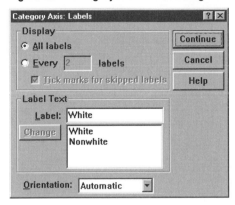

**Display.** Controls the display of axis labels. You can choose one of the following alternatives:

- **All labels.** Displays a label for every category included in the display. To omit entire categories from the display, see "Bar, Line, and Area Chart Displayed Data" on p. 460 in Chapter 39.
- **Every n labels.** Allows you to specify an increment governing the number of categories not labeled between displayed labels. Enter an integer that is 1 greater than the number of labels to be skipped. For example, if you want to label the first category, skip the next two, and label the fourth, enter 3.
  - **Tick marks for skipped labels.** To turn off tick marks, deselect this item.

**Label Text.** Allows you to edit the text of labels. First select a label from the scroll list. It appears in the Label text box. Edit the text and click *Change*.

**Orientation.** Controls the orientation of axis labels. Available only for a horizontal category axis. You can select one of the following alternatives: *Automatic*, *Horizontal*, *Vertical*, *Staggered*, or *Diagonal*. See "Orientation" under "Scale Axis Labels" on p. 502 for more information.

## Interval Axis

The bars of a histogram extend from an interval axis. The Interval Axis dialog box is shown in Figure 40.28.

**Figure 40.28 Interval Axis dialog box**

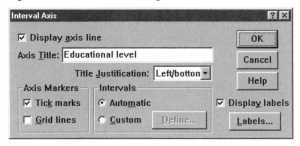

To display an axis line, select the following option:

- **Display axis line.** Turns the axis line off or on. If you want *no line* at this position, you must also turn off display of the inner frame (see "Inner Frame" on p. 520).

**Axis Title**. You can type up to 72 characters for the axis title. To omit the title, delete all the characters.

**Title Justification.** Controls the position of the title relative to the axis. You can select one of the following alternatives: *Left/bottom, Center*, or *Right/top*. Top and bottom apply to vertical axes. Left and right apply to horizontal axes. Justification is with respect to the ends of the displayed axis. See "Axis Title" under "Scale Axis" on p. 498 for more information.

**Axis Markers.** Controls whether tick marks and grid lines are turned on or off. You can choose one or both of the following alternatives:

- **Tick marks.** Controls the display of the tick marks for all categories. Tick marks are at the centers of the intervals.
- **Grid lines.** Controls the display of grid lines. Grid lines are at the bounds of intervals.

**Intervals.** Allows you to define the size of the intervals represented by the bars in the histogram. You can choose one of the following alternatives:

- **Automatic.** The number and size of intervals are determined automatically, based on your data. This is the default.
- **Custom.** Allows you to define the size of equal intervals. Click on *Define* to change the number of intervals, the width of each interval, or the range of data displayed (see the next section, "Defining Custom Intervals").

The following display option is also available:

- **Display labels.** To display axis labels, select this item.

### Defining Custom Intervals

To modify the number or width of intervals in a histogram, select *Custom* in the Interval Axis dialog box and click *Define* to open the Define Custom Intervals dialog box, as shown in Figure 40.29.

**Figure 40.29 Interval Axis Define Custom Intervals dialog box**

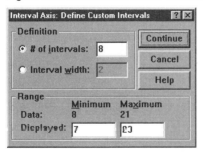

**Definition.** Two methods of specifying custom intervals are available. You can choose one of the following alternatives:

- **# of intervals.** You can specify the number of intervals by entering an integer greater than 1. The system calculates the width of each interval, based on the range.
- **Interval width.** You can enter a width for each interval, starting at the minimum listed under Range. The system calculates the number of intervals, based on the range.

**Range.** Allows you to adjust the range of data displayed. The minimum and maximum data values are listed. You can adjust the range when you change the number of intervals or the interval width. For example, if you specify 10 intervals and a range of 20 to 70, the intervals start at 20 and are 5 units wide. (See Figure 40.30.) You can get the same result by specifying 5 as the interval width, along with the range of 20 to 70.

**Figure 40.30 Histogram with custom intervals**

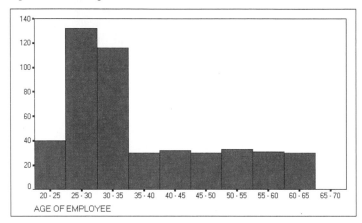

## Modifying Interval Labels

Labels on an interval axis can be suppressed or modified. To modify the labels on the interval axis, click *Labels* in the Interval Axis dialog box. This opens the Interval Axis Labels dialog box, as shown in Figure 40.31. Any changes you make are illustrated in the Example box.

**Figure 40.31 Interval Axis Labels dialog box**

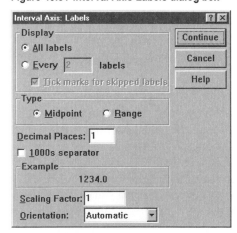

**Display.** Controls the display of axis labels.

- **All labels.** Displays a label for every interval included in the display.
- **Every n labels.** Allows you to specify an increment governing the number of intervals not labeled between displayed labels. Enter an integer that is 1 greater than the number of labels to be skipped. For example, if you want to label the first interval, skip the next two, and label the fourth, enter 3.
  - **Tick marks for skipped labels.** To turn off tick marks, deselect this item.

**Type.** Allows you to select whether each label will denote the midpoint or the range of the interval.

- **Midpoint.** Displays the midpoint of each interval as the label.
- **Range.** Displays the lower and upper bounds of each interval as the label.

**Decimal Places.** You can specify the number of decimal places. Enter a value from 0 to 19.

To insert a thousands-digit separator in numeric axis labels, select the following option:

- **1000s separator.** Displays values greater than 1000 with the separator (period or comma) currently in effect.

**Scaling Factor.** You can enter up to 20 characters. The system divides each label by the factor. For example, the labels 1,000,000, 2,000,000, etc., can be scaled to 1, 2, etc., and the word *millions* added to the axis title. This factor does not affect the scale axis or bar labels.

**Orientation.** Controls the orientation of axis labels. Available only for a horizontal axis. You can select one of the following alternatives: *Automatic, Horizontal, Vertical, Diagonal,* or *Staggered.*

## Bar Spacing

To adjust the spacing of the bars in a bar chart, error bar chart, high-low-close chart, range bar chart, or histogram, from the menus choose:

Chart
  Bar Spacing...

The Bar Spacing dialog box for a bar chart is shown in Figure 40.32.

In a bar chart, you can change the margin spacing at both ends of the series of bars, the inter-bar spacing, and the inter-cluster spacing. The system adjusts the size of the bars to meet the new specifications.

For a histogram, the Bar Spacing dialog box contains only the bar margin specification.

**Figure 40.32 Bar Spacing dialog box (bar chart)**

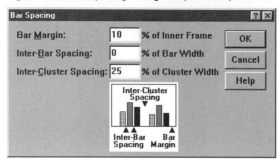

**Bar Margin.** The percentage (0 to 99) of the inner frame left blank on both sides of the series of bars. This percentage is split equally between the two sides. The default is 10% for bar charts and 0% for histograms.

**Inter-Bar Spacing.** The distance between bars within a cluster or the distance between bars in a simple bar chart. Enter the percentage of the bar width (0 to 100) that you want left blank between bars. The default is 0% for a clustered bar chart or 20% for a simple bar chart.

**Inter-Cluster Spacing.** The distance between clusters. Enter the percentage of the cluster width (0 to 100). The default is 25%.

## Adding or Changing Explanatory Text

Explanatory text can be added to charts in the form of titles, footnotes, a legend, and text annotation.

**Titles**

To add a title to the top of a chart, from the menus choose:

Chart
  Title...

This opens the Titles dialog box, as shown in Figure 40.33. If you already have a title for the chart, you can double-click on it to open the dialog box.

**Figure 40.33 Titles dialog box**

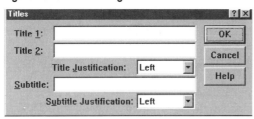

**Title 1/Title 2.** You can enter up to 72 characters for each title. The amount of the title that is displayed depends on the length of the title and the size of the type font selected.

- **Title Justification.** Both titles are justified together. You can choose one of the following alternatives: *Left*, *Center*, or *Right*. Left aligns the first character with the axis on the left; right aligns the last character with the right side of the inner frame.

**Subtitle.** You can enter up to 72 characters for the subtitle.

- **Subtitle Justification.** A subtitle can be left- or right-justified or centered, independent of titles 1 and 2. The default font size for the subtitle is smaller than the font size for titles 1 and 2. You can choose one of the following alternatives: *Left*, *Center*, or *Right*.

To delete any title, delete all of the characters in its text.

## Footnotes

To add up to two footnotes to a chart, from the menus choose:

Chart
 Footnote...

This opens the Footnotes dialog box, as shown in Figure 40.34. If you already have a footnote, you can double-click on it to open the dialog box.

**Figure 40.34 Footnotes dialog box**

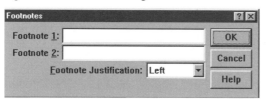

**Footnote 1/Footnote 2.** You can enter up to 72 characters for each footnote. The portion of a footnote that is displayed depends on the length of the footnote and the size of the type font selected.

- **Footnote Justification.** Footnotes are justified relative to the inner frame. You can choose one of the following alternatives: *Left*, *Center*, or *Right*. Left aligns the first character with the axis on the left; right aligns the last character with the right side of the inner frame. See "Axis Title" under "Scale Axis" on p. 498 for more information.

To delete a footnote, delete all of the characters in its text.

## Legends

If you have more than one series in a chart, the system provides a legend to distinguish between the series. A legend is also displayed automatically if you have statistics displayed for a histogram or $R^2$ for a regression line in a scatterplot. To make changes to the legend, double-click on the legend or from the menus choose:

Chart
 Legend...

This opens the Legend dialog box, as shown in Figure 40.35. The legend resulting from the specifications is shown in Figure 40.36.

**Figure 40.35 Legend dialog box**

**Figure 40.36 Legend example**

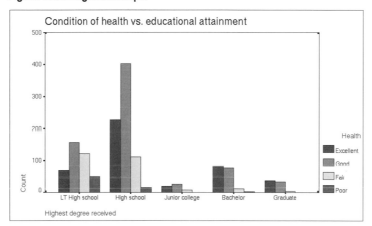

To display a legend for your chart, select the following option:

- **Display legend.** Controls whether the legend is displayed.

**Legend Title.** You can edit the legend title or add one if none exists. The legend title can be up to 20 characters long.

- **Justification.** Aligns the legend title within the area occupied by the legend. You can choose one of the following alternatives: *Left*, *Center*, or *Right*.

**Labels.** The labels in the legend are listed. When you select one of the labels from the list, it appears starting in Line 1 of the Selected Label group. You can edit the text and add a second line if it is not already there. Each line can be up to 20 characters long. When you have finished editing the label, click on *Change*.

## Annotation

Annotation places text within the chart area, anchored to a specific point within the chart. To add annotation to the chart or edit existing annotation, from the menus choose:

Chart
  Annotation...

This opens the Annotation dialog box, as shown in Figure 40.37. The annotations resulting from these specifications are shown in Figure 40.38.

**Figure 40.37 Annotation dialog box**

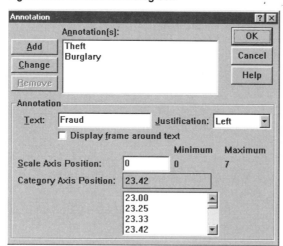

**Figure 40.38 Annotation example**

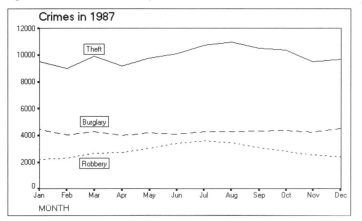

If you already have an annotation in the chart, you can edit it or add others by double-clicking on it. Since you position annotations at axis coordinates, the form of the Annotation dialog box depends on the kind of axes in your chart. Figure 40.37 shows an annotation dialog box for a chart containing a scale axis and a category axis.

For a new annotation, when the text and coordinates have been specified, click *Add* and then *OK*. To make changes to an existing annotation, select the annotation on the Annotation(s) list, edit the text or position, and click *Change*.

**Annotation.** The default position for annotation is the intersection of the displayed axes (the lower left corner).

- **Text.** Type up to 20 characters in the Text box.
- **Justification.** The choices available on the drop-down list are *Left*, *Center*, or *Right*. The default is left, indicating that the leftmost character of the annotation will be positioned at the selected coordinates. In Figure 40.38, the annotations are *centered* above the tick mark for *Mar*.

- **Display frame around text.** Adds a frame around the annotation text.
- **Scale Axis Position.** The scale axis position is a number between the minimum and maximum values.
- **Category Axis Position.** If you have a category axis, the annotation will be positioned at the category you select from the scroll list. In Figure 40.38, all annotations are positioned at the category *Mar*, which makes them appear directly above one another.

## Adding Reference Lines

To add one or more horizontal and vertical reference lines, from the menus choose:

Chart
  Reference Line...

This opens an Axis Selection dialog box appropriate for your chart. Dialog boxes for Category Axis Reference Lines and Scale Axis Reference Lines are shown in Figure 40.39 and Figure 40.40. The dialog box for Interval Axis Reference Lines is similar to the dialog box for Scale Axis Reference Lines.

**Figure 40.39 Category Axis Reference Lines dialog box**

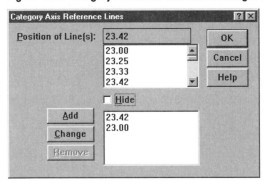

**Figure 40.40 Scale Axis Reference Lines dialog box**

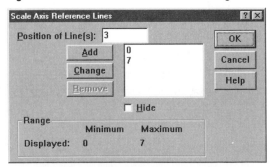

If you already have a reference line in the chart, you can open the dialog box to edit it or add other parallel reference lines by double-clicking on the line.

**Position of Line(s).** For a category axis, to add a new reference line, select one of the available categories and click *Add*. The category is added to the list.

For a scale axis or interval axis, to add a new reference line, type a value and click *Add*. The value is added to the list. If you type a value outside the displayed range, a warning message is displayed.

To remove a reference line, highlight it on the list and click *Remove*. To change the position of a line, highlight it on the list, select a category or type a new value, and click *Change*.

**Hide.** Select this option to hide the reference line that is currently highlighted on the list. Then click *Add* or *Change*. To display a previously hidden reference line, highlight it on the list, deselect *Hide*, and click *Change*.

Figure 40.41 shows a chart that has one reference line perpendicular to the scale axis and two reference lines perpendicular to the category axis, as specified in the dialog boxes in Figure 40.39 and Figure 40.40.

**Figure 40.41 Reference lines**

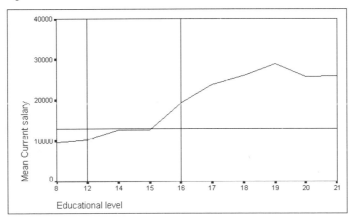

## Inner and Outer Frames

A chart has an inner frame and an outer frame. You can select either one by clicking on it and you can change its attributes. If you want a fill color within a selected frame, be sure that the selection in the Fill Pattern dialog box is a pattern other than empty. Both frames are displayed in Figure 40.42. To set the default display for either frame, from the menus choose:

Edit
  Preferences...

and click *Graphics*.

**Figure 40.42 Inner and outer frames**

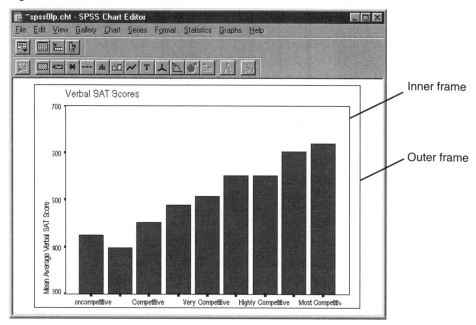

## Inner Frame

The inner frame completes a rectangle, two sides of which coincide with the two axes. For most charts, the inner frame is displayed by default. To suppress or display the inner frame, from the menus choose:

Chart
  Inner Frame

When it is displayed, a check mark appears to the left of *Inner Frame* on the Chart menu.

**Outer Frame**

The outer frame encloses the titles, footnotes, and legend, as well as the chart. To display or suppress the outer frame, from the menus choose:

Chart
  Outer Frame

When it is displayed, a check mark appears to the left of *Outer Frame* on the Chart menu.

## Refreshing the Screen

If your chart does not redraw correctly after you change the size of its window, from the menus choose:

Chart
  Refresh

The chart will be redrawn with the correct proportions.

# 41 Modifying Chart Attributes: Format, Font, and Size Menus

## Modifying Attributes (Format Menu)

The objects that make up a chart have attributes that can be modified:

- Almost all objects have color.
- Lines, including data lines, axes, and the borders surrounding areas, have style and weight.
- Areas have fill pattern.
- Markers have style (shape) and size.
- Bars have bar style (normal, drop-shadows, or 3-D effect) and labels that indicate the exact values they represent along the scale axis.
- Data lines have interpolation style.
- Text items have font and size.
- Pie slices have position (normal or exploded).
- Axes have orientation that can be swapped (for two-dimensional charts) or rotated (for three-dimensional charts).
- Data lines can be discontinuous ("broken") at missing values.

Modifying these attributes requires a mouse. With the mouse, you select an object to modify and then make selections from palettes (see "Selecting Objects to Modify" on p. 455 in Chapter 39). The quickest way to select a palette or perform a Format menu action is to click on the appropriate button on the chart window toolbar.

# Palettes

When you select an item from the Format menu or click on the corresponding button on the toolbar, a palette or dialog box opens. It contains picture buttons illustrating the patterns or styles and several action buttons.

- If you click *Apply*, the selected picture button is applied to the currently selected series or object.
- If you click *Apply All*, the selected picture button is applied to all series in the chart.
- If you click *Close*, the palette is closed without applying the selection.
- If you click *Help*, the SPSS Help window for the palette opens.

The pattern or style of the selected chart object is highlighted by a box drawn around a picture button. If you select a different object in the chart while the palette is open, the attribute of the new selection is highlighted in the palette.

You can drag the palette anywhere on the screen, and you can have more than one palette open at a time.

## Fill Patterns

To fill in enclosed areas such as bars, areas under lines, and background area, from the menus choose:

Format
 Fill Pattern...

or click on [▨]. This opens the Fill Patterns palette, as shown in Figure 41.1.

**Figure 41.1   Fill Patterns palette**

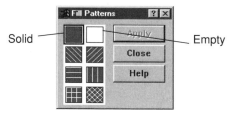

You can use a fill pattern to make distinctions between the areas, especially if the chart is to be presented in black and white or a limited number of colors. In the palette itself, patterns appear in only one color, but your pattern selection is applied to whatever color is in the selected area.

The white picture button represents an empty area. If this fill pattern is selected, the selected object will appear white or have the same color as the background, no matter what color is selected in the Colors palette.

If the bar style is drop-shadow or 3-D effect, you can select any surface of a series of bars and change the fill pattern. For example, you can select the top surface of the 3-D bars for one pattern and the right side for another pattern.

## Colors

You can change the color of chart objects, including areas, lines, markers, and text. To change a color, select the object you want to change and from the menus choose:

Format
  Color...

or click on ▭. This opens the Colors palette, as shown in Figure 41.2.

**Figure 41.2  Colors palette**

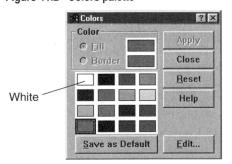

The color of a chart object is associated with a position in the palette and takes on whatever color is currently in that position.

**Color.** You can change the fill color or the border color (if the object has a border).

- **Fill.** Specifies the color inside the element if it is an area, or the color of other elements such as lines or text. To change the fill color, select an object in the chart, choose *Fill*, and then click on the color you want. When you click *Apply*, the selected element changes to the color at the position you clicked on. Be sure that a *non-empty fill pattern* was previously selected and applied.

- **Border.** Specifies the color of the border of an enclosed area. To change the border color, select an area in the chart, choose *Border*, and then click on a color from the palette. When you click *Apply*, the color of the border of the selected area changes.

**Reset.** If you have edited the color palette but have not saved it, clicking on *Reset* restores the colors in the default palette. It also changes the colors of elements in the chart to match the ones in the default palette.

**Save as Default.** If you change the colors in the palette, you can save the palette as the default palette. Then whenever you click *Reset*, the saved default palette will appear and colors of chart objects change to match their associated positions in the palette.

**Edit**. If you want to change a color in the palette, select the color you want to replace in the Colors palette shown in Figure 41.2 and click *Edit*, which opens the Colors Edit Color dialog box, shown in Figure 41.3. (You cannot edit the colors white or black.)

**Figure 41.3   Colors Edit Color dialog box**

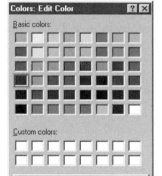

The color you selected in the palette is highlighted. Click on either a basic color or a custom color and then click *OK*. The selected color appears in the palette, in the position you selected before editing. Any chart objects associated with that position also take on the new color.

To define a new custom color, click *Define Custom Colors*, which expands the Colors Edit Color dialog box, as shown in Figure 41.4.

**Figure 41.4   Colors Edit Color dialog box, expanded**

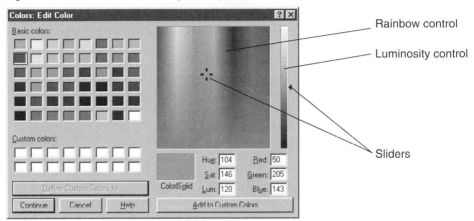

Select one of the rectangles under Custom Colors and use *one* of the following methods to specify the custom color:

- **Rainbow control.** Move the sliders in the rainbow control and the luminosity control until the color in the left half of the Color|Solid box is the one you want. Click *Add to Custom Colors.*

- **HSL.** A color can be specified by typing numbers for hue, saturation, and luminosity. *Hue* corresponds to moving the rainbow control slider horizontally, *Sat* to moving it vertically, and *Lum* to moving the luminosity slider. *Hue* can have any integer value from 0 to 239 and *Sat* and *Lum* can have values from 0 to 240. After typing the numbers, click *Add to Custom Colors.*

- **RGB.** A color can be specified by typing numbers between 0 and 255 for *Red*, *Green*, and *Blue*. This type of specification is commonly used to specify a color to be used in a light-emitting device, such as a video display. After typing the numbers, click *Add to Custom Colors.*

## Markers

Markers are used to indicate the location of data points in a line chart, area chart, or scatterplot, and the data points for the close series on a high-low-close chart. To change the size or style of markers in a chart, from the menus choose:

Format
  Marker...

or click on  ❋ . This opens the Markers palette, as shown in Figure 41.5.

**Figure 41.5   Markers palette**

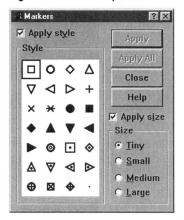

You can change the marker style and size for a single series (click *Apply*) or for all the series at once (click *Apply All*). To change only the style, select *Apply style* and deselect *Apply size*. To change only the size, select *Apply size* and deselect *Apply style*. By default, each series appears in a different color or with a different marker style, according to how your graphic preferences are set.

The speed of drawing scatterplots on the screen may vary with the type of marker. Squares and triangles tend to be faster than circles on a computer with a graphics accelerator. Hollow markers tend to be faster than filled ones.

If you have a line chart in which the markers are not displayed, open the Line Interpolation palette (see "Line Interpolation" on p. 531) and select *Straight* (or another interpolation style) and *Display Markers*.

## Line Styles

The lines in a chart, including the data lines and the axes, can have different weights and different styles. To change the weight or style of a line, select it and from the menus choose:

Format
  Line Style...

or click on 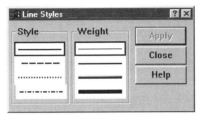. This opens the Line Styles palette, as shown in Figure 41.6.

**Figure 41.6    Line Styles palette**

**Style.** Controls the pattern of the line. The default is solid.

**Weight.** Controls the thickness of the line. The default is thin.

## Bar Styles

To add a drop shadow or a 3-D effect to a bar chart or a range bar chart, from the menus choose:

Format
  Bar Style...

or click on . This opens the Bar Styles palette, as shown in Figure 41.7. Bars for every series in a chart have the same bar style.

**Figure 41.7   Bar Styles palette**

**Normal.** No shadows or 3-D effect. This is the default.

**Drop shadow.** Displays a shadow behind each bar. You can specify the depth of the shadow as a positive or negative percentage of the width of each original bar. The default is 20%. Positive depth places the shadow to the right of the bar, negative to the left.

**3-D effect.** Displays each bar as a rectangular solid. You can specify depth as a percentage of the width of each original bar. The default is 20%. Switching from positive to negative depth changes the perspective of the viewer. With a positive value you see the tops and right sides of the bars. With a negative value, you see the left sides.

If you have already changed the color or pattern of the original bars, the new block surfaces are displayed in the *default color and pattern*, while the front surface retains the attributes you selected previously. Once the shadows or 3-D bars are displayed, you can change the color and pattern of each type of individual surface, including the shadows or the side and top surfaces for each series.

## Bar Label Styles

To label with its numerical value, each bar in a bar chart, range bar chart, or histogram, from the menus choose:

Format
  Bar Label Style...

or click on ▢. This opens the Bar Label Styles palette, as shown in Figure 41.8.

**Figure 41.8   Bar Label Styles palette**

The bar label style applies to all of the bars in the chart. In a bar chart, the number of decimal places in the bar labels is the same as the number of decimal places in the scale axis labels.

**None.** No values appear on the bars. This is the default.

**Standard**. Displays a value at the top of each bar. It may or may not be easy to read, depending on the color and pattern of the bar. You can change the color, font, or size of the value text.

**Framed.** Displays the values in white frames at the tops of the bars. You can change the color, font, or size of the value text and the color of the frames.

## Line Interpolation

In a line chart, scatterplot, difference line chart, mean series in an error bar chart, or the close series in a high-low-close chart, several styles are available for connecting data points. To select a method used to connect the data points, from the menus choose:

Format
 Interpolation...

or click on [ ~ ]. This opens the Line Interpolation palette, as shown in Figure 41.9. The Step, Jump, and Spline picture buttons each have a drop-down list. Examples of various types of interpolation are shown in Figure 41.10.

**Figure 41.9   Line Interpolation palette**

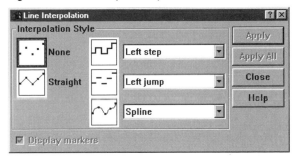

**None.** No lines connect the points.

**Straight.** The data points are connected in succession by straight lines. This is the default for line charts.

- **Step.** Each data point has a horizontal line drawn through it, with vertical risers joining the steps. Selecting left, center, or right from the drop-down list specifies the location of the data point on the horizontal line.

- **Jump**. Each data point has a horizontal line drawn through it, with no risers. Selecting left, center, or right from the drop-down list specifies the location of the data point on the horizontal line.
- **Spline**. The data points are connected by a cubic spline. Lines are always drawn from left to right. For scatterplots, the parametric cubic form is used, and lines are drawn in order of data entry. On the Spline drop-down list are two more types of interpolation:

**3rd-order Lagrange.** Produces third-order Lagrange interpolations in which the third-order polynomial is fitted through the closest four points. The parametric cubic form is used with scatterplots.

**5th-order Lagrange.** Produces fifth-order Lagrange interpolations in which the fifth-order polynomial is fitted through the closest six points. The parametric form is used with scatterplots.

The following option is also available:

- **Display markers**. Displays markers at the data points. To change the style and size of the markers, see "Markers" on p. 528.

For scatterplots, to obtain more interpolation types, from the menus choose:

Chart
  Options...

Then select *Total* or *Subgroups* and click *Fit Options*.

**Figure 41.10 Examples of line interpolation with markers displayed**

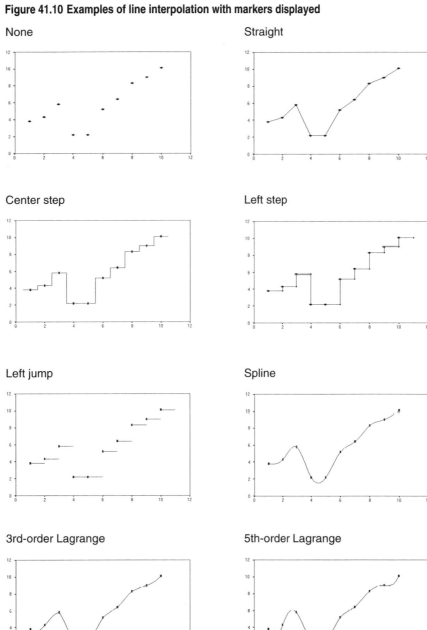

### Text

To change the font or size of a text element of the chart, such as an axis label, select the text and from the menus choose:

Format
  Text...

or click on [ **T** ]. This opens the Text Styles palette, as shown in Figure 41.11.

**Figure 41.11 Text Styles palette**

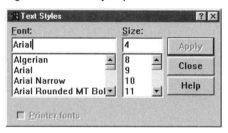

**Font.** The scroll list contains a list of fonts installed on your system. To change the font, select it from the list.

**Size.** To change the font size, select the size from the list or type it.

The following option is also available:

**Printer fonts.** Controls whether the list displays printer fonts or screen fonts. If you're planning to print the chart, use printer fonts.

## Changing or Rotating the Axes

You can change the perspective of a chart by swapping axes or rotating the chart.

### Swapping Axes in Two-dimensional Charts

**Category Charts and Histograms.** In a 2-D bar chart, line chart, area chart, mixed chart, boxplot, or high-low chart with one scale axis, you can swap the axes. Swapping axes changes the orientation between vertical and horizontal. The bars, lines, or areas still represent the same values.

This is different from transposing, where the categories change places with the series named in the legend (see "Transposing Data" on p. 469 in Chapter 39). The difference between swapping axes and transposing data is illustrated in Figure 41.12.

**Figure 41.12 Swapping axes and transposing data**

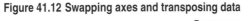

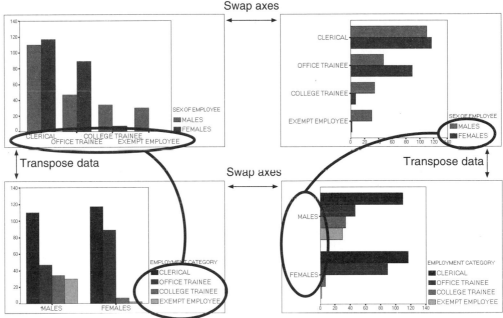

To swap axes, from the menus choose:

Format
 Swap Axes

or click on ⊞. You can also use this procedure for boxplots, and histograms.

**Scatterplots.** To swap the axes on a scatterplot, from the menus choose:

Series
 Displayed...

and assign the variables to different axes, as described in "Simple Scatterplot Displayed Data" on p. 465 in Chapter 39.

## Rotating a 3-D Chart

If the current chart is a 3 D Bar Chart or a 3 D scatterplot, you can rotate in six directions. To rotate a 3-D scatterplot, from the menus choose:

Format
  3-D Rotation...

or click on ⬚. This opens the 3-D Rotation dialog box, as shown in Figure 41.13.

**Figure 41.13 3-D Rotation dialog box**

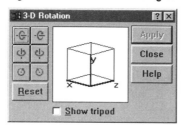

The direction of rotation is indicated on each button. Rotation is about one of three lines: a horizontal line in the plane of the screen, a vertical line in the plane of the screen, or a line perpendicular to the plane of the screen. You can click on a rotation button and release it, or you can click and hold the mouse button until you get as much rotation as you want. The rotation is illustrated in the center of the dialog box. When you have reached the orientation you want, click *Apply* and then click *Close*. Clicking on the *Reset* pushbutton returns the chart to the default orientation.

**Show tripod.** Displays a tripod composed of lines parallel to the *x*, *y*, and *z* axes, with their intersection at the center of the wireframe.

## Using Spin Mode

For another way to rotate 3-D charts, from the menus choose:

Format
  Spin Mode

or click on ⬚. This displays the chart with a new toolbar having the same rotation buttons as the 3-D Rotation dialog box. However, in this mode, the chart is stripped down for the duration of spinning. Only the tripod is shown and solid markers are hollow.The toolbar displays spin tools, as shown in Figure 41.14.

**Figure 41.14 Spin tools**

To rotate the chart in increments, click on one of the rotation tools. You can also click and hold a rotation tool while the chart spins. When you are satisfied with the chart orientation, click on ⬕. The rotated chart is returned to the full version in the new position with its other attributes and options restored. Click on ☒ to return the chart to its default orientation.

To increase the speed of spinning, you can reduce the screen area to be updated by changing the size of the window.

## Exploding Pie Chart Slices

You can **explode** (separate) one or more slices from a pie chart for emphasis (see Figure 41.15).

**Figure 41.15 Pie chart with exploded slice selected**

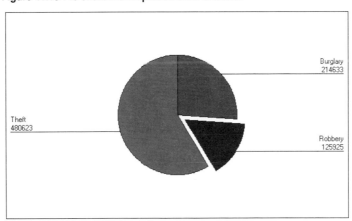

To explode a slice, select it and from the menus choose:

Format
  Explode Slice

or click on ⬕. To reverse the explosion, select the slice and click on the button or menu choice again. A check mark on the menu indicates that the currently selected slice is exploded. You can explode two or more slices, one at a time.

To explode the whole pie, from the menus choose:

Gallery
  Pie...

and then click *Exploded*.

## Handling Missing Data in a Line Chart

You can choose how to display a line chart that has some data missing. By default, the line has a break where the missing values should be. This is indicated by a check mark to the left of *Break Line at Missing* on the Format menu. To connect all existing points, even though data is missing in between, from the menus choose:

Format
  Break Line at Missing

or click on [icon]. To break a line connected at missing values, click on [icon].

    In Figure 41.16, the top chart has no missing data. The other two charts each have a missing temperature value for Day 3. When *Break Line at Missing* is selected, the missing data point is not connected within the chart line. This is the default for a line chart. When *Break Line at Missing* is deselected, the surrounding points are connected, and it is easy to overlook the fact that there is no value there.

**Figure 41.16 Missing data in a line chart**

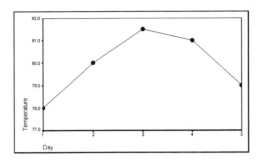

Chart with no missing data

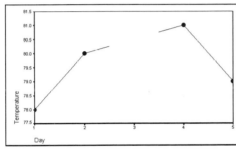

Chart with missing data for Day 3
"Break Line at Missing" is selected

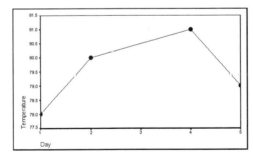

Chart with missing data for Day 3
"Break Line at Missing" is deselected

# 42 Utilities

This chapter describes the functions found on the Utilities menu and the ability to re-order target variable lists using the Windows system menus.

## Variable Information

The Variables dialog box displays variable definition information for the currently selected variable, including:

- Data format
- Variable label
- User-missing values
- Value labels

**Figure 42.1   Variables dialog box**

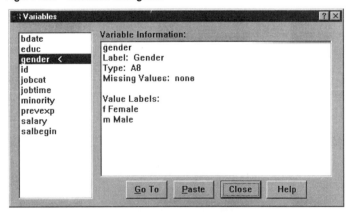

**Go To.** Goes to the selected variable in the Data Editor window.

**Paste.** Pastes the selected variables into the designated syntax window at the cursor location.

To modify variable definitions, use Define Variable on the Data menu.

### To Obtain Variable Information

▶ From the menus choose:

Utilities
  Variables...

▶ Select the variable for which you want to display variable definition information.

# Variable Sets

You can restrict the variables that appear on dialog box source variable lists by defining and using variable sets. This is particularly useful for data files with a large number of variables. Small variable sets make it easier to find and select the variables for your analysis and can also enhance SPSS performance. If your data file has a large number of variables and dialog boxes that open slowly, restricting dialog box source lists to smaller subsets of variables should reduce the amount of time it takes to open dialog boxes.

# Define Variable Sets

Define Variable Sets creates subsets of variables to display in dialog box source lists.

**Figure 42.2    Define Variable Sets dialog box**

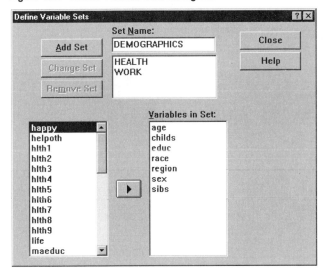

**Set Name.** Set names can be up to 12 characters long. Any characters, including blanks, can be used. Set names are not case sensitive.

**Variables in Set.** Any combination of numeric, short-string, and long-string variables can be included in a set. The order of variables in the set has no effect on the display order of the variables on dialog box source lists. A variable can belong to multiple sets.

## To Define Variable Sets

▶ From the menus choose:

Utilities
  Define Sets...

▶ Select the variables you want to include in the set.

▶ Enter a name for the set (up to 12 characters).

▶ Click *Add*.

# Use Sets

Use Sets restricts the variables displayed in dialog box source lists to the selected sets you have defined.

**Figure 42.3   Use Sets dialog box**

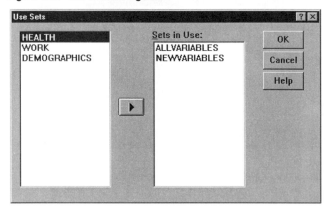

**Sets in Use.** Displays the sets used to produce the source variable lists in dialog boxes. Variables appear on the source lists in alphabetical or file order. The order of sets and the order of variables within a set have no effect on source list variable order. By default, two system-defined sets are in use:

**ALLVARIABLES.** This set contains all variables in the data file, including new variables created during a session.

**NEWVARIABLES.** This set contains only new variables created during the session.

You can remove these sets from the list and select others, but there must be at least one set on the list. If you don't remove the *ALLVARIABLES* set from the Sets in Use list, any other sets you include are irrelevant.

### To Restrict Dialog Box Source Lists to Defined Variable Sets

▶   From the menus choose:

Utilities
  Use Sets...

▶   Select the defined variable sets that contain the variables you want to appear in dialog box source lists.

# Reordering Target Variable Lists

Variables appear on dialog box target lists in the order in which they are selected from the source list. If you want to change the order of variables on a target list—but you don't want to deselect all the variables and reselect them in the new order—you can move variables up and down on the target list using the system menu in the upper left corner of the dialog box (accessed by clicking the left side of the dialog box title bar).

**Figure 42.4   Windows system menu with target list reordering**

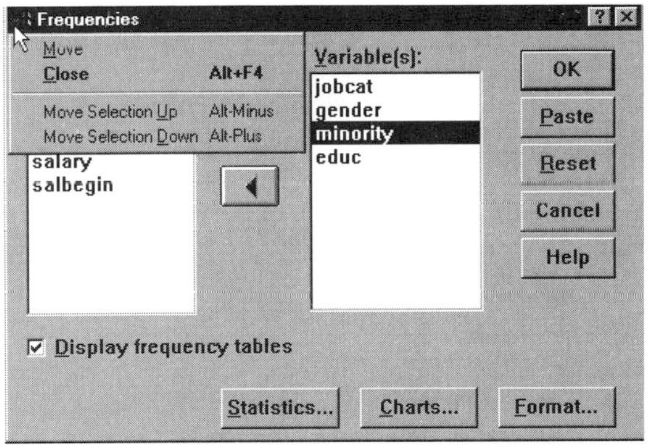

**Move Selection Up.** Moves the selected variable(s) up one position on the target list.

**Move Selection Down.** Moves the selected variable(s) down one position on the target list.

You can move multiple variables simultaneously if they are contiguous (grouped together). You cannot move noncontiguous groups of variables.

# 43 Options

Options controls a wide variety of SPSS settings, including:

- SPSS session journal, which keeps a record of all commands run in every session.
- Display order for variables in dialog box source lists.
- Items displayed and hidden in new output results.
- TableLook for new pivot tables.
- Custom currency formats.
- Autoscript files and autoscript functions to customize SPSS output.

## To Change SPSS Options Settings

▶ From the menus choose:

Edit
  Options...

▶ Click the tab(s) for the settings you want to change.

▶ Change the settings.

▶ Click *OK* or *Apply*.

## General Options

Figure 43.1    SPSS Options General tab

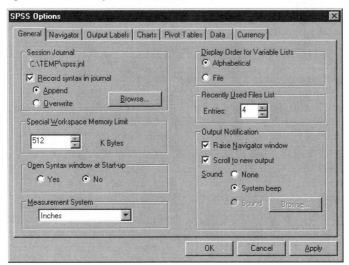

**Session Journal.** SPSS automatically creates and maintains a journal file of all commands run in an SPSS session. This includes commands entered and run in syntax windows and commands generated by dialog box choices. You can edit the journal file and use the commands again in other SPSS sessions. You can turn journaling off and on, append or overwrite the journal file, and select the journal filename and location. You can copy command syntax from the journal file and save it in a syntax file for use with the SPSS automated production facility.

**Special Workspace Memory Limit.** Working memory is allocated as needed during the execution of most commands. However, there are a few procedures that take all of the available workspace at the beginning of execution. Among the procedures that may require all of the available workspace during execution are Frequencies, Crosstabs, Means, and Nonparametric Tests. If you get a message stating that you should change the workspace allocation, increase the special memory workspace limit. To decide on a new value, use the information that is displayed in the output window before the out-of-memory message. After you are finished with the procedure, you should probably reduce the limit to its previous amount (the default if 512K), since an increased workspace allocation may reduce performance under certain circumstances.

**Open Syntax window at Start-up.** Syntax windows are text file windows used to enter, edit, and run SPSS commands. If you frequently work with command syntax, select this option to automatically open a syntax window at the beginning of each SPSS session.

This is useful primarily for experienced SPSS users who prefer to work with command syntax instead of dialog boxes.

**Measurement System.** Measurement system used (points, inches, or centimeters) for specifying attributes such as pivot table cell margins, cell widths, and space between tables for printing.

**Display Order for Variable Lists.** Variables can be displayed in alphabetical order or in file order, which is the order in which they actually occur in the data file (and are displayed in the Data Editor window). A change in the variable display order takes effect the next time you open a data file. Display order affects only source variable lists. Target variable lists always reflect the order in which variables were selected.

**Recently Used Files List.** Controls the number of recently used files that appear on the File menu.

**Output Notification.** Controls the manner in which SPSS notifies you that it has finished running a procedure and that the results are available in the Output Navigator.

## Navigator Options

Navigator output display options affect only new output produced after you change the settings. Output already displayed in the Output Navigator is not affected by changes in these settings.

**Figure 43.2   SPSS Options Navigator tab**

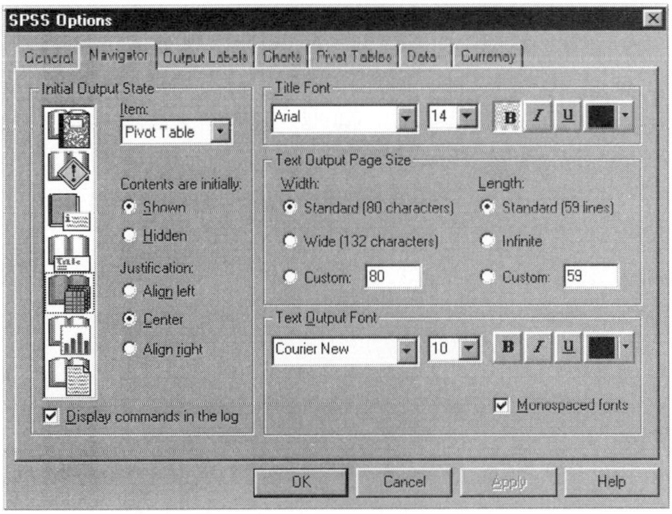

**Initial Output State.** Controls which items are automatically displayed or hidden each time you run a procedure and how items are initially aligned. You can control the display of the following items: log, warnings, notes, titles, pivot tables, charts, and text output (output not displayed in pivot tables). You can also turn the display of SPSS commands in the log on or off. You can copy command syntax from the log and save it in a syntax file for use with the SPSS automated Production Facility.

*Note*: All output items are displayed left-aligned in the Output Navigator. Only the alignment of printed output is affected by the justification settings. Centered and right-aligned items are identified by a small symbol above and to the left of the item.

**Title Font.** Controls the font style, size, and color for new output titles.

**Text Output Page Size.** For text output, controls the page width (expressed in number of characters) and page length (expressed in number of lines). For some procedures, some statistics are displayed only in wide format.

**Text Output Font.** Font used for text output. SPSS text output is designed for use with a monospaced (fixed-pitch) font. If you select a non-monospaced font, tabular output will not align properly.

## Output Label Options

Output Label options control the display of variable and data value information in the outline and pivot tables. You can display variable names and/or defined variable labels, and actual data values and/or defined value labels.

Descriptive variable and value labels (Data menu, Define Variable) often make it easier to interpret your results. However, long labels can be awkward in some tables.

Output label options affect only new output produced after you change the settings. Output already displayed in the Output Navigator is not affected by changes in these settings. These setting affect only pivot table output. Text output is not affected by these settings.

**Figure 43.3   SPSS Options Output Labels tab**

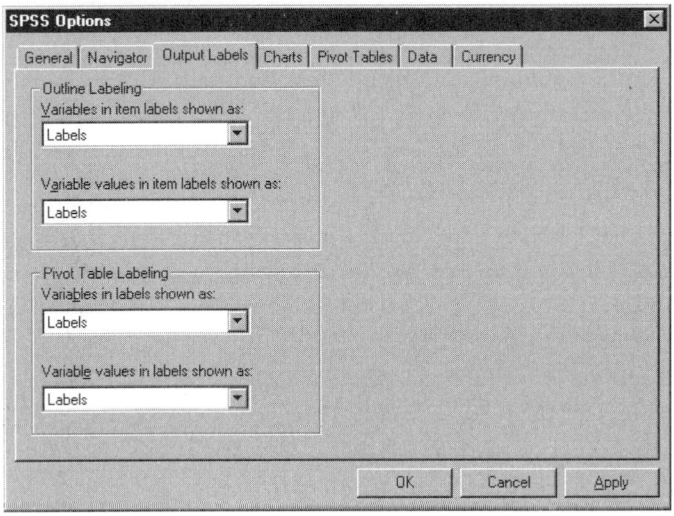

**Chart Options**

**Figure 43.4   SPSS Options Charts tab**

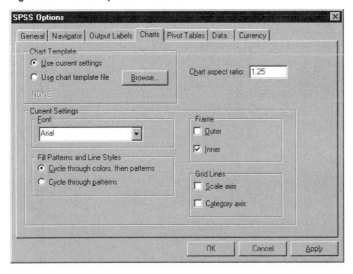

**Chart Template.** New charts can use either the settings selected here or the settings from a chart template file. Click *Browse* to select a chart template file. To create a chart template file, create a chart with the attributes you want and save it as a template (File menu, Save Chart Template).

**Chart aspect ratio.** The width-to-height ratio of the outer frame of new charts. You can specify a width-to-height ratio from 0.1 to 10.0. Values below 1 make charts that are taller than they are wide. Values over 1 make charts that are wider than they are tall. A value of 1 produces a square chart. Once a chart is created, its aspect ratio cannot be changed.

**Font.** Font used for all text in new charts.

**Fill Patterns and Line Styles.** The initial assignment of colors and/or patterns for new charts. *Cycle through colors, then patterns* uses the default palette of 14 colors, and then adds patterns to colors if necessary. *Cycle through patterns* uses only patterns to differentiate chart elements and does not use color.

**Frame.** Controls the display of inner and outer frames on new charts.

**Grid Lines.** Controls the display of scale and category axis grid lines on new charts.

## Pivot Table Options

Pivot Table options sets the default TableLook used for new pivot table output. TableLooks can control a variety of pivot table attributes, including the display and width of grid lines; font style, size, and color; and background colors.

**Figure 43.5   SPSS Options Pivot Tables tab**

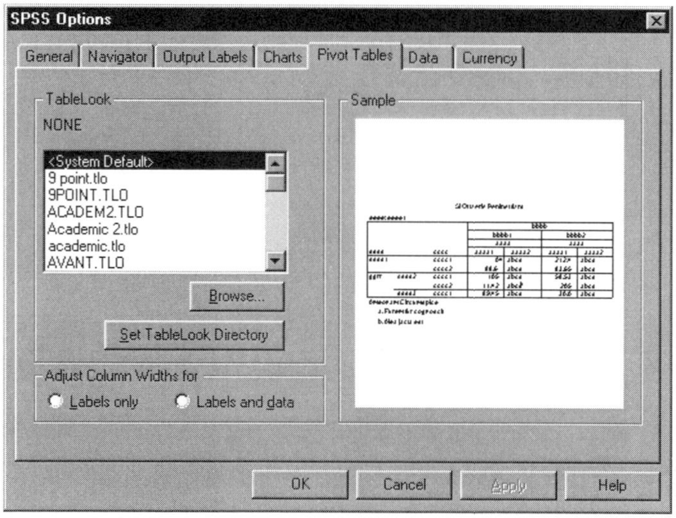

**TableLook.** Select a TableLook from the list of files and click *OK* or *Apply*. By default, SPSS displays the TableLooks saved in the directory in which SPSS is installed. You can use one of the TableLooks provided with SPSS, or you can create your own in the Pivot Table Editor (Format menu, TableLooks).

- **Browse.** Allows you to select a TableLook from another directory.
- **Set TableLook Directory.** Allows you to change the default TableLook directory.

**Adjust Column Widths for.** Controls the automatic adjustment of column widths in pivot tables.

- **Labels only.** Adjusts column width to the width of the column label. This produces more compact tables, but data values wider than the label will not be displayed (asterisks indicate values too wide to be displayed).
- **Labels and data.** Adjusts column width to whichever is larger, the column label or the largest data value. This produces wider tables, but it ensures that all values will be displayed.

## Data Options

Figure 43.6   SPSS Options Data tab

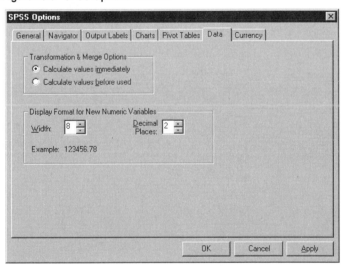

**Transformation & Merge Options.** Each time SPSS executes a command, it reads the data file. Some data transformations (such as Compute and Recode) and file transformations (such as Add Variables and Add Cases) do not require a separate pass of the data, and execution of these commands can be delayed until SPSS reads the data to execute another command, such as a statistical procedure. For large data files, select *Calculate values before used* to delay execution and save processing time.

**Display Format for New Numeric Variables.** Controls the default display width and number of decimal places for new numeric variables. There is no default display format for new string variables. If a value is too large for the specified display format, SPSS first rounds decimal places and then converts values to scientific notation. Display formats do not affect internal data values. For example, the value 123456.78 may be rounded to 123457 for display, but the original unrounded value is used in any calculations.

# Currency Options

You can create up to five custom currency display formats that can include special prefix and suffix characters and special treatment for negative values.

The five custom currency format names are CCA, CCB, CCC, CCD, and CCE. You cannot change the format names or add new ones. To modify a custom currency format, select the format name from the source list and make the changes you want.

**Figure 43.7   SPSS Options Currency tab**

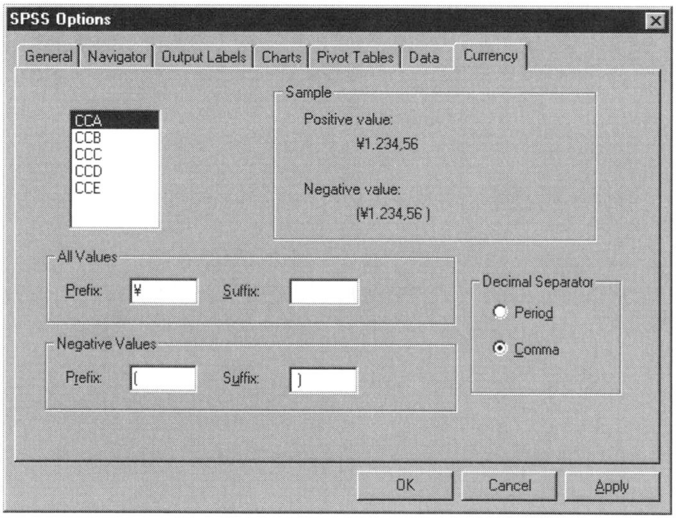

Prefixes and suffixes defined for custom currency formats are for display purposes only. You cannot enter values in the Data Editor using custom currency characters.

### To Create Custom Currency Formats

▶ Click the *Currency* tab.

▶ Select one of the currency formats from the list (CCA, CCB, CCC, CCD, CCE).

▶ Enter the prefix, suffix, and decimal indicator values.

▶ Click *OK* or *Apply*.

# Script Options

Use the Scripts tab to specify your global procedures file and autoscript file and select the autoscript subroutines you want to use. You can use scripts to automate many functions in SPSS, including customizing pivot tables.

**Global Procedures**. A global procedures file is a library of script subroutines and functions that can be called by script files, including autoscript files.

*Note*: The global procedures file that comes with SPSS is selected by default. Many of the scripts that come with SPSS use functions and subroutines in this global procedures file and will not work if you specify a different global procedures file.

**Autoscripts**. An autoscript file is a collection of script subroutines that run automatically each time you run procedures that create certain types of output objects.

**Figure 43.8    SPSS Options Scripts tab**

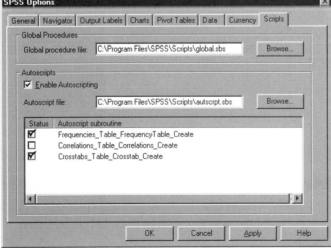

All of the subroutines in the current autoscript file are displayed, allowing you to enable and disable individual subroutines. The autoscript file that comes with SPSS contains the following subroutines:

- **Correlations_Table_Correlations_Create.** In the correlation matrix from Bivariate Correlations, highlights significant correlation coefficients ($p < 0.01$) and removes the upper diagonal of the correlation matrix.

- **Crosstabs_Table_Crosstabulation_Create.** In crosstabulations from the Crosstabs procedure that contain row, column, or total percentages, changes labels to *Row %*, *Column %*, and *Total %*.

- **Descriptives_Table_DescriptiveStatistics_Create**. In the Descriptives procedure, swaps the rows and columns of the table so that the statistics are in the rows and variables are in the columns.

- **Tables_Table_Table_Create**. In tables produced by the Tables option, centers pivot tables in the Output Navigator (affects only printed output, not the display in the Output Navigator).

### To Specify Options for Autoscripts and Global Procedures

▶ Click the *Scripts* tab.

▶ Select the autoscript subroutines that you want to enable.

▶ You can also specify a different autoscript file or global procedure file.

# 44 Printing

With SPSS, you can print:

- Pivot tables, charts, and text output from the Output Navigator
- Data file contents from the Data Editor
- Command syntax from syntax windows

## Output Navigator Printing

You can control the Output Navigator items that print in several ways:

**All visible output.** Prints only items currently displayed in the contents pane. Hidden items (items with a closed book icon in the outline pane or hidden in collapsed outline layers) are not printed.

**All output.** Prints all output, including hidden items.

**Selection.** Prints only items currently selected in the outline and/or contents panes.

Figure 44.1  Output Navigator Print dialog box

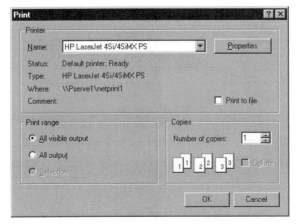

The printing of pivot table layers and the widow/orphan line settings are controlled by the table properties for each table (Format menu, Table Properties, General tab). By default, only the top layer is printed. Print Preview on the File menu displays the layers of a table that will print.

### To Print Output and Charts

▶ Make the Output Navigator the active window.

▶ From the menus choose:
File
  Print...

▶ Select the print settings you want.

▶ Click *OK* to print.

### To Print Hidden Layers of a Pivot Table

▶ Activate the pivot table (double-click anywhere in the table).

▶ From the menus choose:
Format
  Table Properties...

▶ On the General tab, select *Print all layers*.

You can also print each layer of a pivot table on a separate page.

## Print Preview

Print Preview shows you what will print on each page for Output Navigator documents. It is usually a good idea to check Print Preview before actually printing an Output Navigator document, because Print Preview shows you items that may not be visible simply by looking at the contents pane of the Output Navigator, including:
- Page breaks
- Hidden layers of pivot tables
- Breaks in wide tables
- Complete output from large tables
- Headers and footers printed on each page

**Figure 44.2   Print Preview**

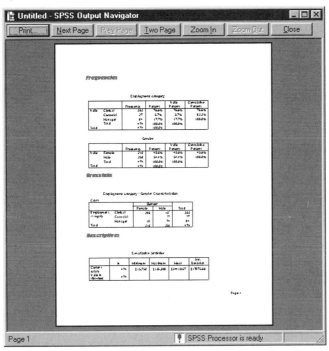

If any output is currently selected in the Output Navigator, the preview displays only the selected output. To view a preview for all output, make sure that nothing is selected in the Output Navigator.

### To View a Print Preview

▶   Make the Output Navigator the active window.

▶   From the menus choose:
File
  Print Preview

## Page Setup

With Page Setup, you can control:
- Paper size and orientation
- Page margins

- Page headers and footers
- Page numbering
- Printed size for charts

**Figure 44.3   Page Setup dialog box**

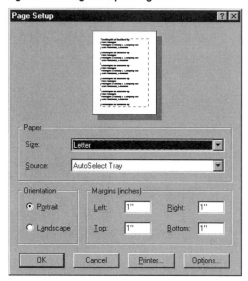

Page Setup settings are saved with the Output Navigator document.

Page Setup affects settings for printing Output Navigator documents only. These settings have no effect on printing data from the Data Editor or syntax from a syntax window.

## To Change Page Setup

▶ Make the Output Navigator the active window.

▶ From the menus choose:

File
  Page Setup...

▶ Change the settings and click *OK*.

### Page Setup Options: Header/Footer

Headers and footers are the information that prints at the top and bottom of each page. You can enter any text you want to use as headers and footers. You can also use the toolbar in the middle of the dialog box to insert:

- Date and time
- Page numbers
- Output Navigator filename
- Outline heading labels

**Figure 44.4    Page Setup Options Header/Footer tab**

Outline heading labels indicate the first, second, third, and/or fourth level outline heading for the first item on each page.

Use Print Preview on the File menu to see how your headers and footers will look on the printed page.

### Page Setup Options: Options

This dialog box controls printed chart size, space between printed output items, and page numbering.

**Printed Chart Size**. Controls the size of the printed chart relative to the defined page size. Chart aspect ratio (width-to-height ratio) is not affected by printed chart size. The overall printed size of a chart is limited by both its height and width. Once the outer borders of a chart reach the left and right borders of the page, the chart size cannot increase further to fill additional page height.

**Space between items.**Controls the space between printed items. Each pivot table, chart, and text object is a separate item. This setting does not affect the display of items in the Output Navigator.

**Number pages starting with.** Numbers pages sequentially starting with the specified number.

**Figure 44.5    Page Setup Options tab**

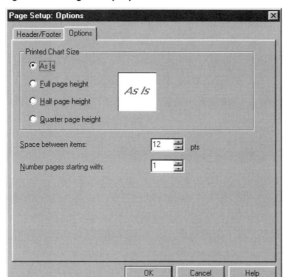

## Controlling Table Breaks for Wide and Long Tables

Pivot tables that are either too wide or too long to print within the defined page size are automatically split and printed in multiple sections. (For wide tables, multiple sections will print on the same page if there is room.) You can:

• Control the row and column locations where large tables are split.

• Specify rows and columns that should be kept together when tables are split.

• Rescale large tables to fit the defined page size.

### To Specify Row and Column Breaks for Pivot Tables

▶ Activate the pivot table.

▶ Click the column label to the left of where you want to insert the break or the row label above where you want to insert the break.

▶ From the menus choose:
Format
  Break Here

### To Specify Rows or Columns to Keep Together

▶ Activate the pivot table.

▶ Select the labels of the rows or columns you want to keep together. (Click-and-drag or shift-click to select multiple row or column labels.)

▶ From the menus choose:
Format
  Keep Together

### To Rescale a Table to Fit the Page Size

▶ Activate the pivot table.

▶ From the menus choose
Format
  Table Properties...
    Rescale wide table to fit page
    *or*
    Rescale long table to fit page

# Data Editor Printing

A data file is printed as it appears on screen. Whether grid lines and value labels are printed depends on whether they appear in the Data Editor window.

Use the View menu in the Data Editor window to display or hide grid lines and toggle between the display of data values and value labels.

**Figure 44.6   Data Editor Print dialog box**

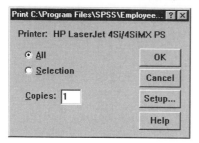

## To Print the Data Editor Contents

▶   Make the Data Editor the active window.

▶   From the menus choose:
File
  Print...

▶   Click *OK* to print the contents of the Data Editor.

# Command Syntax Printing

This dialog box prints the contents of the active syntax window or text document. You can print all of the text in the window, a range of pages, or a highlighted selection in the window.

**Figure 44.7   Syntax Editor Print dialog box**

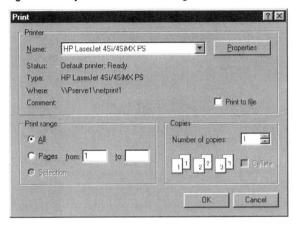

Page Setup options and Print Preview are not available for printing the contents of syntax windows. You can't display, insert, or remove page breaks, so printing a page range can be somewhat unprcdictable.

### To Print Command Syntax in a Syntax Window

▶ Make the syntax window the active window.

▶ From the menus choose:
  File
    Print...

▶ Click *OK* to print the contents of the syntax window.

# 45

# SPSS Production Facility

The SPSS Production Facility provides the ability to run SPSS in an automated fashion. SPSS runs unattended and terminates after executing the last command, so you can perform other tasks while it runs. Production mode is useful if you often run the same set of time-consuming analyses, such as weekly reports.

The SPSS Production Facility uses command syntax files to tell SPSS what to do. A command syntax file is a simple text file containing SPSS command syntax. You can use any text editor to create the file. You can also generate command syntax by pasting dialog box selections from SPSS into an SPSS syntax window or by editing the SPSS journal file.

After you create syntax files and include them in a production job, you can view and edit them from the Production Facility.

**Figure 45.1  SPSS Production Facility**

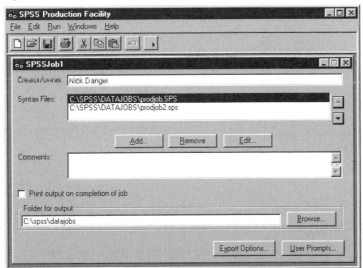

**Production job results.** Each production run creates an output file with the same name as the production job and the extension *.spo*. For example, a production job file named *prodjob.spp* creates an output file named *prodjob.spo*. The output file is an SPSS Output Navigator document.

### To Run an SPSS Production Job

▶   Create a command syntax file.

▶   Exit SPSS if it's running. (You can't run a production job if SPSS is running.)

▶   Start the SPSS Production Facility. This is available on the Windows 95 Start menu.

▶   Specify the syntax files you want to use in the production job. Click *Browse* to select the syntax files.

▶   Save the production job file.

▶   Run the production job file. Click the Run button on the toolbar, or from the menus choose:

Run
  Production Job

## Syntax Rules for the SPSS Production Facility

Syntax rules for command syntax files used in the SPSS Production Facility are the same as the rules for SPSS Include files:

• Each command must begin in the first column of a new line.
• Continuation lines must be indented at least one space.
• The period at the end of the command is optional.

If you generate command syntax by pasting dialog box choices into a syntax window, the format of the commands is suitable for the SPSS Production Facility.

**Figure 45.2   Command syntax pasted from dialog box selections**

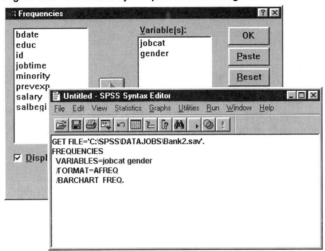

## Production Export Options

Export Options saves SPSS pivot tables and text output in HTML and text formats, and it saves charts in a variety of common formats used by other applications. You can export all output, pivot tables and text output without charts, or charts without other output.

**Figure 45.3   Export Options dialog box**

**Export Format**. Controls the export format for output documents. For HTML document format, charts are embedded by reference, and you should export charts in a suitable format for inclusion in HTML documents. For text document format, a line is inserted in the text file for each chart, indicating the filename of the exported chart.

- Pivot tables can be exported as HTML tables (HTML 3.0 or later), as tab-separated text, or as space-separated text.

- Text output can be exported as preformatted HTML or space-separated text. A fixed-pitch (monospaced) font is required for proper alignment of space-separated text output. (By default, most Web browsers use a fixed-pitch font for preformatted text.).

- Exported chart names are based on the production job filename, a sequential number, and the extension of the selected format. For example, if the production job *prodjob.spp* exports charts in Windows metafile format, the chart names would be *prodjob1.wmf, prodjob2.wmf, prodjob3.wmf*, and so on.

**Image Format**. Controls the export format for charts. Charts can be exported in the following formats: Windows metafile, Windows bitmap, encapsulated PostScript, JPEG, TIFF, CGM, or Macintosh PICT.

Text export options (for example, tab-separated or space-separated) and chart export options (for example, color settings, size, and resolution) are set in SPSS and cannot be changed in the Production Facility. Use Export on the File menu in SPSS to change text and chart export options.

## User Prompts

Macro symbols defined in a production job file and used in a command syntax file simplify tasks such as running the same analysis for different data files or running the same set of commands for different sets of variables. For example, you could define the macro symbol *@datfile* to prompt you for a data filename each time you run a production job that uses the string *@datfile* in place of a filename.

**Figure 45.4   User Prompts dialog box**

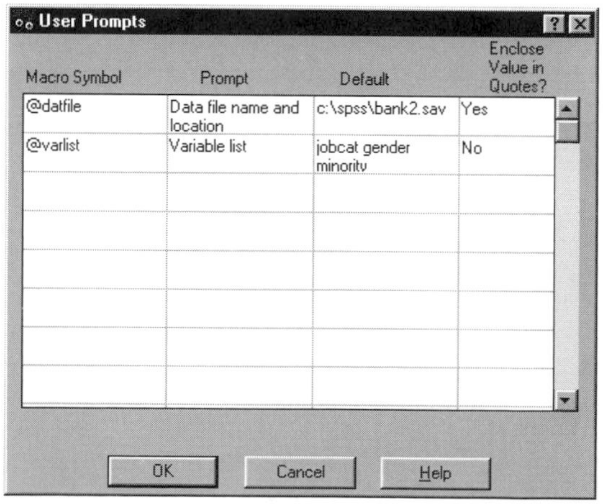

**Macro Symbol.** The macro name used in the command syntax file to invoke the macro that prompts the user to enter information. The macro symbol name must begin with an @ and cannot exceed eight characters.

**Prompt.** The descriptive label that is displayed when the production job prompts you to enter information. For example, you could use the phrase "What data file do you want to use?" to identify a field that requires a data filename.

**Default.** The value that the production job supplies by default if you don't enter a different value. This value is displayed when the production job prompts you for information. You can replace or modify the value at runtime.

**Enclose Value in Quotes**. Enter **Y** or **Yes** if you want the value enclosed in quotes. Otherwise, leave the field blank or enter **N** or **No**. For example, you should enter **Yes** for a filename specification, since filename specifications should be enclosed in quotes.

**Figure 45.5   Macro prompts in a command syntax file**

## Production Macro Prompting

The SPSS Production Facility prompts you for values whenever you run a production job that contains defined macro symbols. You can replace or modify the default values that are displayed. SPSS then substitutes those values for the macro symbols in all command syntax files associated with the production job.

**Figure 45.6   Production Macro Prompting dialog box**

## Production Options

Production Options enable you to:

- Specify a default text editor for syntax files accessed with the Edit button on the main dialog box.
- Run the production job as an invisible background process or display SPSS and the results it generates as the job runs.

### To Change Production Options

From the Production Facility menus choose

Edit
  Options...

# Format Control for Production Jobs

There are a number of SPSS settings that can help to ensure the best format for pivot tables created in production jobs:

**TableLooks.** By editing and saving TableLooks (Format menu in an activated pivot table), you can control many pivot table attributes. You can specify font sizes and styles, colors, and borders. To ensure that wide tables don't split across pages, select *Rescale wide table to fit page* on the Table Properties General tab.

**Output Labels.** Output Label options (Edit menu, Options, Output Labels tab) control the display of variable and data value information in pivot tables. You can display variable names and/or defined variable labels, and actual data values and/or defined value labels. Descriptive variable and value labels often make it easier to interpret your results. However, long labels can be awkward in some tables.

**Column Width.** Pivot Table options (Edit menu, Options, Pivot Tables tab) control the default TableLook and the automatic adjustment of column widths in pivot tables.

- *Labels only* adjusts the column width to the width of the column label. This produces more compact tables, but data values wider than the label will not be displayed (asterisks indicate values too wide to be displayed).

- *Labels and data* adjusts the column width to whichever is larger, the column label or the largest data value. This produces wider tables, but it ensures that all values will be displayed.

Production jobs use the TableLook and Options settings currently in effect in SPSS. You can set the TableLook and Options settings in SPSS before running your production job, or you can use SET commands in your syntax files to control them. Using SET commands in syntax files enables you to use multiple TableLooks and Options settings in the same job.

### To Create a Custom Default TableLook

▶ Activate a pivot table in SPSS (double-click anywhere in the table).

▶ From the menus choose:
 Format
  TableLooks...

▶ Select a TableLook from the list and click *Edit Look*.

▶ Adjust the table properties for the attributes you want.

▶ Click *Save Look* or *Save As* to save the TableLook and click *OK*.

▶ From the menus choose:
 Edit
  Options...

▶ Click the *Pivot Tables* tab.

▶ Select the TableLook from the list and click *OK*.

### To Set Options for Production Jobs

▶ In SPSS, from the menus choose:
  Edit
    Options...

▶ Select the options you want.

▶ Click *OK*.

▶ Exit SPSS.

You can set the default TableLook, output label settings, and automatic column width adjustment with Options. Options settings are saved with SPSS. When you run a production job, the Options settings in effect the last time you ran SPSS are applied to the production job.

## Controlling Pivot Table Format with Command Syntax

**SET TLOOK.** Controls the default TableLook for new pivot tables, as in

SET TLOOK = 'c:\prodjobs\mytable.tlo'.

**SET TVARS.** Controls the display of variable names and labels in new pivot tables.
• SET TVARS = LABELS displays variable labels.
• SET TVARS = NAMES displays variable names.
• SET TVARS = BOTH displays both variable names and labels.

**SET ONUMBER.** Controls the display of data values or value labels in new pivot tables.
• SET ONUMBER = LABELS displays value labels.
• SET ONUMBER = VALUES displays data values.
• SET ONUMBER = BOTH displays data values and value labels.

**SET TFIT.** Controls automatic column width adjustment for new pivot tables.
• SET TFIT = LABELS adjusts column width to the width of the column label.
• SET TFIT = BOTH adjusts column width to the width of the column label or the largest data value, whichever is wider.

# Running Production Jobs from a Command Line

Command line switches enable you to schedule production jobs to run at certain times with scheduling utilities like the one available in Microsoft Plus!. You can run production jobs from a command line with the following switches:

**-r**. Runs the production job. If the production job contains any user prompts, you must supply the requested information before the production job will run.

**-s**. Runs the production job and suppresses any user prompts or alerts. The default user prompt values are used automatically.

You should provide the full path for both the production facility (*spssprod.exe*) and the production job, and both should be enclosed in quotes, as in

"c:\program files\spss\spssprod.exe"  "c:\spss\datajobs\prodjob.spp" -s

# 46 SPSS Scripting Facility

The scripting facility allows you to automate tasks in SPSS, including:

- Automatically customize output in the Output Navigator.
- Open and save data files.
- Display and manipulate SPSS dialog boxes.
- Run data transformations and statistical procedures using SPSS command syntax.
- Export charts as graphic files in a number of formats.

SPSS provides a number of scripts, including autoscripts that run automatically every time a specific type of output is produced. You can use these scripts as they are or you can customize them to your needs. If you want to create your own scripts, you can begin by choosing from a number of starter scripts.

## To Run a Script

▶ From the menus choose:

Utilities
  Run Script...

**Figure 46.1   Run Script dialog box**

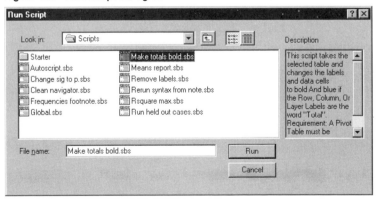

▶ Select the Scripts folder in the SPSS directory.

▶ Select the script you want.

For instructions on running a script from a menu or toolbar, see Chapter 1.

The following scripts are included with the program:

**Analyze held out cases.** Repeats a Factor or Discriminant analysis using cases not selected in a previous analysis. A Notes table produced by a previous run of Factor or Discriminant must be selected before running the script.

**Change significance to p.** Change *Sig.* to $p=$ in the column labels of any pivot table. The table must be selected before running the script.

**Clean navigator.** Delete all Notes tables from an output document. The document must be open in the designated Output Navigator window before running the script.

**Frequencies footnote.** Insert statistics displayed in a Frequencies Statistics table as footnotes in the corresponding frequency table for each variable. The Frequencies Statistics table must be selected before running the script.

**Make totals bold.** Apply the bold format and blue color to any row, column, or layer of data labeled *Total* in a pivot table. The table must be selected before running the script.

**Means report.** Extract information from a Means table and write results to several output ASCII files. The Means table must be selected before running the script.

**Remove labels.** Delete all row and column labels from the selected pivot table. The table must be selected before running the script.

**Rerun syntax from note.** Resubmit the command found in selected Notes table using the active data file. If no data file is open, the script attempts to read the SPSS data file used originally. The Notes table must be selected before running the script.

**Rsquare max.** In a Regression Model Summary table, apply the bold format and blue color to the row corresponding to the model that maximizes adjusted $R^2$. The Model Summary table must be selected before running the script.

For descriptions of autoscripts included with SPSS, see Chapter 43.

# Autoscripts

Autoscripts run automatically when triggered by the creation of a specific piece of output by a given procedure. For example, SPSS includes an autoscript that automatically removes the upper diagonal and highlights correlation coefficients below a certain significance whenever a Correlations table is produced by the Bivariate Correlations procedure.

The Scripts tab of the Options dialog box (Edit menu) displays the autoscripts that are available on your system and allows you to enable or disable individual scripts.

**Figure 46.2   Scripts tab of Options dialog box**

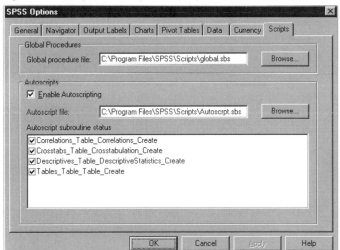

Autoscripts are specific to a given procedure and output type. An autoscript that formats the ANOVA tables produced by One-way ANOVA is not triggered by ANOVA tables produced by other statistical procedures (although you could use global procedures to create separate autoscripts for these other ANOVA tables that shared much of the same code). However, you can have a separate autoscript for each type of output produced by the same procedure. For example, Frequencies produces both a frequency table and a table of statistics, and you can have a different autoscript for each.

For descriptions of autoscripts included with SPSS, see Chapter 43.

## Creating and Editing Scripts

You can customize many of the scripts included with SPSS for your specific needs. For example, there is a script that removes all Notes tables from the designated output document. You can easily modify this script to remove output items of any type and label you want.

**Figure 46.3    Modifying a script in the script window**

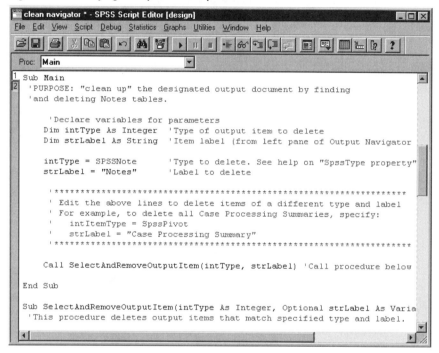

If you prefer to create your own scripts, you can begin by choosing from a number of starter scripts.

## To Edit a Script

▶ From the menus choose:

File
  Open...

**Figure 46.4  Opening a script file**

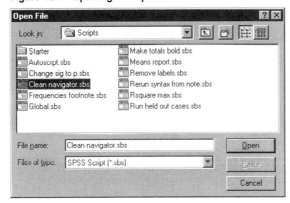

▶ Select the Scripts folder.

▶ Under Files of Type, select *SPSS Script (*.sbs)*.

▶ Select the script you want.

If you open more than one script, each opens in its own window.

## Script Window

The script window is a fully featured programming environment that uses the Sax BASIC language and includes a dialog box editor, object browser, debugging features, and context-sensitive help.

**Figure 46.5   Script window**

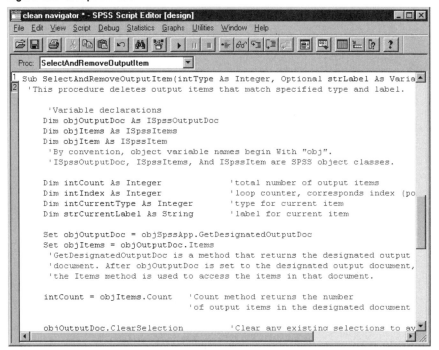

- As you move the cursor, the name of the current procedure is displayed at the top of the window.
- Terms colored blue are reserved words in BASIC (for example Sub, End Sub, and Dim). You can access context-sensitive help on these terms by clicking them and pressing F1.
- Terms colored magenta are SPSS objects, properties, or methods. You can also click these terms and press F1 for help, but only where they appear in valid statements and are colored magenta. (Clicking the name of an SPSS object in a comment will not work because it brings up help on the Sax BASIC language rather than help on SPSS objects.)

- Comments are displayed in green.
- Press F2 at any time to display the Object Browser, which displays SPSS objects, properties, and methods.

## Script Editor Properties

Code elements in the script window are color-coded to make them easier to distinguish. By default, comments are green, Sax BASIC terms are blue, and names of valid SPSS objects, properties, and methods are magenta. You can specify different colors for these elements and change the size and font for all text

## To Set Script Editor Properties

▶ From the menus choose:

Script
    Editor Properties...

Figure 46.6   Script Editor Properties dialog box

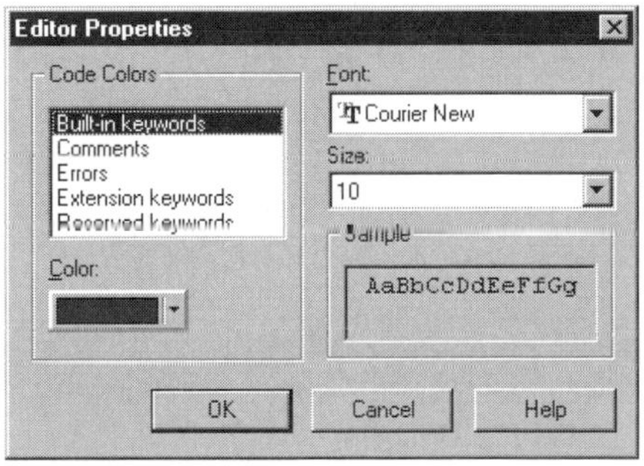

▶ To change the color of a code element type, select the element and choose a color from the drop-down palette.

## Starter Scripts

When you create a new script, you can begin by choosing from a number of starter scripts.

**Figure 46.7    Use Starter Script dialog box**

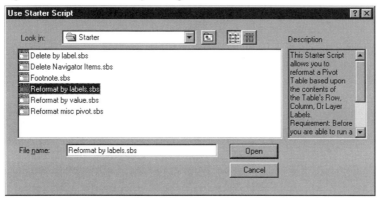

Each starter script supplies code for one or more common procedures and is commented with hints on how to customize the script to your particular needs.

**Delete by label.** Delete rows or columns in a pivot table based on the contents of the Row-Labels or ColumnLabels. In order for this script to work, the *Hide empty rows and columns* option must be selected in the Table Properties dialog box.

**Delete navigator items.** Delete items from the Output Navigator based on a number of different criteria.

**Footnote.** Reformat a pivot table footnote, change the text in a footnote, or add a footnote.

**Reformat by labels.** Reformat a pivot table based upon the row, column, or layer labels.

**Reformat by value.** Reformat a pivot table based upon the value of data cells or a combination of data cells and labels.

**Reformat misc pivot.** Reformat or change the text in a pivot table title, corner text, or caption.

In addition, you can use any of the other scripts that come with SPSS as starter scripts, although they may not be as easy to customize. Just open the script and save with a different filename.

### To Create a Script

▶ From the menus choose:
New
  Script...

▶ Select a starter script if you want to begin with one.

▶ If you do not want to use a starter script, click *Cancel*.

## Creating Autoscripts

You create an autoscript by starting with the output object you want to serve as the trigger. For example, to create an autoscript that runs whenever a frequency table is produced, create a frequency table in the usual manner and single-click the table in the Output Navigator to select it. You can then right-click or use the Utilities menu to create a new autoscript triggered whenever that type of table is produced.

**Figure 46.8   Creating a new autoscript**

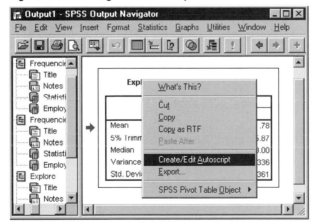

Each autoscript that you create is added to the current autoscript file (*Autoscript.sbs*, by default) as a new procedure. The name of the procedure references the event that serves as the trigger. For example, if you create an autoscript triggered whenever Explore creates a Descriptives table, the name of the autoscript subroutine would be Explore_Table_Descriptives_Create.

**Figure 46.9    New autoscript procedure displayed in script window**

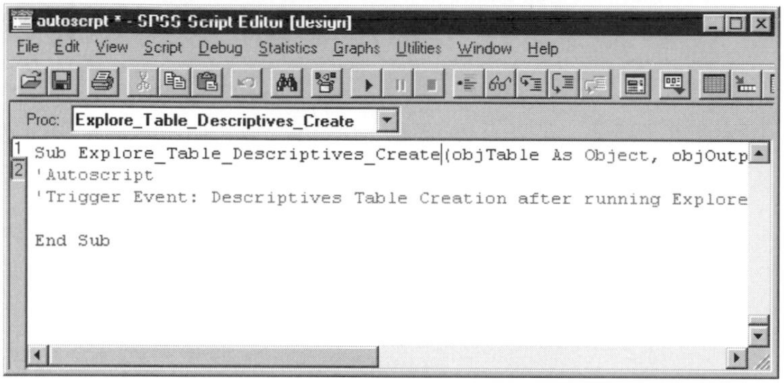

This makes autoscripts easier to develop because you do not need to write code to get the object you want to operate on, but it requires that autoscripts are specific to a given piece of output and statistical procedure.

### To Create an Autoscript

▶   Select the object you want to serve as a trigger in the Output Navigator.

▶   From the menus choose:
    Utilities
      Create/Edit Autoscript...

If no autoscript exists for the selected object, a new autoscript is created. If an autoscript already exists, the existing script is displayed.

▶   Type the code.

▶   From the Edit menu choose *Options* to enable or disable the autoscript.

### Events that Trigger Autoscripts

The name of the autoscript procedure references the event that serves as the trigger. The following events can trigger autoscripts:

**Creation of pivot table.** The name of the procedure references both the table type and the procedure that created it, for example Correlations_Table_Correlations_Create.

**Figure 46.10 Autoscript procedure for Correlations table**

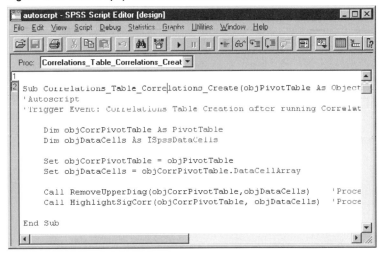

**Creation of title.** Referenced to the statistical procedure that created it: Correlations_Title_Create.

**Creation of notes.** Referenced to the procedure that created it: Correlations_Notes_Create.

**Creation of warnings.** Referenced by the SPSS procedure that created it.

### The Autoscript File

All autoscripts are saved in a single file (unlike other scripts, each of which is saved in a separate file). Any new autoscripts you create are also added to this file. The name of the current autoscript file is displayed in the Scripts tab of the Options dialog box (Edit menu).

**Figure 46.11 Autoscript subroutines displayed in Options dialog box**

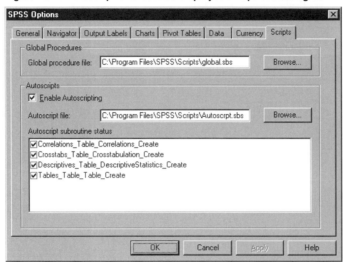

The Options dialog box also displays all of the autoscripts in the currently selected autoscript file, allowing you to enable and disable individual scripts.

The default autoscript file is *Autoscript.sbs*. You can specify a different autoscript file, but only one can be active at any one time.

# How Scripts Work

Scripts work by manipulating SPSS objects using properties and methods. For example, pivot tables are a class of SPSS objects. With objects of this class, you can use the SelectTable method to select all the elements in the table, and you can use the TextColor property to change the color of selected text. Each object class has specific properties and methods associated with it. The collection of all SPSS object classes (or types) is called the SPSS type library.

**Figure 46.12 Tree view of SPSS object hierarchy**

Using objects is a two-step process. First you create a reference to the object (called *getting* the object). Then, you use properties and methods to do something. You get objects by navigating the hierarchy of SPSS objects, at each step using properties or methods of objects higher in the hierarchy to get at the objects beneath. For example, to get a pivot table object, you have to first get the output document that contains the pivot table, and then get the items in that output document.

Each object that you get is stored in a variable. (Remember that all you are really storing in the variable is a reference to the object.) One of the first steps in creating a script is often to declare variables for the objects that you need.

*Tip*: It is difficult to understand how scripts work if you do not understand how SPSS works. Before writing a script, use the mouse to perform the task several times as you normally would. At each step, consider what objects you are manipulating and what properties of each object you are changing.

## Declaring Variables

Although not always required, it is a good idea to declare all variables before using them. This is most often done using Dim declaration statements:

```
Dim objOutputDoc As ISpssOutputDoc
Dim objPivotTable As PivotTable
Dim intType As Integer
Dim strLabel As String
```

Each declaration specifies the variable name and type. For example, the first declaration above creates an object variable named objOutputDoc and assigns this variable to the ISpssOutputDoc object class. The variable does not yet have a value because it has not been set to a particular output document. All the statement does is declare that the variable exists. (This process has been referred to as "renaming the objects you want to use.")

**Variable naming conventions.** By convention, the name of each variable indicates its type. Object variable names begin with obj, integer variables begin with int, and string variables begin with str. These are only conventions—you can name your variables anything you want—but following them makes it much easier to understand your code.

**SPSS object classes.** ISpssOutputDoc and PivotTable are names of SPSS object classes. Each class represents a type of object that SPSS can create, such as an output document or pivot table. Each object class has specific properties and methods associated with it. The collection of all SPSS object classes (or types) is referred to as the SPSS type library.

The following variable names are used in the sample scripts included with SPSS and are recommended for all scripts. Notice that with the exception of pivot tables, object classes have names beginning with ISpss.

| Object | Type or Class | Variable Name |
|---|---|---|
| SPSS Application | IspssApp | objSpssApp - variable is global and does not require declaration |
| SPSS Options | ISpssOptions | objSpssOptions |
| SPSS file information | ISpssInfo | objSpssInfo |
| Documents | ISpssDocuments | objDocuments |
| Data document | ISpssDataDoc | objDataDoc |
| Syntax document | ISpssSyntaxDoc | objSyntaxDoc |
| Output Navigator document | ISpssOutputDoc | objOutputDoc |
| Print options | ISpssPrintOptions | objPrintOptions |
| Output items collection | ISpssItems | objOutputItems |
| Output item | ISpssItem | objOutputItem |
| Chart | ISpssChart | objSPSSChart |
| Text | ISpssRtf | objSPSSText |
| Pivot table | PivotTable | objPivotTable |
| Footnotes | ISpssFootnotes | objFootnotes |
| Data cells | ISpssDataCells | objDataCells |
| Layer labels | ISpssLayerLabels | objLayerLabels |
| Column labels | ISpssLabels | objColumnLabels |
| Row labels | ISpssLabels | objRowLabels |
| Pivot manager | ISpssPivotMgr | objPivotMgr |
| Dimension | ISpssDimension | objDimension |

## Getting Automation Objects

To *get* an object means to create a reference to the object so that you can use properties and methods to do something. Each object reference that you get is stored in a variable. To get an object, first declare an object variable of the appropriate class, then set the variable to the specific object. For example, to get the designated output document:

```
Dim objOutputDoc As ISpssOutputDoc
Set objOutputDoc = objSpssApp.GetDesignatedOutputDoc
```

You use properties and methods of objects higher in the SPSS object hierarchy to get at the objects beneath. The second statement above gets the designated output document using GetDesignatedOutputDoc, a method associated with the SPSS application object, which is the highest level object. Similarly, to get a pivot table object, you first get the output document that contains the pivot table, then get the collection of items in that output document, and so on.

## Example: Getting an Output Item

This script gets the third output item in the designated output document and activates it. If that item is not an OLE object, the script produces an error.

See below for a another example that activates the first pivot table in the designated output document.

```
Sub Main

Dim objOutputDoc As ISpssOutputDoc   'declare object variables
Dim objOutputItems As ISpssItems
Dim objOutputItem As ISpssItem

Set objOutputDoc  = objSpssApp.GetDesignatedOutputDoc     'get reference to designated output doc
Set objOutputItems = objOutputDoc.Items() 'get collection of items in doc
Set objOutputItem = objOutputItems.GetItem(2)  'get third output item
'(item numbers start at 0 so "2" gets third)

objOutputItem.Activate'activate output item

End sub
```

## Example: Getting the First Pivot Table

This script gets the first pivot table in the designated output document and activates it.

```
Sub Main

Dim objOutputDoc As ISpssOutputDoc'declare object variables
Dim objOutputItems As ISpssItems
Dim objOutputItem As ISpssItem
Dim objPivotTable As PivotTable

Set objOutputDoc = objSpssApp.GetDesignatedOutputDoc    'get reference to designated output doc
Set objOutputItems = objOutputDoc.Items()  'get collection of items in doc

Dim intItemCount As Integer'number of output items
Dim intItemType As Integer'type of item (defined by SpssType property)

intItemCount = objOutputItems.Count()  'get number of output items
For index = 0 To intItemCoun   'loop through output items
   Set objOutputItem = objOutputItems.GetItem(index)  'get current item
intItemType = objOutputItem.SPSSType()  'get type of current item
If intItemType = SPSSPivot Then
Set objSelectedPivot = objOutputItem.Activate()   'if item is a pivot table, activate it
Exit For
End If
Next index

End sub
```

Examples are also available in the online Help. You can try them yourself by pasting the code from help into the script window.

## Properties and Methods

Like real world objects, SPSS OLE automation objects have features and uses. In programming terminology, the features are referred to as properties, and the uses are referred to as methods. Each object class has specific methods and properties that determine what you can do with that object.

| Object | Property | Method |
|--------|----------|--------|
| Umbrella (real world) | Size<br>Color | Open |
| Pivot Table (SPSS) | TextFont<br>DataCellWidths | SelectTable<br>ClearSelection<br>HideFootnotes |

### Using Properties

Properties set or return attributes of objects, such as color or cell width. When a property appears to the left side of an equal sign, you are writing to it. For example, to set the font of selected text in an activated pivot table (objPivotTable) to Arial:

objPivotTable.TextFont = "Arial"

When a property appears on the right side, you are reading from it. For example, to get the font of selected text and save it in a variable:

strFontName = objPivotTable.TextFont

### Using Methods

Methods perform actions on objects, such as selecting all the elements in a table:

objPivotTable.SelectTable

or removing a selection:

objPivotTable.ClearSelection

Some methods return another object. Such methods are extremely important for navigating the SPSS object hierarchy. For example, the GetDesignatedOutputDoc method returns the designated output document, allowing you to access the items in that output document:

Set objOutputDoc = objSpssApp.GetDesignatedOutputDoc
Set objItems = objOutputDoc.Items

## The Object Browser

The object browser displays all SPSS objects classes and the methods and properties associated with each. You can also access help on individual properties and methods, and paste selected properties and methods into your script.

▶ From the script window menus choose:

Debug
  Object Browser...

Figure 46.13 Object Browser

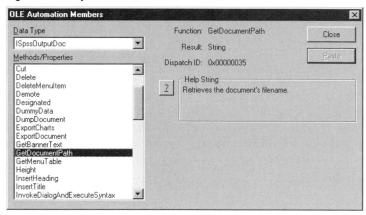

▶ Select an object class from the Data type list to display the methods and properties for that class.

▶ Select properties and methods for context-sensitive help or to paste them into your script.

# Procedures

A procedure is a named sequence of statements that are executed as a unit. Organizing code in procedures makes it easier to manage and reuse pieces of code. Scripts must have at least one procedure (the Main subroutine) and often they have several. The Main procedure may contain few statements, aside from calls to subroutines that do most of the work.

**Figure 46.14 New Procedure dialog box**

Procedures can be subroutines or functions. A procedure begins with a statement that specifies the type of procedure and the name (for example, Sub Main or Function Dialog-Monitor( )) and concludes with the appropriate End statement (End Sub or End Function).

As you scroll through the script window, the name of the current procedure is displayed at the top of the script window. Within a script, you can call any procedure as many times as you want. You can also call any procedure in the global script file, which makes it possible to share procedures between scripts.

## To Add a New Procedure in a Script

▶ From the menus choose:
Script
 New Procedure...

▶ Type a name for the procedure.

▶ Select *Subroutine* or *Function*.

Alternatively, you can create a new procedure by typing the statements that define the procedure directly in the script.

## Global Procedures

If you have a procedure or function that you want to use in a number of different scripts, you can add it to the global script file. Procedures in the global script file can be called by all other scripts.

**Figure 46.15 Global script file**

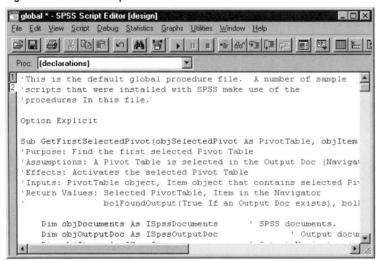

The default global script file is *global.sbs*. You can freely add procedures to this file. You can also specify a different global file on the Scripts tab in the Options dialog box (Edit menu), but only one file can be active as the global file at any given time. That means that if you create a new global file and specify it as the global file, the procedures and functions in *global.sbs* are no longer available.

You can view the global script file in any script window (click the #2 tab on the left side of the window just below the toolbar), but you can edit it in only one window at a time.

# Scripting Custom Dialog Boxes

There are two steps to implementing a custom dialog box: first create the dialog box using the UserDialog Editor, and then create a dialog monitor function (DialogFunc) that monitors the dialog box and defines its behavior.

The dialog box itself is defined by a Begin Dialog...End Dialog block. You do not need to type this code directly—the UserDialog Editor provides an easy, graphical way to define the dialog box.

**Figure 46.16 Creating a dialog box in the UserDialog Editor**

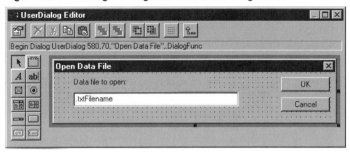

The editor initially displays a blank dialog box form. You can add controls, such as radio buttons and check boxes, by selecting the appropriate tool and dragging with the mouse. (Hold the mouse over each tool for a description.) You can also drag the sides and corners to resize the dialog box. After adding a control, right-click the control to set properties for that control.

**Dialog monitor function.** To create the dialog monitor function, right-click the dialog box form (make sure no control is selected on the form) and enter a name for the function in the DialogFunc field. The statements that define the function are added to your script, although you will have to manually edit the function to define the behavior for each action.

When finished, click the save and exit (far right icon on the toolbar) to add the code for the dialog box to your script.

## To Create a Custom Dialog Box

▶   In the script window, click the cursor in the script where you want to insert the code for the dialog box.

▶   From the menus choose:
    Script
      Dialog Editor...

▶   Select tools from the palette and drag in the new dialog box form to add controls, such as buttons and check boxes.

▶   Resize the dialog box by dragging the handles on the sides and corners.

▶ Right-click the form (with no control selected) and enter a name for the dialog monitor function in the DialogFunc field.

▶ Click the save and exit icon (far right on the toolbar) when you are finished.

You have to manually edit your dialog monitor function to define the behavior of the dialog box.

## Dialog Monitor Functions (DialogFunc)

A dialog monitor function defines the behavior of a dialog box for each of a number of specified cases. The function takes the following (generic) form:

```
Function DialogFunc(strDlgItem as String, intAction as Integer, intSuppValue as Integer)
    Select Case intAction
        Case 1 ' dialog box initialization
            ...    'statements to execute when dialog box is initialized
        Case 2 ' value changing or button pressed
            ...    'statements...
        Case 3 ' TextBox or ComboBox text changed ...
        Case 4 ' focus changed ...
        Case 5 ' idle ...
    End Select
End Function
```

**Parameters.** The function must be able to pass three parameters: one string (strDlgItem) and two integers (intAction and intSuppValue). The parameters are values passed between the function and the dialog box, depending on what action is taken.

For example, when a user clicks a control in the dialog box, the name of the control is passed to the function as strDlgItem (the field name is specified in the dialog box definition). The second parameter (intAction) is a numeric value that indicates what action took place in the dialog box. The third parameter is used for additional information in some cases. You must include all three parameters in the function definition even if you do not use all of them.

**Select Case intAction.** The value of intAction indicates what action took place in the dialog box. For example, when the dialog box initializes, intAction = 1. If the user presses a button, intAction changes to 2, and so on. There are five possible actions, and you can specify statements that execute for each action as indicated below. You do not need to specify all five possible cases—only the ones that apply. For example, if you do not want any statements to execute on initialization, omit Case 1.

- **Case intAction = 1.** Specify statements to execute when the dialog box is initialized. For example, you could disable one or more controls or add a beep. The string strDlgItem is a null string; intSuppValue is 0.

- **Case 2.** Executes when a button is pushed or when a value changes in a CheckBox, DropListBox, ListBox or OptionGroup control. If a button is pushed, strDlgItem is the button, intSuppValue is meaningless, and you must set DialogFunc = True to prevent the dialog from closing. If a value changes, strDlgItem is the item whose value has changed, and intSuppValue is the new value.

- **Case 3.** Executes when a value changes in a TextBox or ComboBox control. The string strDlgItem is the control whose text changed and is losing focus; intSuppValue is the number of characters.

- **Case 4.** Executes when the focus changes in the dialog box. The string strDlgItem is gaining focus, and intSuppValue is the item that is losing focus (the first item is 0, second is 1, and so on).

- **Case 5.** Idle processing. The string strDlgItem is a null string; intSuppValue is 0. Set DialogFunc = True to continue receiving idle actions.

For more information, see the examples and the DialogFunc prototype in the Sax BASIC Language Reference help file.

### Example: Scripting a Simple Dialog Box

This script creates a simple dialog box that opens a data file. See related sections for explanations of the BuildDialog subroutine and dialog monitor function.

**Figure 46.17 Open Data File dialog box created by script**

```
Sub Main
Call BuildDialog
End Sub

 'define dialog box
Sub BuildDialog
Begin Dialog UserDialog 580,70,"Open Data File",.DialogFunc
Text 40,7,280,21,"Data file to open:",.txtDialogTitle
TextBox 40,28,340,21,.txtFilename
OKButton 470,7,100,21,.cmdOK
CancelButton 470,35,100,21,.cmdCancel
End Dialog
Dim dlg As UserDialog
Dialog dlg
End Sub

 'define function that determines behavior of dialog box
Function DialogFunc(strDlgItem As String, intAction As Integer, intSuppValue As Integer) As Boolean
Select Case intAction
Case 1 ' beep when dialog is initialized
    Beep
Case 2 ' value changing or button pressed
    Select Case strDlgItem
      Case "cmdOK" 'if user clicks OK, open data file with specified filename
strFilename = DlgText("txtFilename")
      Call OpenDataFile(strFilename)
      DialogFunc = False
      Case "cmdCancel"'If user clicks Cancel, close dialog
DialogFunc = False
    End Select
End Select
End Function

Sub OpenDataFile(strFilename As Variant)'Open data file with specified filename
Dim objDataDoc As ISpssDataDoc
Set objDataDoc = objSpssApp.OpenDataDoc(strFilename)
End Sub
```

Examples are also available in the online Help. You can try them yourself by pasting the code from help into the script window.

# Debugging Scripts

The Debug menu allows you to step through your code, executing one line or subroutine at a time and viewing the result. You can also insert a break point in the script to pause the execution at the line that contains the break point.

**Step Into.** Execute the current line. If the current line is a subroutine or function call, stop on the first line of that subroutine or function.

**Step Over.** Execute to the next line. If the current line is a subroutine or function call, execute the subroutine or function completely.

**Step Out.** Step out of the current subroutine or function call.

**Step to Cursor.** Execute to the current line.

**Toggle Break.** Insert or remove a break point. The script pauses at the break point, and the debugging pane is displayed.

**Quick Watch.** Display the value of the current expression.

**Add Watch.** Add the current expression to the watch window.

**Object Browser.** Display the object browser.

**Set Next Statement.** Set the next statement to be executed. Only statements in the current subroutine/function can be selected.

**Show Next Statement.** Display the next statement to be executed.

## To Step through a Script

▶ From the Debug menu, choose any of the Step... options to execute code, one line or subroutine at a time.

The Immediate, Watch, Stack, and Loaded tabs are displayed in the script window, along with the debugging toolbar.

▶ Use the toolbar (or hot keys) to continue stepping through the script.

▶ Alternatively, select *Toggle Break* to insert a break point at the current line.

The script pauses at the break point.

## The Debugging Pane

When you step through code, the Immediate, Watch, Stack, and Loaded tabs are displayed.

**Figure 46.18 Debugging pane displayed in script window**

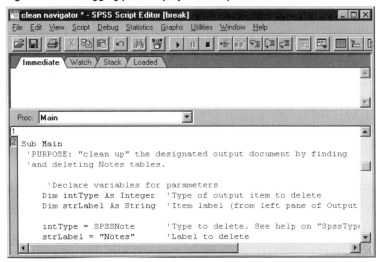

**Immediate tab.** Click the name of any variable and click the eyeglass icon to display the current value of the variable. You can also evaluate an expression, assign a variable, or call a subroutine.

- Type ?expr and press Enter to show the value of *expr*.
- Type var = expr and press Enter to change the value of *var*.
- Type subname args and press Enter to call a subroutine or built-in instruction.
- Type Trace and press Enter to toggle trace mode. Trace mode prints each statement in the immediate window when a script is running.

**Watch tab.** To display a variable, function, or expression, click it and choose *Add Watch* from the Debug menu. Displayed values are updated each time execution pauses. You can edit the expression to the left of ->. Press Enter to update all the values immediately. Press Ctrl-Y to delete the line.

**Stack tab.** Displays the lines that called the current statement. The first line is the current statement, the second line is the one that called the first, and so on. Click any line to highlight that line in the edit window.

**Loaded tab.** List the currently active scripts. Click a line to view that script.

# Script Files and Syntax Files

Syntax files (*.*sps*) are not the same as script files (*.*sbs*). Syntax files have commands written in the SPSS command language that allows you to run SPSS statistical procedures and data transformations. While scripts allow you to manipulate output and automate other tasks that you normally perform using the graphical interface of menus and dialog boxes, the SPSS command language provides an alternate method for communicating directly with the SPSS backend, the part of the system that handles statistical computations and data transformations.

You can combine scripts and syntax files for even greater flexibility, by running a script from within SPSS command syntax, or by embedding command syntax within a script.

## Running Command Syntax from a Script

You can run SPSS command syntax from within an automation script using the Execute-Commands method. SPSS command syntax allows you to run data transformations and statistical procedures and to produce charts. Much of this functionality cannot be automated directly from command scripts.

The easiest way to build a command syntax file is to make selections in SPSS dialog boxes and paste the syntax for the selections into the script window.

**Figure 46.19 Pasting command syntax into a script**

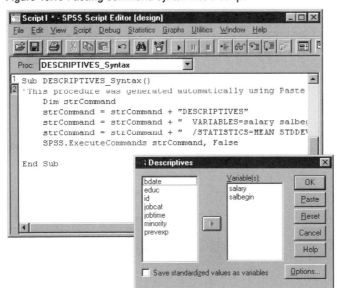

Veteran users of SPSS may already be familiar with the Paste button that can be used to paste command syntax into a syntax window. When you open dialog boxes using the script window menus, the Paste button works in a similar manner, except that it pastes all the code needed to run SPSS commands from within a script.

*Note*: You must use the script window menus to open the dialog box; otherwise, commands will be pasted to a syntax window rather than the scripting window.

### To Paste SPSS Command Syntax into a Script

▶   From the script window menus, choose commands from the Statistics, Graphs, and Utilities menus to open dialog boxes.

▶   Make selections in the dialog box.

▶   Click *Paste*.

*Note*: You must use the script window menus to open the dialog box; otherwise, commands will be pasted to a syntax window rather than the scripting window.

## Running a Script from Command Syntax

You can use the SCRIPT command to run a script from within SPSS command syntax. Simply specify the name of the script you want to run:

SCRIPT C:\MYSCRIPT.SBS'.

# Index